WHAT PRICE LIBERTY?

Ben Wilson was born in 1980 and studied history at Pembroke College, Cambridge, both as an undergraduate and a postgraduate. His first book, *The Laughter of Triumph: William Hone and the Fight for the Free Press*, was published by Faber in 2005 to universal acclaim. This was followed in 2007 by *Decency & Disorder: The Age of Cant 1789–1837*.

What Price Liberty?

BEN WILSON

faber and faber

First published in 2009
by Faber and Faber Ltd
Bloomsbury House
74–77 Great Russell Street
London WC1B 3DA
This paperback edition first published in 2010

Typeset by RefineCatch Limited, Bungay, Suffolk
Printed in England by CPI Bookmarque, Croydon

A CIP record for this book
is available from the British Library

ISBN 978–0–571–23595–7

2 4 6 8 10 9 7 5 3 1

For Claire

... and wrong reasoning sometimes lands poor mortals in right conclusions: starting a long way off the true point, and proceeding by loops and zig-zags, we now and then arrive just where we ought to be.

GEORGE ELIOT, Middlemarch, chapter 3

Contents

—ᴍᴠ—

[ix]

CONTENTS

Prologue

—◊◊◊—

When the teller for the ayes in the House of Commons announced that the government had won a vote on extending to forty-two days the time a person suspected of terrorist offences could be detained before being charged, there were cries of 'Shame,' 'Traitors,' and 'How much were you paid?' from backbenchers. The Speaker wearily rebuked the MPs: 'You know full well that every hon. member has his own vote, on his own conscience.' But as Simon Hoggart, sketch writer for the *Guardian*, put it, 'many politicians put their consciences on eBay a long time ago'.[1]

Gordon Brown's government experienced a significant backbench rebellion on 11 June 2008, but passed its measure by nine votes, thanks to the last-minute change of heart by the nine members of the Northern Irish Democratic Unionist Party who had spent much of the afternoon with the Prime Minister. It was claimed that on that very day an extra expenditure of £1.2 billion was announced for Northern Ireland. Some potentially rebellious Labour MPs had a similar last-minute change of heart after, it was alleged, the government conceded to specific demands, such as lifting sanctions on Cuba and compensation for ex-miners. For the *Guardian* it was 'a shaming victory' and *The Times* proclaimed 'Westminster for sale'.

In the speech of her career made during the debate and before the vote, the Labour MP Diane Abbott said:

People whom the prime minister has never spoken to in his life have been ushered into his presence twice in forty-eight hours. The House should have a shred of sympathy for them. People have been offered Cuba, and no doubt governorships of Bermuda have been bandied about. Any rebel back-bencher with a cause is confident – if they vote the right way of course – that the prime minister will make the statement, give the money or make the special visit. That is humorous, but is it right that our civil liberties should be traded in such a bazaar?[2]

It was a replay of the passage of other pieces of anti-terror legislation through parliament. In recent years the public had been treated to the unedifying spectacle of civil liberties being legislated away: measures were forced through parliament at breakneck speed; deals were struck, and supposedly crucial measures were cynically bargained away at the last moment in return for support.

The resignation the next day of David Davis, Conservative shadow Home Secretary, from parliament in order to re-contest his seat on the principle of liberty was, however, far from usual. In his resignation speech Davis linked the immediate issue of the incarceration of terrorist suspects to what he called 'the insidious, surreptitious and relentless erosion of fundamental British freedoms' over recent years. This included the proliferation of surveillance cameras, the government's enthusiasm for databases, meddling with trial by jury, and new laws which severely restricted freedom of speech and public protest. He was, he said, acting out of disillusionment at MPs' compliance in curbing freedoms for political reasons.[3]

Davis stood up in a one-man protest against the assault on civil liberties, and in doing so became the hero of the hour for liberal Britain. But his quixotic decision also resonated with a strain of anti-authoritarian popular protest long known in this country. Davis was ridiculed by fellow politicians and the media for his pains; what had happened in parliament was unseemly but not particularly unusual. But for many in the world outside Westminster he had done something conspicuously out of character for a British politician and resigned on a matter of principle.[4]

It was an act of desperation. The many members of the public who cheered Davis on did so not necessarily because they supported his politics but because there was a feeling that for years civil liberties had been under assault without any serious opposition and without much debate. The subsequent by-election sparked discussion of this sort in newspapers, the internet and on television and radio shows. But it did not turn into quite the kind of fundamental national debate many had hoped for, mainly because the government refused to defend its record on liberties by contesting the by-election. David Davis duly romped home. In October 2008 the forty-two-day extension was comprehensively defeated in the House of Lords, as had been predicted from the beginning. The measure died an ignominious death, in part because the Prime Minister had too infirm a grasp on his parliamentary party to stomach a fresh battle.

What these events demonstrated most clearly was that, as a society, we had lost the means to talk about liberty. Faced with barely explicable changes and dangers, people found it hard to articulate the kind of liberties appropriate for the twenty-first century. It was a time of revolutionary change in the economy, in world affairs, in technology and in the very identity of the modern nation state. The public was overwhelmed by the fear of terrorism and the sheer complexity of modern life. Talking about Magna Charta, habeas corpus and other historic liberties became harder and harder for defenders of civil liberties: the public just did not respond or understand as perhaps their parents and grandparents would have. And faced with a government dazzled by new technology, spooked by terror and unsentimental – to say the least – about the landmarks of British history ('New, new, new; everything is new,' Tony Blair marvelled at one point[5]) it was instinctive for those concerned about our civil liberties to reach for the traditional language of protest; for others, it was just as natural – and as disheartening – to see the state as an overpowering Leviathan against which resistance was futile.

The conclusion to draw is not that there is a dastardly plot against liberty in Britain or that we are hurtling towards tyranny; it is that the politicians who have run Britain for the last few decades simply have not had a fixed idea of what liberty is. It is certainly the case that while we have been bombarded by 'change' (as politicians constantly remind us), no one has come up with a way of articulating how amid all this newness and revolutionary transformation we are going to develop an idea of the liberty of the individual to match the new kinds of authority and danger all of us have now to confront.

It was regrettable that during the debates which followed Davis's resignation the arguments quickly polarised. Audiences in studio debates and contributors to blogs spoke as if the civil liberties campaign was against things such as CCTV cameras and crime prevention and anti-terror techniques in their entirety. It sometimes seemed as if liberty meant rolling back the state and all its innovations, cancelling anything which might possibly be used tyrannically at some point, and demanding that the clock be turned back to an age of unsullied freedom. Many of those who admitted (reluctantly or not) the value of such innovations were driven to oppose Davis's stand because they assumed that there was a straightforward choice between protection on one hand and liberty on the other; that the plea for liberty meant disempowering the state and dismantling protections; that there are but two unmeeting paths.

The most serious threat to liberty in our society comes from this attitude. It has come in large part from a mentality prevalent among people in power. The plea for liberty is always met with the same excuses: utility, safety first, risk-aversion and so on. Against such bland, principle-free and pragmatic explanations it has been near to impossible for the defenders of liberty to formulate a convincing set of arguments. This is because you are not arguing against a coherent philosophy, merely a range of off-the-peg policies chosen for their immediate utility without consideration of their general impact. And more than that: members of the government seemed determined to pick a fight with defenders of liberty, destroying dialogue by portraying them as enemies of safety and order. As such the very meaning of liberty in the twenty-first century has slipped away. It is hard to talk about, especially to authority, when you can't count on the same assumptions being shared across society. What should be the plainest and most important concept in our civilisation has become overly problematic and impossible to define without cavils and caveats.

Simply opposing everything which is new plays into the hands of those who score political advantage by swatting away liberal sentiment. Indeed part of the problem is that the word *liberty* has been transformed into a philosophy of purely personal autonomy. We should recover its meaning in a public sense: unless you ensure that your political, legal, economic and social institutions are kept in good health then, sooner or later, your personal liberty will suffer as well. Concern about attacks on freedom of speech and pre-trial detention should not focus exclusively on the rights of individuals: it should also be about how new kinds of authority poison our public institutions as well. Liberty in the modern state should be, in large part, an argument about the responsible use of power. The use of power, that is, by people who can be trusted to make use of new technologies and confront new dangers within the traditions and expectations of liberty.

But is this true today? You can no longer count on politicians and officials to be restrained by a regard for liberty or respect for the freedom of the individual. Their language condemns them: not only do they not care, but they do not really understand what they should be pretending to care about. Even such a precious jewel as freedom of speech was ready to be cast away when the government attempted to pass laws designed to counter religious hatred. When David Blunkett, as Home Secretary, dismissed civil liberties as 'airy-fairy', when Tony Blair said they were made for another age, and when the media talk disparagingly about the 'liberati', the effect is to destroy public confidence in our old legal protections. Without a serious attempt to explore what the implications might be or to tell us what we get in return for sacrificing aspects of our heritage it is a dereliction of duty.

It therefore becomes hard to mobilise the public over such issues. In the past politicians were often held to the responsible use of power because they feared the public's response if they began trampling on time-hallowed ideals. This safety mechanism is next to redundant when a common idea of liberty has dissolved into mush. It is in part thanks to seedy parliamentary proceedings, an ideologically neutral style of government and a short-term media that these beliefs have been sapped of much of their power. When ideas like liberty are no longer held sacred or are not capable of holding universal respect their practicality is lessened as well.

And if the concept of liberty has been detached from its moorings it is in large part because the concept of the individual has been made to suffer. This may sound paradoxical in an age of extreme individualism. But while we have gained much in terms of personal rights and choice, our grasp on the autonomous individual has become uncertain. The Enlightenment gave us the idea of the responsible, self-reliant, independent individual. Freedom would allow men and women to flourish and improve; liberty would promote individuality and enlarge the character; risk would lead to discovery. The modern age of individualism (as defined by economic thinking) leads policy-makers to suppose that individuals exist in real or potential conflict. Freedom is, in this case, seen as negative – in excess it leads to antisocial behaviour and unacceptably risky actions.

Nowadays states regard the individual as a potential troublemaker, a selfish economic actor who puts personal gain first: a risk in other words. There is no such thing as a self-regarding act. Every action entails a cost or a consequence – on the environment, on our neighbours, on people on the other side of the world, on the economy, on the social fabric. Even opening our mouths is fraught with difficulties: who knows who we might offend, what conflicts might arise? All these things can, thanks to new technologies, be policed – and many are falling within the grasp of the state. Once risk becomes the bogeyman of modern society the scope for management and control expands. Risk management seeks no philosophical justification – and brooks no philosophical opposition. It is ideologically neutral. This is the true story of liberty in the modern world. Ideas of freedom derive from ideas of the individual. Nowadays pessimism rules.

The great tragedy of modern times is how the notion of liberty has disappeared from our culture. If it had held its position better, then many of the recent assaults on the fundamentals of liberty would not merely have been seen as excessive but as deeply offensive. Politicians would have acted very differently for fear of offending public opinion. Negotiating the relationships between the individual and the state and between individuals – the essence of liberty – is an extremely complex business, and it must often be done on a case-by-case basis, not with a broad-brush ideological rulebook to hand.

Clearly this is a devilishly difficult task. Yet with a better understanding of liberty, and sensitivity to its principles, society as a whole might have been kept in better health. It would at least have been a start.

How are we to recover this cultural attachment to liberty? We could construct a philosophy of liberty. But we would soon find that no theory could possibly be devised that would be watertight enough to withstand all objections. We could write a constitution or Bill of Rights. That might be a start, but a new set of laws could be evaded and suspended as easily as they are now. In the 1930s, when liberty seemed to be dying, the intellectual Harold Laski wrote:

In a time of crisis, particularly, when the things we hold dear are threatened, we shall find the desire to throw overboard the habits of tolerance almost irresistible. For those habits are not in Nature, which teaches us that opinions we deem evil are fraught with death. They come from our social heritage, and are part of a process the value of which we must relearn continuously if we are to preserve it.[6]

By its nature liberty is extremely hard to maintain, and rare are the countries which have enjoyed it. It is rarely a popular cause because it is hard to sum up in a few slogans. It is maintained and defended by values which have grown and thrived within society and which command respect from leaders down to the most powerless, from the left to the right and through fashions of economic thinking. Liberty is the product of human history and of the study of history. The freest countries are those in which these lessons are at the core of the culture, embedded in the DNA.

Examples from the past may be plucked out by journalists and politicians and used to defend liberties. But I argue in these pages that liberty does more than provide a warning or validate accustomed protections and rights. The Labour MP Bob Marshall-Andrews put this well: '. . . the British do not articulate liberties easily any more than they define them in lists or guard them as properties or beneficence gratefully received from their masters above. For us, political and personal freedoms are not gifts or indulgences, they are defining characteristics as a nation.'[7]

As worrying as the attack on fundamental freedoms has been the decline of this sense of history. During the protests over cartoons which satirised Muhammad in a Danish journal in 2006, people asked how it could be that a significant section of the population could countenance censorship without being aware of the implications of such a return to the past. Similarly liberals bemoan the lack of concern adolescents have for privacy when they use social sharing networks, or the public's grudging acceptance of ID cards and suchlike.

Yet it is hardly surprising when the state bargains away old freedoms for temporary advantage and speaks of those liberties with barely disguised contempt or casualness; when politicians themselves attempt to reintroduce controls on free speech without much sign that they know the sorry history of this presumption. It should come as no surprise at all that we find ourselves compelled to re-fight old battles again and again when the history that should teach us about – for example – freedom of speech and privacy is shamefully neglected in education and in everyday political discourse.

Throughout my writing career I have touched upon liberty a lot. It is the most important part of my politics. What I wanted as I read about politics and history was a comprehensive theory or a set of rules which would satisfy my mind and which could be deployed in all kinds of political argument. Researching and writing this book changed that. I was looking for the wrong thing. What I came to realise was that there is no single theory of liberty. Rather there is a way of thinking about liberty.

Indeed it is hard to imagine how else to define liberty but historically. History is full of contradictions and compromises and quirks; it defies any systematic theory or pattern; it is full of individuals pursuing their own unpredictable lines of direction. Thinking historically is an important part of thinking politically, for you learn that things are never as systematic as a planner might hope, and it would be a revolt against the human spirit if the timber could be straightened.

And in the same way it is impossible to conceive of liberty as a single, unchanging philosophy since it only works when it is applied in the confusion of daily life. Giving people the largest sphere of personal autonomy and responsibility is no easy task, and a theory of liberty would be constantly violated when it came up against brute reality. Straightforward and easily explicable ideas are best left to totalitarian systems. Liberty must be remade and rethought continually. We have to live with complexity, compromise and contradiction; for that is to live in freedom.

We learn about liberty by experience – and it gets its value and force from the experience and stories of people living in the past, contending with real issues. I do not mean history here as a static thing which hands us down precious artefacts that we must not sully, or indeed as desiccated morality tales. I mean it as a radical and dynamic force which we can draw upon to formulate and give expression to our own desires and grievances. It provides us with a language of rights, heroes and a way of realising what is at stake in our own struggles. In Britain there is no formal declaration of rights or single document we can memorise or revere. Yet there is a plethora of written documents and accounts of events which shine a light upon the ideas and theories of liberty. In the absence of a fundamental law or a constitution the challenge is to draw together these disparate pieces of paper, these stories and biographies, not to create a narrative of liberty so much as an argument, a way of thinking about society.

It is an admirable feature of British history that, in the main, its people had very low tolerance for even minor trespasses on civil liberties. The true heroes of British history are the radicals and campaigners (often forgotten) who held their so-called betters to a better standard of governance. The petty rules and trivial privileges mattered a great deal to people, and they kept a watchful eye on the state. This was not so much because sporadic violations (as often as not done in the name of security) were seen as the beginning of a slippery slope to despotism (although this cautiousness is a good habit to learn), but because the health of society was measured by the value it put even on petty rights. Civil liberties broadcast the value a state puts on legality and procedure; they set a gold standard which is hallowed by time and so generates respect. Our society has chosen to put things like habeas corpus and trial by jury at the centre of its self-identity. They are the outer ramparts of freedom, and they are surrendered at great peril.

This book is by no means a comprehensive history of liberty: there are many gaps in the long struggle for rights. If I have ignored or skirted over other fights for liberty on the part of, say, suffragettes or Britain's colonies, it is by no means because such struggles are less important than the ones I have included. What I intend to show is how the idea of liberty has retained its hold in British public and private life and why this is in danger today; the specific examples were chosen because I felt they were coherent enough to provide the linking thread for a subject of this complexity. Above all I wanted to show how hard it is to retain liberties – that it is not just sapped by thugs in brown shirts or by Big Brother but by more subtle and less conspicuous enemies. We should not lose sight of the idea that ideals such as liberty – which seem so simple at first glance – must be worked at ceaselessly. The sheer effort of will which is required from all sections of society to keep them in good shape is often overlooked.

As a society, and particularly in our schools, we need to find the appropriate narratives and events which unlock all the various meanings and possibilities of freedom. For unless children are taught this kind of history, then the passions and arguments which sustained liberty will be put to sleep. The concept of the fullest possibilities of a free society will be lost if we box ourselves in with fear and pessimism or lack of imagination. We are contemplating a society which has the forms of liberty without the spirit of liberty. That is to say, a free country should have more than the minimum set of rights; it should search for ways to enlarge responsibility and autonomy for its citizens; it should create an atmosphere of freedom which allows individuals to flourish. Tracing our rights to their source enlarges our understanding and satisfies our curiosity. It is what gives them value.

In her blog, Rachel North – a survivor of the terrorist bombs in London on 7 July 2005 – has written movingly about civil liberties. 'I am not possessed of any special wisdom by virtue of having been on a suicide-bombed train . . .' she wrote in 2007: 'I just care, passionately enough about this to write, and to read, and to learn as much as I can about it. To talk to people, and to listen, and to try to hold a steady course and avoid getting pulled into the malevolent hysteria that sometimes threatens to overtake the issue of terrorism.'[8]

This obligation to equip oneself with knowledge, to care about the state of society and to think beyond the strictly personal is a moral duty, and it might be said that it is a precondition of liberty itself. Without a questing mind and an appetite for exploration the passion for freedom dies away.

History teaches that liberty is something which must be relearnt and rearticulated. By thinking of liberty in this way I do not want to remain stuck in the past or wedded to old ways of doing things. This book is punctuated with great crises and revolutions, wars and economic disasters. Each gave an impetus to the idea of liberty, sharpening old notions to take account of new realities.

We perhaps will live through a period of trauma – economic or environmental or who knows what. Doing so when respect for and knowledge of customary liberties is at a low point is scary. What marks us out from the past is our failure, in a revolutionary time, to think afresh about liberty, drawing upon ideas from the past and applying them to the challenges we face. History is the greatest tool in the fight to maintain and enlarge freedom for it keeps alive that spirit.

I

STRENUOUS LIBERTY

TO 1660

CHAPTER 1

Your Home Is Your Castle

—⚹—

The subtlety of lawyers is far more useful to the king than the violence
of soldiers. By their means suspected persons are ensnared one by one,
and destroyed without noise or danger.

ALGERNON SIDNEY[1]

No man can be a politician, except that he be first an historian or a
traveller.

JAMES HARRINGTON[2]

The ancient law of England declared by the Great Charta . . .

SIR EDWARD COKE[3]

Writing in the first dreadful days of civil war in 1642 the MP Dudley
Digges lamented that ''Tis a bitter controversy that our poor sinful
nation is fallen upon, wherein not only arms are engaged against
arms, but books written against books, and conscience pretended
against conscience.'[4] It was as if the clash of books and free thought
was worse and, in the end, more destructive than the clash of arms.

Out of the controversy came radical ways of thinking about liberty
and authority, ideas that came from English history and law, classical
political thought, Biblical example and natural law. There was a sense
that as the old pillars of society crumbled the world would be made
anew. Ideas succeeded ideas in a rush to rebuild the country. Hence an
explosion of books and pamphlets and a bitter intellectual conflict.
Thomas Hobbes sneered that the 'paper war' was nothing but a
'university quibble' conducted by over-educated young men who had

become intoxicated by classical democracy and specious ideas of liberty. In their 'harangues' they were 'continually extolling liberty and inveighing against tyranny'. They had been trained to look for signs of classical tyranny in modern governments, Brutuses hunting for another Caesar; in the 1640s they used their narrow, anachronistic definition of despotism to analyse the political crisis, mistakenly believing that history was repeating itself. 'The *Universities* have been to this nation, as the wooden horse was to the *Trojans*.'[5] For Hobbes romantic and ill-thought-out notions of liberty, combined with religious fanaticism, had unhinged English minds. And indeed much of the thinking was delusive, utopian or downright silly. But out of the debates has come a particular way of thinking about liberty that echoes down to us today. The experience of the times and the innovative thinking, even if it was never put into practice, provided currents of republican thought which flowed underground, influencing generations of Britons and Americans, occasionally breaking above ground.

The collapse of kingly power and the search for new forms of authority provided people with the opportunity to explore a range of ideas of liberty. For many the intestine violence of the civil wars seemed to have propelled Englishmen back to a primitive state of nature, one where the regulated liberty which existed in civil society under recognised authority had been replaced by the licentious freedom of anarchy. As Digges wrote, 'When every man exercises his natural freedom, no man is free.'[6] Without laws backed by authority there could be nothing but savage competition for resources, in which the fittest always prospered at the expense of the majority who were destined for a short, nasty and brutish existence. According to natural law and human history, the first freedom of primitive man was quickly and voluntarily regulated by laws and magistrates. Over time, wise rulers were invested with greater powers and fewer restraints so that they might act for the common advantage. But it became equally apparent that the freedom which permitted a benevolent ruler to act expeditiously also allowed his degenerate successor to bind and rob the people. But this was an unfortunate necessity for early societies; Henry Parker – a great friend of liberty – wrote that 'Till some way was invented to regulate the motions of the people's maliminous* body, I think arbitrary rule was the most safe for the world.' This was because mankind could not 'find out an orderly means whereby to avoid the danger of unbounded prerogative on this hand, and too excessive liberty on the other'. Occasionally the natural inclination for liberty led the people to revolt, only to find themselves with the choice of taking their chances in ochlocracy (mob rule) or accepting the familiar chains of a new dictatorship.[7]

Reconciling the evils of 'excessive liberty' and unlimited authority was the achievement of civilisation. The civil wars forced Englishmen to confront these elemental urges in human nature, the unending tension between the desire for freedom and the need for security. It represented the perennial need to return to first principles (for which conflict provided the opportunity) and the imperative of designing laws and institutions which would allow for the maximum of liberty and authority. From the ruins of the Stuart monarchy and the waste of revolution the 'bloody generation'[8] had a unique opportunity to rectify the mistakes of their fathers and redesign the state.

Liberty was believed to be something that thrived in English soil. There was a notion that popular liberties and mixed government extended back into the mists of time – to 'time out of mind' as legal jargon held it. The Anglo-Saxons, according to this view, had developed a constitution that respected individual liberty and restrained monarchical power and a system of law, the substance and spirit of which had survived into modernity. The Norman Conquest had not radically altered things; indeed, it was argued that William had undertaken to respect the liberties of his conquered subjects. When things had gone wrong the English, true to their liberty-loving natures, had insisted that they be restored. Magna Charta, therefore, was a restatement of ancient rights, not a grant of new ones. In the turbulent centuries since 1215 the great Charta had been reconfirmed no fewer than thirty times according to Sir Edward Coke.[9]

It was perhaps not a very sophisticated or accurate reading of history. What it represented, however, was a potent national myth.

* Cumbrously moving.

Englishmen were periodically required to restate their 'ancient liberties' and demand them from careless or cruel kings who trampled upon their inherited rights. The very idea of liberty had a magic that was chary of exact definition, but which animated Englishmen of all kinds. Parliament reminded James I: 'no human wisdom . . . however great can pierce into the particularities of the rights and customs of the people . . . but by . . . experience and the faithful report of such as know them'.[10]

The idea that liberty consisted in ancient unwritten laws which predated the monarchy was of crucial importance in the early Stuart period. It made opposition to the king's policies viable. Dudley Digges told parliament in 1628 – during the great debates on the Petition of Right, which attempted to define the fundamentals of liberty – that 'the laws of England are grounded on reason more ancient than books, consisting much in unwritten customs, yet so full of justice and true equity'. There was a thread that linked the men of 1628 to their Saxon ancestors, a tradition that was more ancient than the monarchy itself.[11] This involved the conjuring trick of pretending, with Francis Bacon, that William the Conqueror had himself been conquered – by English habits of liberty and law.[12] The argument held that the common law had no creator and therefore could not be recalled or abridged by royal edict. Indeed, the common law was considered to be a statement of natural or divine law. As one contemporary put it: 'I do not take Magna Charta to be a new grant or statute but a restoring or confirming of the ancient laws and liberties of the kingdom.'[13] Or, in other words, you could declare these rights as much as you liked, but English liberties had a power that transcended written or stated law. Their periodic declaration was merely a verbal statement of something that had an eternal, independent existence. 'The common law', wrote Coke, 'is the absolute perfection of reason.'[14]

At the heart of thinking about English law were two things: the absolute security of property and the constitutional balance. Both supported each other. One of the first thinkers on English government, Sir John Fortescue, writing during an earlier period of civil strife, the Wars of the Roses in the fifteenth century, argued that his country enjoyed liberty because the armed and independent yeomen and nobles provided a counterweight to royal authority. In an absolute monarchy (like France), the king could tax whoever and whenever he felt like it. But in England the right of property was absolute; the king had to rely on the consent of his subjects if he wanted to raise revenue, otherwise taxation was theft. This inevitably (according to patriotic constitutionalists) led to the creation of institutions such as parliament, trial by jury and a balance in the state between sovereign authority and the legislature. It was the development of what some seventeenth-century thinkers called 'modern prudence', or mixed government. According to Walter Raleigh the difference between subjection and slavery consisted in the law of *meum et tuum* – what is mine and what is yours – the basis of property law.[15] In the opening decades of the seventeenth century Sir Edward Coke systematised the common law in his *Institutes*.

A system of law purified of corruption and uncertainty – at which Coke aimed in his reforms – should protect person and property against arbitrary invasions of all kinds. And the early seventeenth century was a time when unscrupulous men could exploit technical flaws in land contracts and pay off judges to deprive families of their inheritance. Coke's belief was that the common law, based as it was on reason, should not leave room for these anomalies. People should have an absolute security in their property.[16] And just as private property could not exist unless there was some remedy in court to prevent its theft, there could be no personal freedom unless there was a remedy for false imprisonment. Englishmen at this time equated their rights of private property with their individual liberties: both were passed down through the generations based on clear and natural divisions of what was *mine* and what was *yours* – whether the external party was your neighbour or the king. This was the substance of the advice that the House of Commons gave to James I: 'our privileges and liberties are our right and due and inheritance no less than our very lands and goods'.[17]

Living in liberty under the law was like living in your estate; you were defended from outside forces by real and imaginary boundaries. Above all, the rules must be known in advance and protected from arbitrary suspension so you could not be trapped into losing your birthright by complex legal quibbles, be it a constitutional right or your house. By the laws of England, the people had an absolute ownership of land. Tenants might be turned off their land by the arbitrary decision of their landlord, but even the king could not alter the ownership rights of his subjects. And Englishmen were not tenants when it came to liberty either: their laws and rights could not be altered by higher authority without the consent of parliament. In a society preoccupied with land the metaphor was powerful. Land was permanent and heritable, and so was liberty; you could not have one without the other. John Milton put this most succinctly. The 'root and source of all liberty' was the power to 'dispose and economise' the land which God had given masters of families. Arbitrary power of any sort – in land or in politics – made men no better 'than slaves and vassals born, in the tenure and occupation of another inheriting lord'.[18] Indeed, in a time when right was traced back to the dawn of time, it was said that the right of property, derived from God, definitively predated the institution of monarchy in England.

Englishmen were freeholders in every sense – and the notion of property ownership became the way that liberty itself was conceived: an inviolable private space defended from trespassers. The worst thing was to be a tenant-at-will in terms of property, and even worse to be one in terms of liberty; perpetual uncertainty would be your lot.[19] Indeed, the king was often cast as the tenant: a monarch ruled in order 'to preserve men's goods, but not to be lord and owner thereof himself'; Charles was but a 'life-renter, not a Lord or proprietor of his Kingdom'.[20]

The distinction was made time and again, for it went to the heart of Englishness. Royal authority and personal freedom had separate existences, and they should never muscle in on each other. This idea that the two could be divided by something like contract or property law was put into a vivid metaphor by Sir John Selden in the parliament of 1628: 'The king and the subject have two liberties, two manors joining one another.'[21]

This kind of language was appropriate at a time when, like the British American colonies in the 1760s, politics was dominated by lawyers.[22] *Meum et tuum* was supposed to set the boundary between state authority and individual liberty.[23] The monarchy had powers, of course, but the challenge was to define them to allow the individual and the king the maximum amount of liberty to fulfil their respective functions. 'The king has no prerogative, but that which the law of the land allows him,' stated Coke.[24] But working out a true boundary between the state and the individual was more fraught than examining the title deed of a house. The more people tried to define the exact rights of the subject, the more it came to seem as if they were under daily attack. In reality king and subject could not inhabit different estates without some conflict over the party wall. When Charles's opponents tried to build up their side of the fence, there could not but be conflict over those points where subject and king inevitably overlapped.

Yet many did feel that kingly power and individual freedom could be reconciled without trauma. Some believed that the monarch's powers could be divided between that which was called 'ordinary' and that which was 'absolute'. The former concerned matters of property, inheritance and criminal justice, where the subject might successfully challenge royal edicts in the courts. The latter was indisputable for it touched on matters of statecraft – the declaration and prosecution of war, the defence of the realm and the national coinage being the supreme examples. Some tried further to divide the powers of the prerogative between those in which the king himself would be affected by his bad decisions in common with his subjects (war, the economy etc.) and those erroneous decisions where a private subject would be the sole loser by an unwise decision (cases of property, imprisonment and pardon). The first examples were a legitimate prerogative, the second illegitimate without a legal remedy because there was no limit to the king's potential to do accidental harm.[25] This might appeal to tidy legal minds, but real life was littered with instances where no rule could divide 'petty' matters and great issues of state with any precision. That a hard and fast line between state and personal rights could be maintained with rigour in all cases and without controversy would have been a dangerous delusion in ordinary circumstances; as the political temperature began to climb it became the ground for destructive conflict.

These became matters of urgency in the late 1620s. In 1625 an Elizabethan-style expedition to seize the Spanish treasure fleet at Cadiz went wildly awry. Parliament blamed the commander, Charles's favourite, the Duke of Buckingham, and impeached him. Faced with a hostile parliament unwilling to squander more money on such madcap adventures, and ambitious to capture La Rochelle (where Huguenot protestants were holding out against the King of France), Charles asked for a loan from the country. In the king's 'Instruction for a Free Gift', he argued that as there was no parliament sitting he needed to raise money himself or else 'the common safety of us and our people cannot be defended and maintained', and the country would be 'assailed and swallowed up by a vigilant and powerful enemy'. The troops who returned from the disastrous campaign were billeted at the expense of ordinary subjects. Charles justified his actions: 'no ordinary rules can prescribe a law to necessity'.[26]

For Charles war represented a national emergency that required the suspension of laws. For many in parliament the king's policies were costly and foolhardy foreign adventures at best and, at worst, a bid for absolute power; his every move became big with menace for constitutionally minded men. In the past what were called 'grievances' – or trespasses on the rights of Englishmen – were discussed separately. The suppression of free speech in parliament, the granting of trade monopolies to royal favourites, the occasional abuse of power or the corruption of office holders were treated as controversies disconnected from each other and the general life of the nation. But from the accession of Charles I many were coming to believe that there was a widespread plot to undermine the liberties of Englishmen: monopolies undermined free trade; office holders used their power to steal from their countrymen; the law was infected with complexity to benefit a small group of corrupt men. The linking thread was the chipping away of constitutional liberties under the common law so that the ordinary subject was left neither security nor protection.

The Forced Loan in 1627 involved a very obvious collision of constitutional rights and property rights. Five prominent men were arrested and held without charge for refusing to pay the loan. These were Sir Thomas Darnel, Sir John Corbet, Sir Walter Earl, Sir John Heveringham

and Sir Edmund Hampton – the so-called Five Knights. Facing indefinite detention for as long as Charles said a national emergency was
underway, they brought proceedings in the court of King's Bench for a
writ of habeas corpus showing the cause of their arrest and the legal
authority upon which it was based. The outcome, they hoped, would be
either that they were bailed by the court or that the exact specifications of
the charge against them would hasten a trial before a jury. Their lawyers
argued that their imprisonment could not be legal because the judges of
the King's Bench had not been given reason for it by the king's Attorney
General. What they had, simply, was a warrant saying that the knights
had been arrested by the special command of His Majesty, stating no
reason and offering no evidence.

The Five Knights' lawyers did not stint their eloquence in trying to
convince the judges that this was a violation of the 'birth-right and
inheritance' of all Englishmen. The very meaning of liberty in England
was that a man should be taken before a court at the earliest opportunity and given the right to seek justice. This was the essence of the
common law, put into words by Magna Charta. As one of the lawyers
said, 'it appears by the books of our law, that liberty is a thing so
favoured by the law, that the law will not suffer the continuance of a
man in prison for any longer time than of necessity he must'. The treatment of the Five Knights therefore offended not only against the *words*
of Magna Charta but the *spirit* of English law and immutable natural
law. Their lawyers joined in warning that without this fundamental
liberty, an English man had no other right whatsoever, including
the right of property. Habeas corpus was at the heart of a web of
interconnected rights; take it away and liberty would be no more.

A return of a writ of habeas corpus should state a reason and
justification of a person's arrest. The king's Attorney General agreed
with this, but with an exception: That a king commits a man to
prison is in itself cause enough that he *should* be committed. Who says
that a king is wrong, even if his actions cause annoyance or misery?
Who says that he can judge matters of state better than a king? The
Lord Chief Justice agreed: 'if no cause of the commitment be
expressed [on the return of the writ of habeas corpus], it is to be
presumed to be for a matter of state, which we cannot take notice of'.

The word of a king was more than enough proof any court needed that an action was legal. The judges assumed that the case in hand was a matter of exceptional need rather than the normal way of proceeding. They could not deprive the state of emergency powers, even if the means might be abnormal or obnoxious.

But it was clear that Charles could do what he liked and the silent assumption would always be that it was a 'matter of state'. He could tax his subjects' property at will, imprison those who disagreed, and hold them on a matter of national interest (which he need not tell anyone about) for as long as he liked. It might not be prudent, but it was legal. There was no liberty that was not vulnerable to his conception of the national interest. Coke's assumption that the prerogative was limited by the laws that guaranteed the subject's sphere of liberty was not accepted by the court. The Chief Justice had his own 'immemorial' law and history to call upon, that which said the king could do no wrong; the judges, he said, were walking in the footsteps of their forefathers.

When parliament met at the beginning of 1628, Sir Francis Seymour answered the judge directly. 'I must confess he is no good subject that would not willingly and freely lay down his life, when the end may be the service of his majesty and the good of the common-wealth: but he is no good subject, but a slave, that will set his goods to be taken from him against his will, and his liberty against the laws of the kingdom. In doing this we shall but tread in the steps of our forefathers.'[27]

Other MPs agreed that the case of the Five Knights showed that there was no liberty left in England other than that which existed at the tender mercy of Charles. It was bad enough when the king had taken his subjects' property (in the form of the Forced Loan) without their consent. But why talk of English liberty of any kind at all when men might be put in prison indefinitely on the say-so of men in power? Was this not an invasion of the 'estate' that had been passed down from the Saxons? Charles, desperate for a vote of money, had to tolerate the sitting of a parliament determined to find a way of cur-tailing his powers in the name of liberty. Led by MPs such as Coke, Seymour, Digges and some of the lawyers who had represented the

Five Knights, the Commons set about framing a bill to secure the liberties of the subject, which became the Petition of Right.

The Commons resolved on four main points based on what they saw as the law of the land. No one should be detained without cause shown; habeas corpus should not be denied even if ordered by the king; if no reason was given for an arrest the prisoner should be bailed forthwith; and lastly by 'ancient and indubitable right' and by statute law, the subject should be not be made to pay tax unless it was consented to in parliament. The Lords agreed to the Petition, but wanted to introduce a sentence which would allow the king 'sovereign power' to defend the lives of the people. MPs knew that this would make the Petition of Right a nullity by giving Charles unlimited power whenever he felt it was necessary.

The solution, according to many, was that absolute royal power should co-exist with absolute liberty of the subject in matters of justice and property; indeed, when it came to a conflict liberty should take precedence. The problem with this is easily apprehended. The Commons were acting in a negative way, cutting back on kingly power without suggesting an alternate way of governing. They spoke of liberty and authority as clean separate things; it was confrontational with little in it that was constructive.[28] 'I know that prerogative is part of the law,' Coke said, 'but "Sovereign Power" is no parliamentary word. In my opinion it weakens Magna Charta, and all the statutes; for they are absolute, without any saving of "Sovereign Power" . . . Magna Charta is such a fellow, that he will have no "Sovereign".'[29]

The Lords dropped their proposed addition, and the finished Petition, according to Coke, 'contained the true liberties of the subjects of England, and a true exposition of the Great Charta'.[30] Charles replied in words that were conciliatory and vague enough for his purposes: he declared that he was bound by conscience and his own inclinations to defend the 'just' liberties of his subjects; that his people should have as much liberty as was enjoyed in the times of the 'best of kings' in English history. Soon after he prorogued parliament for some months, and when it returned it was dissolved amid bitter recrimination over matters of indirect tax and religion. In a declaration on the controversies of the previous year Charles was forthright. The lengthy discussions of the Petition had, he said, disordered weak minds which could 'not well distinguish between well-ordered liberty and licentiousness'. The controversy had made men air a welter of inchoate grievances; they now openly criticised the courts, the judges, the king's counsellors and the king's policies. As a direct result there was a violent mood in the country. MPs had 'swollen beyond the rules of moderation and the modesty of former times; and this under pretence of privilege and freedom of speech, whereby they take liberty to declare against all authority of Council and Courts at their pleasure'.[31] For good measure, Charles had nine of the freest-speaking MPs arrested, several of whom were to die in prison and one remain there until 1640.

The Petition of Right, therefore, was a dead letter from the start. Throughout the 1630s people continued to pay taxes which had not been sanctioned by parliament and were arrested when they withheld their money; people were imprisoned and tortured for speaking out on matters of religion. Most notorious is the question of Ship Money. As part of the common law of the land, subjects were obliged to provide manpower, weaponry and money to help the monarch defend the realm. And it was the monarch's highest duty to protect his country against foreign enemies. As with the Forced Loan Charles understood this to mean something different from an emergency levy of men and money when a foreign enemy was approaching the coast. Rather it was a permanent situation in which the king should have the discretion to fulfil that part of his duty. Ship Money was an ancient and disused part of national defence whereby counties and towns provided warships for their monarch. For Charles it would provide a steady income and free him from the inconvenience and indignity of haggling with difficult parliaments for cash. One MP from the parliaments of the 1620s, John Hampden, resisted, on the grounds that it was a tax not sanctioned by parliament (which had not sat since 1629). Under the common law, monarchs might require their subjects to lay down their property and lives for their country. But where was the enemy in the 1630s? No one could pretend that another country was about to invade, or at least invade before parliament could be summoned to raise a tax. But this sense of rule by virtue of emergency powers was becoming ever more permanent.

When Hampden's case was brought to court the judges supported him in principle, but could not deny that the king had legal powers to raise supply for purely military purposes; put another way, he was not confiscating private property but redirecting it towards an end in which the whole community had an interest. The power in the state must have this right, said the judge, or else 'I do not understand how the King's Majesty may be said to have the magisterial right and power of a free monarch'. The court was not prepared to divest the king of powers that might prove essential in an emergency. But for others Charles was straining the ordinary meaning of prerogative, which was needed to defend the country in exceptional circumstances, and in the process he was making a mockery of the common law and parliament by setting them at naught in times of peace.[32] This cavalier approach to the spirit of the law and the dignity of parliament was subjecting liberty to the king's conception of necessity. There could be no settled rule of law and no security of property if this became a general policy. This was put in emotive language for his contemporaries by Sir John Strangeways when parliament met again in 1640: 'If the king be judge of the necessity we have nothing and are but tenants-at-will.'

In the Palace of Westminster the statue of John Hampden faces that of Lord Clarendon, supporter of Charles I, Lord Chancellor to Charles II and historian of the civil wars. That is how the English liked to see their history: the clash and eventual reconciliation of opposites. Hampden symbolises the rule of law and liberty; Clarendon the conversion of the monarchy to constitutional forms and parliamentary government. For generations of historians the events of 1628 and the ensuing decade of disputes laid the foundations for habeas corpus and all other liberties. It was the bridge between the crude liberty of distant history and more refined modern liberty. Indeed, the parliamentary cause in the run-up to conflict in 1642 was, in the Whig interpretation, all about the vindication of English liberty against arbitrary government.

Most modern historians reject this interpretation. The gentry who sat in Charles I's parliaments had a host of grievances. It wasn't so much the arbitrary power inherent in the Crown so much as the way it was abused. The 1620s were not a happy time: the economy was in tatters; Charles's military adventures were costly farces; religious policies seemed to be lenient towards Catholics and authoritarian towards Protestants. England seemed to be in decline, a poor shadow of what she was under Elizabeth. In Coke's famous metaphor, the bounteous garden of the commonwealth was being eaten away by caterpillars – parasites who abused their power by enriching themselves. And of all looming dangers, Charles's inept foreign policy was allowing England's enemies to creep closer to the Channel ports. Facing such threats to prosperity, to national prestige and to their Church the gentry who sat in parliament focused their opposition into the all-embracing issue of liberty. It was a call for regular government and the rule of law when so much seemed to be in disarray, a search for a cure for misgovernment more than for over-government.[33]

For Englishmen were not unaccustomed to over-government. Stuart parliamentarians might shudder to recall it, but Elizabeth had suppressed free speech in parliament, subjected critics to the rigours of Star Chamber and trumped the common law with martial law when it suited her. But reading the debates and publications of the time it was as if Charles had suddenly usurped power and trampled underfoot the time-honoured rights of Englishmen. When lawyers such as Coke and yeomen like Hampden recalled the struggles for liberty of the past they were plugging directly into the emotions of their countrymen, touching on what was considered a national instinct and a unique feature of their history and religion. They depicted themselves as restorers of rights which were nonetheless integral to the nation for their long abeyance. 'We must vindicate: What? New things?' asked Sir Thomas Wentworth. 'No: our ancient, legal, and vital liberties; by reinforcing the laws enacted by our ancestors; by setting such a stamp upon them, that no licentious spirit shall dare henceforth to invade them.'[34]

But this language, noble as it is, masked just how explosive were parliament's demands. The powers to which they objected and the liberties they extolled all belonged to a common past; they bore the traces of distinct periods in English history. Voltaire would later observe that 'liberty was born in England out of the quarrels of the tyrants'.[35] And what was seen as immemorial liberty was, on closer inspection, something very different from the kind of constitutional freedom beloved of lawyers and parliamentarians. At no time in the past had liberty meant *personal* liberty; rather it meant privileges for certain groups in society. Periods of so-called liberty in the English past were little more than conflicts between sets of powerful men – the jockeying for power between kings and nobles. Medieval liberty was essentially the independence of over-mighty subjects – and its consequence was often licentiousness and anarchy when central authority succumbed to the ambitions and avarice of the barons. The loser was the humble subject. The rhetoric of 'liberty' in medieval parliaments and texts covered a multitude of sins with a beguiling ideology. Indeed, the increase of royal prerogative, especially under the Tudors, had meant the subordination of a factious aristocracy and a powerful Church and the end of intestine violence that had recurred in England for centuries. The 'liberty' that had been lost was really the power of lawless aristocrats, which was incompatible with popular rights. Royal authority under Henrys VII and VIII, Edward VI and Elizabeth had created stability and extended law over licentious or power-hungry groups, be they nobles, priests, factions or rebels.

English history had periods when central authority had been weak and factional strife common, and times of strong royal power and relative peace, and seventeenth-century government was marked by elements of both. Habeas corpus was part of the common-law inheritance; but so too were the doctrine that the king could do no wrong and the absolute power of a monarch to secure the defence of the realm as he or she felt fit. A clear-cut *meum et tuum* simply did not exist when it came to the government and the individual, or at least not one that could be drawn from either law or history. As David Hume wrote in the eighteenth century of this time, if the diverse precedents had been pursued it would become apparent 'that the constitution of England was, at that time, an inconsistent fabric, whose jarring and discordant parts must soon destroy each other'.[36]

So, by making Charles out to be a usurper of popular liberties, parliamentarians were moving on to swampy ground. There was a realisation that government was not working and a growing desire for liberty. But it was seventeenth-century liberty that was needed, not a romantic recreation of medieval lordly independence. Modern civilisation, with its increase in commerce, learning and arts, required reconciliation between authority and liberty, between monarchical power and parliamentary participation. When parliamentarians used 'liberty', therefore, it was unclear what they meant. In essence, it symbolised the clash with Charles and the impossible situation whereby MPs and the Lords swapped money for minor constitutional concessions and the sporadic redress of grievances, and where the king was bent upon ignoring the Petition of Right and ruling without parliaments at all. There was no check or balance that could be imposed upon Charles but by force if he was not prepared to compromise. The decisions of the courts and the ease with which Charles ignored parliament showed that there was no constitutional means by which the parliamentary cause could be vindicated. As the king saw matters, his enemies were trying to divest him of authority which would propel the state back into the kind of anarchy that beset it in its licentious past. And as far as parliament was concerned, every move the king made was an irrecoverable step towards tyranny.

There was a hunger for liberty, evinced in parliament and without. The appeal to history was sincere. It gave Englishmen of all hues something to seize upon in their dispute with the king, a sense of right and a language with which to formulate their desires. It was a rhetorical inheritance of immense value. It provided the descent into civil war in 1642 with a vivid language and a basis for opposition, even if we cannot ascribe the reasons men took up arms as a revolution on behalf of liberty; other, more complex reasons, explain this.

As Charles's reign unravelled with disastrous defeats in Scotland and rebellion in Ireland he became beholden to parliament for finance. And parliament seized the opportunity 'to reduce him to the necessity of granting'.[37] This had been the strategy since it tried to impeach the Duke of Buckingham and pass the Petition of Right, only this time the king's need was greater and his resistance weaker. In return for income and help to subdue Scotland and Ireland Charles had no choice but to concede to parliament. Star Chamber (which enforced royal proclamations) and other prerogative courts were abolished; parliaments were to be called automatically, not by whim of the monarch; royal revenue was settled on a regular footing; Ship Money was declared illegal; bishops were deprived of their right to sit in the Lords; habeas corpus was given new legal meaning; and Archbishop Laud and the Earl of Strafford, Charles's chief advisers, were impeached.

Charles said that parliament had 'taken the government all in pieces, and I may say it is almost off the hinges'. Parliament's actions were negative: it aimed to prevent the king from doing any greater harm as the three kingdoms fell further into crisis. It took control over certain areas – taxation and the militia principally. There was no attempt to refashion government; alternatives to monarchy were never discussed. They did not want to take royal power 'out of the crown', but merely to 'suspend the execution of it for this time and occasion only'. This was the prevailing opinion in the Commons; most realised that they were in the midst of a crisis which Charles could only exacerbate by his stupidity.[38]

By the end of 1641 parliament and king were in a position of mutual loathing and suspicion; each feared the other would resort to violence. When parliament tried to take control over the royal household itself and reform the Church, the king reversed his humiliating policy of compromise, and, having failed to break parliament by force when he arrived with his guards to arrest its leading members, retreated from London. Unable to conceive of an alternative to monarchy, parliament was acting like a kind of regent, as if Charles was a child or a lunatic. It had, according to Lord Saye and Seele, become impossible 'to trust him with the power whereby he may do himself and us hurt'.[39] It was an uneasy state of undeclared war in which, as Hobbes said, 'there was no blood shed; they shot at one another nothing but paper'.[40] In July 1642 Sir Benjamin Rudyard told parliament that 'we have gone as far as words can carry us'.[41] Within a month Charles had raised his standard at Nottingham in a last desperate bid to regain his authority. On 23 October the royalist and the parliamentarian armies engaged each other at Edgehill.

CHAPTER 2

Teeming Liberty

—⚬—

Fire and *water* may be restrained, but *light* cannot; it will in at every cranny, and the more it is opposed, it shines the brighter: so that now to stint it, is to resist an *enlightened, enflamed multitude*.

LORD BROOKE, 1642[1]

If the liberty of a man consists in the empire of his reason, the absence whereof would betray him unto the bondage of his passions; then the liberty of a commonwealth consisteth in the empire of her laws, the absence whereof would betray her unto the lusts of tyrants; and these I conceive to be the principles upon which Aristotle and Livy . . . have grounded their assertion that a commonwealth is the empire of the laws and not of men.

JAMES HARRINGTON[2]

I fear yet [the] iron yoke of outward conformity hath left a slavish print upon our necks.

JOHN MILTON[3]

Speaking of the unsuccessful attempts of the Elizabethan parliaments to stand up to the Virgin Queen, David Hume said that their arguments provided 'a rude sketch' of the principles of liberty. The same could be said of the parliaments of Charles I. The ideas and language of liberty were there, but the means of putting it into action were wanting. The gains were considerable – and they live with us still as the bedrock of liberty. The rhetoric of the parliamentarians, of habeas corpus, the independence of parliament and courts, the primacy of laws and institutions over arbitrary government and so on, became, in due course, sacrosanct. It came from *their* idealised view of English history, one where resolute yeomen – the backbone of the nation – stood up to vindicate their natural and inherited rights when they were invaded by encroaching power. Yet their imperfect vision of liberty and free government was never realised; the necessary admixture of authority had collapsed under the pressure of war, rebellion and constitutional wrangling since 1639. Yet this vision entered the soul of English politics – and shaped it in later generations – even though liberty was effectively dead from the moment king and parliament embarked on their separate paths.

The praiseworthy 'passion for liberty' which animated people leads to alarming and unpredictable consequences. Political philosophers such as Thomas Hobbes (who lived through the anarchy of the seventeenth century) and David Hume (who genuinely feared its reappearance in the eighteenth century) took authority as the starting point for analysing liberty. The men of 1642 (and 1628 for that matter) became besotted with the idea of liberty, but it was a utopian notion that owed more to their vision of things as they should be than to what they *were*. Liberty, then, was a slogan with great emotional punch but very little content; it wrecked men's attachments to power without solving humankind's need for authority. Hobbes wrote that 'to obey the laws, is the prudence of the subject; for without such obedience the commonwealth (which is every subject's safety and protection) cannot subsist'. Parliamentarians who withheld money or obedience from the king had a 'want of knowledge of what is necessary for their own defence'. The call of liberty seduced even wise heads, and the passions stirred up rendered liberty impossible. Much later Hume wrote of this time that the undue power of the monarchy begat 'an immeasurable appetite for liberty' just as at other times violence and *excessive* liberty made people envious of the stultifying peace of an absolute monarchy.

But this love of liberty had only one elemental instinct: how to strike at power; it had nothing to put in its place. Civil liberty was the fruit of civilisation; what was called 'liberty' by malcontents and zealots was really selfish independence better called 'licence'. Milton wrote at the height of the wars:

Licence they mean when they cry liberty;
For who loves that, must first be wise and good;
But from that mark how far they rove we see,
For all this waste of wealth and loss of blood.[4]

For Hume the Civil War was a replay of other times in English history when the important men in the kingdom rose up against onerous power, but soon succumbed to authority again from fear of licentious violence; it was not the founding of modernity but the last throes of a primitive instinct for independence that was blind to the baleful consequences. The moderate path between authority and freedom – the true meaning of liberty – had not yet been discovered: that was the achievement of enlightened modern men.

But it might well be asked how liberty could ever be achieved unless by the zeal of enthusiasts. Liberty has more often been won in moments of storm and passion, when everything is in flux. It has rarely progressed in times of dozy tranquillity – or even times of scholarly enlightenment. This brings to mind Milton's famous line about people preferring 'bondage with ease' to 'strenuous liberty'. The clash of ideas and events in times of struggles for liberty produces energy and innovative thinking to a degree that is impossible when things meander along in the same old accustomed manner. What Lord Brooke (a parliamentarian and Puritan) called 'an enlightened, enflamed multitude'[5] which sought liberty was more a consequence than a cause of the civil wars. Breakdown in the state came not from revolutionary libertarians indiscriminately removing old barriers, but from other factors. The king's inaptitude for power and his final inability to govern his three kingdoms brought the country to the brink; his determination to evade constitutional settlement, by force if necessary, made peace all but impossible. And the absence of any group of politicians blessed with the ability to seize events and shape them meant that parliament and king veered off into irreconcilable loathing and mistrust.

The result was an extraordinary period of freedom as authority withered away – freedom of thought and discussion. It was unprecedented. In 1640 twenty-two political pamphlets were published; in 1642 this had rocketed to 1,966, and this does not include newssheets and ballads.[6] The books and pamphlets from this short period in English history, which make up the Thomason Collection in the British Library, number in excess of twenty thousand. As Milton wrote in his famous *Areopagitica*, the sudden release of cramping authority unleashed the imaginative powers of the people. Ideas that had been simmering away in secret burst into print, given urgency by national crisis. And this represented the dawn of liberty for Milton: the restraints on human thought had been smashed and the mind had room to think for the first time. The final descent into violence opened the floodgates; perilous times encouraged new and radical ways of thinking about liberty hard to imagine in times of 'bondage with ease'.

Thinkers such as Hobbes and Hume saw Charles's opponents as enthusiasts who were inflamed by specious arguments, whether the romance of historic liberty or the intoxicating passions of religion. And this is partly true. But Hume and Gibbon both admit that fanatical zeal is frequently the moving force in history. For all its terrors, the monomaniac passion of a true believer has the explosive energy to revolutionise the world when men of more sanguine tempers prefer to sleep in peace. Change comes from revolutions, but revolutions are made by the hotheads who pull down but do not construct; that task is left to other people. This time was well supplied with men who were prepared to take up the sword in vindication of their sacred beliefs. The 1640s was a decade of extraordinary religious excitement. For some the prophecies of the Book of Revelation were being fulfilled in terrible violence. Others saw it as millennial, when the enemies of Christ would be vanquished. One writer compared parliament to Samson fighting the Philistines, describing it as a 'quiver so full of chosen and polished shafts for the Lord's work'. Lord Brooke justified the war to the House of Lords with the chilling words, 'but let us proceed to shed the blood of the ungodly'.[7]

The notion of liberty was given powerful augmentation by the religious divide which was opening up between the king and many of his subjects. The break with Rome under Henry VIII, the aggressive process of Reformation under Edward VI, Mary's brutal suppression of the new religion, and the Elizabethan settlement of the Church of

England had penetrated deep into the national consciousness. The early Protestants had rebelled against the spiritual authority of the pope, but had accepted secular authority as the guarantor of reformed religion. The process of reformation had only gone so far; certainly not as far as the austere Protestantism of Geneva or Edinburgh. The Church of England retained traces of Catholicism, especially in some of its rituals and its retention of bishops. James I resisted Puritan demands to accelerate the process of reformation, and was firm in his support of bishops. Yet he did nothing to offend godly sensibilities. His son was less tactful. For one thing Charles was married to a Catholic, and he allowed her court to hear mass and entertain papal prelates. To the irritation of his first parliaments he was lax in enforcing the laws against recusant English Catholics. Worst of all he abandoned England's defensive networks of allegiances with Protestant kingdoms on the Continent. So not only did he leave fellow Protestants helpless, but he let the great Catholic monarchies of Europe march their armies and establish their ports within striking distance of the English coast. If Charles could not reconvert the country he could open the gate for the superpowers of the Catholic world.[8] This apocalyptic scenario was symbolised in his reforms of Church ritual and his hostility to preaching and printing. His Archbishop of Canterbury, William Laud, dragged him further into confrontation with Protestant England.

King and archbishop were convinced that religious dissent was an affront to God and a seditious, anti-monarchical doctrine. Both firmly believed in order and unity in Church and State. As archbishop, Laud set about a fresh reformation. Ornaments and statues of saints and the crucifixion were installed, and popish altars, stripped during the Reformation a century before, were restored. And just as the fabric of the Church was replenished, so was the language and form of the service. Congregations were required to bow at the names of Christ and Mary, music became a key part of ritual, priests had to wear surplices, and preaching was suppressed to give pre-eminence to a formulaic service. This was not just obnoxious to Puritans who believed in 'plain worship', but downright blasphemous. Puritans put great emphasis on the religious spirit; the most important aspect of devotion was preaching the word of God. Anyone should proselytise as long as they were moved by the passions of divine inspiration.

But this kind of spontaneous fervour Laud saw as a fatal enemy to the order of the Church; religious devotion should be expressed only within the structures of prescribed services. The Church, under the authoritarian Laud, was also in charge of censorship and it clamped down on free opinion during Charles's reign. For Puritans this kind of repressed doctrine prevented the direct communion with the word of God and the intellectual aspect of devotion. But much worse in their view, Laud was overtly re-establishing the worst abuses of Catholicism. Superstition and idolatry were replacing the true meaning of the Bible. And, as Englishmen viewed Catholic Europe, papal control was an assault on the mind of men. It represented the crushing of faith under the heel of dogma. Authentic believers should discuss and argue. So Charles and Laud resembled Catholic prelates in their coercive policies and determination to silence the godly. John Milton said that 'he who prays must consult first with his heart', but Laudism made this duty impossible, replacing unprompted devotion with rituals that merely presented 'God with a set of stale and empty words' and corrupting the minds of the godly with distracting imagery and profane music.[9]

Charles's madcap scheme to have English worship imposed on the fiercely Protestant Scottish Kirk led to the Bishops' War which precipitated the civil wars. In England his Church reforms and his employment of Irish Catholic mercenaries when he was attempting to bring parliament to heel in 1641/2 made him seem dangerously tyrannical. It was also seen as a further attack on liberty, but in this instance liberty of conscience. Worst of all, many saw Charles fitting into the mould of a continental Catholic despot, or even an idolatrous tyrant of the Old Testament. It awoke radicalism and fanaticism in many who had tolerated the lukewarm Protestantism of Elizabeth and James. In the 1630s the most zealous of the Puritans were tried for seditious libel and found guilty. They were whipped, their ears cropped, their noses slit, and their cheeks branded with 'SL' for Seditious Libeller, or, as they managed to joke, 'Sign of Laud'. Beleaguered Protestants everywhere had martyrs to look to, bearing, as they saw it, the irrefutable marks of an impious tyranny.

As Lord Brooke wrote, Charles's actions opened a 'Soul-Schism' in which the duty of loyalty led to the rocks of blasphemy. Which authority came higher, God's or the king's? For by obeying the king many felt they were betraying the 'liberties and privilege of all Subjects of Christ'.[10] Or, as John Goodwin put it, reason and judgement in pursuit of spiritual enlightenment were the foundations of the sincere religious life; uniformity imposed from above made people 'yield to blind obedience, never to search in the truth'.[11] That was the fundamental difference between freedom and slavery: enlightenment or darkness, a personal spiritual journey or mind-numbing deference.

Worse still, according to John Milton, external authority like this reduced everything to custom. Laud's censorship was identical to the Inquisition. It destroyed the master spirit, making minds run in grooves cut the deeper by repetition. There could be no intellectual progress when people lived under the dominance of a bishop's court or the king's justice in Star Chamber. And enforced conformity killed the essence of Christian liberty, free choice. Custom and tradition made people dull and passive. No one could be truly good if he or she was led like a child and prevented from making a judgement. The Reformation had supposedly freed people from this kind of external control, but Laudism was rushing the country back to Catholic autocracy. A nation of conformists – in an intellectual as much as a religious sense – would sink into sluggishness and decline. Humans who assumed the authority to put restraints over their fellow humans' thoughts sinned and caused others to sin. Allowing customs or other men to determine your belief was to put something other than God in authority; it was to betray the God-given freedom to choose and take responsibility. Would the self-elected sifters of the truth stand as representatives at the Day of Judgement for the people whose minds they had presumed to govern? It was a fundamental question: for how could men and women give account of themselves to God if someone else had kept them from knowledge and spoonfed them untested assertions?

This was a new perspective (at least in England) in which not just the common law and history but divine law supported liberty. But it chimed with the traditional argument about property-based liberty.

The whipping, slitting and branding of the Puritan enthusiasts coincided with the prosecution of John Hampden, himself the scion of a Puritan family. Giving in to kingly exactions of money was to condone theft, and accept an external authority. Moreover, Puritan writers accepted the negative definition of liberty as wholeheartedly as the lawyers. Charles's creatures aimed at taking people's goods and property; but in dictating religious matters they also had designs on your 'estate' in the afterlife. People who managed to 'lord' it over you as ministers and officers of the Crown could also lord it over your thought and worship. Once the defences of your 'estate' were breached you had either to retreat to the wilderness (where there is no authority but also no protection) or to find a secret place for free contemplation, retreating further into a private world. The third option was to defend your 'sanctuary' (the private mental sphere) by defending the freedom of your 'public assemblies'.[12]

To talk of shielding this 'close and secret' citadel of the spiritual life was considered by many – on the parliamentary as much as the royalist side – to be the most dangerous of the slew of dangerous ideas at this time. For it made every person his or her own judge over religious matters; it made everyone a perpetual rebel against authority. Out of the confusion of civil strife came the radical view that liberty was inherent in mankind. Milton wrote that no one 'can be so stupid to deny that all men naturally were born free, being the image and resemblance of God himself'.[13] What followed from the concept of the all-powerful individual was a fledgling theory of the social contract. Republican writers such as Henry Parker and Samuel Rutherford argued that 'man is the free and voluntary author, the law is the instrument, and God is the establisher of both'. Humans in early society set up laws and magistrates to govern them in good order. But it was a free choice. The Bible commanded that 'one from among thy brethren shalt thou set king over thee' (Deuteronomy XVII.15). But at the same time, the power was still in the possession of the people who, as Rutherford argued, 'must only have made him King *conditionally*, to be a father, a feeder, and tutor'.[14]

Power given on conditions can be recalled, however long that right remains dormant. The republican writers were happy to agree with royalists that monarchy was a divine institution. But they disagreed that Charles had personally been ordained by God. People may agree on a king, but that did not bind them to accepting his weak-minded successors in perpetuity. And God certainly did not give powers to kings to set up false images, introduce impious religious innovations and subject free choice to tyranny. Christians had a sacred obligation to refuse to obey the king if he acted against biblical injunction; if they did not have this right they would be nothing more than 'brute beasts'.

Nothing could be more dangerous as far as orthodox thinkers were concerned. Theories that used popular liberties to limit monarchical powers were answered by a deluge of publications. '*Royal Power and Sovereignty of the King*', wrote John Maxwell, 'is from God primarily, formally, immediately.' Rulers were not chosen by 'a headless, a disordered multitude'. If kingly power was a gift of the people, they could ask for it back, 'and may find exigents, which will warrant them to resume, and to exercise this power'. The right to resist a ruler – which was implicit in the radical interpretation of individual liberty – was irreligious, for when a monarch's power could be disputed or denied the country would no longer 'belong in quiet, in peace; no governors can be secured; by these maxims we may change kings and governors as often as moons'. Englishmen need only look at their own bloody history, particularly the Wars of the Roses, to see this – if they did not first look at the cyclical violence of the ancient world. The evil of regarding monarchy as contractual was being shown in 'letters of blood'.[15]

As government crumpled, men were compelled to search for a new source of authority. As many pointed out, liberty could have no meaning in war and confusion: for all his faults, Charles represented an ancient form of government which could allow for individual liberty. Were the occasional abuses of power and injustices a small price to pay for stability? And did any other system of government exist which would be any better? Many doubted that sinful and naturally selfish humans could ever devise an alternative. As the king said during the war, parliamentary government was itself arbitrary. In January 1649, after his final defeat, when he was on trial for his life, Charles pointed out that power had fallen into the hands of a self-selected group of men who had no discernible legitimacy or obligation to the people. Parliament had never articulated an alternative mode of government or vision of liberty. What kind of brave new world awaited England? The ancient form of government had been torn up, Charles told his judges, and replaced by a military dictatorship which had assumed the authority to kill a king without consulting the people: 'it is not my case alone, it is the Freedom and the Liberty of the people of England; and do you pretend what you will, I stand more for their Liberties.'[16]

The unequivocal destruction of traditional government in 1649 was nevertheless seen as a starting point for a new form of government and liberty. Historians such as J. G. A. Pocock, Quentin Skinner, Blair Worden and others have provided brilliant studies of the emergence of classical republican thinking in England at this time. If before and during the war liberty was cast as inherent in the ancient constitution, Charles I's execution provided the opportunity for redefining liberty in the context of a dramatically altered constitutional environment. Gone were kings and bishops; the state could be rebuilt with the rights and freedoms of the citizen in mind.

For many writers in 1649–50 England seemed to be poised for a revolution in government. And the new state needed free institutions to secure the liberty of the people. But the people were rather inconveniently the stumbling block: given the choice they would flock back to the magic and sacredness of monarchy. They must learn to see their own interests. First they must give up their sentimental longing for monarchy. 'If men within themselves would be governed by reason,' wrote Milton, 'and not generally give up their understanding to a double tyranny, of custom from without, and blind affection from within, they would discern better, what it is to favour and uphold the Tyrant of a Nation.'[17] According to the great political writer James Harrington, the irrational side of man represented sin and slavery, while reason made him virtuous and free. And the state mirrored the man: liberty existed in the sober reason of free institutions and the impartiality of the rule of law, while the capricious desires and personalised character of a monarchy led to tyranny. A free state was one governed by known laws rather than fallible men – by wisdom rather than whim.[18]

Sovereign power belonged to the people. But for the time being that power had been transferred to the House of Commons and a Council of State to preserve the embryo free state. One republican propagandist bluntly told the people that their liberties and rights had been given to parliament for safe keeping because 'your selves are so apt to mistake in your Desires, not truly understanding what may tend to make you happy'.[19] Freedom was a precious jewel which the people would fling away because they were so thoroughly conservative and besotted by monarchy. Full-scale reform should await the time when 'the inhabitants of this Nation shall have drank awhile of the sweet waters of that Well of Liberty, which the Army have digged and opened with their Swords'.[20] The Free State should be a lesson in liberty for the people who, after all, had sacrificed so much.

The unexpected turn of events which had brought the three kingdoms to war and the final, unpredicted, fall of the monarchy were seen by a new generation of writers as one of those events in history which presented people with a unique opportunity. The key writers of the republican interlude – James Harrington, John Milton and Marchamont Nedham, among others – were all steeped in classical literature and the writings of Niccolo Machiavelli, principally his *Discorsi* on the histories of Livy. Harrington and Nedham were among those figures of the republic who had been associated with the king's cause. Harrington was a scholar who was close to parliament in an intellectual sense and to Charles I in a personal one. Nedham was a man of different stamp. He was a journalist who had alternated between king and parliament depending on his personal circumstances. He backed the wrong horse towards the end of the wars, and found himself in Newgate prison when the Commonwealth was founded. Happy to repent, however, and responding to the new regime's demand for journalists, he edited the government's newssheet, *Mercurius Politicus*. This he did with the help and connivance of the state licenser, John Milton, a passionate republican. Neither Harrington nor Nedham had been hotheaded anti-monarchists before the execution of Charles; the monarchy abolished, however, they shared a determination to accept the sudden and irrecoverable break with the past and help design a free republic.

History – this time non-English history – provided guidance and warnings for the emergent Commonwealth. Harrington had little time for his countrymen's veneration of medieval government – the constitutional balance of monarchy, nobility and the people. The answer lay further back, in the history of the ancient republics. From distant times freedom and tyranny had been locked in perpetual conflict. And waiting in the wings was always a dictator strong enough to quell the antagonistic elements. Nothing was harder in human affairs, Machiavelli said, than for a state or a people to remain in freedom. The English republic should be aware that even the strongest states were vulnerable to the levelling hand of fortune; there seemed to be an inevitable process where states fell to competitors, or destroyed themselves by falling, by stages, into enervating luxury and factional strife. According to Machiavelli the cycle of history that dictated the rise and fall of free states could be broken by the energy and virtue of its citizens. The freedom and, consequently, greatness of a state depended on the liberty of its members. They must learn the arts of self-government and civic virtue – by choice or, if necessary, by identifying their private, selfish ends with the needs of the state.

In the context of England in 1649, this meant designing a state with institutions which called upon the talents and energies of its people. This was to place liberty at the centre of political life. It was a version of what today we tend to call 'positive liberty' – the idea that freedom was given meaning by one's participation in the political life of the nation. This forced republican writers to try to give a clear definition of liberty, for, if it was to have any value, it must lead to specific ends. This contrasts with the older model, whereby liberty was simply the absence of restraint which allowed subjects to do as they wanted in their private sphere. Positive liberty embraced engagement and citizenship.

The chief benefit of liberty, therefore, was its role in maintaining the health of the nation. It also profited the citizens themselves, for they would learn the arts of civilisation and augment their wealth as members of a flourishing community. This follows Machiavelli's cynicism about human nature: people won't naturally be good citizens unless their direct interests are involved. Writers such as Nedham and Harrington went out of their way to stress the benefits of living under a free state. Like Machiavelli they believed that an armed population was better than a standing army: the people must take it upon themselves to defend their country and further its ambitions abroad. Such an arrangement would be cheap; it would also involve citizens in the decisions of the state. And it would bring liberty to the people, for so armed they would counterbalance the power of the nobility or would-be dictators.

The republic must also be one of property holders – because an independent gentry class was historically the most eager to defend liberties against arbitrary rule.[21] (Harrington rendered himself dangerous when he wrote that the desire for liberty had grown up in the sixteenth century as more people became property owners and that the logic of a republic would be the continual division of property until everyone was a landowner and hence a participant in government.[22]) The republic should find ways other than militia service and gentry status to involve people in the running of government. Most clearly, everyone, including the propertyless and poor, should perceive that the republic was more peaceful, predictable and cheap than a monarchy. It allowed the citizens to prosper, because the gain of one was the gain of the community. Kings and their courtiers benefited from the degradation of subjects because they taxed and spent as they saw fit. So it was in the people's direct interest to watch over their institutions and prevent selfish and ambitious men from insinuating their way into power and restoring, as in ancient Rome, the principles of monarchy. The ordinary folk should be the watchdogs of liberty because, as Nedham said, they knew best where the shoe pinched.

But how could this work? Looking at history, Nedham said that the English in the 1650s were like the Romans when they expelled the Tarquins: they got rid of the *name* 'King' whilst the *thing* remained, the power transferred to the hands of a small class of senators.[23] Liberty required 'more than an ordinary art and industry to preserve it'.[24] It was especially hard to discern the signs of constitutional takeover: the enemies of free states moved quietly and artfully, sapping freedom gradually or exploiting some grave emergency. As Machiavelli warned, any state was vulnerable to the *ambizione* (ambition) of the great men who would always be on the lookout to increase their power over the small fry; this was a fact in any polity. Nedham's solution was to put control of popular liberties in the hands of the people themselves, in the forms of tribunes and popular assemblies. The great men might put their wealth and talents towards running the state (this was necessary for efficiency's sake), but they should not have complete impunity. The people should take the responsibility of guarding popular rights – that is to say the legislature (the people's representatives) should scrutinise the executive (the nobility who, in Machiavellian terms, were prone to *ambizione*).

But why would the great families tolerate this? If they were prone to power-lusts, the people were attracted to licentiousness rather than liberty. The answer was to find a way of harnessing the advantages the different classes possessed – in other words, designing forms and procedure. Harrington followed Machiavelli's advice of turning the deficiencies of human nature towards public benefits and he explained it in a vivid metaphor. If two girls have a cake to share then the only way that both can get a fair outcome is for one to cut the cake in half and the other to choose the piece she wants: the girl cutting the cake can't choose first because she will naturally cut a larger portion for herself. And so the diversity of people in terms of intelligence, courage, strength and wealth makes an equitable solution hard to determine. How can these conflicting interests be reconciled? 'Ask the girls,' says Harrington. If the ruling class decided on how much to tax the people and how to spend it then they would tend to take too much. The answer is for the senate (or the assembly of the nobility) to debate and 'divide' and for the people to choose from the options offered to them. This is to separate deciding, paying and doing – so that each estate has a defined role and limits the other. The 'two silly girls' with the cake have discovered the way in which the interests of the few and the many can be reconciled. Everyone's liberties and interests can be defended if in all matters of state (as much as in matters of cake) the interested parties say, 'Divide, and

I will choose; or let me divide and you shall choose.' In the free state the apparently incompatible benefits of aristocracy (the senate), democracy (the people) and monarchy (the executive) are therefore brought into harmony: 'the commonwealth consisteth of the senate proposing, the people resolving and the magistracy executing'.[25]

This is what Harrington called 'the empire of laws' – cool procedure takes over from the storms of factionalism. Freedom could be maintained if the state was a balance not only of its legislative and executive functions but also of the classes and conditions of its citizenry. In short, no one should dominate over another, or else liberty would disappear. To prevent this, all offices in government should be rotated by ballot. This satisfied personal ambition without making power permanent and it drew greater numbers of citizens into fulfilling their public duty: 'the very life of liberty is in a succession of powers and persons'.[26]

This is state-building with the liberty of the individual at the centre. In spatial terms the liberty of the citizen is of such a great extent that the state has to grow round it. The principle at the heart of the state should be the defence of the rights of its people; all institutions should be designed with this as the start and end point. All power therefore *ascends* (the opposite of a monarchy), and it is grounded in the rights of the individual. At the heart of this concept is the *negative* liberty of the citizen. His private sphere is sacrosanct, and cannot be invaded; therefore all actions of the government have to adapt themselves to take this into account. Power must flow in regular channels to protect the people's rights. But the *positive* liberties of the individual also affect the constitution of the state. By choosing and/or limiting his rulers, the citizen ensures that the sovereign power is directed towards the public good. The outcomes of his negative liberties are justice and limited government. Those of his positive liberties are the best individuals in power, good government and a balance of interests. In turn the citizens have a government which is efficient and cheap, because its officers are chosen by the people and accountable to them, and open, because the people demand scrutiny. And the governing power can count on an obedient population and public peace because the people have a share in the state and something to gain from the common endeavour.

Thomas Hobbes sneered at such visions. He argued that the quantity of liberty in a state would be the same in a monarchy or a so-called 'free state'. The mistake that Harrington and Nedham made was to confuse power and liberty. Citizens or subjects would always be oppressed in some way or another because they would have to obey, at some point, laws to which they had not assented. Whether it was a king or a parliament or the majority which made the law did not matter – it was still a sovereign power remote from the individual. The best which could be said was that at some point fate might thrust you into a position to make the law, and then you would have a glimpse of liberty for the moment. What was important, Hobbes said, were negative liberties – that space the citizen had in which the laws were silent. The character of the government did not matter a jot, save for one thing – the ability it had to protect its subjects and make laws to regulate the antagonistic relations of human beings. When men throughout history used the 'specious name of Libertie' to rebel they were really trying to control their controllers in a fit of arrogance, and thereby exchanging the protection of the law for the horrors of war. Machiavelli's 'active citizens' were in truth factious rebels who read too much fanciful ancient history about noble Roman citizens and who brought their states interminable violence by their inability to accept power: just look at the decrepitude into which Italy had fallen. There existed in every state, whatever its character, absolute power to accomplish its tasks. And this power would always trump the fancied rights of citizens to limit or share authority. 'There is written on the turrets of the city of *Lucca* in great characters at this day the word LIBERTAS,' wrote Hobbes; 'yet no man can thence infer that a particular man has more Liberty or immunity from the service of the Commonwealth there than in *Constantinople*. Whether a commonwealth be monarchical or popular, the freedom is still the same.'[27]

But given the choice I'd rather live in seventeenth-century Lucca (a nominally free state) than Constantinople (an autocratic one). It is nonsense to suppose that the quantity or quality of liberty was the same in these cities. Negative liberty varies in the size of the sphere that is allowed to the individual; in despotic states it can be very small indeed. And a bigoted, fanatical state might give you a thousand privileges: you might be free to keep a harem, feast on delicacies every day, rampage through the streets or whatever; but what is this worth if you are made to believe what you are told and your worship is compelled? As Quentin Skinner argues, any theory of liberty must begin with negative liberties, that aspect of life which is one's own and in which what is conventionally known as freedom can be enjoyed.[28] Yet these liberties will always remain precarious unless the citizen has the power to hold rulers to account; that is to say, by the exercise of positive liberty. Machiavelli's point, picked up by his English followers, was that personal freedom flourished best in a free commonwealth. True liberty – which contained elements of the positive and negative – was the result of pursuing social duties and fulfilling political obligations. Liberties therefore did not exist as desiccated rights that could be given to you by a benevolent government; they only found existence in the daily, unremitting struggle of the citizen. Once the forward movement of energy and participation ceased then the liberties disappeared – you became a passive recipient of whatever rights a ruler happened to give you.

For the neo-classical writers this called upon Englishmen to be strict, serious and sober. Guardians of their own polity, citizens first had to adopt the manners and habits of a republic. (And, as has been pointed out, this concept of citizenship chimed with the Puritan mentality.[29]) 'For as there is no happiness without liberty,' wrote Algernon Sidney, 'and no man more a slave than he that is overmastered by vicious passions, there is neither liberty, nor happiness, where there is not virtue.'[30] If these modes of conduct were not learnt, then indolence and corruption would creep in, paving the way for a restoration of monarchy or dictatorship. True freedom depended on your attitude and ability to subject yourself to rigorous discipline – 'strenuous liberty' indeed.

And here is the problem. The people's liberties cannot exist but in a free state, and a free state cannot be built unless the people have liberty. Do the wise citizens design a republic in the hope that the people will reform themselves and not abuse their responsibilities? Or do they assume authority to train the people in the principles of liberty, even if the vulgar only want 'bondage with ease'? This leads to a morass when trying to define liberty. Milton believed that the condition of liberty would render men good because, by removing the restraints of tyranny and servile custom, it released the active powers of mind and spirit. He believed that 'substantial liberty . . . is rather to be sought from within than from without; and whose existence depends not so much on the terror of the sword, as on sobriety of conduct and integrity of life'.[31] This places a serious obligation on the individual: if his liberty is dependent on self-regulation rather than external authority then there will be an eternal conflict in the human mind between the desire for freedom and the need for discipline. Liberty is no easy thing. Do you therefore have to earn it? And can you free men by imposing discipline on them? The answer is not made clear. Milton wrote this in 1659/60, when the people were rushing towards Charles II; it is a last plea for Englishmen to perceive the glory of republican values. In these circumstances liberty becomes a distant prospect, the free state a vain dream that has been scorned by the unworthy people.

A decade before, writers like Milton had assumed that liberty on its own would purify the people as they moved from the darkness of corrupting monarchy into the light of reason. He was much influenced by the Roman writers Tacitus and Sallust, who both argued that under the control of monarchy people dwindled into passivity and mental inhibition, fearful lest their talents attract the jealousy of their masters. Republics, because they demanded participation, unlocked creative energy.[32] In *Areopagitica* (1644), Milton conferred on liberty an integral value: 'Behold now this vast City: a city of refuge, the mansion house of liberty . . .' full of 'pens and heads . . . sitting by their studious lamps, musing, searching, revolving new notions and ideas . . . others as fast reading, trying all things, assenting to the force of reason and convincement'.[33] In the free marketplace of ideas truth will always prevail over falsehood and charlatanry. 'The minds of men are the great wheels of things,' wrote John Warr at the same time; 'thence come changes and alterations to the world; teeming freedom exerts and puts forth itself.'[34]

The fruits of liberty, then, are unbounded, unknowable and necessary for human flourishing. Milton imbues it with a high moral worth, a purpose beyond merely excluding irksome authority. Liberty becomes the starting point of endeavour. But it must lead somewhere, to some tangible benefit. It also takes courage, for only by exchanging the trammels of conventional thought for individuality can one find freedom. Are these just high words? Do not artists sometimes reach the height of creativity in authoritarian and censorious regimes? Or is liberty awoken by the struggle for liberty, so that we perceive mankind's ingenuity and courage best in the sparks of collision rather than during the torpid luxury when liberty is attained? At the very least Milton's words are a glimpse of the possibilities of freedom written at a time when anything seemed possible. Liberty meant, for him and others, the beginning of an era when humans could indeed be humans in the fullest sense – once the artificial straitjacket and the stupefying drug of absolute power are taken away. If Milton does not – or cannot – determine the road there, it is no less incumbent upon mankind to exert its energies to find the route.

This flowering of English political thought coincided with a time when liberty was not in fashion, at least not with the country's new rulers. The government did not dare test its popularity by calling an election, and parliament remained the one which had been called by Charles I, albeit purged of many of its original members. The real power in the state lay with soldiers who had fought in the parliamentarian armies. The freedom of the House of Commons and the liberties of the people were, according to one petition, 'under the visible, detestable force and sword of a rebellious and mutinous army, who have imprisoned, excluded, and forced away most of their fellow members'.[35]

Cromwell was the only man of stature who could stand between the army and parliament. He also knew that the new state would only survive if it reached out to the property owners and merchants – the naturally conservative. Reform was slow, and Cromwell had to take on the quasi-monarchical role of Protector to maintain order. The knot of republican writers were carried along unwillingly. The dreams of founding a new Rome were impossible. The priority switched from building a free state to keeping out the Stuarts at any price. Cromwell was a regrettable necessity. Perhaps the people were simply not up to the rigorous demands of active citizenship; they must learn to love liberty before they could be trusted. The radicals were left feeling distinctly let down by the timidity of their new leaders. 'Certainly we looked for the good hand of peace, but behold oppression,' opined one writer. 'We looked for liberty, but behold slavery! and our end is worse than our beginning.'[36]

By the end of Cromwell's life, people were talking openly of the benefits of an hereditary monarchy and strong government to prevent the tumults of the common folk.[37] By 1659, after Cromwell's death, there was a power vacuum in the country, and another civil war seemed likely. After so many years of uncertainty and tepid experiment, the people were more than happy to see the restoration of the monarchy in the person of Charles II. If 1649 was what Machiavelli called an *occasione* – the moment when history could be transformed by wise men – it was a road not taken.

This section started with the concept of liberties in the ancient constitution. It ends with the radical injection of new ideas into English thinking and their utter failure to alter the events of civil war, Commonwealth and Restoration. But these ideas would retain their vitality, even when the books of Harrington, Nedham, Milton and other radicals laboured under official ban. They never lost their grip on politicians and thinkers; their effects were yet to be felt – which they would be, not least in the American Revolution.

Most importantly, the memories of this period became a moment in the English psyche. Liberty was a thing of the emotions, what people believed to be the natural state of English life. The belief in national liberties stretching back into time immemorial retained a hold on people; the sense that it was their birthright gave them the stomach to resist rulers and a justification for doing so. The Levellers, who had the heart to stand up to Charles, parliament and Cromwell, insisted on fundamental English freedoms as much as the MPs who framed the Petition of Right. The Levellers, who had the heart to stand up to Charles, parliament and Cromwell, insisted on fundamental freedoms as much as MPs who framed the Petition of Right. Indeed, they went beyond the cautiousness of other thinkers who grounded their notions of liberty on property rights, insisting on equality of rights for all 'freeborn' Englishmen. Underlying these claims was the unwelcome truth that absolute property rights – so useful in resisting absolute monarchs – might be yet another barrier to the liberties of men and women oppressed not only by political authority but by the economic clout of their superiors. Injustice must be continually fought by people conscious of their liberties; it went beyond constitutionalism. Silenced and punished by monarchs, parliamentarians and Cromwellians, this radicalism survived in English popular culture, never completely extinguished but never completely fulfilled.

This spirit was embedded deep in the culture, and the men who stood up to Charles in 1628 and from 1640 became national heroes for many and examples of anti-authoritarianism, until long into the twentieth century. Their core demands – for limited government, the rights of parliament, trial by jury and habeas corpus – set a kind of gold standard of basic rights, even if their demands were never resolved into a coherent programme. They helped sow the idea of a national trait of anti-authoritarianism and stubbornness which sustained generations of radicals. And perhaps this is just as important as winning concrete victories. Liberty became a vital thing in English politics and sense of nationhood. The *spirit* of liberty remained alive, and it had a history to be embellished and to provide inspiration.

During the painful struggle of these decades the notion of liberty became easier to perceive. The ancient notion of civic freedoms which came from Greece and Rome was fused with a native tradition. The rough and ready ideal of English freedoms based in property and a balanced constitution was augmented by ancient ideas of positive liberty and republicanism. Later thinkers would blend them into the idea of a republican monarchy in which modern liberties could exist within the structure of an ancient monarchy – the belief of the early Whigs which dared not admit its name of republicanism. Added to this was the Puritan's right of resistance and sense of individuality. They all left their traces on the development of liberty in England. Conceived in moments of crisis and conflict these opposing ideas forced their way into compromise with each other.

II

DE FACTO FREEDOM

1660–1760

CHAPTER 3

The Good Old Cause

—∿—

He who will support what hurts himself, because he thinks it the support of the whole liberty we enjoy, shall meet with nothing from me but
what he deserves from all mankind, the utmost respect.

HENRY ST JOHN, VISCOUNT BOLINGBROKE[1]

Liberty is a right which every individual must be ready to vindicate for
himself, and which he who pretends to bestow as a favour has by that
very act in reality denied. Even political establishments though they
appear to be independent of the will and arbitration of men, cannot be
relied on for the preservation of freedom; they may nourish, but should
not supersede that firm and resolute spirit, with which the liberal mind
is always prepared to resist indignities and to refer safety to itself.

ADAM FERGUSON[2]

The *spirit* of liberty burned bright in England in the late seventeenth
and throughout the eighteenth century. If the parliamentarians and
radicals of the Civil War period believed that liberty was part and
parcel of being English, their grandchildren knew that they had not
only restored ancient freedom but enlarged it beyond all historical
precedent. Modern liberty was unique to Britain and the British, they
believed; the history of their lucky country was nothing more than
the history of the progress and perfection of liberty – of civilisation
itself. The Scottish historian and philosopher John Millar wrote that
'The British government is the only one in the annals of mankind
that has aimed at the diffusion of liberty through a multitude of
people, spread over a wide extent of territory.'[3] This is a stunning

assertion. It supposed intentionality on the part of rulers and also a monopoly on the meaning of liberty. That British ideals of freedom did take hold in a vast continent was owing to the spirit of its people, who carried ideas across the Atlantic which had withered in Britain. That liberty failed to be extended across equally vast extents of territory was owing to the very idea that liberty was not universal at all, but the privilege of civilised men – a unique privilege at that.

The idea of liberty was firmly connected to the national temperament and explained the remarkable success of Britain in the eighteenth century; it was never far from the lips of any politician, writer or man on the street. Most importantly its reality was believed in by people of all types and conditions. It distinguished them from the rest of the world, and even from history: not even the great civilisations of antiquity had achieved the same degree of liberty, learning, scientific advancement, commerce, wealth and power as Britain. And it was no accident. Britain in the mid-eighteenth century was humming with energy and wealth; her empire was expanding; and all this came from the boldness and entrepreneurial zeal which was a by-product of liberty.

And where did this come from? Montesquieu and others asserted that the supremacy of the rule of law and the mixed form of government gave every subject a sense of security to say what he wanted and conduct the business of his life with confidence. Others, most notably Hume (in his younger days), believed that the spirit of liberty had woven itself so far into the national character that no one, not even a king, dared offend this sentiment. It was not necessary to *understand* liberty so much as to worship it. Hume wrote that what stopped arbitrary power reappearing in the Britain of the 1740s was not simply regular law or constitutional forms: it was the certain knowledge that even the smallest encroachments on rights or bid for power would be shouted from the rooftops and resisted as tyrannical.

The spirit of the people must frequently be roused, in order to curb the ambition of the court; and the dread of rousing this spirit must be employed to prevent that ambition. Nothing is so effectual to this purpose as the liberty of the press, by which all the learning, wit, and genius of the nation may be employed on the side of freedom, and every one be animated to its defence.[4]

Pursue it to a cast-iron definition and this notion of liberty will crumble in your hand. When every political party and journalist is wielding the term about like a battle-axe against opponents, liberty can have no precise meaning. And when the majority of the people had no political rights and a meagre hope of justice it might seem like a bit of a joke or the hypocrisy of the fortunate free. But Hume is right. For all the vagueness regarding liberty, it had a reality. It was certainly not complete. It was often delusive political cant. But the spirit of freedom gave Britain (and her settled colonies) something that was the envy of less fortunate people throughout the world. Most importantly, it nurtured the habits of liberty which would remain a vital aspect of political and popular culture.

The achievement of this British liberty was believed to have happened against the odds. The Glorious Revolution of 1688 was a 'miracle' whereby the best parts of the liberty envisaged by the Commonwealthsmen of the 1640s and 50s ('the good old cause') were engrafted upon the monarchical system. John Toland, the publisher and writer who kept alive the flame of the republican theorists such as Harrington, said that the achievement of the Revolution was to 'find out the secret of so happily uniting two seemingly incompatible things, Principality and Liberty'.[5] But it was a close-run thing. And it would remain so; liberty was always vulnerable to power and only a vigilant citizenry could defend it.

Those who lived in the years between Charles II's Restoration in 1660 and the Glorious Revolution in 1688 fully expected to see the death of constitutional freedom. Charles had returned promising 'a Liberty to tender consciences', or toleration of the non-Anglican Protestant dissenters, following Lord Chancellor Clarendon's advice that after the civil wars and interregnum the monarchy could only survive if it reconciled all the groups in society. He also extended this theme of healing and forgiveness by incorporating some of Cromwell's ministers and soldiers into his government. The reforms of 1640–2 were kept: there was no revival of Star Chamber or royal monopolies, although bishops were restored. But Henry Neville, a key republican writer, called this Charles's 'honeymoon': the promise of liberty masked a deeper desire to restore monarchy in the long term. This is how it looked in hindsight. By the 1670s, the representatives of 'the good old cause' – the survivors of the Cromwellian period – had left government and, under the leadership of the Earl of Shaftesbury, had formed the embryonic Whig party. The battle lines of the 1640s seemed to have sprung up again. The old cavaliers, scarred by the dark days of the interregnum and haunted by the spectre of anarchy, were steadfast in support of Charles II, while elderly parliamentarians and their scions were reviving fears of absolute monarchy.

And it was over the linked issues of religion and foreign policy that the country split. Charles seemed dangerously partial to Louis XIV, the supreme example of an absolute Catholic ruler, with whom he waged war against the Protestant Dutch Netherlands; his brother and heir, James, Duke of York, was openly Catholic; the leading royal mistress was as well – and French to boot; and the Secretary of State, Lord Arlington, was unmasked as a secret member of that faith. The old notion of an international Catholic conspiracy was more potent than ever. Louis's dream of Universal Monarchy – in France but also throughout Europe – seemed close to realisation. And Charles appeared to be aiding the plan. By allowing Louis to overrun the Low Countries, England was sacrificing the last defence barrier on the European mainland and handing over her principal Protestant and strategic ally to the most powerful, ambitious and destructive monarchy. The liberties of England to exert herself as a great power were under real threat; the liberties of Englishmen would inevitably follow the same fate as French power and French methods of government conquered territory and official mindsets.

A realistic fear that modern Europe (England included) would be shaped along absolutist principles manifested itself in wholly unrealistic fantasies. In 1678 the country was in ferment when the 'Papal Plot' was brought to light by Titus Oates. The substance of it was that the king would be assassinated, James would come to the throne and the bulwarks of Protestant Europe would fall to predatory France – James's natural ally. As France expanded, England's strategic leverage in Europe – and hence the wider world – would disappear; eventually the country would be forcibly converted to Catholicism and anyone foolish enough to resist would be gladly added to the list of Protestant martyrs. Look at the Great Fire, the rabble-rousers said; that was an early attempt by Catholic terrorists to bring the country to its knees. It was preposterous, but it was believed and sent the country into a fever; it also chimed with fears that had been simmering throughout Charles's reign. Catholicism was firmly associated with autocracy, force and injustice. 'There has now', wrote Andrew Marvell in his best-selling *An Account of the Growth of Popery and Arbitrary Government in England*, 'for diverse Years, a design been carried on, to change the lawful Government of *England* into an Absolute Tyranny, and to convert the established Protestant Religion into down-right Popery.'[6]

Riding the wave of anti-Catholic hysteria, the parliamentary opposition, led by Shaftesbury, tried to defend English liberties pre-emptively by excluding James from the succession to the throne. What was at stake, many MPs believed, was the future of England. Lose, and the country would be deprived of its religion and become something like France – a centralised, bureaucratic autocracy with few freedoms left for the people, who crouched under fear of a large professional army. The Exclusion Crisis lasted for three years, and Charles would not compromise.

But out of this fraught period came one huge gain for liberty. In 1679 parliament, desperate to build up defences against an imminent Catholic tyranny, passed the Habeas Corpus Act. Under this law, no one could be held in prison for more than one night under any circumstances without charges being brought. At the time it seemed to have caused few ripples, there being bigger issues at stake; but in later years it would be regarded as the bulwark of liberty. William Blackstone called it a 'second Magna Charta' upon which all other liberties were dependent. Another writer said that the absolute right of remedy in court against injustice and the right to be tried in front of a jury meant that Englishmen 'enjoy a liberty scarce known to the ancient *Greeks* and *Romans*'. Later, Hume would say that the Act gave Britons an almost excessive liberty, which was often incompatible with good policing on the part of the state, but which was the price the country paid for freedom. Habeas corpus had, of course, been part of the common law and had been bolstered by the Petition of Right and act of parliament. What this act did was to close the loopholes which governments had learnt how to exploit. It deprived the executive of the right to act expeditiously without consent of parliament. If an emergency compelled the government to hold dangerous people without charge it would have to ask parliament to suspend the law.[7]

Like so many English liberties, its origins were an unremarkable and unheroic incident. A City man called Francis Jenkes was arrested for making an inflammatory speech at Guildhall and held under order. This man's name does not grace the pantheon of liberty. The words which provoked the authorities were probably hotheaded. Whatever the case, they led to a fundamental change in the relationship between parliament and the executive. Were MPs at the time aware of its significance? Like many other liberties, habeas corpus was born, not out of quiet reflection and theoretical agonising, but from a minor event shadowing one of the great crises of English political history.

This gain would be a chimera anyhow if the worst fears were realised. Charles resisted the calls to exclude his brother from the succession, but at the price of a bitterly divided and apprehensive country. He solved the problem by dispensing with parliaments altogether in 1681. Whigs were purged from all levels of politics, and MPs left parliament with doleful predictions. 'A troop of horse and a file of musketeers will turn us out of doors. Let us know what we have to trust to,' said one MP, anticipating the next reign: the accession of James would mean that Louis's armies would be one step nearer the Dutch ports, the platform for conquest.[8] When James did finally come to the throne it could hardly be said that he introduced the dark night of Catholic persecution that had been predicted. When Charles II's bastard son, the Duke of Monmouth, attempted a rebellion on behalf of Protestant England the country failed to rally to the banner.

Parliament, which was packed with loyal Tories, gave James unqualified support. Thanks in part to the memories of bloodshed and cruelties in the Civil War, most of the country was prepared to forsake the warcry of *Liberty*. The hope was that the more obsequiously loyal and crazily royalist the Church and parliament and the courts were, the more inclined James would be to tolerate the Anglican monopoly of religion and the laws of the country and the happier he would be to welcome such lickspittle friends as his partners in power. James had nothing but contempt for puppy-dog behaviour. Rather than reward their unconditional professions of love and loyalty he was emboldened to treat them with cavalier haughtiness. He believed he had ascended to the throne against all reasonable expectations; it was a sign of the divine blessing shown to him and his religious cause by God. As a libidinous prince he had sinned again and again; despite this he had been given a chance to find redemption. A brittle man, accustomed for so long to commanding others as a military leader, but bowing to the higher command of his elder brother, he was not partial to compromise now, especially when what was at stake was his soul and the souls of his benighted countrymen.

And his confidence and sense of self-belief coincided with a collapse of opposition. Any of that 'appetite for liberty' which had been evinced in 1641–2 was confined to the private dinner-party grumblings of publicly muted Whigs or overblown rantings from across the water. The full horrors of Catholic absolutism lay in the future, or more accurately in the nightmares of Whigs and dissenters. For James's tyranny was of the mildest sort. Few could complain of actual oppression or walked in terror of assassination. Perhaps that was the king's problem. Gilbert Burnet would later write that James's rule was 'broken with a touch'. If he aimed at absolute monarchy he fell a long way short of constructing an oppressive state.

There is no doubt something shaming about living under a benevolent dictatorship. The full horrors of an absolute tyrant are at least impressive – impressive enough for even the bravest to give up hope of resistance. But a soft-hearted tyrant who oppresses in small things is the more vulnerable to resistance because it is humiliating to obey a weak dictator. Moreover the bar of bravery is set considerably lower for casual rebels. The king's every move was big with significance. James used Monmouth's rebellion to station an army on Hounslow Heath. A standing army was traditionally a sign of Catholic absolutism. It might even be seen as a proxy for a French army, sparing Louis the hassle of encircling England with a ring of steel to deprive her of elbow room on the Continent. This suspicion was not confined to Protestant zealots and Whig hotheads. 'It seems to me', Louis XIV's ambassador, Paul

Barillon, wrote to his master, 'that the King of England is very glad to have a pretence for raising troops, and he believes that the Duke of Monmouth's enterprise will serve only to make him still more master of his country.'[9] And this army was not only within striking distance of Westminster but included Catholics when James suspended the law which required officers to take an oath abjuring transubstantiation. Even the fearsomely loyal parliament became nervous, and it was prorogued, never to sit again, when it tried to censure the king's policies.

And, in an echo of Charles I's reign, when the legality of permitting Catholics to serve in the army was challenged the courts upheld James's prerogative to dispense with statute law. This was an ancient part of the governance of England, the thinking being that the royal prerogative could free individuals from the rigours of general law when a particular law was too broad to account for peculiar circumstances. But suspending the law for everyone named in the statute (in this case, Catholics), rather than individuals, was entirely different; it effectively repealed the act. 'There is no law whatsoever but may be dispensed with by the supreme lawgiver,' said the Lord Chief Justice; 'as the laws of God may be dispensed with by God himself.'[10] This was the language of naked absolutism, albeit applied to freeing an oppressed minority rather than oppressing the majority.

James went on to bypass the law concerning Church appointments and ripped up the ancient statutes of Magdalen College, Oxford, when he imposed a Catholic master there. (Oxford had promised unconditional loyalty to James when he took the throne, but when he did exercise his unlimited powers to bend college rules the fellows of Magdalen found reasons to resist, albeit in a non-violent way.) As the growing opposition noted, if the king had a negative voice to dispense with laws made in parliament and a positive power to make law whenever and however he saw fit then there was no need for parliament and no power that could be denied the 'supreme lawgiver'.

And if the people did not like it, there was an army lurking in readiness. His Commission for Ecclesiastic Causes was set up to investigate the Church of England. Since Elizabeth it was an English monarch's duty to uphold the Church at home and protect Protestants abroad: for religious motives, to be sure, but most importantly for reasons of strategy. The reverse was happening. At the same time as James fretted at the fabric of the Anglican establishment, Louis XIV revoked the Edict of Nantes which gave protection to his Protestant subjects. England was awash with French Huguenot refugees, who brought horrific tales of forced conversion, destruction of property and burning libraries.[11] Tellingly James had little sympathy with the Protestant victims, and ordered the burning of books which detailed their sufferings. His Commission was considered 'a sort of Inquisition, or at least a certain forerunner of the new way of converting people, by the irresistible eloquence of armed dragoons'.[12]

James believed that he had to use a level of legal chicanery and royal prerogative to prise open what he saw as the all-powerful tyranny of bigoted Protestantism which had persecuted Catholics for generations. He wanted Catholicism to compete more or less equally with the established Church. Perhaps he saw the English clarion call of liberty as hypocrisy. Whigs, who believed in freedom of conscience, were distinctly squeamish when it came to Catholics.

Liberty meant liberty for Protestants. 'If we have a general liberty, we may have good as well as bad people amongst us,' said one MP who might have been haunted by the paradox of freedom had he given it some thought.[13] James tried to speak the language of tolerance, but his brittleness, haughty manner, deafness to criticism and single-minded zeal made him seem like a classic tyrant. Everything was bent to his one aim – that of breaking the monopoly of the Church of England and allowing his subjects to hear what he considered to be the true word of God, denied to them since the dark days of Elizabeth. In 1687 when seven bishops and archbishops petitioned him to release the Church from the obligation of supporting his pro-Catholic policies he had them imprisoned for seditious libel. The gentlest and most ardently royalist members of the established Church were thus transformed into the guardians of liberty. A mild tyranny got mild rebels.

The country had for three years been loyal; now patience was at an end. In 1688 James tried to have a general election and to that end put pressure on Lords Lieutenant and office holders in the town corporations to return MPs to his liking. His agents were met with coldness, so the office holders were replaced with men thought more compliant. Even these creatures were unable or unwilling to do the king's bidding. There was no rebellion brewing, just plain reluctance to help the king: so-called 'passive obedience', the Church of England's lukewarm form of rebellion. James's policies, it was noted with glee, were going at 'a rapid motion without advancing a step'.

When William of Orange invaded the country, therefore, few had the heart either to defend their king or rally to the challenger. Prince William, Stadtholder of the United Dutch Provinces, was James's nephew and son-in-law – Charles II had married James's eldest daughter to the fiercely protestant Dutch prince as a gesture to the Anglican community. William had assumed that when James died his wife Mary would come to the throne, and unite the might of England with the Netherlands against France. In 1688 James finally had a son with his second, Catholic, wife, dashing William's hopes. It also confounded English expectations that James's Catholic interlude would be of short duration, ending with his death. No one could quite believe the evident truth. This must be another Jesuitical wile: the international Catholic conspiracy had arranged for James's wife to have a fake pregnancy and then smuggled a baby into her bed in a warming pan. By now no one trusted James, and the rumours gave William the chance he wanted. He was invited by seven prominent Whigs to put pressure on James to call a free parliament which would restore the law and investigate the validity of the birth of the Prince of Wales. Under the cover of asserting his rights, William assembled an army on the Dutch coast. Whig propaganda swung into action, with Major John Wildman, a former Leveller and political prisoner under Cromwell and Charles II, asserting that James had renounced his right to be king by trampling the fundamental laws and rights of his subjects. In such circumstances Englishmen 'cannot in conscience comply with illegal commands, and will not treacherously surrender their legal rights and privileges to the King's will'.[14]

William duly invaded, and James's government fell apart from the inside. His court had always operated in a kind of siege mentality, completely out of touch with the nation. The king was given to hysteria, paranoia and depression on a good day, and 1688 was his *annus horribilis*. Louis, despite the sobriquet of Universal Monarch, could not be everywhere at once, and in the autumn of 1688 his army was diverted to the Rhine and his fleet to the Mediterranean. The Dutch fleet and armies had a once-in-a-lifetime opportunity: the United Provinces were spared a menacing foreign force at her land borders and her fleets had absolute freedom of movement in the Channel and North Sea. James's strategic assumptions were blown away; even if he was unpopular at home or threatened by another state the might of France would restrain Dutch or Whig ambitions. But when he most needed support he found himself isolated at home and abroad. His nerves gave up the struggle when his second daughter Anne defected to William with a handful of army officers. Without testing the residual loyalty of the nation or the mettle of his army, he fled to France. 'A great King with strong armies, and mighty fleets, a vast treasure, and powerful allies fell all at once,' wrote Bishop Burnet. 'And his whole strength, like a spider's web, was so irrecoverably broken with a touch, that he was never able to retrieve what for want of judgement he threw up in a day.'[15]

And this was the start of a story the English liked to tell themselves: liberty always triumphed in the end, as if it liked breathing English air. They had not committed the sin of rebellion; no blood had been shed; and God had given them the chance to vindicate their ancient liberties. It was a miracle beyond the play of human intention. This was not so at the time. James's unexpected flight left the thorny problem of how the throne would be settled. The Whigs in the hastily called Convention Parliament were keen to suggest that James had broken a fundamental contract with the people. But the Tories took their oath to James as a matter of faith. He was not dead and he had not technically abdicated. The Bishop of Ely said that they would be guilty of 'accumulative treason' if they declared the throne vacant and set about looking for a replacement.

Yet what could they do? The Tories did not want James back, but they could not live with the alternative. If they let James return, their religion would be in greater danger; if they did not they would undo the ancient monarchy. The country seemed to be back in the hands of the Roundheads. The committee of the House of Commons set up to consider the constitutional settlement was under the chairmanship of Richard Hampden, son of John the Ship Money rebel, and there were plenty of other Whigs associated with republicanism and the Cromwellian protectorate. Indeed, were they not proposing *electing* William as a king, making him a new Cromwell? The Lords held out against the radicalism of the lower house, refusing to accept that the throne could be vacant and that it was given to mere mortals to set up a new monarch. The Tories did not want to crown William because he was not next in line; to do so would be to destroy the sacred nature of the monarchy.

This wrangle could have gone on forever, were it not for the bracing logic of William. He would go home if the English carried on wrestling with their consciences by affecting to be James's loyal subjects while doing everything they could to prevent him coming home. This would leave the country with neither their old monarch nor the strong leader whom everyone wanted. The Tories capitulated, mollified slightly by the fact that Mary was next in line (if you contrived to forget James's son) and therefore preserved the line of succession. They managed to salve their consciences *and* face up to reality by telling themselves that they could accept William because he was king de facto and it would be a sin to resist the powers that be. But he would never be king *de jure* – by will of God.[16] Parliament discussed and voted the Bill of Rights, to which William and Mary assented before being crowned joint monarchs in 1689.

William III and his Hanoverian successors suspected that the English liked having their cake and eating it: they professed themselves monarchists but had few problems about limiting a king, throwing one out or even executing one. They preached absolute loyalty but insisted on absolute liberty. This was confirmed by some of the more outspoken MPs, such as Colonel Birch: 'If King William should destroy the laws, foundations, and liberties, I doubt not but you will do with him as you did with King James.'[17] 'They are strange people one has to work with here,'[18] William told his Dutch friends, and frequently expressed his extreme distaste at the indignity with which an English king was forced to beg money and favours from his subjects. In 1714, when George I was preparing to travel to London to take up the throne, his entourage believed that the British were all hypocritical republicans who would have no trouble killing a king, weeping crocodile tears all the while. ('All the king-killers are on my side,' George reassured his mistress, correctly assuming that the Whigs would be dependent upon him, for fear of the Stuarts.)[19]

But the men who settled the succession in 1688–9 were conservative. They declared the throne to be vacant and settled on Mary, who after her baby half-brother – the little prince whose legitimacy everyone doubted – was first in line, and her husband, who was third in line. They stressed their innocence: they had found the throne empty and merely *confirmed* the most likely successors, whom God and circumstances had put in front of their noses. They might say that James had broken the fundamental laws of the nation and exceeded the just powers of an English monarch – implying he had violated a contract with the people – but William and Mary were not offered their crowns with conditions attached. James and the Prince of Wales were excluded from the throne because it was 'found by experience' that Catholics could not rule a Protestant nation.

The Bill of Rights contained no breathtaking vision of liberty for the future. It was a litany of complaints against obnoxious things that had happened since 1660: the dispensing of statute law, the retention of a standing army, interference in elections, irregular parliaments. In the future the monarchy could not raise tax, suspend laws or retain an army without the consent of parliament. So it did not make these powers obsolete; it made parliament partner in power with the Crown. A standing army was not abolished as an affront to the people, but instead parliament renewed its existence every year by passing a temporary Mutiny Act which allowed men to be enlisted under military law. Almost as soon as William was in place, parliament agreed to suspend the beloved Habeas Corpus Act in order to deal with pro-James (Jacobite) rebels. And parliament has been happy to 'dispense' with laws – 'fundamental' or not – in what it considers to be emergency situations ever since. The Bill of Rights had little to protect the individual; the 'Rights' were the collective rights of the nation, which were held in trust by parliament. Those who called for a new Magna Charta to establish basic liberties were ignored. Both Tory and Whig were concerned to preserve the 'ancient constitution'.

But this is not to say that the Glorious Revolution did not mean a break with the past. It was not so much what was written or decided in 1688-9 but a change in attitudes. The lustre of divine monarchy was tarnished by the twists and turns, the hypocrisy and fictions of constitutional wrangling, and by the personality of William, an austere Dutch Calvinist who had no time whatsoever for the theatre and pageantry the Stuarts had deployed to devastating effect. William – and his successors – were shocked by the disrespect shown them by their subjects. For at least a century and a half 1688 would stand as Year Zero in the history of liberties – the year when everything changed.* Wrongly or not, this sense that it *was* a revolution exerted a powerful hold on minds. It emboldened people to stand up for what they saw as their rights – for the *spirit* of '88 more than its reality.

In the absence of a constitutional declaration of rights it was left to people to find and preserve what liberties they could. This is what liberty has meant in Britain. The vision of Milton or Harrington or their followers of a new state with a definite moment of creation which would set in stone liberties and rights never happened. Their successors ('True Whigs', as they called themselves to avoid the taint of republicanism) believed in de facto liberties, just as their Tory rivals believed in de facto monarchy. That is to say, the constitutional forms may not have been there but the substance of liberty could exist without their formal declaration.[20] Later in the eighteenth century, historians would say that the loser in 1688 was the idea of *political* liberties, which had been the dream of Machiavellian/Harringtonian republicans. The power of the Crown actually increased in the eighteenth century, but a new kind of liberty grew and flourished. This was called 'modern liberty', or commercial, intellectual and social freedom which thrived to an extent unimaginable in the 'free' states of ancient

---

* I say a century and a half: the celebrations of the centenary in 1788 were lavish, not to say ecstatic; Macaulay popularised the Whig interpretation of history in the mid-nineteenth century; but in 1888 *The Times* did not contain a paragraph marking the bicentenary of William III's landing on the west coast on 5 November, formerly a key date in the British calendar. Perhaps two Reform Acts rendered it relatively unimportant.

Athens or Rome. The achievement of Britons was to have discovered the means by which liberties – or an *atmosphere* of freedom – could flourish within a monarchical framework. The people might not have political freedom, John Millar wrote much later, but the increase in wealth, commerce and learning had 'diffused a feeling of independence and a high spirit of liberty, through to the great body of the people'. The emphasis is on 'feeling' and 'spirit'.[21]

In the years after the Revolution there was an acknowledgement that things had not resolved themselves into a solution to England's problems. It required men to make things work in a more equitable way than under the Stuarts. William still had undeniable powers under the prerogative. What changed was the manner of government. The new king's sole ambition always had been to drive France from the Low Countries and further the Protestant cause in Europe. He was not as constitutionally finicky as his Stuart predecessors; he was prepared to barter his power for the money and men that would allow him to wage war. It made him a political king, compelled to negotiate with parties in the Commons. He was never popular, and he made no pains to make himself so; this was to have a profound impact on politics. He could not – and nor could his early Hanoverian successors – tap that reservoir of loyalty which had bolstered the Stuarts even at their lowest ebb.

This pushed William into an uneasy and often fraught partnership with politicians. Parliament was apprehensive that he might be using England to further Dutch ambitions and that he might degenerate into an absolute monarch. Experience taught that parliament should not grant a monarch permanent revenue at the beginning of a reign, otherwise parliaments would lose their teeth. One MP said that 'the King's necessity will bring the King to the people and the people to the King'.[22] Elections were held every three years, not at the king's pleasure, and the revenue and the army were kept under parliamentary control which meant that if the monarch did not call a parliament every year he would be left without money or an army, an unthinkable indignity for any self-respecting sovereign. Lurking behind these explosive issues was the increasing intolerance for monarchs who stepped over the line; William was always aware that James II was still alive and a possible, if somewhat distant, alternative. One of his Dutch associates remarked that 'in the coffeehouses here people are saying, "We have beheaded one King and thrown out another and we know how to deal with the third." '[23]

And if parliament was more than ever before a forum for the nobility and gentry to discuss and exert control over the monarchy, there was another force in the state, a new one. John Toland wrote that the greatest benefit of the Revolution was that he and other journalists were able to write 'freely, fully, and impartially'; this was the greatest bulwark against arbitrary government and a sign of new respect for the people. But he deliberately downplayed how accidental that was. Few in 1688–9 had the gumption to pretend that free speech was one of the ancient liberties of the realm. After the fall of Star Chamber and bishops' courts in 1660, the press had been governed under a system whereby every publication had to be examined by the Secretary of State, the Lord Chancellor or one of the archbishops and licensed by the Stationers' Company prior to publication. Printers had to post a bond of £300 and present the name of an author on demand. This was done by royal prerogative in 1660 and thereafter by act of parliament which lapsed every few years. When in 1695 the act came before parliament in a bundle of expiring acts which needed to be renewed something very strange happened. Its renewal should have been done on the nod. But someone used the opportunity to demand a more stringent censorship. The new plan was for all printers to register their presses and deliver copy, page by page, to the censor as they came off the press (in the past printers had frequently changed the content of books after the first draft had been given an imprimatur by the Stationers). Furthermore, every licensing body would have a general warrant to conduct searches and presses could be confiscated if the rules were broken.

This new measure failed to pass the Commons. Was it because of post-Revolution zeal for freedom? Not a bit of it. The Stationers' Company did not want to lose its monopoly, the book trade objected because it would be too expensive and the lawyers in the Commons did not like the badly drafted clauses. The new bill did not pass and the old one lapsed because it had been taken out of the schedule of renewable acts. So it was the silence of the law which gave the press its first glimpse of freedom, based on an accident. Writers and publishers could still be prosecuted under the common law for seditious or blasphemous libel. This meant that writers and printers still went to gaol, but only *after* a crime had been committed, once their books had gone on the market and their ideas been disseminated to the community. There was no pre-publication censorship under common law. The legislative fumble of 1695 was momentous, but it had not been intended and its consequences were not foreseen. As in so many things, no new right had been created; an old restriction had been lifted.

The press was far from free. Parliament could, on its own authority, arrest a printer for reporting or criticising its business. The government could prosecute its opponents for seditious or blasphemous libel, and, since juries were hardly free from class and political bias, could secure convictions when political conditions suited them. Throughout the eighteenth century and into the nineteenth there were what might be called seasons of relative freedom and seasons of repression. It was in the periods of the law's silence that ideas or principles of the freedom of the press hardened and came to be seen as integral. It was the start of a battle for liberty of speech. It was never declared – as in other countries – but depended upon public opinion and the self-restraint of governments to keep the restrictive laws of libel in abeyance. The conflict between the press and the state would continue until the nineteenth century, and even then incredibly restrictive laws would exist unrepealed, the liberty of the press remaining de facto rather than established in law. And this is how liberties existed in Britain: the mechanism for repression existed, and individual freedom depended on the efforts of people to put political pressure on the state to stay its hand. This they could and did do as members of juries, as part of a mob or as articulate, peaceable voices.

One of the immediate consequences of the disappearance of licensing was the re-publication, or publication for the first time, of the classic works of English republicanism – books by Milton, Harrington, Algernon Sidney, Henry Neville and their ilk. It also spawned discussions of their ideas as they were applied to modern problems by young journalists. When William signed a peace treaty in 1697 he proposed retaining the army as a strategic measure. But the 'True' or 'Real' Whigs who had been bred up in the republican tradition saw it as a means of unbalancing the constitution. This is the beginning of the myth of 1688. The Real Whigs saw the Glorious Revolution as a restoration of an ancient form of government. In their view liberty had emerged spontaneously in Europe after the fall of the Roman Empire. It existed in what they called 'the Gothic balance' – that is to say equal power given to king, nobles and people. This had collapsed in the Middle Ages when subjects gave up their weapons and monarchs started employing professional soldiers.

The balance had been restored by the English in 1688. It had brought back that which had previously existed throughout Europe – limited, mixed monarchy which, it was said, was natural to mankind. Now here was William bringing an army back not ten years after the second dawn of liberty. He was harmless, no doubt; but who could answer for his successors? This was a political controversy that engaged all kinds of people for a variety of reasons. The Real Whigs used it to slip previously suppressed ideas that derived from Machiavelli and his English followers into the debate, rewriting history to vindicate their concept of freedom. Liberty would be retained only if the citizens were armed and prepared to man a volunteer militia when circumstances demanded. A professional, permanent army would turn a modern king into another James II with his permanent encampment on Hounslow Heath or Charles I with his praetorian guards. But more pertinently, an army had to be clothed, fed, armed and transported; it called upon the creation of a 'fiscal-military state' managed by politicians who would command men, money and lucrative contracts; in other words considerable civil, military and financial clout.[24]

On the other hand, absolute liberty might endanger the state if there was no army to prevent a Jacobite invasion or pre-empt a hostile king's march across northern Europe. The balance between liberty and security reached a symbolic level in discussions concerning standing armies. True Whigs might see an army as incompatible with constitutional freedom. But an unarmed England was incompatible with modern freedom, which required keeping out Jacobites, Universal Monarchs and every other threat to stability. As Brendan

Simms has shown, the phrase 'the liberties of Europe' was rarely far from the lips of statesmen in the eighteenth century. By this they meant the liberties of Britain, or maintaining a state system which prevented the dominance of a single nation.[25]

And the liberty of the individual was bound up with the liberty of the state: if the country was threatened or contained by another state then your freedom to trade and travel would be severely limited. The government, in the manner of a private individual ensuring his own liberties, had to prevent the omnipotence of another country powerful enough to give arbitrary law to the rest. An army was a perquisite of maintaining the balance of power – or *liberty* – of Europe and hence domestic liberty. People might grumble, but William III's aim to drive France from the Low Countries cut Universal Monarchy down to size, and gave England (and Britain after 1707) the elbow room to expand as a great power and enrich individuals by extending the horizon of trade. There was considerable political opposition to a standing army. It was not just the cost, or its possibility of subduing popular liberties, although that was worrying enough. What was of great concern was that soldiers were governed under a different legal regime from other citizens. It was to be feared that a soldier, long estranged from social liberties and habituated to discipline, billets and requisitioned victuals, would become a subject apart from his fellows with no interest in freedom or respect for private property.

In order to make this constitutionally acceptable parliament suspended ordinary law for soldiers for one year only by passing the annual Mutiny Act allowing military law, and hence discipline, to be enforced upon enlisted men. This meant that the army, and the odious things which came with it, could not strictly be called 'permanent' or 'standing'. Subjects and, most importantly, foreign monarchs knew that it would be renewed each year in perpetuity, not least because the Mutiny Act, like the tax bills, guaranteed the survival of parliament because kings depended upon it. But an ambitious commander or a venal politician knew that bad intention could lead to the non-renewal of the act. Throughout the eighteenth century the standing army issue flared up regularly. The instinctive suspicion of a standing army had a good effect. The army was kept small and ministerial conduct was kept under continual scrutiny.

The army crisis of 1697 was the first time the press found a voice in politics, and the *symbolic* issue of the standing army was the focus for a wider discussion of liberty, a means of educating the people in Machiavellian republicanism when their interest was piqued by a political squabble. This was useful, and continued to be so during the coming century: the *ideal* of liberty (in the sense of the absence of a professional army and an armed citizenry as the guarantee of the Gothic balance) was impossible in a factious Europe, but people continued to believe in it as an ideal, and hence kept their eyes open for abuses in a system they tolerated with the greatest reluctance.

This was a habit which was hard learnt. Hume liked to call domestic conflicts 'intestine' strife. And the memories of the civil wars provoked visceral responses from most people in the British Isles. A relatively homogeneous nation, with scant experience of invasion and only one land border to worry about, the English found the idea of countrymen armed against countrymen abhorrent. What was learnt in England perhaps more than in any other country in the seventeenth century was the real and symbolic importance attached to obeying legal forms. Deviation from them – what was euphemised as 'dispensing' with laws – was taken to be the harbinger of much worse: the unsure tenure of property, attacks on the Church and extralegal punishments. A dose of legal pedantry combined with instinctive overreaction to deviations from constitutional propriety was no bad thing – indeed, as Hume argued, shouting from the rooftops every time a minor infraction of liberty was merely suspected kept a country free, even if it looked somewhat paranoid. Much better venerating legality than allowing another James – or even a Cromwell – to chip away at the laws one by one. Other countries endured more and rebelled less. The lesson of England in the seventeenth century is that it is too late when your books are being burnt and you face imprisonment. Resistance should come much earlier, when the as yet undangerous ruler is breaking petty laws and trespassing on minor rights: resist when he is amending the statutes of a college, not when he is at your door.

CHAPTER 4

Licentious Liberty

—⁓—

The great liberty and independency which every man enjoys allows
him to display the manners peculiar to him. Hence the English, of any
people in the universe, have the least of a national character, unless this
very singularity may pass for such.

DAVID HUME[1]

It is commonly said, that no nation in the world would allow such
papers to come abroad as England suffers; which is only saying,
that no nation in the world enjoys the *liberty* which England enjoys. In
countries where there is no liberty, there can be no ill effect of it.

JOHN TRENCHARD AND THOMAS GORDON,
'CATO'S LETTERS', 10 JUNE 1721

The Gothic balance was integral to Whig thinking. It was under this
timeless form of government that human liberty could find existence.
Meddle with the essentials and its antithesis, arbitrary government,
would creep back. This would dominate thinking throughout the
eighteenth century and into the nineteenth, until the Great Reform Act
in 1832. The radical Whigs might try and use this as a cover for
discussing Machiavellian ideas of participation via things like a citizen
militia, but it was a greater force for conservatism and a check to reform.
Liberty became a matter of living under a certain type of government,
one where parliament was sovereign. And because the franchise was
restricted to a small number of male electors in unevenly distributed
constituencies, 'liberty' in the fullest sense – and especially in the sense
in which it was used in parliament – became the preserve of an elite.

Political liberties might reinforce general liberty, but they were not deemed essential for the bulk of the nation. What the people enjoyed was 'civil liberty', the protection of the law, security of property, habeas corpus, trial by jury and the freedom of the press. The liberties of parliament and the small political nation were vital in maintaining the separation of powers and limiting government.

John Trenchard and Walter Moyle, two Whig republican writers, believed that this was the foundation for a kind of republican monarchy or 'limited, mixed monarchy': 'the Man is loose, and the Beast [of arbitrary power] only bound; and our government may truly be called an Empire of Laws, and not of men'. The 'Beast' was always there; it could not be otherwise, for every society had to live with the danger of unlimited power if it was to defend itself against internal and external enemies. In the past and in less developed countries, existential threats would lead men to unchain the beast for their own defence – and they would have to live with their savage deliverer when the danger was gone. The answer was to locate this supreme authority in such a way that the beneficial exercise of power did not become a double-edged sword. If the power was broken up, divided among different participants, scrutinised by the courts and hedged by procedure then modern Englishmen could reconcile Leviathan with liberty. This would be the central idea of the eighteenth century. The 'Beast' could always escape its chains. It was up to the public, guided by the press, to keep alive the passion for liberty to balance exorbitant power, whether it manifested itself as a king or a minister or a faction in parliament.

The press, and the burgeoning public sphere of printing and debate, therefore was elevated to a part of the constitution which fulfilled a quasi-republican role of public tribune. Popular culture in the eighteenth century was awash with motifs of liberty. Songs, novels, journalism, poetry, cartoons, Hogarth's art kept alive this patriotic notion of liberty. And this was of great use to politicians. The national passion for liberty could be worked up and used to pillory and shame rival parties and politicians. 'Liberty' in this loose sense was kept at the heart of politics for a reason. It was a term to hurl about the House of Commons, to accuse opponents of treachery or legitimise one's own policies. It could be used to elevate the sordid game of politics to a higher plane, and thus hypnotise the public. But over time it would become a very dangerous horse to ride, especially when Britons, in whatever continent they lived, dreamed up their own definitions of what liberty they had or deserved to have.

But this is not to say that liberty was merely a piece of political humbug and overheated rhetoric. The liberty that allowed the elite to argue with kings, form parties to govern the nation and publish furious satires against each other created the conditions for freedom lower down the social scale. David Hume said that Britain enjoyed 'the most entire system of liberty that was ever known amongst mankind'.[2] But it was less a system bolstered by rigorous philosophy than a compromise within society that had emerged from the political revolutions since 1688. The Whig commitment to small government restrained the hand of the state not only from meddling with the gentry but, de facto, the population as a whole. The disenfranchised did experience a species of liberty that was enjoyed in few other places in the world. And this was classic negative liberty, or, as it was put then, a fiercely defended spirit of personal independence. 'What is it to the magistrate how I wash my hands, or cut my corns, what fashions or colours I wear, or what notions I entertain, or what gestures I use, or what words I pronounce, when they please me, and I do him and my neighbour no hurt?'[3]

This may be called the quintessence of British liberty: being left alone. The state should not compel people to serve in the army, wear certain styles of clothing or believe in its doctrines (which happened in other countries), but nor should it intervene to make people better. And the evidence of it was seen every day in the streets and coffee-houses and taverns. There was a marked lack of uniformity of dress, action and thought compared to anywhere else in Europe. Britons prided themselves on their individuality and nonconformity. Just look at any of William Hogarth's paintings or prints. He celebrates the diversity and individuality of Londoners whose freedom thrives in the wild variety of everyday life. They have the freedom to sin, and sin badly: the harlots, scapegrace apprentices, rakes and street-side drunkards can choose their path through life without any moral guardian intervening between them and ruin. Punishment does come; but it is at the hands of nature rather than a moral policeman.

The author of the above quote about being left alone was 'Cato', whose letters in the *London Journal* were one of the most widely read pieces of journalism in the 1720s. 'Cato' was the product of a collaboration between John Trenchard, a veteran of radical Whig writing since the 1690s, and Thomas Gordon, a younger man. Their 'Letters', which appeared between 1721 and 1723, were among the high points of writing on liberty in the eighteenth century. They taught their readers not only that there was liberty in Britain, but that it was worth having: 'The privileges of thinking, saying, and doing what we please, and of growing as rich as we can, without any other restrictions, than that by all this we hurt not the public, nor one another, are the glorious privileges of liberty.'[4]

Liberty found expression in the way that Britons led their lives. As David Hume made abundantly clear in his history of England, the country had been poor, unstable and divided until the end of the seventeenth century. In the eighteenth century she was rich, energetic and poised to master the world as a trading and military power; the people were free to think, discuss, trade and use their talents as they saw fit. This is what he meant by the perfection of liberty in modern Britain. It was a rare situation, the consequence not of a master plan but the conjunction of circumstances; the result of events (such as the Revolution) which established not cast-iron rights but a political landscape *favourable* to freedom.

Hume called liberty 'the perfection of civil society': it was something that flowered only with the culmination of civilisation – commerce, politeness, art, learning and science. He mocked those Whigs who venerated the liberty of the Saxons – what was their freedom but the inability of men to submit to authority? As for the rebels of the 1640s, they were religious fanatics who took up the sword in a passion of deluded zeal to impose their notions of religion on the country. Throughout the seventeenth century the people struggled against prerogative, but could not find an alternative; ideas of absolute monarchy clashed with the desires of the people with no prospect of an equitable solution. England had reached a condition whereby greater numbers of people owned property, and this gave them the desire for liberty. This is the idea that connects Harringtonian republicans to Hume: power and property went together. By the seventeenth century there was a dislocation between an ancient system of government and modern economic conditions. It resulted in conflict.[5]

This could have gone on for ever. As Hume argued, 'in all governments, there is a perpetual intestine struggle, open or secret, between AUTHORITY and LIBERTY; and neither of them can ever absolutely prevail in the contest'. This is the eternal fact of all political systems. The secret was to find a system that blended the two, in which this inevitable conflict was resolved into something other than a zero-sum game between power and the people which found its periodic expression in violence. The Revolution of 1688 and the subsequent settlement was one of those accidents of history: 'a more uniform edifice was at last erected: The monstrous inconsistence, so visible between the ancient Gothic parts of the fabric and the recent plans of liberty, was fully corrected: And to their mutual felicity, king and people were finally taught to know their proper boundaries.'[6]

Matters of liberty were transferred from actual conflicts between those who wanted to rule and those who were ruled, into politics. The rise of parties and the press, which was a remote consequence of the Revolution, might look sordid, but was a good thing. Modern parties did not fight it out with anything other than words: today's Outs stood a chance of being tomorrow's Ins; they were not perpetually excluded from influence, like the Puritans of Charles I's reign compelled to take up arms when their interests were threatened. Politicians, in the pursuit of power, made pragmatic and sometimes surprising temporary alliances with minority groups, who exacted their own concessions. Parties in power compromised and blended the diverse views of the nation. Adam Ferguson wrote that 'numbers of men . . . become, by their jarring pretensions and separate views, mutual interruptions and checks'.[7] The political reality after 1688 created forums for the peaceful expression of dissent and complaint, principally parliament, the press and the courts. The savagery of the civil dissensions of the seventeenth century had made it clear that religion should be taken out of politics. Dissenters were tolerated and the Church of England slipped into an agreeable torpor, which offended evangelicals but at least meant that the sleepy established religion remained inoffensive, drained as it was of proselytising zeal and political ambitions. Dissenters, Catholics and Jews may have suffered disqualification from office, but they were tolerated. Indeed, the multiplication of Protestant sects, with traditions of active dissent, combined with a reluctance to tinker with individual conscience meant that the established Church could never gain a monopoly. 'If there was only one religion in England, there would be danger of despotism,' remarked Voltaire, 'if there were only two they would cut each other's throats; but there are thirty, and they live in peace.'[8] Diversity, therefore, and a lack of a national rallying point – particularly a homogeneous religious culture – helped create liberty.

Civil society existed where freedom had been established; and freedom could only flourish in civil society. As civilisation grew and expanded, so did liberty. Indeed, liberty was said by thinkers such as Hume to be the discovery of the eighteenth century: everything before was a 'rude sketch' of what was emerging and becoming ever more clearly defined in conditions of enlightenment. The liberties of modern Britain were entirely new. The negative liberties which were the fruit of eighteenth-century government allowed for the growth of commerce and learning. And so the active powers of man were unleashed. They had fresh spheres in which to exert themselves; whole new worlds, mental and physical, to discover, explore and subdue. That was liberty.

'To the ancient Greek or Roman, the individual was nothing, and the public everything,' wrote Ferguson. 'To the modern . . . the individual is everything and the public nothing.' The ancients were taught to venerate their city and identify their freedom with the freedom of the state. Moderns had less of that zeal for public affairs, but dedicated themselves to their own advancement and profit – or, in eighteenth-century terms, commercial pursuits.[9] Luxury and commerce had been seen throughout history as incompatible with liberty: freedom depended upon self-sacrifice and unsullied virtue. But this ethos was falling out of fashion. Hume wrote that economic progress would benefit greater groups of people, giving them 'material independence and moral fulfilment'. Classical republicans saw luxury as the enemy of liberty and citizenship; for Hume, and later Adam Smith, the triumph of modernity was to make wealth creation the cornerstone of civilisation and the prerequisite of citizenship and the support of liberty.

Trenchard and Gordon, in the guise of Cato, stressed that the benefits of wealth and trade were utterly dependent on liberty. The rule of law and security of person and property were absolute prerequisites of a flourishing economy. 'Who would establish a bank in an arbitrary country, or trust his money constantly there?' they asked.[10] One of the Williamite innovations inspired by military need had been the greatest of all financial institutions, the Bank of England. The government borrowed from it, and the people who invested in the Bank of England had a guaranteed return because it enjoyed the long-term security of parliamentary taxation. The state became debtor to investors in the bank, but the debt was managed and the loan provided an income far in excess of yearly tax revenue. Would the monied classes tolerate an absolute king? As one government journalist asked rhetorically, 'Do not the *proprietors* therefore of the *funds* [investors in the Bank of England], lie under the strongest ties and motives of interest and self-preservation, vigorously to oppose such a *Prince*, and maintain the just liberties of the people, and the power and authority of parliaments?' For an arbitrary ruler would have no problem in tearing up the records in the vault of the bank.[11] And absolute kings could and did go bankrupt, ruining their creditors. This resembles Coke's concept of liberty being grounded in property – only by now it included a modern kind of property: liquid assets.

The state was therefore bound by threads of gold. Institutions, laws, constitutional procedure, the press and trade all supported each other, and, thereby, the people's liberty. And as so many people were bound up with the economic life of the nation, they could not but support, or at least tolerate, the wealth-creating energy of the people. This involved lifting restraints. 'Cato' imagined a free trade in commodities and a free trade in opinion as mutually supporting: 'in those wretched countries where a man cannot call his tongue his own, he can scarce call any thing else his own. Whoever would overthrow the liberty of the nation, must begin by subduing the freedom of speech.'[12]

As Milton had said long before, a person who assumed the authority to tell you what to believe would have the power to do just about anything. A free market in ideas lay behind the advance in science and discovery and hence the advance in trade. Subjected people could not think, and that is why they were unadventurous and timid. Peoples who were conventional in their thinking were conventional in their behaviour – that is to say stagnant. 'Freedom of speech is ever the symptom, as well as the effect, of good government,' said Cato.[13] And as Voltaire commented when he visited England, the power of commerce connected men to men in new ways and freed people from clannish or ethnic animosities, universalising their experiences and values. Of all things, money had this power to bust the rivets of custom: at the Royal Exchange 'the Jew, the Mahometan and the Christian transact together as though they all professed the same religion, and give the name of Infidel to none but bankrupts'.[14]

In the same spirit, Descartes said that seventeenth-century Amsterdam was 'an inventory of the possible'. A free state therefore was alive with discussion and experiment. It was noisy and it could be disagreeable. It could also look dangerously like licentiousness, especially when writers used their new liberty to advocate radical ideas or fired off scurrilous libels. For those who hankered after the discipline and order of a monarchy the nation could look as if it was permanently on the brink of disorder and combustion. But that was the price one had to pay for freedom: to live in a country advancing in civilisation and wealth called upon habits of liberty, key among them tolerance for the tares that grew among the wheat. To use authority to crack down on a single abuse would be to awaken authority – 'the Beast' – from its slumber. It would be to confer on some government hireling the judgement of what idea was valuable and what should be silenced. 'As long as there are such things as printing and writing,' commented Cato, 'there will be libels: It is an evil arising out of a much greater good.'[15] There could be no progress without the freedom to go down a dead end, or even to stray perilously close to the abyss.

This is the modern kind of liberty Hume celebrated. It arose from the mutual needs of all the jarring and diverse elements of the community, not simply politics. The Tory farmer might grumble at modern licentiousness, but his investments in the bank were augmented by the wealth creation of the merchant, who required the lifting of restraints, and he too was dependent on the intellectual freedom which allowed scientists to experiment. Living in liberty, therefore, was something which had to be learnt; you had to see beyond the things which harmed or annoyed you to perceive the greater good. Out of the complexities of a modern, capitalist society had come liberties, rather than from revolutions or people sticking out for independence.

Or that is what Hume was keen to emphasise. He was afraid lest people were seduced into demanding more liberty by historians who venerated the ancient freedom of the Saxons or the glamorous rebelliousness of the Roundheads. Liberty would continue to grow so long as the mind of mankind was not restrained from roving into undiscovered territory. That was a freedom a Saxon could not conceive. Liberty still lay in the future, because increasing civilisation would produce greater opportunities, more choices and unforeseeable outlets for human endeavour. Adam Ferguson neatly divided the two kinds of freedom. Either you sought it in the desert or you engaged with modern society where, if you did not possess the pristine independence you had in the uninhabited wilderness, you had boundless opportunity to benefit from the amenities of civilisation.[16] Liberty gave you the means to construct new liberties. But that was dependent on your self-motivation and ability; no one was going to put opportunity in your way.

Disciples of Machiavelli would recognise the need to connect self-interest with the greater good. Defending collective liberty and preventing the return of arbitrary government was a duty that all shared if they wanted to see themselves and their country prosper. There was a realisation that people would lose sight of the need for keeping alive the struggle when there was no clear and present danger to fight. There were plenty who warned of the consequences of letting slip the instinct of vigilance over the powers that be. Ferguson called this tendency gladly to surrender political participation for private ease 'political refinement': on one hand it was a luxury of modernity, on the other it was a terrible danger.

If national institutions, calculated for the preservation of liberty, instead of calling upon the citizen to act for himself, and to maintain his rights, should give a security requiring, on his part, no personal attention or effort; this seeming perfection of government might weaken the bonds of society, and, upon maxims of independence, separate and entangle the different ranks it was meant to reconcile.[17]

In other words, people would, by living in freedom, become unworthy of freedom and unable to defend it. Individuality, the precious fruit of liberty, could easily become selfish individualism. It was a terrible paradox.

And politicians might actually try to foster this complacent attitude and chain up the active spirit of the people. It was absolutely essential that people keep a jealous watchfulness over the powers that be, and that there were constant 'alarms' to rouse the latent spirit of liberty and keep politicians on their toes – a kind of zero tolerance for encroachment on rights.

The attitude seemed to be that it was better to demand too many liberties lest you were given too few. And there were plenty of people eager to fulfil this role of public watchdog. Publishers such as Toland aimed to establish a 'canon' of seventeenth-century republican writing to animate people in the eighteenth. Historians wrote with passion about the supposed continuities of history which meant that 'Britons never, never will be slaves'. Trenchard and Gordon mobilised 'Cato' in response to the South Sea Bubble crisis in 1721, when over-speculation in the South Sea Company resulted in a stockmarket crash, financial ruin and accusations of political corruption. A time of high political excitement was ripe for a lesson in liberty. The bursting of the Bubble therefore resembled the 1697 army controversy. 'Cato's Letters' were popular weekly pieces which ranged over classical and British history, republican theory, Machiavellian thought and new liberties such as the freedom of the press, commerce and individualism. 'Cato' explicitly referred to Machiavelli's belief that an *occasione* allowed for a *ricorso*, or return to first principles after a period of languor and bad habits. 'Let us exert a spirit worthy of Britons, worthy of freemen who deserve liberty. Let us take advantage of the opportunity, while men's resentments sail high, whilst lesser animosities seem laid aside, and most men are sick of party and party-leaders.'[18]

Above all the lesson of 'Cato's Letters' is that liberty and power sit in an uneasy relationship. Power is like fire: it is essential to life, but it is better for mankind that it is kept in the grate. And liberty runs to licentiousness if not regulated by stated rules. British civil liberties existed because of the extraordinary combination of opposites and reconciliation of interests: republicanism and monarchy; authority and liberty; commerce and public service; religion and toleration; selfishness and duty; reason and passion.[19] Rather than destroy each other in an intestine struggle, they found strength in concord: 'Dominion will always desire increase, and property always to preserve itself; and these opposite views and interests will be causing a perpetual struggle: But by this struggle liberty is preserved, as water is kept sweet by motion.'[20] All the good things in society came from a collision of interests and the heat generated by competition. It was not enough to hate power in order to worship freedom. Liberty and authority were both kept in a state of evolution and freshness by the 'perpetual struggle' recognised alike by Hume and 'Cato'.

Dependent on this kind of complex balance, politics was vulnerable to instability. Men naturally loved power, for instance, and would find ways to expand and hold on to it. Bolingbroke wrote that 'it follows undeniably that, in the nature of things, the notion of a perpetual danger to liberty is inseparable from the very nature of government'.[21] In the eighteenth century one of the major threats was corruption. The creation of a massive national debt, institutions to manage it and politicians who operated the levers of financial control had unbalanced things. The enemy was not now an old-fashioned absolute king, but the 'cash nexus'. Robert Walpole, the first Prime Minister, had carved out a position whereby, on behalf of the Crown, he doled out rewards of lucrative offices, pensions and sinecures, buying up power and votes in the Commons from greedy MPs.

Walpole therefore bridged executive and legislative authority and power grew and expanded into all the nooks and crannies of the country. Liberty was subordinated to money.

And most disturbingly it was not recognisable classical tyranny: thanks to the complex relations of modern capitalist society it was invisible. Commercial freedom, which had brought real benefits, also incubated vices. Government and the City were in unholy alliance; the public became a milch-cow, whose sole purpose was to supply taxes to satisfy the greed of politicians on the make and their friends in the counting houses who creamed off the wealth of the country. Sir John Barnard said that Walpole's system 'divided the nation into two ranks of men, of which one are creditors and the other debtors. The creditors are the three great corporations [of the City] and others, made up of natives and foreigners; the debtors are the landholders, the merchants, the shopkeepers, and all ranks and degrees of men throughout the kingdom.'[22] And the debtors became the slaves of the creditors, who subverted the essentials of the constitution whilst preserving its outward forms.

Parliament, therefore, could usurp liberty as easily as a king. It was up to the people to fight for their own liberties and throw out the would-be modern dictators. It was the job of journalists such as 'Cato', historians, poets and playwrights to keep alive the spirit of liberty. Public opinion and electors in the constituencies had to be roused to chuck out the guilty men. 'Cato' appealed to the patriotism of electors at the time of the 1722 general election, playing on their pride as 'freeborn Englishmen': 'This, gentleman, is your time; which, if you suffer to be lost, will probably be for ever lost.' People should use the opportunity to vote out the 'saleable vermin' who were utterly corrupted creatures of the ministry.[23]

But nothing interrupted Walpole's long premiership. In the 1730s the dissident Tory Lord Bolingbroke revived the call of liberty, saying that the Whigs had betrayed the principles of 1688 and subverted the freedoms of the people. Most damagingly, they had blurred the lines that separated the powers in the constitution, fusing the executive and the legislature into a fatal instrument of unbounded power. He wrote of the decline of the independent gentry and yeomen who had been the backbone of freedom and their replacement with a nouveau riche class who cared nothing for British values. Power, which had traditionally been tied to landed property, had fallen into the hands of seedy businessmen, and they poisoned everything with their avarice and contempt for the people. The result was moral decline and a new kind of slavery.

Bolingbroke had been Secretary of State under Anne, but had supported the Jacobites against the Hanoverian succession in 1714. After years of exile as a named traitor he returned to help the Tory opposition to Walpole through the pages of the *Craftsman*. He was accused of the grossest hypocrisy in appropriating Whig-republican arguments for the Tory cause. Liberty was on everyone's lips; every party claimed to be defending it against the others, who were bent on stealing freedom in one way or another. The supporters of Walpole claimed that *they* represented liberty. What looked like the worst kind of corruption was in fact part and parcel of the constitution. If the ideas of Bolingbroke and the 'True Whigs' concerning the purity of mixed government were followed through, then an over-powerful House of Commons would lord it over a weak Crown. The government would be forced to intercede between the two, and would in the end become the slave of MPs. The dispersal of jobs and pensions among MPs gave the executive some leverage over the legislature, restoring balance where otherwise there would be mutual competition. What people called 'corruption' was in reality patronage – and patronage was the only power the Crown had left in the eighteenth century. Take it away and there would simply be no mixed government: democracy would unbalance the scales. And democracy would not mean the combined strength of the British people, but the richest few who elected MPs. Hume admitted that what was commonly called corruption was 'inseparable from the very nature of the Constitution'.[24] This was because the constitution did not entail a *separation* of powers but an equal and mutually supporting and checking combination of Crown, Lords and Commons: a *mixture* of powers which could only be maintained by artificial means.

So corruption was tyranny. Or corruption was liberty. In the debates of the 1720s and 30s libertarian arguments were scattered about like shot from a blunderbuss. The rhetoric of 1688 was deployed by all sides. The Whig government claimed to be defending a pristine constitution which had sprung fully formed and incapable of improvement in 1689; this was an excuse for keeping the door bolted against further innovation and, inter alia, preserving the ascendancy of the great Whig families and their acolytes. Tories laid claim to ancient liberties which *predated* 1688 in an effort to show that the Whigs' rhetoric of liberty was mere cant and a mask for their seedy ambitions. The 'Real Whigs' tried to present the Revolution as unfinished business, a starting point for the development of liberty which had been betrayed by ministerial Whigs who were interested only in power. 'Liberty' was dropped into every sentence of every speech, every paragraph in every political pamphlet.

Among political parties and their hired pens there was a rather Manichean view of liberty emerging. Any measure or slight abuse that diverged from a person's ideal of what the constitution should be was seen as an assault on the very foundations of liberty. The Gothic balance would be upset, and a slight deviation from constitutional propriety would take the country on the road to tyranny or licentiousness, according to political prejudices. But the constitution admitted of no rigorous definition. The relationships of powers and rights which existed between Crown, ministers and parliament were so complex and fluid that there was no single definition of what the constitution was or should be.

This kind of constitutional analysis was the product of a classical education. The Roman republic was brought low when constitutional purity was sullied. But that age was past. Modern freedom was judged by the effect on the individual rather than by a mathematical formula to deduce the exact relationship between all the branches of the government. When Hume talked of a 'system' of liberty he meant the host of interrelated and interlocking arrangements in society – the result of the cumulative activities of millions of people in civil society. It was better to live with the myths, half-truths and customs of a political system for the sake of peace and freedom than bend the system to some precise theory of natural rights: for then the messy compromises and conspiracies of silence which allowed a mature society to function would be overtaken by dissatisfaction and violence.[25] If the constitution was too imprecise, untidy and changeable to suit a Harringtonian constitution-designer or a classical purist then it had little bearing on individual liberty. A free government was one which allowed the complex webs of modern society to be spun. It was de facto or practical liberty which emerged thanks to various historical contingencies – including making the best of luck – not an absolute liberty dependent on a government designed by experts, worked on mechanical principles and encoded in a constitution.

There was a neo-Hobbesian view that the character of the government did not matter as much as the liberty the individual had *from* interference and *to* pursue his or her own interests. Corrupt elections, hired MPs and government-by-patronage could be tolerated as long as one was left free to make money, write books, get drunk, avoid the prescriptions of state or Church discipline and live under the rule of law. This was the kind of liberty that was readily understood and eagerly supported, even by those who did not benefit from it in a positive way.

In other words, popular liberty was a small price government had to pay for political peace. It was little wonder that politicians were eager to keep the state small; a laissez-faire government was less likely to tread on toes and incur a sustained campaign for political reform as a penalty for real, imagined or suspected oppression. When it came to government, the British in the eighteenth century had a high threshold of tolerance for corruption and an exceedingly low one for meddling and interference.

Yet nothing could alter the fact, as De Lolme famously said, that parliament could do absolutely anything except make a man a woman (British radicals would often point out that parliament could legislate that white was black and black was white). Parliament had, in theory, absolute sovereign power to pass acts which could not be challenged even by the highest courts in the land as unconstitutional. Today's liberty could be legislated away en masse tomorrow. The people's only security was to elevate the principle of liberty (however it was understood) to the level of sacred value. In other words, keep up moral and political pressure on their powerful leaders to respect the rule of law. The people got worked up about trifling infringements of liberty and made their displeasure vociferously known; the state, limited in small things, was constrained in big ones too.[26] As Montesquieu wrote of the British, 'They have a great reason to be jealous of this liberty; were they ever to lose it, they would be one of the most servile nations upon earth.'[27]

Visitors to Britain from other European monarchies such as France, Germany or Spain were amazed by the atmosphere of intellectual and social freedom. The country was conspicuous for eccentrics, free-thinkers, free-talkers and the downright boorish. It was also doing exceptionally well as a colonial and commercial power, eclipsing larger and more resource-rich nations. It was no coincidence, many believed, that the country which produced *The Decline and Fall of the Roman Empire* and *Tristram Shandy* also had a flourishing trade and a vast empire. The same thing which made them buffoons allowed them to make strides in business, discovery, philosophy, science, maths and the arts: a general contempt for custom and convention. One tourist wrote:

A rich Englishman, and in general every inhabitant of that fortunate island, knows no other restraint on his conduct than the laws, and his own inclination. If he does not infringe on the jurisprudence of his country, he is entirely master of his own actions. From these proceed those numerous follies, and those extravagancies, at which the nations among whom they are unknown seem so much shocked ... *The opinion of the world*, so formidable in other countries, is there disregarded. Nobody consults any thing but his own judgement.[28]

Rousseau said that this was a fiction. Every seven years a handful of men went to cast their votes, while their disenfranchised neighbours enjoyed a kind of saturnalia: drinking, mild violence and baiting political opponents. But others said that Rousseau was confusing political power (which was conferred by voting – staking a small share in power) with personal liberty. The two should be distinguished. The British way was to live under the rule of law. Laws which had been made to defend barons and parliamentarians against arbitrary power in the distant past, such as Magna Charta, juries and habeas corpus, had been extended as like rights to everyone else. The laws which were designed to protect property also protected the individual. A member of the government or the nobility had no legal immunity, and he could be dragged in front of the courts like anyone else if he invaded the rights of a less exalted subject. The rule of law was the basis of Whig supremacy; the constitution they had created was the culmination of legal restraints which had been placed on kings. The grandees could not claim legitimacy as a ruling class therefore unless it was a general principle rather than a class privilege. 'Liberty is thus made the common cause of all,' wrote De Lolme; 'the laws that secure it are supported by men of every rank and order; and the Habeas Corpus Act, for instance, is as zealously defended by the first nobleman in the Kingdom, as by the meanest subject.'[29]

The keystone of Whig Britain was the majesty of the law: an independent judiciary, free juries, equality under the law and the consistent application of known laws. Fair play should be done and be seen to be done. The impartiality of the law was the guarantee that the political nation held out to the people as the basis of their liberties. It is an ideal of law which has endured as the hallmark of a free society. And in general the people went along with it. As one visitor wrote, 'One is astonished to hear some of the very lowest of the populace reason concerning the laws, the rights of property, privileges, &c.'[30]

But the existence of a rule of law cannot tell us very much in itself. England, the haven of freedom, had the bloodiest legal code in Europe. Other countries might have exercised their laws in an arbitrary way and yet the laws themselves were mild. In Britain the belief that the common law was distilled reason was considered by some the equivalent of worshipping fool's gold. Jeremy Bentham wrote that his countrymen yielded 'the same object and indiscriminate homage to the laws . . . which is paid to the despot elsewhere'.[31]

The people worshipped the relics and dusty artefacts of their past, the old laws and legal parchments, the records of the achievements of their ancestors. They called it liberty, but they no longer reflected, tested or questioned; they were blinded by custom. Bentham reprobated the spew of ancient laws and procedures that made up English law; no one would design such silly laws and arcane rules of procedure if they started from scratch. But most people believed with

Blackstone that the glory of English law was its continuity with the past:

We inherit an Old Gothic castle, erected in the days of chivalry, but fitted up for a modern inhabitant. The moated ramparts, the embattled towers, and the trophied halls, are magnificent and memorable, but useless. The inferior apartments, new converted into rooms of convenience, are cheerful and commodious, though their approaches are winding and difficult.[32]

It was grand, confusing and venerable.

Such a system demanded, and received, respect. As modern historians have argued, a state which bases its legitimacy on the pristine quality of its legal system and the detached nature of its judiciary can be repressive in more subtle ways than an absolute regime. The ruling class make sure to submit to the same laws as their inferiors and accept the occasional defeat in court. But this is a very small price to pay for the benefits that the system provides. The lower sort of people come away impressed by the majesty of the law at work and the equality of their treatment. As Douglas Hay et al. argued in *Albion's Fatal Tree*, this serves as an instrument of control in itself: combining bloody punishment for a host of crimes with mercy and discretion in the use of this punishment, the elite neatly masked terror with overt fairness. And by being deliberately lax in a host of trivial instances, the authorities could present a front of permissiveness that made people *feel* free in the daily round of life. The idea of a professional, co-ordinated police force was fiercely and effectively resisted until long into the nineteenth century by all classes because it would be an intrusion into privacy. They might have walked the streets with less fear if there had been a Parisian-style gendarmerie, but that would be an enormous price to pay for being watched and harried by a uniformed jobsworth or by political spies. Bentham grumbled that otherwise sensible people believed that if their property was guarded they would be less free: 'I wonder what liberty it is they are so afraid [of losing]? The liberty of robbing or their liberty of being robbed.'[33]

Liberty was what you could get away with, and enjoying the freedom of pleasure was probably the more delicious for being officially prohibited. Oliver Goldsmith wrote that a 'perfect state of civil liberty' was living under a strong government which never chanced its arm:

There is scarcely an Englishman who does not almost every day of his life offend with impunity against some express law, and for which in a certain conjunction of circumstances he would not receive punishment. Gaming-houses, preaching at prohibited places, assembled crowds, nocturnal amusements, public shows, and an hundred other instances are forbid and frequented.

It was quite right for these to be prohibited, continued Goldsmith, but equally prudent that they were permitted.[34]

So you could drink and dance and disport yourself with abandon under the indulgent eye of a libertarian magistrate. This generosity in matters of pleasure could make the ordinary folk submissive and respectful to their betters who 'dispensed' with the rule of law to lubricate the wheels of social life. The restraint in small matters was not extended to other crimes. The rule of law was intended to protect people against arbitrary power, but it also protected individuals from other individuals. In eighteenth-century terms, this second purpose meant the defence of private property. And even the most minor sin against property was punishable by death. Thus the exercise of law might be fair, but the laws themselves were biased towards certain groups in society.[35]

The rule of law and the rhetoric of liberty therefore benefited Whig politicians and Whig property owners. In his book *Whigs and Hunters*, E. P. Thompson wrote of the passing of the Black Act in 1723, which was aimed explicitly at the farmers and tenants who lived on former royal parks which had been purchased by arriviste Whig families for the purpose of hunting. The Act covered 250 offences against property, including cutting down trees and damaging the head of a fish pond. Farmers in these areas were restricted by ancient law as to what they could and could not do with their land. They could not do anything that might interfere with the hunting of deer, including keeping dogs, cutting turf, building fences or felling trees.

The Whigs who took over the land did not pull down these legal anomalies in the name of liberty, but entrenched their privileges in the savage Black Act. As Thompson wrote, this was not done for reasons of public order or for class privileges; the law was passed to get rid of people who were nuisances. In time the act – along with the multi-purpose Riot Act – was used to deal with all sorts of other trouble-making and minor disorder. This is what Thompson calls 'the Whig state of mind': the defence of private property must come above all else. It derived from the long-standing view that absolute security of property against absolute power equalled liberty, only by the eighteenth century it had been bent to mean absolute security against other Englishmen.

David Hume feared that the passion for liberty which was so great in Britain would cause people to resist power for the sake of a misbegotten ideal of freedom and destroy the complex balances and relationships which held together the system of liberties. In society, authority represented reason and liberty passion. This was natural, for we are a mixture of reason and passion; but an excess of either leads to trouble. The appetite for liberty should therefore be channelled into respect for existing benefits. Experience of living in civilised society taught people to suppress their 'primary instincts' and to accept that artificial restraints were compatible with, not opposed to, refined liberty.[36] Otherwise Englishmen might scotch their gains by demanding utopian freedoms and upsetting the balance. In his *History* and his *Essays* he tried to show that liberties varied in time and in place. There was no single concept of liberty but that which was suitable to a society's state of development. You could not derive present rights from studying the Anglo-Saxons or philosophising about the natural rights primitive man had in the state of nature. He urged people to accept the imperfect liberty of the mid-eighteenth century because, for all its flaws, it was unparalleled in human history and because it gave Britons benefits denied the rest of the world.

This chapter has argued that for all the laudations of British liberty after the Revolution, it was often used cynically in party political disputes, to tranquillise public opinion or as a way of legitimising class power. For all the talk then – whether it came from patriots or foreigners intoxicated by the free atmosphere of England – a certain kind of liberty had emerged which by no means represented the full possibilities of human freedom.

When John Millar wrote that the British government extended liberty around the world, it was this kind of liberty. And the state's role in promoting freedom was a negative one; it guaranteed a way of governing which kept interference to a minimum rather than actively liberating people. It was a liberty that suited those who had the means to unleash their potential in whatever field they chose. But for those who had not the means of realising their talents – from a lack of education, social inferiority or the luxury of time needed to perfect those talents – this liberty might be something of a sorry joke. The absence of oppression and prescription is the essential starting point of liberty; but unless this freedom leads to something more enriching it can be a frustrating doctrine. It *is* only a starting point, a basic minimum.

As A. V. Dicey would later write, there is nothing so sweet as that which can be favourably contrasted with your neighbours. This is what gave eighteenth-century British liberty its lustre.[37] In the years during which he researched *Whigs and Hunters*, E. P. Thompson learnt to hate the early Whigs and the hypocrisies of English justice. But in a concluding chapter he defended the concept of the rule of law, the application of which he had attacked in the book. It might have been humbug, but at least it was noble humbug. The establishment of legal forms and procedures and the righteous language of law and liberty took on its own idealism. In time, abstract notions of right would take over from the original intent; lawyers, legal writers, politicians and public opinion would come to believe in the principles of justice for all and reform the abuses of the bloody code. But that lay in the future. The architecture of liberty under law was there, and it sank deep foundations. Charles James Fox wrote on liberty: 'If it be an illusion, it is one of those that has brought forth more of the best qualities and exertions of the human mind than all other causes put together; and it serves to give an interest in the affairs of the world, which without it would be insipid.'[38]

So the belief that Britain was a country of liberty was more important than the reality. Oliver Goldsmith wrote an imaginary conversation between three Londoners gathered at the gate of a debtors' gaol speculating on a French invasion. The prisoner worried what would become of his freedom; a porter feared that he would be enslaved by the French and made to carry burdens; and a soldier fretted about the fate of the Church as he swigged his grog and spat out blasphemous oaths.[39] Deluded and arrogant they may have been, but the conception of being the freest people in the world elevated people's minds and gave them confidence to think and speak. In the nineteenth century John Stuart Mill wrote that in the preceding century people closed their minds to the idea that the government could do good: 'The cry of the people was not "help us", "guide us" . . . the cry was "let us alone".'[40] But the kind of good the government would have tried to accomplish would have been harmful. Contemporary beliefs of what would benefit the people may not have included a programme of education or inspection of sanitation. Judging by the activities of the Society for the Reformation of Manners in the early eighteenth century and the Society for the Suppression of Vice in the early nineteenth the respectable portion of the public would have confined their efforts to restraining petty deviations of strict morality and improper publications.

As it was, the licentious liberty of the time gave Britain the atmosphere of freedom. People *believed* in it, and it had positive effects on them. Britain did not have the freest government or the mildest laws in the world. But it had something else. The people did not *feel* oppressed or cramped and the beneficial effect was to give them characteristics of candour, outspokenness and resilience. They did not conform readily to the prescriptions of moralists or busybodies in thought or behaviour. Edmund Burke said: 'If any ask me what a free government is, I answer, that for any practical purpose, it is what the people think so.'[41]

Liberty in Britain at this time became a conservative principle, used to elevate property and stifle demands for reform. The social freedom that thrived in Britain led to a Panglossian view of the world that all was for the best, or at least better than any radical foreign ideals. It diverted people from improving the system or searching for solutions to problems. 'We had a government, which we respected too much to attempt to change it, but not enough to trust it with any power, or look to it for any services that were not compelled,' wrote Mill.[42] It benefited those in power. But when you use a concept like liberty for cynical reasons it can prove explosive.

In those times when the government did not use the libel laws to stifle debate the press made the most of its season of freedom, and it became seen as the norm rather than an exception. Likewise, the frequent lapses of the law made people perceive social liberties as their right. It was often practical or de facto liberty, which breathed only by the silence of the law rather than by a constitutional right, but thanks to long existence it would come to be regarded as absolute despite any explicit guarantee. The language of liberty equipped people with a sense of justice and principle which they could throw back in the faces of their betters. An imperfect liberty, to be sure, but an inheritance which has been sorely missed in countries which have suddenly been given freedom after generations of oppression. Those gentlemanly Whig ideals of independence filtered down and imbued the people with habits of liberty. As Thompson wrote, it bred 'a very ancient cultural tradition in Britain of bloody-mindedness towards the intrusion of authority'.[43]

III

ENLIGHTENED LIBERTY

1760–1820

CHAPTER 5

Every Tainted Breeze

—∾—

What an eventful period is this! I am thankful that I have lived to see it . . . After sharing the benefits of one Revolution, I have been spared to be a witness to two other Revolutions, both glorious. – And now, methinks, I see the ardour for liberty catching and spreading.

RICHARD PRICE, 1789[1]

The people of the colonies are the descendants of Englishmen. England, Sir, is a nation, which I still hope respects, and formerly adored, her freedom. The colonists emigrated from you, when this part of your character was most predominant; and they took this bias and direction the moment they parted from your hands.

EDMUND BURKE, 1775[2]

Writing back in the 1630s Thomas Browne said: 'We carry with us the wonders we seek without us: there is all Africa and her prodigies in us; we are that bold and adventurous piece of nature which he that studies wisely learns . . . what others labour at . . . in [an] endless volume.'[3] The proper study of mankind was, in the eighteenth century, man. It was based on empiricism, philosophical enquiry and science. The connection between reason and liberty, between material progress and personal freedom was one which remained strong until it was blown violently apart in the twentieth century. Liberty meant so much because of this indissoluble connection – it was the sense of a real liberation from superstition, ignorance and conformism; from the ties of churches, hierarchies and traditional authorities.

People, therefore, could build themselves anew, based on the fruits of their own enquiry. The individual was moved to the centre of philosophical and political thinking. Reason and liberty were placed side by side, and it was this self-confidence and optimism which was to give shape and content to the religious, legal and constitutional freedoms contended for in the seventeenth century. Our ideas of, for example, absolute freedom of expression or the separation of Church and State come from Enlightenment ideals more than they do from law books. Liberty and modernity were seen as indivisible. The future would be defined by freedom, and classes and kings which stood in its way went against the trend of history.

Enlightenment thinkers liked to identify people and places on the line which extended from barbarism to civilisation. Cosmopolitan Europe, with its learning and culture, its commerce and refinement, had progressed far along the line. But this vision of modernity got its most rigorous definition from those who did not live in these centres of civilisation but on the periphery. Most of the philosophical opinions quoted in the previous chapter are from Scots – Hume, Millar and Ferguson. This chapter concentrates on the revolutionary generation in America – Jefferson, Madison, Adams and Hamilton. They lived far from the metropolitan centre, but for this very reason had a greater conception of progress, living, as they saw it, as pockets of enlightenment in a new world previously untouched, or uncluttered, by civilisation. They imbibed the virtues of enlightened thinking – urbanity, sociability, learning and public service. And, most importantly, the values they admired the most and the status they aspired to – as disinterested public gentlemen who carried the flame of enlightened rationality – had to be earned. Such things were not a birthright, as they were elsewhere; American leaders were self-made and they had to work hard to live up to their aspirations of learning and gentility. They were not self-made men in the sense in which we use the term now; they aimed at something higher, something taught by classical writers and modern philosophers. They did not wear their responsibilities lightly; as Alexander Hamilton – first Secretary to the Treasury under President Washington – explained when refusing the offer of a lucrative property deal: 'there must be some public

fools who sacrifice private to public interest at the certainty of ingrat-
itude and obloquy'.[4] The elite leaders of the American Revolution
were happy to be such fools.

The founding of the United States coincided with the time when
these ideas and values were at their height. And, unlike in England and
Scotland, the pre-eminent enlightenment thinkers in America happened
to be active political leaders. In other words, there was a unique combination of political ideals with political power. And it happened at a
moment in history when *liberty* – rather than God, nationalism, economic equality or other things for which humans have contended – was
vaunted as the noblest of mankind's aspirations.

Speaking in defence of the American rebels, Edmund Burke told
parliament that the true currency of the British Empire was liberty.
Suspend or devalue it and Americans would simply mint it for themselves. The original colonists had left England during the disputes of
the seventeenth century to found their own political communities
and worship their God as they chose. As Burke warned parliament,
the spirit of liberty burned brightest in America:

It has grown with the growth of the people in your colonies, and increased
with the increase of their wealth; a spirit, that unhappily meeting with an
exercise of power in England, which, however lawful, is not reconcilable to
any ideas of liberty, much less with theirs, has kindled a flame that is ready
to consume us.[5]

The American Revolution severed all political connections with the
British Empire in a war which began with the Declaration of
Independence in 1776 and ended with the Peace of Paris in 1783.
But the culmination of the Revolution was the ratification of the
Constitution by Rhode Island in May 1790, the last and most reluc-
tant of the original thirteen colonies to do so. As Burke suggested,
Americans had not only nurtured the spirit of British liberties but,
when the spring of those liberties turned sour, improved upon them.
In the course of the struggle for first independence and then a viable
political society, Americans drew upon ancient principles of freedom,
but redefined it with recent discoveries in political science. It was a

bold experiment. The Constitution combined that which had been thought to be incompatible – political and individual liberty. Americans had liberated themselves from George III, but also, as significantly, from the trammels of history and custom that imprisoned men in a knot of practices and modes of thinking which could not be undone without great harm.

The American colonists did not find that rebellion came naturally to them. They were conscious that their colonies had been founded by Britons who had fled the religious intolerance and limited options of the Old World. Generations had contributed to carving out territories from the wilderness and constructing political communities modelled on English institutions. And if American Britons enjoyed like liberty under the law to their fellow subjects in the British Isles, they experienced a greater practical liberty to make the best of their talents and energy and to conduct themselves as they saw fit. Above all there was that precious commodity, religious freedom, which had dictated the emigration of the original settlers. In terms of political liberty, they submitted themselves to parliament's control of the empire's trade and tolerated the Crown's right to veto their assemblies' legislation. In return, the Crown and parliament upheld the rule of law, provided authority and defended colonial liberty from the predatory moves of other European empires.

The exact constitutional relationship between the colonists, their assemblies and the government at Westminster was left unclear and untested as long as the Crown confined its activities to a limited sphere. Americans were reasonably confident that they were Britons enjoying the same rights and liberties as Britons in Europe. The great shift in imperial policy during the Seven Years War (1756–1763) changed all this. The combination of British and Prussian military campaigns against France in Europe and the activities of the Royal Navy drove France from her North American possessions. The ring of French forts which had hemmed in and indeed threatened the existence of the thirteen colonies was gone, and the possibility of expansion westward opened itself up to ambitious colonists who faced no imperial rival.

The vast Ohio valley awoke the dream of fresh settlements on virgin territory. It was the fruit of victory in the Seven Years War – or the French and Indian War as it was known across the Atlantic – and a new chapter for Americans. But the British had treaty obligations with the Indians and were fearful of provoking a new war with the Spanish who held lands west of the Mississippi; the territory was closed off by royal proclamation, against which there was no appeal.

Americans were left with the bitter taste of thwarted ambition. Throughout the war American officers and soldiers had shown themselves to be not merely the equals but the superiors of their British counterparts. This experience was the forging of a nation and a national consciousness. The reward of victory – indeed the destiny of Britons in America – was to make good the advantages of war and expand into the opened territories. But George Washington's projected Mississippi Land Company – which aimed to take control of 2.5 million acres on both sides of the Ohio – was rendered null by the proclamation. The option was to ignore an unenforceable order, and Washington joined a surge of settlers who claimed lands beyond the Alleghenies.[6] In the northwest, Britain aimed to give new lands to Quebec as a way of buying the affections of its French Catholic inhabitants lest they rebel on behalf of their motherland. Ambitious colonists found that nothing had changed after the war: if it wasn't the French pinning them down to the eastern seaboard it was the British. Britain and the colonists now appeared to be competitors in America where once they had been partners. This was a physical restraint of liberty.

Where once there had been indifference on the part of British statesmen towards America there was now interference. Those colonists who had joined militias in the war had had a taste of actual liberty; they had co-operated with each other in a fight against tyranny; they had experienced something like the self-governing virtue celebrated by Machiavelli as the spring of civic engagement. The policies of Great Britain were thus read in a radically different light. 'At a time', Washington wrote, 'when our Lordly Masters in Great Britain will be satisfied with nothing less than the deprivation of American freedom, it seems highly necessary that something should be done to avert the stroke and maintain the liberty which we have derived from our Ancestors.' Who were these ancestors? Americans were conscious that their forebears had found (as they saw it) an empty land and settled it. They had made a voluntary decision to accept the laws and governing traditions of Britain. The colonies had, as John Adams said, been 'sought and settled as an asylum for liberty, civil and religious'.[7] There was a line of inheritance which connected them with the founders of their colonies, a line which was clearly traceable, going back perhaps for many just three or four generations. The settlers could easily perceive how their lands had been brought within the pale of civilisation. If Europeans had to live with an accumulation of history which had made political and social life an artificial labyrinth, surely the blank page of the New World could teach, or remind, men how to live. In the eighteenth century many thinking men believed that the science of government could be discovered in this kind of way. God had not told men how to arrange their political societies, but he had planted clues in nature. Wise men could read them by using their rational faculties.

The Bible and religious history had been the first ports of call for deducing the basic forms of political society, but philosophical progress provided a rational basis for speculation about human nature and the fine details of a constitution. Famously John Locke argued that the laws of nature could be deduced if you imagined a society uncluttered by history and tradition. Or, as people in the eighteenth century conceived it, what sort of society would a Robinson Crusoe build? All men would be equal and independent; therefore the first natural law must be that 'no one ought to harm another in his life, health, liberty, or possessions'.[8] Men, in the state of nature, would be free according to reason; government came into being to defend these original rights, the secure enjoyment of property and livelihood.

Governments which conformed to the law of nature were legitimate; those which deviated from the duty of protection and mutual defence deviated from the laws of God. This was not an historical account of human development, but a rational justification for all types of government. 'Men being . . . all free, equal, and independent,' wrote Locke, 'no one can be put out of his estate, and subjected to the political power of another, without his consent.'[9] And, most importantly, as American colonies had been founded in the dawn of the age of reason, Locke's argument seemed to conform to reality. The original settlers *had* come together and formed government by consent, with the express intent that they secure the enjoyment and enlargement of property. There were, as yet, no robber barons to reallocate land. And so it was easy to believe that the American way of life conformed to the law of nature; easier than in complicated commercial societies such as Britain.

But their ancestors were also Britons who had fought against Stuart absolutism to live under the rule of law and representative government. The colonists were steeped in English history and republican political thought. And it was the Whig version of history rooted in the Civil War which they accepted most readily – often to the complete exclusion of other readings of history, which somewhat coloured their view of contemporary Britain. The key authors were John Smith, Milton, Sidney, Henry Neville, Locke, Trenchard and Gordon ('Cato'), and the Tory wildcard, Bolingbroke. It was the republican inheritance which had flourished (in literature if not politics) during the Commonwealth and which had gone underground after the Restoration. It was one which held that a rational, mechanical, properly balanced government was the only security for liberty. It stressed the positive aspect of individual liberty – participation in the life of the polis. It was a Puritan and republican inheritance which put great emphasis on freedom of thought and worship as a precondition for personal salvation. It put the development of character as a man's lifelong ambition. Existing in self-governing political and religious communities, many colonists lived by what they saw as this kind of republican code long before they lived in a republic.

Viewed through this prism, history showed that government always became overbearing, corrupt and absolutist when the virtuous 'country' party took its eyes off politics. The colonists believed, like Coke and the parliamentarians, that the 'natural' state of human freedom had been transmitted through the generations – and against the odds – by the distilled reason of the common law. It thrived in a constitution which was balanced and a government which was mixed between its competing elements. Liberty was always on the knife edge: perpetually threatened by malign forces which had triumphed everywhere in the world apart from Britain.

Above all this history showed that the first test of freedom or tyranny could be determined by the way the state taxed its subjects. Until the 1760s Britain had confined its fiscal activities to indirect taxation and regulating Atlantic trade. The war had been expensive, and politicians wanted to find a way to make the colonies pay for their defence retrospectively. The answer was the Stamp Act of 1765. Americans considered it to be an arbitrary tax imposed without their consent. Their protest framed the growing friction with British imperial policy as a constitutional issue of liberty. It involved their rights as Britons. It was more than an echo of the conflicts of the seventeenth century. Edmund Burke reminded English MPs that in English history the issue of taxation had been the barometer of politics: for seventeenth-century MPs and modern Americans 'Liberty might be safe, or might be endangered in twenty other particulars, without their being much pleased or alarmed. Here they felt its pulse; and as they found that beat, they thought themselves sick or sound.'[10]

As Burke argued, the ancestors of the colonists had left England when the passion for liberty was at its height; they had inherited the language of liberty and nurtured the republican philosophy of the radicals of the previous century when this had withered in the motherland. Parliament was picking a fight with people who were disposed to resist, and it was choosing its intellectual battleground unwisely – on issues with great historical resonance. Behind this lay their perception of the world as Protestants – dissenting Protestants in English terms. As Burke told parliament, 'the religion most prevalent in our Northern colonies is a refinement of the principle of resistance; it is the dissidence of dissent; and the protestantism of the protestant religion'.[11] It was the belief that God's word and laws could only be followed in self-governing communities which sustained resistance. Like the Puritans of the English Revolution, Americans knew that the issues of taxation and standing armies foreshadowed attempts to subvert religious autonomy. Thanks to a number of philosophical, religious and historical ideas the colonists, said Burke, 'snuff the approach of tyranny in every tainted breeze'.[12]

Parliament repealed the Stamp Act in response to furious resistance in America. But this act of conciliation was accompanied by the Declaratory Act which stated that the colonial assemblies were subordinate to the parliament in London. It was a rude shock to colonial assumptions that they enjoyed autonomy over their own affairs, and that parliament had only a superintendent authority over external affairs. It was a problem that had been avoided for decades, largely because no one had thought of taxing the colonies. What was the exact constitutional relationship between the colonies and the metropolis? Even those who objected most to the Proclamation Line and the Stamp Act wanted to preserve what they saw as their ancient rights as Britons. They saw their position as analogous to that of Ireland, which was linked to Britain by the Crown but had its own parliament.

What had changed in the 1760s was a growing intolerance for taxation of any sort and the means by which it was being collected, i.e. by soldiers. The colonists had tacitly accepted indirect taxation in the past. After the Townshend Duties of 1767 it was added to the catalogue of constitutional violations. They were nudged in this direction by Townshend himself, who said that it was 'perfect nonsense' to draw a line between direct and indirect taxation, internal and external affairs.

The scales fell from American eyes. Benjamin Franklin wrote that either parliament could make all laws for America or it could make none. Those who believed that there was a middle way, in which Americans could be subordinate to parliament in external affairs and autonomous in local affairs, were deluding themselves. Their case was justified by law and history. Their states were independent from their creation, but parliament had imperceptibly usurped this independence over time – first by regulating their trade in a hands-off kind of way, then by using this as a lever to meddle in the affairs of a Bostonian or a Virginian. The full extent of this trespass had only become apparent in 1770. But what right did the parliament in Westminster claim as a basis for its actions? The colonies had their own assemblies. Parliament did not represent the people of the colonies either directly or 'virtually', and therefore could not tax them. The apparent distinction between regulation of trade and revenue-raising was chimerical. They were interconnected, and parliament could not carry on this power without undermining the tenets of its own constitution – that there is no taxation without representation. Otherwise the colonials would be subject to another people – the British in Britain – who benefited from taxing a distinct people – the British in America.

From 1763 Americans deployed all the reasons for resisting the encroachments of parliamentary authority that they could find. The idea of the absolute sovereignty of the people to make and unmake their governments was not countenanced, as Carl Becker argued, until all other arguments had been tried. Even at the first Continental Congress only a few saw natural rights as a viable reason for resistance. John Adams persuaded Congress to include natural rights for the pragmatic reason, as he later said, that it was 'a resource to which we might be driven by Parliament much sooner than we were aware'. And so the Declaration and Resolves of Congress on 14 October 1774 had one mention of 'natural rights' against many appeals to the rights of the English constitution, the common law and colonial autonomy.

As Jefferson argued in 1774, Britons had come to America and set up governments as individuals, not as representatives of the British public. They had voluntarily agreed to live by English law, but this did not mean they had reserved to the mother country any superior right. Since the Restoration, however, the monarch had come to treat the subjects of the various states of which he was king entirely differently. In Britain, kings did not veto bills or dissolve assemblies; British subjects were tried by their peers in their communities, were allowed to trade freely and retained some form of control over their representatives in parliament. Americans had been deprived of these rights. Executive power, which was controllable in Britain, was increasing in America. And what was worse, the pretended authority to meddle in colonial affairs came from parliament, 'a body of men foreign to our constitutions, and unacknowledged by our laws'. It was

George III's duty to mediate between the peoples of the states he ruled over and govern them equally, but he was supporting one set of men against another – one large state against thirteen small ones. Britain was encroaching 'upon those rights which God and the laws have given equally and independently to all'.[13]

The idea persisted that English laws and the Constitution, when correctly applied, were conformable to the laws of nature and God. But if these principles were not upheld there was a further appeal at the last resort. 'The God who gave us life gave us liberty at the same time,' wrote Jefferson; 'the hand of force may destroy, but cannot disjoin them.'[14]

Until 1776 Americans held on to the belief that they could be reconciled to the British Empire if and when their appeals to law and history were recognised. This assumption was blown apart with the Prohibitory Act, in which George III put his American subjects beyond his protection. This extreme measure was the response to years of disobedience, protest and the spectre of violence. But it was a blunder. When authority and protection were withdrawn, men were placed back in the state of nature, where they were obliged to seek new political authority. Ideas of natural rights took on new power. At war with Britain and their king, Americans were forced to form alliances with other powers and fill the vacuum created by the Prohibitory Act with their own authority.

The Declaration of Independence stated that in the course of human affairs it sometimes becomes necessary for 'one people to dissolve the political bands which have connected them with another'. This could only come from the idea that powers were derived from the consent of the governed. The Declaration contained many reasons for Independence, mainly concentrating on George's descent into tyranny and acts of war against his own people. Revolution was justified for other reasons, one of them being the natural rights of mankind. In its conclusion the representatives of the people declared that 'these United Colonies are, and of right, ought to be free and independent states; that they are absolved from all allegiance to the British Crown, and that all political connection between them and the state of Great Britain, is and ought to be dissolved'.

Notice the *is/are* and the *ought*. The people of the colonies *are* free according to the history, laws and constitution of Britain; they *ought* to be free according to the immutable natural law that governs human beings.*

The Declaration did not mention parliament. To have done so would be to acknowledge that it had possessed a legal right. The issue was with the king, for he was the only link the colonies had had with the empire. There had been no connection in law with parliament. Americans had been freed from their ties to the king because he made war on them. This played on the elemental in politics. As the Virginian politician Arthur Lee had warned the king, loyalty – 'the first duty of subjects' – could be converted into resistance 'which the great and primary law of nature, self-defence, makes necessary'. When George III put his colonial people outside his protection he deprived Americans of their rights and released them from their duties as subjects. It left them independent human beings in a state of nature, and it was as human beings that they would have to rebuild their political societies.

As Thomas Paine argued, men throughout history – including Americans – had been governed by the dead hand of history. Now, in an enlightened age, mankind would arrange their affairs according to reason. Americans would not rebel unless they believed they were doing so for logical, legal and legitimate reasons.† They had tried to achieve their aims as subjects within the British Empire; they had deployed constitutional arguments again and again. This proved a dead end: by obeying laws made in Westminster over decades they had implied their subjection to parliament. In 1776 Americans were

---

* 'This phrase *ought to be*', wrote the constitutional historian Carl Becker, 'is the fundamental premise of the whole colonial argument. It is the expression of a new right that did not exist before; a plea for things as they should be, rather than as custom said they were. It is a search for liberty beyond the legal and constitutional when those things failed to provide an answer.'[15]

† 'Prudence . . . will dictate that Governments long established should not be changed for light and transient causes,' read the Declaration; 'and accordingly all experience hath shown, that mankind are more disposed to suffer, while evils are sufferable, than to right themselves by abolishing the forms to which they are accustomed.'

compelled to appeal to the highest authority – natural human rights which transcended all positive law devised by man.

Jeremy Bentham famously dismissed the idea of natural rights as 'nonsense on stilts'. Tom Paine's rights of man, he said, amounted to 'the right of being starved and conquered'. Many of his countrymen would have been happy to agree. Apart from a handful of radicals, the Declaration of Independence and its appeals to natural law and the right of resistance were dismissed as a farrago. Americans were rejecting the ideals of British freedom – individual liberty – and sailing into the uncharted waters of political liberty. And history taught that the outcome of popular political rights was anarchy.

The most famous proponents of political liberty in Britain were Joseph Priestley and Richard Price. They attracted venomous ripostes for the intellectual succour they held out to the American Revolutionaries and the encouragement they gave their own countrymen to demand a specious political liberation. Priestley's thinking on liberty derived from the idea of the ultimate political sovereignty of the people. He stressed clearly that there were two kinds of liberty: political and civil. The latter was the security a citizen had that his government would conduct itself with regularity and legality. A government of almost any character could offer civil liberty, but these rights would always be vulnerable unless the people had political control. And the more political power an individual had the better the civil liberty he would enjoy. But given that political participation in a state required equality of wealth, education and opportunity, full political liberty was impossible in a large and complex state.

There was, however, a spectrum between absolute freedom and slavery in which varieties of liberty were available. It was perfectly possible to enjoy liberty without having the vote, for instance. Political sovereignty was not immediately enjoyed by the disenfranchised masses, but existed remotely. Priestley saw the people's right of resistance as the ultimate security for civil liberty. This right would hardly ever be exercised, but the knowledge that it did exist kept governments in check.[16] Others, such as Burke, believed that the sovereignty of the people was expressed indirectly, through representatives in parliament and the influence of public opinion. Liberties thrived when the monarchy and the executive heeded the voice of the public. In such circumstances, it could be no surprise that the liberty of the press was pushed to the forefront of national liberties: for the freedom of discussion was the forum where the will of the people, disenfranchised as most were, could be heard.[17]

Richard Price was far more radical. His *Observations on the Nature of Civil Liberty* followed hot on the heels of the Declaration of Independence. His vision of liberty consists entirely in autonomy. Any external power which makes decisions on behalf of another has usurped the privilege of humanity – the privilege of being governed by one's own will. The danger to your liberty came from others limiting your movement and from your own base instincts. Overcoming these bad appetites made you a moral creature, as God intended. But you could only do it on your own. If you did not have full freedom of choice in terms of movement, morality, religion and civil matters then it meant that someone else had power over you – directly or in more subtle ways. Either way, someone had presumed to take authority over you without your consent. To submit to the control of another was slavery; there was no middle ground in which liberty could be enjoyed, merely a stark difference between absolute freedom and varieties of slavery.

Therefore liberty could only be enjoyed if you had power over your faculties, to develop as a human being in conformity with natural laws. And if individuals should have power to participate in making the laws, it followed that this was only possible if the political community itself was free from outside control. The worst form of tyranny was one state controlling another. The danger of this was that a remote and badly informed foreign power would have nothing to limit its cruel or capricious policies; its good policies would be a matter of forbearance or luck. And the subjected people would have to shake off not just a single tyrant but a united people. A declaration of a country's independence was the first step towards the freedom of man, and the freedom of man justified such a declaration.

This kind of thinking was dismissed as mere speculation on the imponderables of the human condition; as 'the hazard of appealing from settled laws to wild opinion'.[18] For by Price's definition, every law to which you did not consent and every tax you did not conceive as a free gift would be an act of coercion, a suppression of your natural liberty, whether it came from a king, an elite or the majority. Unless there was authority in the state to tax, make laws and govern multitudes of diverse people, said Price's critics, there could be no practical government. Dr Price's liberty was really anarchy, where every man was an autonomous unit, justified in rebelling against every rule he felt inhibited his natural rights. And for Price read American rebels.

Price contended for 'ideal liberty'; 'real liberty' was what existed in Britain. Its strength consisted in its freedom from metaphysical speculation. The history of the world was that of clashes between individuals and between liberty and authority; human life was messy. Only in Britain had liberty and authority been resolved. It meant that Britons were free from arbitrary invasion of their person and property and free from the obligations of public service. Americans revolted against the legislative sovereignty of parliament, and they did so because they conceived a greater right – the sovereignty of the people. 'Do we in this island rest uneasily in our beds because we know the parliament has a right to govern us in all cases whatsoever?' retorted the writer John Gray. 'Do we expect to be enjoined at what hour we shall rise in the morning, how many glasses of wine we may drink after dinner, how many cabbages we may plant in our garden, how often we shall wash our hands?'[19]

Of course not. Parliamentary sovereignty and liberty had been found, by experience, to be compatible. That, in an imperfect world, was the best kind of freedom to be expected. Price said that people were justified in rebelling – as the Americans were – if they were compelled to obey laws to which they had not consented. That millions of Britons could not vote and that the American colonists were subject to parliamentary superintendence did not make them unfree; in fact they enjoyed the laws and liberty of Britain – the liberty to live as free individuals. MPs were returned by a small number of people, but that was not the point: the House of Commons represented the people in a wider sense, checking power and safeguarding individual liberties. They were not led by the people they represented, and so were therefore a check on the capricious passions of the people as much as the arbitrary actions of the government.* In other words, legislative independence for the colonies would not automatically make *individuals* more free. It would lead to what Thomas Jefferson called 'elective despotism'[21] – the predominance of a popular assembly, the power of which would be, thanks to its democratic mandate, unlimited.

Indeed it was thanks to the *absence* of political rights that Britons had liberty. Parliament was independent of the clamour of the multitude – the kind of unthinking clamour which *would*, if it gained authority, start telling people how many cabbages to grow, how many glasses of wine they were permitted, how property should be redistributed and every other passing whim or fancy of the day that would be fatal to individual liberty.[22] Power emanated from the Crown, not the people – but it was a power divided and distributed among bodies and individuals who were accountable in courts for their actions as private individuals. If power flowed from the people – if they were self-legislating and self-governing – they would renounce authorities which were wiser than they and had a greater conception of the good. It was the authority of tradition and history, of religion and morality, of the wise and respectable. Human wisdom had not made the British constitution, but it was the singular good luck of Britons to live under a constitution which, however messy and irrational it appeared, had discovered modern liberty; one which had gradually built up barriers against arbitrary government over centuries of actual experience. By throwing it away in favour of utopian notions of unrealisable liberty, Americans were choosing anarchy and losing individual freedom, which had only ever existed in the history of the world in Britain.

Such was the fond delusion that British freedom was the only kind that could flourish. It was a pretty poor argument which merely

---

* See an example of this from Charles James Fox in his less radical youth: 'their [the people's] business is to choose us; it is ours to act constitutionally . . . Whether that independency is attacked by the people or by the Crown, is a matter of little consequence; it is the attack, not the quarter it proceeds from, which we are to punish.'[20]

claimed to be the least worst and took such a dim view of human nature. As Burke said, the colonists revolted not for speculative notions of liberty, not because they rejected the paper arguments about the purity of the British constitution, but because they experienced an *actual* diminution of their liberty. That was evidence in itself that the system was not working; that those barriers against executive interference had worn themselves out.

And the same thing was happening in Britain. The House of Commons was failing to operate as a check on executive power; indeed, executive and legislative power had merged – MPs were corrupted by royal handouts and its leading members exercised real power. The people's representatives were becoming their masters, rather than the guardians of their rights. From the accession of George III in 1760 ministers were picked without heeding the voice of public opinion – a reference to the 'popular party' had previously been an important factor in cabinet formation; now ministerial appointments depended on royal favouritism. The voting public was itself tiny and its independence curbed by money, intimidation and plain old-fashioned electoral fraud. The Commons lost its connection with the wider public. At the same time the press was subject to repeated assaults by the government and civil liberties were invaded with melancholy regularity. The result of government by a narrow cabal was that the sentiments of the population were now expressed in violent protests (in London) and revolution (in America).[23] It was left to a small band of Whigs in parliament to point out that the war against America was a war against liberty itself. Any attempt to check those passions which had once given Britain liberty would turn on itself and become a scourge against domestic freedoms.

The war against the colonies showed just how fragile British liberties were. Habeas corpus was suspended for crimes committed abroad or on the high seas, meaning that British forces could arrest whoever they wanted and hold them wherever they chose. There were cases of people who had been secretly stowed in the hold of a ship and taken from court to court throughout the empire until they were convicted.[24] 'A person only suspected, or pretended to be so, may be doomed to the dampest, most noxious dungeon, on the most swampy coast,' said John Wilkes.[25] It was extraordinary rendition, eighteenth-century style, and a complete betrayal of all the liberties which Britons had taken for granted since the Glorious Revolution.

Parliament had risen to power within the state because it had always sided with the people in the struggle for liberty. In the Whig view this was how it had evolved from *a* branch of the state charged with the administrative task of revenue-gathering to *the* supreme body in the nation. It had risen to power by enlarging liberty; it would surely fall when it abdicated that responsibility. The justification that the legislative authority of parliament guaranteed civil liberty against executive authority was becoming ever more threadbare. The radical Whigs grouped around Charles James Fox and Edmund Burke hoped that Britain would lose in America. The growing power of the Crown had caused the war, they argued, and the war was increasing the power of the Crown. These Whigs believed that the constitution was being undermined. The monarchy was making a bid for power, they thought; and, as other Whigs defected to Toryism, they held on to 'Revolution principles'. They toasted the sovereignty of the people and George Washington, and like their True Whig predecessors, aimed to limit the power of the monarchy. It was not until 1832, when Fox and Burke were long dead, that the Whigs were returned to power to reform the old system.

Fox's frustration with the corrupt and lickspittle 'system' burst out in 1781 when he demanded that MPs accept that the war was lost and make moves for peace: 'He called upon them as the representatives of the people, and not as the creatures of ministers, to do their duty; to execute the trust reposed in them, and act up to the sentiments they really felt.'[26] But his fellow MPs lived down to expectations and voted to continue the doomed war in accordance with the deluded wishes of George III.

For Americans it was a clear indication that British liberty had spent its energies. The motherland was decadent and effete. The constitution had lost its former balance, entailing corruption and aggression. Having forgotten her habits of liberty, Britain was now turning on its colonies' liberties for plunder and profit. It hardened the feeling that liberty was only possible in America, where agrarian virtue, religious freedom and habits of self-reliance were still widespread. Britons had lost their freedoms when they lost the capacity for virtue and self-government. The baton of liberty – which had been passed down from the Anglo-Saxons – had been transferred to the American people, who had learnt exactly what it meant to be modern citizens. It happened first during the Seven Years War, then in the years of soul-searching and finally in the perilous task of building a state. 'But what do you mean by the American Revolution?' John Adams asked in 1818.

Do we mean the American war? The Revolution was effected before the war was commenced. The Revolution was in the minds and hearts of the people; a change in their religious sentiments, of their duties and obligations . . . *This radical change in the principles, sentiments, and affections of the people was the real American Revolution.*[27]

CHAPTER 6

Liberties Old and New

—∿—

> But why is the experiment of an extended republic to be rejected merely
> because it may comprise what is new? Is it not the glory of the people of
> America, that whilst they have paid a decent regard to the opinions of
> former times and other nations, they have not suffered a blind vener-
> ation for antiquity, for custom, or for names, to overrule the suggestions
> of their own good sense, the knowledge of their situation, and the lesson
> of their own experience?
>
> JAMES MADISON[1]

> Since we live in modern times, I want a liberty suited to modern
> times . . . Individual liberty is the true modern liberty. Political liberty
> is its guarantee.
>
> BENJAMIN CONSTANT[2]

Writers in Britain assumed that the talk of a new liberty was ridiculous. Political liberty based on democracy would destroy the fledgling
republic in short order. Yet far from having utopian notions of liberty
Americans were determined to build systems of government which
preserved the kind of individual freedom which had emerged in
Britain.

The leaders of the American Revolution set out to show the world
that power emanating from the people did not necessarily subject government to the instinctive, unreflective fits of passing prejudice. They
attempted to perfect modern liberty by safeguarding it within rational
mechanisms of government. Lying behind the attempts to construct a
government was the belief that 'liberty may be endangered by the

abuses of liberty, as well as by the abuses of power'.[3] As Burke was later to retort to people such as Dr Price who gave unqualified welcome to the French Revolution, one might as well congratulate a highwayman who escaped from gaol on his liberty as a people who had thrown off traditional authority, however oppressive it was, and stood liberated but undefended against the storms of their passions and the schemes of designing men. For to commend liberty indiscriminately would be to hold up the wildly independent savage in a state of nature as a model of humanity. Robinson Crusoe would therefore become the perfect being, and everyone else a slave or vassal of some sort.[4] The Framers of the United States Constitution, almost alone in the history of revolutionary leaders, succeeded in fulfilling Burke's criteria of subjecting themselves to a rational, regulated liberty. And unlike revolutionaries, they looked to history rather than subjecting themselves to notions of a perfect future.

The Declaration of Independence made clear that all governments rested on the consent of the people, a promise that could not be easily denied or easily fulfilled. The people would not be satisfied by anything other than free republican government. But the wiser among them realised the dangers to which they were vulnerable. It was true that in history all republics had sooner or later been pushed to the extremes of anarchy or tyranny. As the Framers of the Constitution would say, they proceeded with ancient examples in mind, but were able to use the discoveries of modern political science to build barriers against both tyranny and mob rule. The discovery of modernity, wrote Alexander Hamilton, included the 'regular distribution of power into distinct departments; the introduction of legislative balances and checks; the institution of courts composed of judges holding their offices during good behaviour; the representation of the people in the legislature, by deputies of their own election'. These were unknown to the ancients, but were the tools by which republics and republican values could be upheld and their weaknesses isolated.[5]

The Constitution of the United States was based upon republican experiments made in several of the states after the end of the War of Independence. Most significant among the liberties demanded at this point was religious freedom – what Thomas Jefferson numbered among the 'natural rights of mankind'. For gentlemen of the Enlightenment something was deeply wrong if a set of beliefs had to be defended by law or official sanction. It offended against reason: things were either true or they were not. This was put nowhere better than by Priestley:

Should free enquiry lead to the destruction of Christianity itself, it ought not, on that account, to be discontinued; for we can only wish for the prevalence of Christianity on the supposition of its being true; and if it fall before the influence of free enquiry, it can only do so in consequence of its not being true.[6]

That, after all, is the essence of being free; and a society which grants *anyone* such a privilege to shatter – or attempt to shatter – its most sacred tenets qualifies as being open.

European settlers in America had a long history of demanding freedom of conscience, and, chiming with the tenets of enlightened thinking, it was *the* fundamental right of free men. As Jefferson said, at the time he was framing the Bill for Establishing Religious Freedom in Virginia, the 'impious presumption' of state authority in religion and attempts by punishments or inducements do not strengthen faith but 'tend only to beget habits of hypocrisy and meanness'.[7] The assumption from the first was that religion was perverted by association with temporal authority, and that the mixture of the two created evils for which there was no harmless solution in history. James Madison wrote that the separation of religion from the state is essential to the purity of both. As with much thinking at this time there was never a conviction that the truth *was* there waiting to be discovered. The only conviction was that, left to mere mortals, the least worst outcome of setting up some truth as infallible would be that the men in charge would be benign. Jefferson's statute was written in national law as the First Amendment, ensuring what was a vision for enlightened thinkers in Europe: the neutrality of the state in matters of religion – the key component of liberty and a foundation of social peace.

The attainment of liberty, however, brought its own problems. British authority had been driven out, and democratic authority had been put in its place. But this existed at a local level, often very local indeed. The links which riveted the thirteen states were weak, and most citizens regarded themselves as members of their state or their community rather than as a nation of Americans. The people were scattered over a wide territory. They feared the reappearance of a distant authority over which, by reasons of geography if nothing else, they could have little control. The states called conventions to draw up constitutions, which were ratified by the people. Having built viable republics many believed that liberty was only possible in small self-governing communities where the citizens had direct political control. Proposals to extend republicanism as the central governing power over thirteen disparate states were regarded by many as a doomed experiment.

To the consternation of some of the glittering stars of the Revolutionary period – those enlightened men who had provided the intellectual nourishment of independence – republican democracy had not awoken republican virtue. State legislatures were as susceptible to parochialism and populism as many critics had suspected. The loose confederation of the states was facing chaos. This was the background to the passage of the Constitution. The intellectual lead came from those enlightened gentlemen and friends John Jay, James Madison and Alexander Hamilton in their collaboration, *The Federalist Papers*. As with all writing of this time, it was undertaken by working politicians who were concerned with everyday realities as much as political theory. United by the fundamentals of liberty and what were the necessary preconditions of a free society they may have been, but, like any set of human beings, the details and purposes of liberty divided them in irreconcilable factions.[8]

The three authors of the *Federalist* had to convince the inhabitants of the states that a federal government would not only provide security for the liberties they already had but augment those liberties. A federal union, they said, would pool the resources of the vast territories of the states, providing a collective strength which would free Americans to make the best of their wealth and talents. Only a strong and efficient state could have the muscle power to defend American traders and negotiate treaties with foreign powers. It would have the ability to borrow money which would provide the 'sinews' of national defence;

roads and canals could be co-ordinated which cut across great tracts of land, and general laws would allow citizens to trade and travel with freedom across the states. Thirteen loosely united states with their own governments, laws and currency would undo the blessing of independence. They would not be able to defend themselves against predatory powers, and they might fall into dispute with one another. One state might draw up laws or impose customs duties which benefited its own people but harmed a neighbouring state. Only a federal government would be able to reconcile that which was of national importance with local interests. The political instability which had beset the United States since independence, and any future crisis which would be met with panicky solutions at the brink of disaster, were far greater threats to liberty then a central government. Therefore union and strong central authority would enlarge the liberties already won by giving Americans the chance to compete in the world and dominate their continent.

Indeed the Framers claimed that a federal republic would mean greater civil and political freedom than a small commonwealth. History taught that small republics were prone to a majority or a party taking power and ruling with contempt for a minority and against the long-term interests of the state. James Madison warned that when the weaker members of society had little or no power against the strongest you were back in the state of nature, where might triumphed over right in an anarchical free-for-all.[9] But, as he argued, the sheer size and diversity of the United States, which many saw as a barrier to republican democracy, would prevent this. Under the Constitution the bicameral legislature comprising the House of Representatives, elected by individuals, and the Senate, elected by the legislatures of the states, would represent the multiplicity of interests across the United States at the centre. The diversity of a people spread across an extent of territory was a security for liberty because it made it hard for a majority of identical interests to form – much harder than in a city or even in a fairly homogeneous state. An individual in, for example, Rhode Island, who felt oppressed by his state government or his community, would have another government and other people with whom to seek protection and solidarity. A single homogeneous state, however free were its institutions, could not provide this defence for liberty; it was thanks to the geography and character of the people of the United States that this experiment in federal republicanism could be tried.[10]

The Framers were much influenced by Montesquieu's theory that the separation of powers in a state prevented one branch of government predominating over another. Montesquieu based his ideas on the British constitution; but, as Americans knew all too well, power in the British state was liable to fluctuations. They had seen the result of legislative supremacy. The competition for power among the separate branches of the constitution had endangered the people's liberties. The republican principle, which had been articulated in political thought since the Commonwealth, of an empire of laws and not of men, was not being fulfilled. Over time the popular part of the legislature, the House of Commons, had ceased to act as a guardian of the people's rights against the executive and had taken on executive functions.[11] As such MPs had become corrupted by the other branches; they had ceased to be the representatives of the people when they became partners in power. This was all too natural. Paper barriers would not work because it was in the nature of a popular assembly to swell in power over time. The several offices and assemblies in which different authorities were located would gradually merge, and the men who held office would develop a corporate mentality which might estrange them from the interests of the community. It had happened even in the short existence of the American states – and it had happened despite the best intentions and virtue of the people involved. As Jefferson wrote of Virginia:

All the powers of government legislative, executive and judiciary, result to the legislative body. The concentrating these in the same hands is precisely the definition of despotic government . . . One hundred and seventy-three despots would surely be oppressive as one . . . As little will it avail us that they are chosen by ourselves. An elective despotism was not the government we fought for; but one which should not only be founded on free principles, but in which the principles of government should be so divided and balanced among several bodies of magistracy, as that no one could transcend their legal limits, without being effectively checked and restrained by the others.

The Framers of the Virginian constitution had made the executive and judicial parts of the state dependent on the legislature, and, without an overt bid for control, the balance of power had naturally tipped towards the legislature.[12]

Again, this problem could be remedied in a larger state. The more places there were to locate power, the less likely it would be for one to predominate over the other. Americans would have a state government to manage their affairs, with a bicameral legislature, an executive and judiciary; the same would be replicated at a higher level. Both governments would check each other's encroachments. Madison called this a 'double security' for the rights of the people. The powers would be kept separate not just by paper guarantees but by mutual checks and by differences in the function and election of the members. The popular assembly – the Representatives – would be directly elected by the people; the Senate by the state legislatures; and the president by an electoral college. The Supreme Court would guarantee judicial independence. The branches were distinct in their election, their function and their accountability. None was responsible for appointing, rewarding or punishing the other. Therefore they each provided actual 'obstructions' against one of the others encroaching upon power, rather than just balancing each other. Faith in local centres of authority and accountability, for example, would provide a check against the growth of power at the centre.[13]

The thinking behind this complex mechanism of government was that power corrupts. Therefore power should not be allowed to corrupt weak-willed men. 'The aim of every political constitution', wrote Madison, 'is, or ought to be, first, to obtain rulers for men who possess wisdom to discern, and most virtue to pursue, the common good, of the society; and in the next place, to take the most effectual precautions for keeping them virtuous, whilst they continue to hold their public trust.'[14] Rules and procedures would prevent the accidental or contrived emergence of a single authority in the state. But if the Constitution was designed to prevent the untoward exercise of power on the people, the barriers also worked the other way. Because a diverse people were spread over a big area they would find it harder to combine and act like a London or Parisian mob. The character of the Senate as comprising men who had been chosen by state legislatures would mean that they would be wise and respectable and isolated from the tumult of public opinion. Senators and the electoral college which chose the president were deliberate barriers against the emergence of crowd-pleasing demagogues. They were also responsible for that exercise of power with which the people could not be trusted: foreign treaties and the regulation of trade.[15]

The principle of the United States was that the people were sovereign. But there was also a strong belief among political leaders about the ends of government. Madison wrote that 'it is the reason of the public alone, that ought to control and regulate the government. The passions ought to be controlled and regulated by government.' The Constitution was supposed to be an ascending conduit for the 'reason' of the public and a brake on its passions.[16] It would therefore create the conditions in which freedom could exist – one in which the mistakes to which governments were prone and the evils inherent in mankind could be conquered. As the Framers believed, taking an exalted view of humanity was an oft-repeated error in history. They were true to their Protestant heritage. Secular power always managed to sully religion, whether it meant to or not. That alone justified its restraint. For what was the struggle of Protestantism through the centuries but the fight to exclude authority from intervening between the community of believers and the word of God?

The Constitution and the Bill of Rights were negative in design. The history and literature of republicanism and Puritanism, with their pessimistic analysis of power, meant that this would always be the case. They limited the power of government, but had little to say about the development of the individual. This was because, like Milton and others in the English Revolution, American republicans believed that the experience of liberty and self-responsibility would naturally turn people into citizens as they sought to overcome the obstacles inherent in their own nature and the outside world without being cosseted or coerced by authority.

But the Framers also assumed an active citizenry already existed who would make the system work. Republican liberty was to be expressed in public forums, in the township and county or at state and national levels. The yeomanry scattered about the territory of the US and cultivating their lands had a role as participants in the process, and they *would* govern themselves, out of duty or sheer necessity. The Framers presupposed this quality in the free male population, and they also presupposed that a majority of the citizenry would be members of Protestant communities, not isolated individuals. Power could remain distant because society provided the self-acting discipline to mould citizens.[17]

Their revolution was not one which aimed to liberate the oppressed masses, because the oppressed masses did not exist as they did in European cities (the oppressed in the US happened to live in plantations). It was no levelling revolution because every free male was, or could become, a property owner. There was therefore none of the work of destruction of ancient forms of oppression which was a feature of the French Revolution. And consequently no revolutionary urgency to free people from pain and submission and lead them, willingly or not, to the good. There was none of Robespierre's 'despotism of liberty' whereby people must be made to learn to be free, to join a movement of national destiny and conform to public virtue; no Terror.

The Jacobin leaders of the French Revolution believed that liberty was only possible when all the old forms of social relations were obliterated, society was reconstructed and conventional ideas of morality revolutionised. They wanted to create *le nouveau Adam*, a modern man who lived according to his true nature. This required intellectuals who knew what the true nature of man was in order to remould human consciousness. Benjamin Constant noted of his country's revolution that it conformed to ancient ideas of liberty, whereby society called upon the individual to join a collective endeavour and identify his interests with the interests of the whole. It was an ideological revolution, in which the price of deviating from the 'will of the people' (or what the rational ends of human beings were determined to be) was high. 'They believed that everything should give way before collective will,' said Constant, 'and that all restrictions on individual rights would be amply compensated by participation in social power.

'We all know . . . what has come of it,' Constant continued. What share of power of any sort could any man lost amid the multitudes of modern societies expect? Constant answered his own question: 'The nation did not find that an ideal share in an abstract sovereignty was worth the sacrifices required from her.' The plan that liberty was realised only by being an atom in the collective endeavour of the social organism was believed to be a new and noble phase for humanity. Instead the austerity required by this kind of 'liberty' was more onerous than tyranny and more savage and inquisitorial than a despotic government. Dissidents became, in the eyes of the brave new leaders, not merely seditious rascals (as they were under a monarchy) but rebels against the progress of humanity itself. Having the like political rights as your neighbour – and a million other neighbours – meant that your individuality was lost in the great crowd called society.[18]

Modern liberty consisted of being free to participate in all that modern civilisation had to offer, as David Hume and others had noted. It was the liberty to choose from a range of commercial, professional and intellectual possibilities which could only spring from individual effort and which the collective voice could not prescribe. The republican ethos which made participation and service obligatory was irreconcilable with the privacy which gave citizens this opportunity. In Britain and America, although the route to the same end differed, modern freedom – individual liberty – was only possible when political power was represented in responsible institutions. The individual must be free to delegate his political rights to others, rather than having them exacted from him. By making the citizen the source of power, but releasing him from daily participation in politics, the Constitution of the United States had discovered the means whereby republican forms of freedom could be reconciled with modern commercial society. The Constitution therefore bears the fingerprints of the Enlightenment in Britain. Politics was not intended to awaken men's souls by redirecting them to a higher cause; rather, it found the best means to channel self-interest into beneficial – or at least harmless – activities.

As the Framers made clear, the United States was not a pure democracy but a federal republic. The will of the sovereign people was the ultimate arbiter of power, but power itself was exercised by a small body on behalf of the people. Represented by political parties which reflected his interests and defended by bodies which upheld his legal privileges the citizen's particular grievances would be heard and his idiosyncrasies defended by law. In short, his personal liberty was considerable and his political rights equal, even while his personal influence was negligible – a disparity impossible in all previous models.

In 1768 Joseph Priestley had written:

... the sense of political and civil liberty, though there should be no great occasion to exert it in the course of a man's life, gives him a constant feeling of his own power and importance; and it is the foundation of his indulging in a free, bold, and manly turn of thinking unrestrained by the most distant idea of control.

Political participation and active citizenship may be the highest expression of liberty; but it should never be compulsory or the very notion of liberty would be destroyed.

To transfer immediate responsibility, however, to people and institutions which could be trusted to govern for the public good and which could never become tyrannical was the outcome of political liberty and the source of civil liberty. And, as Priestley argued, this kind of freedom has a positive outcome in developing character rather than a negative quality of merely restraining authority.[19] It was a wholly modern discovery. When Priestley wrote it was experienced only by elites rather than masses of people. By the end of the century the experiment had been made in one part of the world at least. Constant said in a lecture in 1819,

Individual liberty is the true modern liberty. Political liberty is its guarantee, consequently political liberty is indispensable. But to ask the peoples of our day to sacrifice, like those of the past, the whole of their individual liberty to political liberty, is the surest means of detaching them from the former and, once this result has been achieved, it would be only too easy to deprive them of the latter.[20]

The American Revolution gave the world its most powerful instance of the rights of man as the justification for power. It gave us the language and heroes of modern political liberty, examples which nourish and set a gold standard for us today. 'The sacred rights of mankind', wrote Alexander Hamilton,

are not to be rummaged for among old parchments or musty records. They are written, as with a sunbeam, in the whole volume of nature, by the hand of the Divinity itself, and can never be erased or obscured by mortal power. I consider civil liberty, in a genuine, unadulterated sense, as the greatest of terrestrial blessings. I am convinced that the whole human race is entitled to it, and that it can be wrested from no part of them without the blackest and most aggravated evil.[21]

Fine words indeed. But this was also the Hamilton who declared that the British system of government was 'the best in the world'. When challenged by John Adams to qualify such remarks by admitting that the mother country was tarnished by corruption and a restricted franchise, Hamilton dismissed these as 'supposed defects' and reiterated that the British constitution and state had reached perfection.[22] The eloquent words of the fight for independence thereby collided with reality. James Madison found that the constitution he helped design had subordinated the states – particularly his beloved Virginia, pre-eminent among them – to the control of central government. As Secretary of the Treasury under President Washington, the hard-headed realist Hamilton had centralised the American economy and laid the foundations for a modern state – one which resembled Britain in its financial architecture, administrative functions and system of patronage. Madison had envisaged central government as a higher power in a more noble sense – something which would have a moral and intellectual legitimacy to keep less enlightened states in republican good health rather than a fiscal and administrative clout to rule the states directly. An ardent Virginian nationalist, he found that the new government was easily shaped by United States nationalists such as his erstwhile friend and collaborator Alexander Hamilton, who, born in the British West Indies to a Scottish father, had no such connection to any other state than the brand new USA.[23]

In Madison's eyes Hamilton was reviving British power – Virginians were as exposed to taxation from a distant legislature and as subordinate to a metropolitan elite in the 1790s as they had been in the 1760s. And, just as invidious, American agrarian virtue was being overtaken by mercantile vice and the Wall Street mentality. When you had a centralised state, aggressive commercialism and a military establishment you had what went with them – a nationwide network of state employees, banks, patronage and everything else which had made Britain seem so corrupt a quarter of a century before. What came under pressure was the vision of the virtuous agrarian republic – or republics. Liberty had been mortgaged to greed, selfish interests and big government. But Secretary Hamilton was a close student of David Hume. Modern liberty survived and was perfected once a viable and financially competent nation state had been established. Capitalist self-interest, therefore, took over from the public spirit which had been assumed to be uniquely American during the days of Independence. Sociability, urbanity and commerce became the glue of a democracy when the republican ethos of selfless public participation no longer was. And, following the Humean analysis, economic, social and intellectual freedoms *were* compatible with a strong state. The differences between Hamiltonian federalists and the republicans who followed Jefferson and Madison were stark, even if they shared, and defined, the starting point.

The dream that a new kind of liberty could be created in the utopia of the New World proved short-lived. The United States would become as much a modern nation state as any European country, with all the vices Americans had rejected as an affront to liberty: centralised government, a military infrastructure, an administrative cadre, paper money, public credit and taxation. But if many saw states' rights subordinated to Leviathan, it was clear that this cut both ways. How could America claim to be the new home of liberty when it permitted slavery? Springing seemingly out of the imagination of the Enlightenment, the Constitution and the settlement of the government in the 1780s and 90s were every bit a compromise. Having reluctantly accepted federation, it was believed to be beyond the realms of politics for the new central government to enforce emancipation as well. If it *had* been tried it was feared that the United States would have been one of the most short-lived nations in history. And so the nation conceived in liberty was born with a terrible curse. In such circumstances silence was preferred to confrontation; the pursuit of a unique experiment in democracy was considered more important than completing the plan of liberty. Hamilton lauded civil liberties, and the passage of the Bill of Rights affirmed their centrality to the republic. Yet even at the time, anti-federalists said that hedging government with such neat perimeters was a red herring, an attempt to divert substantive cravings for freedom from the Hamiltonian big state by granting perfunctory concessions. For many the great plan of substantial liberty had been put off by political expediency and human greed.

As I have argued, the American revolutionaries were fortunate in point of historical and social and geographical circumstances that liberty could be at the forefront of their movement. The disjunction between the above two quotations from Hamilton reminds us of the contrast between the hope of revolution and the realities of human politics. *The Federalist Papers* and the drafting of the Constitution satisfied politicians as diverse as Madison and Hamilton because such documents were general enough in wording and satisfying as a solution to the problems of government; the use to which such plans were put and the subsequent split in the ranks of the revolutionary generation showed how malleable were the ideas of liberty.

Americans won their liberties thanks to outright conflict against an unwelcome alien authority, and this gives the notion of liberty a centrality to American politics. In Britain the struggle for liberty resembled guerrilla war. Most radicals did not want to pull down traditions and start again at Year Zero, like the French Jacobins. Their tactic was to chip away at authority, bit by bit; to hold it to account; to play their rulers at their own game. There was no attempt to reframe the constitution or strip it of its essentials; they worked within the system. America has heroes of liberty who risked all and whose pronouncements on the subject could fill a book of quotations: Franklin, Jefferson, Paine, the Adamses, Washington, Madison, Hamilton. French philosophers injected wholly new ways of thinking about the world. Britain owes many of its liberties to somewhat seedy adventurers: John Wilkes, John Entick, Brass Crosby, Thomas Hardy, William Cobbett, William Hone . . . the list could go on, but even the well-informed reader would be puzzled at the obscurity of most of the heroes of the intermittent guerrilla campaign. Few of them have statues (Brass Crosby's memorial obelisk has been transferred from the City, and is now the battered and anonymous centre point of a roundabout near the Elephant and Castle). And few of their victories were accompanied by the banging of drums and tantantara of trumpets. Change crept in so slowly and unremarkably that there can be no start date of any one of our liberties when the ray of light burst through the clouds. But that is the nature of British liberty.

You won't find any great pronouncements on liberty from John Entick. Yet he gives his name to one of the fundamental cases in English constitutional law and one of the most important precedents in British civil liberties. Entick was one of forty or so printers and journalists arrested in 1762–3 over criticism of the government in the pages of the *Monitor* and the *North Briton*. Behind it was John Wilkes MP, a contributor to the former paper and editor of the latter. The opposition and radical press was in full cry against the policies of the government, the influence of the young George III's favourite, Lord Bute, and Britain's inglorious exit from the Seven Years War.

The ministry answered the satire and censure in kind, and then by harsher methods. In November 1762, Lord Halifax, Secretary of State, issued warrants against two *Monitor* writers, John Entick and Arthur Beardmore. Entick's house was searched thoroughly by the King's Messengers; locks and chests were broken and pamphlets and private papers were loaded up and carried away in a search for evidence of sedition. Halifax drew up warrants against the *North Briton*, but they were not served.[24] In April of the next year, Halifax struck against Wilkes after the forty-fifth edition of the *North Briton* dared to say that King George's speech closing parliament had been written by his ministers. John Wilkes was arrested on suspicion of seditious libel, and his house and papers ransacked by the Messengers, as Entick's had been.

The ins and outs of Wilkes's fascinating career need not be repeated here. It is the subject of a very good recent book, and the story of his clashes with authority in the 1760s is key to the development of liberty in Britain.[25] Burke would later say that the ministries after 1760 were hostile to the idea that the common folk could have an influence on politics. Wilkes was an offender on several counts. He was a popular journalist, and later in the decade he would be returned by the people of Middlesex, a constituency which was one of a handful which had a large, independent electorate. Wilkes claimed to speak for the country against a cabal of ministers and court favourites. He was condemned by parliament for seditious and blasphemous writing and found guilty in the courts. When he was returned for Middlesex parliament voted down his membership of the Commons because he was still serving a prison sentence. There were unsubstantiated claims that men in power had tried to have him assassinated. Very quickly he became a symbol of resistance and a one-man opposition to an unpopular government, who contrasted with the hundreds of supine MPs. And the efforts to which the government went to crush him made Wilkes a popular hero and embodiment of the people's thwarted liberties.

What is of significance is the behaviour of the crowd throughout Wilkes's campaign to vindicate his name, protect the liberty of the press and defend the rights of critical MPs. Wilkes was adept at stage-managing his trials. He was helped by Charles Pratt, Lord Chief Justice of the Court of Common Pleas, and conveniently a political opponent of the government, who tolerated Wilkes's irrelevant panegyrics on liberty in court. When the judge told the MP's supporters to keep quiet, Wilkes was ready with one of his memorable bon mots: 'This is not the clamour of the rabble, my lord, but the voice of liberty, which must be heard.'[26] This was the stirring of urban radicalism in all its goriness. Liberty was becoming the cause of the people against government and parliament.

Of great interest to the average subject was the means by which Halifax had given the King's Messengers carte blanche to scour London for evidence of seditious libel. This was called a general warrant, one which specified a crime but not a suspected criminal. This had implications for everyone. For if this was within the power of a minister no one would be free from arbitrary searches. It made a mockery of privacy.

If you want to understand the way liberty works in Britain, the case of *Entick* v. *Carrington* speaks volumes.[27] John Wilkes, his printers and John Entick had all successfully sued the Messengers for damages when they raided their property. However Nathan Carrington, the chief Messenger, appealed against the damages awarded to Entick at the Court of Common Pleas. Fortunately for the Wilkesites, Charles Pratt, now Lord Camden, was still Chief Justice of the court. What right, asked Entick's barrister, had the Secretary of State to issue a warrant to a Messenger to search for papers? For a start, Messengers were not known to the law. Secretary of State Halifax might as well have issued a warrant to his footmen, or a gaggle of prize fighters. And why did they go to Entick's house? – he was not named in the warrant. Or rather, what stopped them searching not just Entick's house, but every house they felt like? Armed with a general warrant, the Secretary of State's creatures could search any building in the country. Therefore this was an issue of trespass. If someone complained to a magistrate that his snuffbox had been stolen, the justice could make out a warrant to search for the snuffbox in a specific place. If the justice's officers found and took a candlestick they believed to be stolen property when they were searching for the snuffbox they could be charged with theft, not to say trespass. When you were dealing with opinion, this was trespass of an aggravated kind. As the barrister put it, 'ransacking a man's secret drawers and boxes, to come at evidence against him, is like racking his body to come at his secret thoughts'.

Camden did not spare himself when he gave judgement. It would influence the way that British and American governments worked and protect the civil liberties of the subject until the twentieth century. At the heart of the argument is the principle that the state cannot break the law in the name of necessity. If ministers bend or break the laws in the exercise of their duty they are accountable in the courts like any other subject. Carrington and his Messengers had argued that they had only carried out their duty as they and their predecessors had done since the Glorious Revolution. And the Revolution was, after all, the dawn of liberty. The Secretary of State was charged with defending the state against traitors and libellers, and he was within his rights to issue a warrant and give the Messengers the responsibility of carrying it out. Under an act of parliament, Justices of the Peace and their deputies were given wider powers to search for evidence of crimes, and they were indemnified against criminal charges if they acted within their prescribed duties. Surely a Secretary of State had at least the authority of a JP?

Camden disagreed. The act did not mention a Secretary of State or a Messenger. A Secretary of State was, strictly speaking, the king's private secretary; what authority he had could only be as a proxy of the king because there was no formal job description, let alone an act of parliament which conferred legal powers. That Secretaries of State had, as the government system gradually matured, taken on greater powers and adopted procedures could not justify the Messengers' actions. The court could not convert departmental method into law just because it had been the norm for generations; to say otherwise would be 'to mould an unlawful power into a convenient authority'. The silence of the courts did not make law; and the time-honoured practice of officials did not create custom.

But the meat of the argument concerned itself with trespass. 'The great end for which men entered into society was to secure their property,' said Camden. 'That right is preserved sacred and incommunicable in all instances, where it has not been taken away or abridged by some public law for the good of the whole.' Where did the law state that agents of the Crown could search a man's study and take away his papers? 'By the laws of England, every invasion of private property, be it ever so minute, is a trespass.' Camden showed how a search for libel was worse than a search for a physical object. Private papers were the 'dearest property of a man'; looking at them was as intrusive as taking them away. If a constable came looking for a snuffbox, he would look only for a container for powdered tobacco. If a Messenger came looking for a libel, what should he look for? Everything and anything. In this case, the libel has not been proved. If your snuffbox was stolen, you would swear to the fact of theft before a magistrate, and it could then be recovered. If a libel was alleged, it remained alleged until a trial established its criminal character – whereas the snuffbox is deemed stolen property already. Therefore searching for libellous papers was a contradiction in terms, given that no paper could in itself be libellous.

This fact meant that even if the Secretary of State *did* have the legal authority to issue a warrant, he could not issue a general warrant to look for a seditious libel. If he did so he would be forcing the Messengers to break the law. Constables and keepers of the peace had to obey their warrants one hundred per cent. If they did less they were lax; if they did more they were straying into the realm of discretionary power. The point of a warrant from a higher authority was to release lower officials from 'the perilous task of judging'. The government did not have arbitrary authority, so there was no reason why a constable should. A general warrant by its very nature conferred unlimited discretionary authority to an agent of the state. And, because a libel was a thing of words, the Messenger would have to search and take everything with words on it – what we would today call a trawl for evidence. The minister had, by signing the warrant, made the Messengers break the law because the warrant was too general to be obeyed without straying into illegal actions.

Nathan Carrington argued that the Secretary of State must have power to prevent sedition. But this was not so. No one could judge state necessity on his own, and no court could indemnify a minister and his agents. 'If the king himself has no power to declare when the law ought to be violated for reason of state, I am sure we his judges have no such prerogative,' Camden said in his judgement. If general warrants for seditious libels were allowed by the courts, even for the best of reasons, there would be nothing to stop ministers launching an inquisition into the thoughts and beliefs of every one of the king's subjects by rifling their drawers and opening their mail. This probably would not happen, but the principle of the Revolution was surely that laws could not be dispensed with by individuals, even for good reasons, and even if the courts consented. Men did not rebel in 1688 so that a minister of state, a political party or a benevolent statesman could turn himself into a James II.

General warrants were never abolished by statute, even though a few attempts were made. What happened was that Camden clarified the situation whereby a Secretary of State is considered a private individual in the eyes of the law. If I search my girlfriend's desk for reasons of jealousy, I am guilty of trespass, just as the Secretary of State is if he does the same thing for reasons of state. If he errs, he errs as a private individual, not as an official. This is crucial for explaining the development of civil liberties in Britain. A. V. Dicey would claim the supremacy of private rights and the absence of an administrative law as the glory of England. The essence of this is that a citizen can sue public administrators in their capacity as private individuals subject to the rule of law.[28] We should not be so admiring. But it is a fact of English law and English history. It has conditioned our liberties. No constitutional principle or written law gives force to Camden's condemnation of trawls through private papers to incriminate people on moral grounds. The arbitrary action of the state was stopped not by a commitment to liberty (though this may have lain behind it as a motivating factor), but because it involved trespass on private property. This is true of many civil liberties in Britain, where rights have not been conferred but the possibilities of excessive state action have been hedged in by legal condemnation of certain types of procedure which are incompatible with *private* rights, especially property rights.

There were other ways of trapping the government into a position where it had silently to concede a right. If you want a seedy hero of liberty then Brass Crosby is a fine example. He was a bibulous, plain-talking, oath-spouting City man, Lord Mayor in 1770 and an MP. At the same time John Wilkes was an alderman of the City. The two City dignitaries, backed by other liberty-loving guerrillas, decided to ignite a conflict between two ancient institutions, both with privileges in law. At stake was the freedom of reporting parliamentary proceedings. The Bill of Rights defended parliament from outside criticism. This might have meant the Crown or other rival authorities that threatened its existence, but it was extended to include *any* criticism. At the time parliament could, on its own authority, arrest journalists who trenched upon its dignity. This included printing reports of speeches; note-taking was not permitted in the galleries, and anything that purported to be a record of a debate was liable to be punished. Wilkes and his friends set up the government by having a City printer deliberately go beyond the rules. When the Speaker sent the Sergeant-at-Arms and a messenger to arrest the printer, a City constable had the parliamentary officers arrested for assault.

They were brought before Brass Crosby in his capacity as mayor to adjudicate on whether parliament's officers had the right to make an arrest. The hearing took place in Crosby's bedroom, where he had retired suffering from gout. He was told that the Sergeant-at-Arms of the Commons and a Messenger had dared to make an arrest on a City printer. Crosby asked if parliament's men had obtained permission from a City magistrate. No they had not, he was told. This was all part of the performance. 'No power on earth', Crosby said from his bed, judicial wig clashing somewhat with his nightshirt, should seize a citizen of London without authority from him or some other magistrate of the franchise.[29] The City had special privileges as a self-governing community, and it appeared that parliament – or any other authority – had no right to enter it and arrest criminals without permission. The printer was released, and he thereupon made a complaint for 'assault', or wrongful arrest, against the parliamentary officers. Crosby made out a warrant to arrest the Sergeant-at-Arms.

Brass Crosby found himself in the Tower for his pains. The Commons was furious that its privileges had been destroyed from the bed of a gout-ridden City politico. Crosby and his colleagues were summoned to parliament, condemned, and sent to the Tower. On every occasion the City men were escorted to Westminster by a raucous crowd of dignitaries, middle-class men and the mob, who cheered their favourites and assaulted ministerial MPs and the Sergeant-at-Arms. When Crosby et al. were released from the Tower, they received a twenty-one-gun salute from the soldiers and a huge welcome party. From Wilkes's arrest in 1763 onwards the mob had moved to centre stage. When the press was attacked by parliament they intruded into the streets of Westminster, providing a chorus of disapproval to the desperate attempts of parliament to grasp on to its old authority. In the end parliament gave in. Every time it resolved to arrest a City printer or journalist it would end in a morass of City litigation, a dispute with the London authorities and an angry mob. Again, no rights were conferred; parliament just learned to ignore reports in the newspapers of its debates.

The battle for the liberty of the press would go on. The efforts of Entick, Wilkes, Crosby and the rest were moves towards practical freedom. They joined a succession of cases where legal judgements were obtained, precedents were set or public opinion tested, and which restricted the state's freedom of movement, making efforts to control the press irksome – not impossible. The government would still strike at hostile critics by prosecuting them for seditious or blasphemous libel, often with success. But every time a journalist deliberately provoked the government and risked imprisonment the state looked ever more hypocritical and vindictive. Writers such as William Cobbett, Jonathan Wooler, William Hone and Richard Carlisle all took on this role, exposing ministers to public disapproval. When things changed, from the 1820s, it was because juries became less biddable. The law has never been changed. What had changed was public opinion (represented by juries, the electorate and newspaper readers) and the political calculations of politicians, who grew tired of risking popularity on quixotic sallies against the press.[30]

The constitutional law expert A. V. Dicey wrote that liberties were inductive in Britain. In more modern constitutions rights of, for example, free speech had been *deduced* from agreed principles of human nature. In Britain they had been *induced* from experience.[31] They were the result of legal precedents that had come from criminal and civil trials involving real events. The law had kept pace with liberty, and vice versa, the two evolving together as the needs of British society and politics changed. Verdicts which ruled in favour of private individuals were extrapolated to include the public in general. It was the continuance of a process of finding barriers against authority – and new manifestations of authority – which had been going on since the Norman Conquest.

What Dicey does not celebrate, however, is the individuals who made this happen. If civil liberties are extensions of private rights, then the development of constitutional law has been dependent on bloody-minded people such as John Entick, politically motivated judges like Lord Camden and opportunists like Crosby. What Dicey's account does not realise is that the law did not evolve naturally. It required people to provoke power. It is significant that the liberties secured in *Entick* came from exploiting the existing law of trespass and Wilkes's victory over parliamentary privilege came from upholding the ancient rights of the City. Liberty has come from calculated provocation and opportunism. It has also been thanks to large mobs of people who have scared the government away from exerting its powers. Liberties were not given up with much pleasure; they were wrested bit by bit.

The effect of this is to downplay the progress of liberty by giving liberally minded judges and self-denying politicians the credit for 'discovering' liberties. The evolutionary account has emphasised the peaceable development of liberty, and therefore tranquillised the public by extolling the wisdom of gradualism. It has masked the true account: that such a system required active citizenship in securing favourable decisions and to defend them against encroachment. A constitutional guarantee survives even when the public have slipped into passivity; the British way was dependent on people scrapping against authority in an undignified manner, and defending their gains in the same way. For even fundamental rights such as those secured in *Entick* can be overturned. It is a history without many national heroes, but with many lesser heroes who stood forward to fight for their private rights and therefore enlarge the liberty of their fellow citizens.

From the 1790s through to the 1820s civil liberties in Britain came under renewed attack. Habeas corpus was frequently suspended to deal with sedition, the press was harassed by prosecutions and expressions of dissent were suppressed by troops. This was in response to the French Revolution and the wars which lasted until 1815. In 1794 twelve members of the London Corresponding Society were tried for treason. Their crime was to have advocated a republic, which would have sped George III to the same fate as Charles I and Louis XIV. It was what is called 'constructive treason' – a case built up by assembling pieces of disparate evidence which taken on their own were not criminal, but which cumulatively added up to treason. By this means the state could construe scattered statements into a crime.[32]

'Good God!' said Thomas Erskine, the barrister of one of the defendants. '. . . Was it in England – was it in the year 1794 that such a trial was brought into a Court of Criminal Justice?'[33] It was a notorious attempt to have radicals executed by manipulating ancient statutes referring to 'imagining the king's death', and it smacked partly of the Spanish Inquisition but mainly of fevered suspicion on the part of the government. The law was not always a bulwark of liberties; it could cut both ways when ancient statutes were dusted down. It was typical of this age of reaction, when the government tried, successfully and unsuccessfully, to bend the law in its favour. Erskine told the court:

In times when the whole habitable earth is in a state of change and fluctuation, when deserts are starting up into civilized empires around you, and when men, no longer slaves to the prejudice of particular countries, much less to the abuses of particular governments, enlist themselves like the citizens of an enlightened world into whatever communities shall best protect their civil liberties, it never can be for the advantage of this country to prove that the strict unextended letter of our law is no certain security to its inhabitants. On the contrary . . . it will be found to be the wisest policy of Great Britain to set up her happy constitution, the strict letter of her guardian laws, and the proud condition of equal freedom, which her highest and lowest subjects ought equally to enjoy.[34]

In the years of emergencies and emergency laws between the 1790s and 1819 (when the notorious Six Acts were passed, which restricted protest of all sorts) it certainly seemed like the twilight of liberty in Britain, made more sinister by the extinguished freedoms of the European people after the defeat of Napoleon in 1815 and the triumph of reaction over the principles of revolution. But, as Erskine said, the enlightened world had a new force – the natural rights of man, which had burst forth and could only be temporarily arrested by oppression.

And the only legitimacy the British state had in this new world was when it restrained itself, if not by inviolable constitutional principles, then by 'an almost superstitious reverence' for liberty.[35] When from the 1820s the state began to reform itself and backed away from emergency powers and restrictive laws it regained that legitimacy. Governments learned to respect civil liberties and listen to the voice of the nation, rather than scorn these as the symptoms of Jacobinism. They learned, or relearned, the eternal lesson, advocated by James Mackintosh at the time of *ancien régime* repression in 1815, which is the only sure basis for liberty, be it in the nineteenth or the twenty-first century:

The example of reverence for justice – of caution in touching ancient institutions – of not innovating beyond the necessity of the case, even in a season of violence and anger, may impress in the minds of men those conservative principles of society, more deeply and strongly, than the most uninterrupted observation of them in the ordinary course of quiet and regular government.[36]

America achieved this through deliberate design, taking passion out of politics so that procedural coolness safeguarded liberty; Britain's route to the same ideal was windier, and it was learnt through experience.

Tom Paine wrote that in Britain liberty was 'wholly owing to the constitution of the people and not to the constitution of the government'.[37] Liberty was kept alive even during these dark years not least because liberty became a popular cause. Radicals adopted the language of historic Whiggish freedom in reaction to various governments' contempt for these laws and customs. The events of this time reinforced the cultural tradition of bloody-mindedness towards authority – 'the dissidence of dissent'. No amount of repression stopped the people protesting in the streets or in the press. The memory of these years sustained what used to be a British habit of peaceful and often humorous resistance to the intrusions of government and the belief in liberty as a right to be flaunted in the face of presumptive officials.

This spirit was the first step and the last defence of liberty. 'The people ought to feel a continual jealousy of power,' wrote Lord John Russell in 1821,

... and when they see any one man borne down unjustly, they ought to perceive immediately, that the cause of that man is the cause of the whole nation . . . So, I trust, it may always be, when any individual, however humble, however odious or however despicable, is pursued by illegal, or unjust methods.[38]

IV

Mind Your Own Business

1820–1914

CHAPTER 7

Character

—∿—

'If everybody minded their own business,' the Duchess said, in a hoarse growl, 'the world would go around a deal faster than it does.'
LEWIS CARROLL, *ALICE'S ADVENTURES IN WONDERLAND*

. . . you think to cover everything by saying 'We are free! we are free! Our newspapers can say what they like!' Freedom, like Industry, is a very good horse to ride – but to ride somewhere.
MATTHEW ARNOLD[1]

The English, said Alexis de Tocqueville, had 'an aristocratic temperament' when it came to liberty. It was the belief that an Englishman's home was his castle. Those seventeenth-century ideas that liberty was a freehold estate to be enjoyed as one saw fit permeated society from highest to lowest. People jealously guarded their private sphere. John Stuart Mill told him that 'The taste for making others submit to a way of life which one thinks more useful for them than they do themselves, is not a common taste in England.' The evidence of this was variety, a pronounced individuality and a tolerable level of disorder. An English election, Tocqueville said, was full of 'shouting speakers, stones and fisticuffs and all the orgies we witness of English liberty'.[2]

Tocqueville observed that the English were intoxicated with the pride of liberty, a passion inflamed by French writers in the eighteenth century, such as Voltaire, Montesquieu and De Lolme, who said that England had reached a perfection of freedom. Some English writers dissented from the self-congratulation, saying that the liberal use of the word liberty was a deliberate strategy to confuse the people, who were free in small things (such as swearing, drinking and other social privileges) but deprived of the right of good government and political freedom. Liberty was what Whig aristocrats said it was – what we call 'negative liberty'. It was defined against the historical and contemporary standard of arbitrary government and found expression in such institutions as trial by jury, habeas corpus, the independent judiciary, religious toleration and a free press. These liberties were inherited wisdom from the seventeenth century and they were also *literally* inherited, like an entailed estate which could not be broken up, traded in or taken away.[3]

These were the arguments deployed by radicals in 1628 to entrench their rights against the ambitions of Charles I; by the nineteenth century they had become the clarion call of conservatives. If liberty was a freehold estate defended behind sturdy walls that no government durst invade, then some lucky few enjoyed a richly endowed park whilst others squatted on a patch of blasted scrubland on the outskirts, perhaps next to the neighbouring great house's sewage outlet. You could drink and swear, to be sure, or pray to your chosen idols in your miserable shack, and no one would violate your darling liberty; but no one would come and teach your children to read or clean up the rich man's effluent. Tocqueville observed that the rich and the poor had the same rights; they obeyed the same laws; and nothing could prevent a ploughboy becoming Lord Chancellor (once he had overcome his lack of education, found the means to support himself and battled the closed ranks of the legal profession and social snobbery). The liberty a Briton enjoyed was the 'possibility of endless individual action either to make the administrative power act, or to protect against its excesses'. It was a kind of liberty that encouraged strenuous effort, fierce competition and risk-taking.[4]

By the end of the nineteenth century this self-acting energy was known as individualism. It was seen as a national characteristic, built on the rebellious spirit of seventeenth-century commonwealthsmen, matured under the unobtrusive government of the eighteenth century and reaching the acme of perfection in the mid-nineteenth. It was an attitude which doubted the ability of government to improve society; indeed, one which believed that centralised power naturally became tyrannical even if the men in power were liberally minded. Britain had become the greatest industrial and imperial power in the world thanks to millions of individuals pursuing their private interests and disposing their property as they saw fit without the interference of the state. The opposite of individualism was held to be collectivism, when central government contrived means to improve the individual and marshal the resources of the state to combat social problems. It was attacked as un-British. Walter Bagehot said that his countrymen of all classes possessed 'inbred insubordination' and despised all outside intervention, even if it was benevolent, as an unwelcome alien force bent upon tinkering and tailoring, nagging and scolding.[5]

Liberty in nineteenth-century Britain was at the heart of the sense of national identity and at the centre of politics. It was a new kind of liberty – different alike from British history and every other country in the world, including the United States. From all sides of politics there was one uniting thread, and it was the assumption that the purpose of liberty was to elevate the character of individuals. There can be few other times when liberty was conceived of as an end in itself. There were bitter disagreements about the kinds of conditions in which the individual flourished. But this was a time when the language of liberty, in its many guises, suffused politics.

The heyday of liberty was considered by many to have been the middle decades of the nineteenth century. One of the most famous exponents of individualism, A. V. Dicey, wrote that it marked 'the omnipotence of individual effort which ruled England during the existence of the middle-class parliament created by the first Reform Act [of 1832]'.[6] The coming of a democratic age heralded reform. But it was the reform of clearing out centuries-old clutter and detritus, not that of construction. The old town and borough corporations, which had their ancient privileges and franchises entrenching local power into an oligarchy of local potentates, were replaced with town councils based on male household suffrage. In the 1840s the Navigation Acts and Corn Laws were repealed, freeing traders from tariffs and customers from artificially inflated prices. The Bank Charter Act of 1844 ended government control over the monetary system. By the late 1850s the so-called 'taxes on knowledge' – taxes which made newspapers and pamphlets expensive – were withdrawn, extending free-trade principles to opinion.

The state seemed to be rolling back in all areas, using its energies to remove old abuses and restraints. Samuel Smiles wrote in 1859 that 'it is every day becoming more clearly understood, that the function of government is negative and restrictive, rather than positive and active; being resolvable into protection – protection of life, liberty and property'.[7] Tolerance was extended to unorthodox religions; entry to the universities was opened up to non-Anglicans; criminal and commercial law was reformed to help give the poor equal access to justice; disqualifications on certain men becoming MPs were removed. This clearly involved the abolition of old rights (of, inter alia, slave traders, the Anglican Church, monopolies, ancient borough corporations and the professions), but it was a suppression of ancient *liberties*, which were the privilege of specific groups from time immemorial, in favour of individual *liberty*. Traditions which gave some institutions unequal advantage were stripped away in order that the principle of free competition might play itself out.

It coincided with a time of greater civil liberties as well. Prosecutions of political dissidents became rare; it was called a bloodless revolution in which the old vindictive state restrained itself from suppressing critics and troublemakers. 'At home the half-century has changed the aspect of society,' commented the *Spectator*; 'where all was Tory suppression at the beginning is thrown open now. We have gained freedom, political, religious and commercial.'[8] London became a haven for European revolutionaries of all kinds, who could preach as much revolution as they liked without being bothered by a constable or a spy. Tourists who went to the Continent were irritated when compelled to prove their identity with passports and put up with the tedious and intrusive inquiries of officials.[9]

At the mid-point of the century there was a belief that, after nearly a century of recurrent repression and passive observation of foreign revolutions, British liberty was once more a moral example to the world. The country and its people gave actual and moral support to movements for freedom abroad, from Garibaldi's bid for Italian freedom to the North in the American Civil War; this was augmented by a sense of imperial mission, in which white colonists were given liberties and systems of government modelled on the mother country. Liberty was at the centre of national identity, made real by contrast with the varieties of unfreedom seen throughout the civilized world: Napoleon III's kid-glove dictatorship in France, slave plantations in the American South, authoritarianism in Bismarckian Germany, the police state of Tsarist Russia. Britain was the freest country in the world and the richest; no coincidence, it was said.

Britain was then, according to Dicey and others, a pure laissez-faire state. The intention of reform was to promote individualism based on free competition. The retreat of authority meant the consequent expansion of the private sphere. People were encouraged to act (and were treated) as individuals, to prosper according to their own efforts and ingenuity, to make of the world what they could. Tradesmen were at liberty to dispose of their resources and energy as they saw fit; labourers and artisans entered into free contracts with their employers. The rationale behind banning trade union activity, for example, was that people banding together to exert pressure on an employer was an unacceptable use of collective force which went against the principle of individual responsibility and was, worst of all, a barrier in restraint of free trade, which was itself illegal. Joining a trade union, moreover, meant submitting your free will to the dictates of a group. Individualism was seen as noble. It encouraged people to fulfil their civic duties of their own volition; it made them self-reliant, moral and 'manly'. It was the culmination of a struggle against the dead hand of authority (in all its guises) that had been stifling individual effort for centuries. State activity, it was alleged, was now limited by the 'absolute principle of civil liberty' and political orthodoxy held that 'the best medicine for all social ills is liberty'.[10]

'Every man possesses a free activity in himself,' one provincial newspaper commented, expressing the received opinion of the middle of the century. '. . . We are not the mere slaves of circumstances . . . but are to a large extent free agents, independent existences, endowed with power to battle and contend with adverse circumstances.'[11] One of the most famous proponents of individualism as a moral project was Herbert Spencer. His ideas on liberty were derived from natural science (he came up with the phrase 'survival of the fittest' before Charles Darwin published *On the Origin of Species*).[12] Individuals and societies prospered alike according to competition, he argued. In nature those who worked and overcame the harsh natural environment flourished, whilst the weak lost out. In the modern world economic competition took the place of nature. Pure liberty consisted in everyone exerting his or her energies for private, selfish ends; the outcome of self-interest would result in harmony, the free market naturally supplying all the needs and wants of a diverse population. Every citizen had a moral duty to better himself independent of hindrance and help alike from the state. Any attempt by the state to interfere for the good of the poor might seem benevolent, but it would in fact have disastrous consequences. It would diminish liberty, and liberty of action in the economic field was the 'vital' condition of a progressive society driven forward by the unrestrained exertions of its members. Any theory of freedom should contain the freedom to fail, even if it was painful for members of society to witness the deprivation of their neighbours. Relief of poverty would make the lowest members of society dependent and therefore less inspired to work hard. 'Society in its corporate capacity, cannot without immediate or remoter disaster interfere with the play of these opposed principles under which every species has reached such fitness for its mode of life as it possesses, and under which it maintains its fitness.'[13]

Written in the age of Darwin, these words had an immediate resonance. They were also familiar from the language of modern political economy and Protestantism: that of self-reliance and self-abnegation in the present for benefits in the future. It was the idea that the world was so ordered that the industrious enjoyed the fruits of their diligence while the slothful and immoral were visibly punished in this life by the rags of poverty. Liberty was the space that modern man had to expend his energies and exercise his talents; the outcome was natural justice – the survival of the fittest. The poor should not be given help for this would dull their capacity for self-help and ingenuity. The solution was to make them, by education or simple necessity, exercise their energy to make life tolerable or comfortable. They needed more liberty not more help. If the state was tempted to make their lives better by artificial means it should be restrained from meddling in this system of justice by the 'sacredness of property'. Any attempt to relieve the distress of the poor would involve taxation – or the confiscation of one person's property for the benefit of another. This Spencer held to be immoral – a form of theft from the better members of society and a diminution of their freedom to spend their money as they saw fit. It would corrupt the natural purity of the free economy with man-made incentives, compulsions and controls.[14]

The privacy and independence which property supplied was the prerequisite of liberty. Dicey and Spencer alike believed that civilisation represented the liberation of mankind from the collective whole. Barbarians submitted themselves to the superstitions and mutual protection of the tribe; medieval peasants sacrificed their independence to the solidarities and security of the feudal community and the Church. Freedom of thought had been unleashed from the time of the Reformation and the economic freedom of the nineteenth century represented the culmination of the process of liberation from the oppressive bonds of the community. The individual was finally freed to pursue his interests as he saw fit, unencumbered by the dogma of authority or the arbitrary rules of tradition. But this was under threat. Dicey wrote that there was an 'essential conflict between individualism and collectivism' which ran through human history.[15] People were led to believe that their immediate problems could be solved by a force greater than themselves – the force of authority and men acting in their collective capacity. But however seductive this force might be, it would degenerate the individual's powers of thought and action. The tribe would live again. This was the chief danger of the later nineteenth century, when the state began to involve itself in collective solutions to manifest problems.

If, for example, the state compelled a local authority to do something, even if it was beneficial like an order to protect the health of the community, it was just that – compulsion, an increase in authority, a diminution of individual responsibility, and therefore a suppression of liberty. 'The difference between free institutions and despotic government', wrote Joshua Toulmin Smith, 'is simply the difference between men taking care of their own affairs, and submitting to have their affairs taken care of, for them, by others.'[16] The framework of civil liberties built up over the ages limited executive action, while the rule of law existed to defend private property rights and was the basis for an unprecedented flowering of economic liberty. It was an absolute concept of liberty. It brooked no compromise with the forces yclept 'collectivism'. Liberty lay behind the progress of civilisation; and it would continue to progress so long as the individual was allowed to flourish without hindrance to his energy by well-meaning compulsion. Britain was a free country because the state was small; it was a rich and powerful country because its citizens were free to unleash their energy.

There were those in Victorian Britain who took the view that a theory of liberty conceived solely in terms of economic freedom encouraged selfishness, greed and conformity. People were becoming enslaved to their passions, which were awoken by the lure of consumerism and legitimised by a theory which said that self-interest indirectly benefited the community. The Victorian period is replete with *cris de cœur* against materialism and appeals to medieval chivalry in novels and poems; but the age was proud of its industrious spirit.

John Stuart Mill and Alexis de Tocqueville famously explored the political implications of democracy. Aristocratic liberty – the kind that flourished in Britain – had over centuries built up barriers against central authority. The legacy of this was responsible government and legality. The existence of a powerful and independent leisured class had also made for a diverse society in which the arts and sciences flourished. Unconventional thinkers had, thanks to the aristocratic phase of history, been shielded alike from the profit motive and the whimsies of public opinion. In his two reviews of Tocqueville's *Democracy in America* and other essays in the 1830s, Mill compared this to a young republic where there was no such class. Political and social equality among white males and the possibility of rapid advances up and tumbles down the social scale meant that individual effort was confined to money-making and self-advancement. It was a highly competitive society – one in which everyone was free to succeed or fail by his own efforts and talents. But the blessings of political liberty and economic individualism did not necessarily lead to a richly textured society in which people were free to explore the mysteries of human life and cultivate their characters. On the contrary, Americans were as conformist, philistine and intellectually timid in their cultural and social life as they were innovative and adventurous in their business life.[17]

Mill compared this competitive ethos with the British middle class for whom everything in life became the means to an end – that of self-enrichment. It crushed the desire for education or artistic pursuits for their own sake. It made deference to public opinion an absolute prerequisite for an ambitious businessman on a neighbourhood or national level. The worst crime was to fall behind in the race of life; the sure way to fail was to stand out as an unorthodox thinker or eccentric. In a society in which people dressed the same, received a like education, had a choice of a handful of newspapers and accepted conventional manners it became harder to evaluate a stranger's integrity. In this situation people were obliged to drop confusing, unreadable personal idiosyncrasies which might offend others and adopt 'mere marketable qualities' in character, dress and deportment.[18] People lived up to what was expected of them by customers, employers or neighbours. This was as true of a young man seeking employment as a clerk as it was of a statesman seeking office. If people of a previous generation did not care what the world thought of them, and politicians in the age of aristocracy were secluded from public opinion, their children and grandchildren felt the pressure to conform from public opinion, on whatever level it operated. 'No rank in society is now exempt from the fear of being peculiar, the unwillingness to be, or to be thought, in any respects original,' wrote Mill.[19]

The importance of 'individuality of character' and the freedom to overcome restraints to the flourishing of the mind inform all of John Stuart Mill's writing. And the process of recognising, and overcoming, these restraints was what gave value to life. It was what he would refer to as 'experiments in living', and for him such experiments were what propelled society forward. Liberty was the ability people had to seek richness in their lives and explore unpredictable routes; the conservative reflexes of society always discouraged this kind of seeking in the unorthodox. As Isaiah Berlin said, Mill did not believe in one unalterable goal of life 'because he saw that men differed and evolved, not merely as a result of natural causes, but also because of what they themselves did to alter their characters, at times in unintended ways'.[20]

Mill should have known. His view of liberty was not just the result of quiet rumination in the library but of a life lived. The extraordinary way in which his father tried to mould the young John Stuart into a desiccated thinking machine is well known: how he read Demosthenes in the original at the age of eight, mastered political economy at twelve and so on; how he was left emotionally bereft.[21] There followed the most famous nervous breakdown in history, when at the age of twenty he felt 'A stifled, drowsy, unimpassioned grief' (to use the words Mill borrowed from Coleridge). The discovery of the imaginative in poetry and emotional depth in his intense love for the married Harriet Taylor gave him an insight into the hurly-burly of life which collided with the cold logical mental habits in which he had been schooled. It was a process of liberation, of breaking free from deeply ingrained beliefs: as he wrote to Thomas Carlyle, 'my own thinking faculties were called into strong though partial play; & by their means I have been able to *remake* all my opinions'.[22]

And like him individuals flourished when they sought liberation from restraints which only became apparent to them as they enlarged their moral and mental horizons. Like him, people should not just have freedom to remake their lives and rethink received opinions, but they should live in a society where these things were encouraged. His achievement was to see these restraints on liberty as existing not only in relations between the individual and the state, but in the home, the school, the workplace and the media. This informs much of his writing: the attack on conventional thinking and social tyranny; his plea for 'individuality of character' in *On Liberty*. His experiences of liberation from his past and society's condemnation of his love for

Harriet were expressed in *The Subjection of Women*, wi.
lation of much of his work. Women were the victims of an u.
ing deference to custom which made them dependent on men,
retarded the development of their character and, which was worse,
made them complicit in their own subjection. The fate of women in
the nineteenth century was the fate of mankind through the ages;
where once men had offered unconditional obedience to kings and
priests, the female sex continued to do so to the male. As Mill wrote,
'every restraint on the freedom of conduct of any of their fellow
human creatures . . . ties up *pro tanto* the principal fountain of human
happiness, and leaves the species less rich, to an unappreciable
degree, in all that makes life valuable to the individual human
being'.[23]

Liberation in this sense was made immeasurably harder in a
society which discouraged original thinking and prized economic
individualism. 'The private money-getting occupation of almost
every one is more or less a mechanical routine,' Mill wrote,

it brings but few of his faculties into action, while its exclusive pursuit tends
to fasten his attention and interest exclusively upon himself, and upon his
family as appendage of himself; making him indifferent to the public, to the
more generous objects and the nobler interests, and, in his inordinate regard
for his personal comforts, selfish and cowardly.[24]

The original mind becomes a solitary one in such a snakes-and-ladders
society; the tendency of the institutions and associations of modern
society was to foster self-love and purely private endeavour. Education
was one chance to cultivate the habits of independent thought and self-
exploration; but even for a well-off student in Britain's most venerable
academic institutions education was more committed to turning out a
competent clerk than 'the strengthening and enlarging of his own intel-
lect and character'.[25] Mill quoted a conversation between a clergyman
and a modern tutor from the novel *Eustace Conway* by J. F. D. Maurice:
'You believe that the University is to prepare youths for a successful
career in society: I believe the sole object is to give them that
manly character which will enable them to resist the influences of
society.'[26]

In a democracy the 'influences of society' would become almost irresistible. The individual would be subject not to a king or a class but to the majority. Democracy would bring benefits, Mill said, but unless society learnt to restrain itself the price to pay would be 'the tyranny of public opinion over the individual mind'. The tyranny of the majority might be vulgar, nagging and disapproving, productive of average minds and mediocre culture, as it allegedly was in America; at worst it would be intolerant and persecutory. Later he would write: 'The power of the majority is salutary so far as it is used defensively, not offensively – as its exertion is tempered by respect for the personality of the individual, and deference to the superiority of cultivated intelligence.'[27] Tolerance was the first step in liberty; it was a hard lesson to learn. It was essential if you did not want society to accept as its standard merely average thought, as it surely would if equality became some sort of idol. Democracy held great promises for human development. But this would only work if a democracy provided the forum for a multitude of voices, opinions and personalities. The great danger was slipping into consensus, be it doctrinal laissez-faire, nationalism, socialism, communism or whatever came along to besot people with a vision of progress.

For Mill the idea that there was *one* road anyway was anathema. Individual and society benefited alike from rethinking its sacred tenets, from the jarring and clashing of different personalities and minds. He called it 'the multiform development of human nature', perfected by the 'stimulating collision' of ideas and intellects.[28] Valuing diversity of opinion and experimenting in a variety of possible routes to the attainment of the good life was more likely to lead to a satisfactory outcome than clinging on to preconceived ideas or having faith in one single answer. The individual built his personality upon many different experiences and sources; society progressed thanks to the compromise and conciliation of opposites. The very purpose of working-class representation in parliament, for example, would be to make it 'the arena where opposing forces should meet and fight out their battles, that they may not find themselves reduced to fight in a less pacific field'.[29]

The idea that complete economic liberty would satisfy all mankind's needs and wants was a false one. There was a complacency in mid-Victorian Britain that the self-restraint of government in allowing men of all conditions to compete in a free marketplace would naturally lead to greater standards of living; that it would develop character and benefit all alike. Herbert Spencer believed that one day the state would wither away, society instead ruled by the unwritten laws of the market and collective solutions achieved through the uncoordinated and unintended interaction of millions of individuals making rational decisions regarding their personal interests. This might have been above the heads of most. But many held views of freedom which were just as idealistic. The 'Manchester School' of economists believed that free trade would lead to peace between man and man, state and state. Press and politics were suffused with the moral ideal of laissez-faire government. Even working men, true to their radical heritage, distrusted the state intensely and did not see it as the source of salvation. Mill took another view:

> I confess I am not charmed with the ideal of life held out by those who think that the normal state of human beings is that of struggling to get on; that the trampling, crushing, elbowing, and treading on each other's heels, which form the existing type of social life, are the most desirable lot of human kind, or anything but the disagreeable symptoms of one of the phases of industrial progress.[30]

Individualism, then, was not the same as individuality. They could be natural enemies. 'The progress of individualism on the one side and the gradual extinction of individuality on the other', wrote Balzac, '. . . constitute a double abyss . . . in which we are precipitated.'[31] It was argued that a society besotted with the ideal of individualism would actually lose the ability to remain free. People were encouraged to leave government to professionals and retreat into political passivity and public indifference. Passivity on one side and competitiveness on the other further made them suspicious of others, fearful of social breakdown and obsessively protective of their gains. Such a society was, as we can see at some remove from the Victorian era, suffused with discipline – particularly discipline for people who threatened private property by their disorderliness and who became burdensome by their infirmities. The working class bitterly resented the Poor Law, which coerced the idle and unproductive, the unfortunate and infirm alike into supervised labour in return for food; they mistrusted the new police force, which was seen as the defender of property and the suppressor of what more respectable people considered to be their 'antisocial' entertainments. Indeed, the police spent a disproportionate amount of its time meddling with working-class recreation, and was harsh on drunkenness. The workplace was also a place of discipline and enforced deference to managers and their ideas of respectability. This was true in industrial and clerical jobs; the disciplinary aspect was doubly relevant for the millions of people who were servants, domestic or agricultural.[32]

Alexander Herzen, a Russian refugee, was perceptive enough to point out a paradox in British liberty:

The freer a country is from government interference, the more fully recognised its right to speak, to independence of conscience, the more intolerant grows the mob: public opinion becomes a torture chamber; your neighbour, your butcher, your tailor, family, club, parish, keep you under supervision and perform the duties of a policeman.[33]

If the state was inactive, there were plenty of others who were willing to patrol the borders of virtue and vice, to ensure that the mob and the lowest in society were regulated and that unsightly displays of unorthodoxy in social matters did not break out among middle-class people. By limiting its sphere of action the government gave authority to voluntary groups within society, a different but nonetheless real tyranny. The economically better off did enjoy unprecedented freedom as government rolled back and the market was freed. But the insecurity which accompanied such a leap in the dark demanded greater control of the 'dangerous classes', and indeed greater self-control among the well-to-do.

The liberty-loving race tolerated, for example, the Contagious Diseases Act which allowed the authorities to subject working-class women whom they suspected of being prostitutes to summary medical examinations and a six-month period of quarantine if they were believed to be carriers of VD. A prisoner released on licence could be returned to gaol and further punished if the police merely had reasonable grounds to *suspect* he was breaking the terms of his release.

The mid-Victorian state could be intrusive, but it depended upon who you were. 'What conception', asked one journalist, 'can the ignorant poor form of the government at all, save as a species of magnified policeman, impassive at the sight of every form of suffering not contagious or dangerous to "society"; yet sternly repressive of the enjoyments they covet, as "low".'[34] Victorian society was hardly one of forbearance, forgiveness or kindly tolerance for people who transgressed narrow expectations of conformity. This is a feature of economically liberal economies: permissiveness in one department of life makes people fearful that society is out of control and hence they embrace direct and indirect social control. Taken to its extreme, negative liberty gives you complete independence from the state, independence from its positive injunctions to participate as well as its intrusions. You can retreat to your sphere to enjoy your own, protected but also detached from society. You have this right; but if it is positively encouraged then you had better leave your external security to others: Mrs Grundy, the busybody, the policeman. As long as you are left alone the liberty of your neighbours can go hang: for it is a potential threat to you.

Mill's *On Liberty* is a call for authority of all kinds, including the force of society, to give spiritual elbow room for the individual to flourish. Some interpret this as a denial of the state's role to interfere in the lives of the citizen. But Mill's vision of liberty goes beyond this. As he argued elsewhere, 'Energy and self-dependence are . . . liable to be impaired by the absence of help, as well as by its excess.'[35]

Throughout his career he struggled to reconcile individual liberty with the beneficial activity of the state. Contrary to long-held beliefs, the two were not incompatible. Mill believed that when the state forbade people to do something it chained up the individual's active powers. 'But', he asked,

does it follow from this that government cannot . . . beneficially employ its powers, its means of information and its pecuniary resources . . . in promoting the public welfare in a thousand means which individuals would never think of, would have no sufficient motives to attempt, or no sufficient power to accomplish?

Mill's originality was in seeing threats to liberty coming from all areas of life, wherever people interact in society. There were times when the state had to intervene to free the citizen from these pressures and restraints. It possessed a creative power of its own. The state should be seen as a gigantic benefit society, which had the power to help those members of society who were powerless to help themselves.[36] There was no one road sign which pointed to liberty.

Mill argued that social problems would be reconciled by compromise and experiment, not by adhering to one system. In his *Principles of Political Economy* he wrote:

There is a circle around every individual human being, which no government, be it that of one, of a few, or of the many, ought to be permitted to overstep. The point to be determined is, where the limit should be placed; how large a province of human life this reserved territory should include. I apprehend that it ought to include all that part which concerns only the life, whether inward or outward, of the individual, and does not affect the interests of others.[37]

Given the difficulty of saying how much one individual affects another, even unintentionally or remotely, this sounds vague indeed. Determining where the line lay had to be the work of actual experience, not absolute rules.

And politicians in Victorian Britain were not constrained by hard-and-fast concepts of inviolable liberty.[38] Spencer, Dicey and their followers were lucky enough that their early adulthood coincided with extraordinary circumstances. Britain's economy was riding high in the 1850s – she had taken the lead in the Industrial Revolution, which gave her a mighty advantage over slower starters (especially in the conditions of a 'free' international market) – and the country, alone among the major world powers, was threatened by neither internal violence nor invasion. The freedom they experienced was partly a result of this; but as old men they would look back on these times as the standard of normality.

By equating liberty with laissez-faire the libertarian thinkers of the nineteenth century went further than the classical political economists who, as far back as Adam Smith, stressed important exceptions to complete economic freedom. 'The principle of laissez-faire', wrote J. R. McCulloch, the great expounder of liberal economics, 'may be safely trusted in some things but in many more it is wholly inapplicable; and to appeal to it in all occasions savours more of a parrot than of a statesman.'[39] Economists and politicians realised that there had to be exceptions to complete freedom of contract. The hours and conditions imposed upon women and children in mills and factories were regulated in the so-called 'age of individualism' despite the protests of diehard capitalists.[40] Politicians of all hues were aware that the market, if left to play itself out in complete freedom, did not necessarily lead to a just outcome.

Men in office were not doctrinally laissez-faire, but they did, like most people in mid-Victorian Britain, believe that the state's effectiveness was limited. It was allowed to tell people what they could *not* do, but it could not tell them what *to* do or how they should do it. There was a feeling among all classes that central government, even if it did try to interfere for the best motives, was incapable of fulfilling the task and would become overbearing. This was based on experience rather than philosophy. There was a formal commitment to individualism, but a realisation that the principle need not be violated if, for example, squalid and dangerous conditions on emigrant ships were regulated or if the providers of water were made to prevent noxious substances from entering the supply. These cutbacks of liberty for some were outweighed by the benefit to the helpless, or, put another way, by restraining the liberty of one person so that others' liberty was enlarged. But in general, the role of the state was still seen as negative; it legislated against the abuses of industrialisation where it could, but it should not interfere with the operation of the free market without a compelling reason. If you had a problem it was up to you, in the first instance, to sort it out.

The hesitation of central government to blunder into the web of social and economic relationships was not so much a matter of hard and fast ideology as an expectation that individuals could do the job better than the state. This did not necessarily mean they assumed the free market would naturally co-ordinate the laying of drains or found schools because people wanted such things. The provision of water, for example, was in the hands of large private companies. Here the principles of the free market could not operate, for it was ridiculous to suggest that anyone could pick and choose between competing suppliers. The boards and owners of water companies might say their concerns were private property, but they were monopolies pure and simple. And with that, they had power over the individual. The arrangement between the water company and the private person involved compulsion as surely as between central government and the individual. How could public opinion be represented as a check on this unassailable power? Mill said that in this situation there were two choices. The government could nationalise the supply or it could subject the company to regulation and supervision. The latter was the course which best resolved the conflict between business and public provision; but it should be the responsibility of local authorities.[41]

The reform of municipal corporations in the 1830s was supposed to inject elan into local politics; people would come together in a voluntary way and act collectively in solving problems. Decentralised government gave room for successful middle-class businessmen to involve themselves in their localities, improving their immediate environment and reforming where they could. This new class of local administrators would be the basis of the British system; they would fulfil their civic duty, the modern version of Machiavelli's active citizen. Life was not as clear-cut as the Manchester School imagined or Dicey argued. Liberal politicians believed strongly in liberty and the Whiggish concept of small government, but they also believed in resolving antagonism between classes and elevating the character and condition of all sectors of society.[42] The essence of modern liberalism, which was articulated by Benjamin Constant, was that the first freedom was negative – the right to live a life free from the interference of the state and the obligations of service. But it did not mean that people should be encouraged to retreat into a world of privacy and isolation. Indeed, the tradition that connects Constant, Mill and Victorian liberals made clear that negative liberty and the non-interfering state could best be achieved by positive involvement in the community. The state would remain small and laissez-faire if citizens participated in local politics, local self-improvement schemes and the local provision of services, including policing. The two provisos were that, first, service should be voluntary and, second, that if the job was neglected the state would be compelled to step in. Central government had a role, but it should never be a substitute for individual effort; indeed, the role of central government was to find ways to awaken and guide public energy. The state *could* be a force for good; what mattered was where power was located.

Communities had always been able to make improvements, but the means of doing it were frustrating and expensive. Every scheme, from putting in sewers to widening a road, had to be passed by private act of parliament.[43] The sponsors of the project (local bodies, joint-stock companies or individuals) had to petition parliament and pay for lawyers to draft the act. The preliminaries cost at least £1,000, and there was no guarantee that the act would be passed. As the needs of every community in the country became greater and more complex in the nineteenth century this system was clearly unworkable. In line with the policy of making life easier for self-motivated reformers governments from the 1830s passed more enabling acts, or what was called 'permissive legislation'. A general act would be passed by parliament, and every city, town or village in the country was free to adopt its provisions, and equally free to ignore it. Acts were passed which gave authorities the ability to establish libraries, improve paving and roads, provide essentials such as water and gas at the ratepayers' expense and other worthy things without the need to petition parliament every time they wanted to make improvements. The County and District Constabulary Act of 1839 was just such a permissive piece of legislation, allowing counties and boroughs to establish a police force in their area. Twenty-four counties adopted it, seven adopted parts of the act and twenty refrained, so it was common for a well-policed county or borough to be next to a lawless one. Disraeli said that 'permissive legislation is the characteristic of a free people . . . you must trust to persuasion and example as the two great elements, if you wish to effect any considerable change in the manners and customs of the people'.[44]

This was the bedrock of Victorian liberty. The true conflict was not between such absolutes as individualism and collectivism but between central and local authority.[45] Local autonomy was seen by some as the key difference between free England and centralised European countries and by many more as an inheritance that went back to the Anglo-Saxons. The soul of liberty had been preserved not in the struggle between barons and kings or Whigs and Tories, nor in the wisdom of the common law, but in the decentralisation of power to its most ancient and fundamental unit – the parish.[46] For Toulmin Smith, the fiercest proponent of parish autonomy, the relationship between central and local power was like the relationship between individuals. 'Imbeciles' or children were unable to look after their affairs, and had to be spoonfed and coddled at all times. Managing your own affairs was the privilege of sanity and adulthood, and any do-gooder who tried to meddle was depriving you of self-determination. In the same way, a community which allowed another agency to tell it what it needed had sacrificed its responsibility and therefore became dependent. It could not complain if some distant bureaucrat started foisting unwanted improvements upon it and if a politician taxed its inhabitants to pay for his paternalistic schemes.

And the more freedom a parish had, the more an individual had. Indeed, a person who lived in a self-governing community had a lesson in citizenship. A person who abdicated his responsibilities was dependent and had robbed himself of the ennobling qualities of involvement in the life of the community. Collective action could be workable if it was entered into voluntarily and if it encouraged participation. 'True Freedom', Toulmin Smith wrote, 'consists in the continual active consciousness of the position and responsibilities of a Free Man, a Member of the State, and a positive Item in it. The Free Man will feel that he has something to live for beyond the attainment of mere personal ease and comfort.' For people like Toulmin Smith, liberty did not consist in the Bill of Rights, laws or the parliamentary system; it was a living thing that people had to make work every day.[47]

Unfortunately quite a lot of ratepayers did not like expressing their liberty by putting their hands in their pockets. The cholera outbreak of 1848–9 showed just how lax sanitary reform had been in most parts of the country. Such epidemics could never be resolved by the miracle of the free market or the constitutional propriety of decentralisation. Providing clean water for slums or cleaning up the effluent generated by industrialisation and urbanisation was not immediately attractive for businessmen or middle-class councillors. What was needed was a dose of authority. The Public Health Act of 1848 allowed councils to impose minimum standards on new houses (making them have a privy and proper drainage), take control of sewage and water systems, regulate slaughterhouses and cesspools and irrigate cemeteries – if they wanted to.

The act was permissive – but only up to a point. The General Board of Public Health could impose the act on a community if the death rate was higher than the national average or if just ten per cent of the inhabitants complained that their fellow ratepayers were putting low tax before the health of their neighbours. If either of those things were reported to the board its inspectors would descend on the community. Localists like Toulmin Smith were furious; here was a clear example of the over-mighty state barging in on individual freedom. By the end of 1853 the board had received 284 complaints and imposed the act on areas covering a total of 2,100,000 people whose councils had decided, for example, that slaughterhouses should have the freedom to dispose of rotting offal as they liked even in the midst of dense population. *The Times* attacked the Public Health Board for filching undue authority during a national crisis, and then using its extraordinary powers in a way 'which a beleaguered community would hardly confide to a military dictator'.[48] The board signed its death warrant when it dared to interfere in London's business and it was abolished thanks to anti-statist Liberals, Conservatives and Radicals.

The health of the poorest people was at the centre of a contest about the just limits of local liberty and central compulsion. In the end the presumption was on the side of liberty. The Town Council Act of 1858 did not repeal the Public Health Act, but it extended the principle of voluntary adoption of national acts. Britain was a patchwork of authorities, some very small; cross the boundary from one to another and you could go from a clean, well policed area to a squalid and lawless township.[49] But disease did not respect parish borders. Another cholera epidemic would originate in a laggardly district and spread to the whole country. Was this not a national problem? If so, medical experts argued, it was up to national government to compel councils to adopt the legislation.[50] But in the 1850s and 60s those municipal authorities which had not adopted health legislation were ignoring everything that was not compulsory, as if it was a matter of conviction. The voluntary principle was fine, but not if some authorities did not volunteer to do the right thing. What was called a 'system' of government was nothing of the sort. One critic said that local government taught that 'what is everybody's business is nobody's business'.[51]

The whole of permissive legislation was coming into serious disrepute, and practical politicians who did not want to have another national crisis on their hands were coming to believe that compulsory legislation was the only answer. There was emerging 'a patriotic craving for a higher national life' with responsible central government curing the deficiencies of local parsimony.[52] A handful of councils had, in their intransigence, ruined the principle of voluntary co-operation which, in some areas, had been a success. The historian W. L. Burn said that it was quite wrong to dignify the anti-interference attitude of the time with a political philosophy called laissez-faire; plain stinginess would be more appropriate.[53]

CHAPTER 8

Administrative Despotism

—m—

O whether devil planned or no,
Life here is ambushed, this our fate,
That road to anarchy doth go,
This to the grim mechanic state.

A.E., 'THE IRON AGE'

Liberty has lost its spell; and democracy maintains itself by the
promise of substantial gifts to the masses of the people.

LORD ACTON[1]

For A. V. Dicey, everything went wrong from about 1865. This, for
him, was the beginning of collectivism, when 'the intervention of the
State, even at some sacrifice of individual freedom, for the purpose of
conferring benefit upon the mass of the people' became an acceptable
doctrine – or rather, a general do-gooding sentiment. Public health
was taken in hand by central government; education became compulsory; industries and transport came under administrative inspection;
and trade unions were recognised by the law. Even in commerce the
tendency was a drift away from the single entrepreneur towards joint-
stock companies, which were run by corporate boards and shareholders and regulated by act of parliament rather than the self-motivated
and enterprising businessman who had the courage to take risks.

It marked, for Dicey, the end of 'the omnipotence of individual
effort'. Free compulsory education signalled the end of the principle
of individualism which said that parents should, first, come to realise

the importance of education and, second, give it value by sacrificing income and savings to pay for it. A social good was worthless, in other words, unless it had been earned. From 1870 municipal authorities took over the supply of gas and water, thus violating the free market. Redistributive tax gave the poor schools, houses and utilities – but private property was invaded to pay for it. The benefits were there for all to see. What was not perceived, said Dicey, was that self-sufficiency had been replaced by benevolent dictatorship and free government by socialism. The bulwarks of liberty, erected in the aristocratic phase of history, had been bulldozed by democracy.[2]

Lord Acton believed that modern democracy and classical liberty were not necessarily compatible. The needs of the majority overrode the traditional scrupulousness regarding the individual; rights must not be allowed to stand in the way of the good of the collective whole. Democracy possessed a power and absolutism unknown by a king; as Acton said it would be better to be enslaved by a minority than by the majority because you can at least resist, rebel and find sanctuary somewhere when your master is not the whole people.[3]

Civil liberties were not created in a democratic age; they were set up to retard the operation of authority. But when authority was used to feed, house, heal and educate the majority it was to be welcomed not feared. In every stage of civilisation, Acton wrote, freedom came low in the list of mankind's priorities, threatened by 'ignorance and superstition, by lust of conquest and the love of ease, by the strong man's craving for power and the poor man's craving for food'.[4] As some of the most eloquent and perceptive writers of the century pointed out, including Tocqueville and Mill, freedom would be even harder to maintain under a democracy. For the sovereign will of the people could become a force of compulsion greater than any other, and the solitary citizen who defended his personal interests could easily be perceived as standing in the way of the collective endeavour. Had the majority ever believed in freedom as a good in itself? As Acton pointed out, 'Liberty, for the mass, is not happiness; and institutions are not an end but a means.' Unless precautions were made a democracy could become the worst tyranny known in the human experience.[5]

The great fear in the latter part of the century was that the demands of the majority would mean strong, centralised government capable of solving problems and satisfying demands. In the process, the vital power of the nation would be sapped as individuals became dependent on the state as the provider of everything. Tocqueville wrote of the benign tyranny of active government:

It covers the surface of society with a network of small complicated rules, minute and uniform, through which the most original minds and the most energetic characters cannot penetrate, to rise above the crowd. The will of man is not shattered, but softened, bent, and guided: men are seldom forced by it to act, but they are constantly restrained from acting: such a power does not destroy, but it prevents existence; it does not tyrannize, but it compresses, enervates, extinguishes, and stupefies a people, till each nation is reduced to be nothing better than a flock of timid and industrious animals, of which the government is the shepherd.[6]

Attitudes were changing. Matthew Arnold wrote that 'the nation in its collective and corporate character entrusted with stringent powers for the general advantage, and controlling individual wills in the name of an interest wider than individuals' was the only solution to the social ills of the century.[7] The idea of the powerful state dictating modes of conduct to the population might have been alarming in times when the state was controlled by a narrow group at the top, but now power was in different hands. In fact, the view that the state was the inveterate foe of liberty could no longer hold sway. There were plenty of ways in which liberty was denied or withheld that had nothing to do with central government.

In 1866 there was an explosion at Oaks Colliery in Barnsley killing 420; a year later 178 died in a colliery in the Rhondda. All the dead and injured had freely made a contract with their employers in accordance with the principles of laissez-faire. But what kind of freedom was it to accept work in a dangerous mine or factory? Contract was supposedly the keystone of economic and civil freedom; it represented the principle of voluntarism and free agreement. By this time radicals were talking of the 'Tyranny of Contract':

Talk of freedom, indeed! – why, if a man brought up as a collier refuses to go down a pit which he knows to be fiery, he starves on the ground that he will not work, and if he works he is suffocated or burnt. A puddler is perfectly free to contract to produce iron, but his freedom is to work at an occupation that tends to shorten his life.[8]

To be sure, the miner or puddler could negotiate a better contract with his employer, guaranteeing safe conditions and good pay. But he would do it as an individual, man to man with his employer, not in league with other workmen or with the support of the state. The owner could say no, and the workman could go and revel in his freedom in the workhouse. Similarly, a homeless family was at liberty to make whatever deal they could with a slum landlord. The principles of individualism, it seemed, did not put much emphasis on individuals.

This was to regard the state with new eyes. Where the rich saw liberty as an absence of restraints – restraints imposed by government – the poor could see that restraints existed throughout society, many of which were created thanks to the superabundant liberty of the fortunate few. For working-class radicals, history taught two major lessons. The first was that an elite, whether it consisted of Normans or mill owners, had progressively taken privileges in land and law from freeborn Englishmen. The second was that these robber barons (of whatever era) had taken freedoms which had been established by the Anglo-Saxons. Throughout history it was the stubbornly independent little man who had stood up against injustice – rebellious peasants, Puritans, Cromwell's yeomen, Wilkesite rioters, Paineite radicals and trade unionists – not the grandees, be they barons at Runnymede, Whigs at the Convention Parliament or judges in the common-law courts. Working-class radicals were deeply imbued with the tradition of nonconformist dissent. They instinctively hated privilege. And there were plenty of privileged sections of the community, whether rapacious industrialists, the owners of unsanitary slums or aristocratic landowners whose vast domains included a still subjected peasantry.[9]

Radicals were no less suspicious of the state than thoroughgoing Whigs; indeed, hostility to distant authority was bred in their bones. But the state could be used to bulldoze those things that restrained the lower class, just as an earlier generation of middle-class reformers had used it to sweep away different barriers – those which impeded free trade, entry to university and corrupt municipal corporations. The end point need not be 'grandmotherly government' (what we call the 'nanny state') or the extinction of individualism, merely modifications in favour of justice. An employer saw liberty in the laws which prevented his workers combining for collective bargaining in the name of free contract and free trade. The worker saw such laws as skewed in favour of the minority, another example of the things that prevented the working class from realising their aims. The sacrosanct right of property held – but many believed that property was a privilege in itself, one which derived from robbery and injustice. And it represented power in the state, one that the unpropertied majority could not rival. Collective bargaining was the only element of strength workers had; it was, for them, a matter of liberty to demand better conditions on a footing of equality. F. D. Maurice wrote that politicians must realise 'that the manhood they [the working class] share with others is greater than the property which they do not share with them; that there is a higher title to belonging to the nation than that'.[10]

If the chief symbol of British liberty had been property then libertarians had a rude shock in the 1880s. The land metaphor, which brings to mind Fortescue, Coke, Locke and Burke, treated liberty as an inviolable estate. It gave colour to the idea of liberty as a 'private sphere' which no one could enter. A freeholder was no tenant-at-will (who could be turfed out of his let at short notice) when it came to liberty, but a proud inheritor of rights which he in turn passed down the generations. Exponents of liberalism said that an Englishman's home was his castle; his ownership was the basis of all other rights. But this was conveniently to ignore the fact that millions owned barely a stick of property. They were, and always had been, tenants-at-will – literally and in the sense that they were beholden to their betters. Without any property to back up their rights, workers held their labour to be a form of property. The problem was inequality between the rights of labour and the rights of property. Changes in the ownership of land partially reformed this. Under the old law, tenants on landed estates had to leave game – such as deer, pheasants, hares and rabbits – for their landlord's sporting and culinary pleasure. They had to put up with damage to their crops and in times of dearth they could not take a rabbit for the pot. Tenant farmers were also put off investing in improvements to their land, because their landlord could put a premature end to their lease. Reforms to the law gave tenants greater rights. They could protect their crops against deer and rabbits. They were given security of tenure for life so they could raise productivity confident that they would benefit from their hard work. Landowners complained that the ancient liberty of disposing of land as one wished had been destroyed by the Victorian state; now their hands were tied while their tenants were protected for life. Industrial workers also won greater protection from profit-hungry businesses; the Employers' Liability Act forced employers to compensate workers injured in workplace accidents.

These acts of parliament in effect tore up contracts made between workers and employers, farmers and landlords.[11] The implication was that the working classes had been compelled to sign contracts that went against their best interests. They had been unequal arrangements, made between a strong party and a weak party; the state stepped in to create an artificial balance. It was intended for practical reasons – raising productivity in agriculture and industry – but it was deeply symbolic. British liberty was said to be based upon legal contracts which no one could violate, not even a monarch. But contractual freedom was biased towards freeholders, not tenants. Land is always emotive, especially in Britain where it was firmly tied to the concept of liberty. The reforms weakened absolute security of ownership, and placed good husbandry above it. It is an illuminating change in priorities. That which was of benefit to society should prosper and be protected; that which retarded human development could claim no automatic protection. Mill pointed out the unwelcome truth that property rights had not always been sacrosanct; various forms of property had been abridged or abolished, most recently the franchise, patent offices and commissions in the army. 'The idea of property is not the same one thing, identical throughout history and incapable of alteration,' he wrote, 'but is variable like all other creations of the human mind.' No custom should stand in the way of a public good.[12] If Britain was a country of tenants, they now, unlike tenants throughout history, enjoyed security. Hard work was in effect given the status of property.

These acts passed through parliament without serious opposition. People such as Dicey may have seen these reforms as a betrayal of liberalism, but for many others it was the logical next step in terms of liberties. Liberalism, wrote Millicent Fawcett, 'is in the main the force which cuts at the root of injustice; not so much by tinkering and patching up particular instances of wrong, but by giving the people the power to protect themselves'.[13] The second Reform Act of 1867 had brought greater numbers of working men within the franchise. Liberals and Conservatives believed they had to respond to the new electorate or risk extremist parties emerging. But the enfranchisement of workers also brought instances of abuse to national attention. In the past men in politics, journalism and academia might have assumed that equal laws would lead to a just outcome. As knowledge increased it was readily apparent that it was not as simple as this; that it took more than simply loosening restraints to ensure that 'free play' occurred. But there were many who assumed that the Liberal Party was, by doctrine, committed to liberal economics. This was not so; British Liberalism was committed to healing divisions in the country and providing modern, efficient government. At the centre of this was the concept of the individual, which must be respected. 'Liberalism', said Gladstone, 'has ever sought to unite freedom of individual thought and action, to which it largely owes its healthy atmosphere, with corporate efficiency.' He admitted that such a balance 'is noble, but it is difficult': there was no sure path to this outcome, only the courage to experiment.[14]

Leading members of the Liberal Party argued that laissez-faire had been appropriate for a certain period of economic development; it was good at producing wealth but it was unable to distribute it. In the nineteenth century every department of life had become increasingly complicated with numerous conflicting interests which could only be resolved at the centre. If the state had in the past been incompetent and sometimes cruel, by the 1880s it was in different hands, run by men who did not grasp at power and personal enrichment. One of Gladstone's leading ministers, G. J. Goshen, said that since mid-century the 'attitude of the public towards "Laissez-faire" on the one hand and State action on the other has entirely changed'. He was part of the second generation of middle-class industrialists, those who had benefited from their parents' individualism and entrepreneurial energy and from the smashing of restraints from the 1820s onwards.

But people like Goshen believed that it was the duty of the state and local government to heal those class tensions and inequalities which the free market, on its own, could not. For people like him state intervention was a moral issue, not an economic one; people could not bear to stand by and allow monstrous inequalities and misfortunes to exist in the name of personal freedom. It was also a product of modernity that was independent of doctrinaire interpretation. In the recent past, he said, the street had policed itself. But as population grew and the nation's energies were stretched to their utmost, traffic and congestion gradually increased, turning long-held freedom into a kind of anarchy in which the strong muscled through. Rules needed to be drawn up and a policeman had to direct the vehicles. 'The principle of individual liberty yielded to organised control.'[15]

If pure unfettered individualism had never existed in Britain (or anywhere else), even in the days of reform and free trade, it was in the last part of the century when tentative steps towards social reform were being taken that it was elevated to a sacred ideal. Herbert Spencer wrote that modern Liberals erroneously believed that 'a rectified evil is equivalent to an achieved good'. They wanted to eradicate evils and win benefits immediately by using the state rather than waiting for the free play of individual action. Besotted with immediate victory in the fight against poverty, they had wantonly used methods which sapped liberty from society. With each paternalistic bit of legislation a little more energy was taken from the individual, a multiplication of rules, introduced gradually, wound red tape around all private activity, and greater numbers of people were drawn into dependence on the state. It was like history in reverse, only this time the people were offering up their liberty to a democratical Leviathan rather than a king.[16]

'If men use their liberty in such a way as to surrender their liberty,' asked Spencer, 'are they thereafter any less the slaves?'[17] Under the intellectual guidance of Spencer, the legal brain of Lord Justice Bramwell and the political leadership of the Earl of Wemyss, a heterogeneous group of

Whigs, Liberals, Peelite Tories, radicals and anarchists formed the Liberty and Property Defence League in 1884. Indeed many members of the group believed that in the future society would be conducted 'on the principle of absolute philosophical anarchy'; the present was an unfortunate aberration, but the state would one day wither away.[18]

The main business of the League, however, was not in promoting anarchy but resisting the slow march towards what Tocqueville called 'administrative despotism'. It lent legal and parliamentary support to diverse groups, from big businessmen to trade unions, who opposed certain pieces of legislation. In other words, the League gave ideological and political help to single-issue groups. Like every lobby group it saw wider conflict in an issue in dispute, even if its client of the day was acting for a particular reason. They opposed weighty bits of government policy – the advance of 'municipal socialism' in the cities, social legislation of all kinds, trade-union law reform, the reintroduction of tariffs, the regulation of industry. The battle could be fought over anti-competitive laws which affected business as much as the liberty-suppressing tendency of public libraries, which were a form of redistribution whereby everyone, including the wilfully ignorant, had to provide books for poor autodidacts.[19] But they also supported women workers against misogynist trade unions and attracted working-class support for their campaigns against local and national temperance movements. The League was against 'over legislation' without much discrimination between the relative value of pieces of legislation. In 1899 it helped defeat a bill which required employers to provide seats for girls in Scottish shops, provoking a rather strange letter from Wemyss to Lord Salisbury: 'Let us hope that the House of Commons, having taken shop girls' seats in hand, has thus touched the bottom in social legislation.'[20]

This was to use the plea of liberty as a defence against democratic reforms, whether those reforms were annoyingly meddlesome or genuinely progressive. Some of the League's members were Liberals who had resigned in disgust at the direction of modern liberalism in the last quarter of the century. But most Liberals did not see a contradiction between classical notions of liberty and the progress of the working class. The 'second nature' of liberalism, wrote the MP

James Stansfield in the 1880s, was a strong respect for individuality and distaste for disciplinary coercion, as it always had been.[21] By altering the law of contract and the balance of property, by making education compulsory and improving working conditions they were enlarging liberty, indeed reinventing it for the twentieth century as the radicals and Whigs of two centuries earlier had constructed liberties for *their* times. Mill had centred his concept of liberty on the sanctity of individual character. This concept of freedom would be but a chimera if millions of men and women were shackled by unfair disadvantage from the start. Mill argued that accident of birth, which concentrated property in a few hands, was not an inviolable liberty but something which put barriers in the way of the majority. He wrote that the laws of private property 'have not held the balance fairly between human beings, but have heaped impediments upon some, to give advantage to others; they have purposely tolerated inequalities, and prevented all from starting fair in the race'.[22]

There was a difference between removing restraints to give people an equal opportunity of enjoying the benefits of liberty and intervening to make them better. Mill's philosophy of liberty held that the free range of an individual's liberty should be limited when it conflicted with another: the so-called 'harm principle'. Actions which were prejudicial to the community should be restrained; but the all-important inner citadel of the individual should not be violated by outside action. For a start, people had a tendency to rebel against prescribed modes of conduct, especially in Britain where there was considerable prejudice against state intervention. Mill believed that people should be masters of their own destiny, volunteers for the virtuous life not press-ganged by society. Education was one of the tests of this. On the one hand consumers in a free market were unlikely to choose the best form of education, and might very well put material accumulation above the mental cultivation of their children. On the other a state curriculum would stifle the very bedrock of liberty, diversity, choice and freedom to think beyond the orthodox. 'A general state education', he wrote, 'is a mere contrivance for moulding people to be exactly like one another.'[23] Making people better, as opposed to coaxing them towards the good, was always likely to end in failure. People were best when they were authors of their own destiny; they might fail, but they would be free.

'As if it were a sin to control, or coerce into better methods, human swine in any way,' wrote Carlyle in response to *On Liberty*. '*Ach Gott in Himmel!*' And many others saw Mill's philosophy as untying the moral leadership of the nation, asking society to step back and allow people to experiment in modes of life on their own, indulgently tolerating their vices in a misguided respect for their liberty. The diversity Mill preached would lead to anarchy, moral collapse and a cultural Tower of Babel. Leslie Stephen, for example, asked how the line could be drawn in Mill's harm principle: 'The very same qualities which make a man useless to himself inevitably make him noxious to others; the external circumstances make the difference, and not the character.' Society must possess moral force; being permissive in private affairs would be to encourage vice to seep out of the home or the club, infecting society.[24] His brother, James Fitzjames Stephen, similarly argued that removing the restraints of custom, religion, morality and order was like 'freeing' the separate parts of a clock, allowing pendulum, springs, hands and rotary instruments to whirl and whiz about as they pleased.[25] Independence in matters of personal opinion in a society which put emphasis on diversity would not make people think great thoughts; free and alone they would only confront the chasm in their souls. Average people had always had average thoughts; you could not expect liberty to elevate them. It was given to a very few to think, reason, teach and lead. Freedom would not vivify the arts and sciences, despite what Mill said; the greatest products of the human mind had, more often than not, flowered under tyranny, guided by a privileged elite.[26]

In other words, the question was not about liberty – the romantic language of which had encouraged people through the ages to despise all restraint – but about the right sort of restraint. Liberty had no real meaning; it was the vacant space where no order reigned. But order and rules there must be. Society should not couch its arguments in terms of liberty, but in finding the kind of laws and compulsion, teachers and leaders, which would take it to greater enlightenment.[27] Until their twenty-first birthdays, Fitzjames Stephen wrote, young people had every imaginable restraint. But the moment they reached that day 'liberty claims her prey': the individual was 'liberated' to ruin himself on Mill's experiments in living. The fact was that society required moral force and people needed to be protected from themselves:

If freedom does not like it, let her go and sit on the heights self-gathered in her prophet mind, and send the fragments of her mighty voice rolling down the wind. She will be better employed in spouting poetry on the rocks of the Matterhorn than in patronizing vice on the flags of the Haymarket.[28]

Fitzjames Stephen represented an older authoritarian instinct, which saw modern liberalism as besotted with social freedom. The argument for filling in the gap of liberty with something worthwhile also came from the left. T. H. Green was the foremost British exponent of what we call 'positive liberty'. His arguments were an attempt to awaken liberalism from its Whiggish past. True freedom, wrote Green, consisted of 'the liberation of the powers of all men equally for contributions to a common good'.[29] Freedom which allowed the individual to frustrate the ends of the joint endeavour was a right no one should possess. If a person was compelled to do work that gratuitously wasted his health, shortened his life and degraded his morals then this lowered the aggregate energy of the nation – immorality was added to inefficiency.

What was different about Green's thinking was that liberty could be equated with self-realisation. If a person cannot read then you could very well say that he is not strictly unfree because no one is deliberately preventing him from learning – that is the essence of classical liberalism. Green said that the illiterate person would not be free because some outside force (such as the concentration of economic power or social prejudices) was hindering the full realisation of his potential. Society has a duty to maximise the liberty of this man by teaching him to read – and teaching him a great deal more as well so that his energy can be directed towards the tasks which suit best his talents. So it is not a matter of removing restraints so much as putting things in their place.[30]

Green said that a sober man was a free man. This gets us closer to the danger lurking in his arguments. A lot of what he says does not have much to do with liberty as it is understood either philosophically or on the street. Most people associate liberty with liberation from some sort of restraint – especially one which obviously impedes and makes us feel constrained. For Green the restraints are everywhere, including in our own weak natures; if we don't acknowledge that we are constrained by some vice or prejudice it does not mean it is not there. The battle for freedom can have no end – not till we have sought out and exerted every last drop of our talents and knocked down every hindrance to them. If you have not fulfilled all your potential then you have not achieved full freedom. What is your potential? It is impossible to say. What if a teacher or a person wiser than you spots a talent that you have not noticed? Are they entitled to intervene to make you a better person and add to the sum total of the community's collected energies? Even if you are Leonardo da Vinci then you can never be absolutely sure that you are firing on all cylinders. The goal can never be won because you are aiming at things which can never be quantified. Life becomes one of self-sacrifice, self-restraint and submission. It is hardly one we would immediately recognise as free. Liberty is always contingent in such an argument; the hindrances which Mill identified as the barriers to liberty are omnipresent, lurking yet to be discovered.[31]

Green wanted 'freedom in the higher sense', not the 'delusive' kind of freedom championed by most Britons. Modern freedom, he argued, would come when people came to identify themselves with the common whole. The distinction between individual liberty and the state would come when the state came to represent what he called the 'collective will'. His aim was to knock down negative liberty, which he saw as blocking progress and making the working class complicit in their own degradation by feeding them on romantic notions of independence.[32] The thrust of his arguments was intended to resolve the ideological conflict at the heart of liberalism, which wanted to intervene to improve lives but was hesitant about betraying its founding principles by becoming authoritarian or by trampling on individual rights. In other words, he wanted to break the Millite spell which taught that 'Leaving things to the government, like leaving them to Providence, is synonymous with caring nothing about them, and accepting their results, when disagreeable, as visitations of Nature'.[33] For Green the state was – or should be – a thing of high moral purpose which people approached reverentially, on bended knee. It was the source of modern freedom, not its enemy: 'So to submit is the first step in true freedom, because the first step towards the full exercise of the faculties with which man is endowed.'[34]

This kind of liberty, it was supposed, would work when people were not broken up into mutually antagonistic units, competing to rule for class interests, but when the state was dedicated to the common good. The individual would, through participation in social and political life, come to identify his interests with the state. The state would not shy away from compulsion, but learn to confine its activities to liberating its members and guiding them towards self-realisation. L. T. Hobhouse, proponent of the New Liberalism, wrote that 'freedom is only one side of social life. Mutual aid is not less important than mutual forbearance, the theory of collective action is not less fundamental than the theory of personal freedom.'[35] I am the state, and the state is me: liberty is best enjoyed when we subsume ourselves into the common endeavour. And true freedom is not the absence of restraints but the voluntary, grateful adoption of restraints which we acknowledge to be good for us. 'Liberty and compulsion have complementary functions,' wrote Hobhouse, 'and the self-governing state is at once the product and the condition of the self-governing individual.'[36]

Such arguments, whether they came from Fitzjames Stephen or Green and Hobhouse, seemed to illuminate the contradictions in Mill's arguments. They argued that there was no such thing as the kind of self-regarding act which Mill would protect as the choice of an individual. Private acts are public ones too: a drunkard harms more than just himself and an uneducated, unfulfilled man diminishes the nation's active powers. If you wanted to develop the individual's character, as Mill wanted, he had to be led by a force greater than himself: the collective whole. And he had to be restrained from harming the community or retarding the uphill march of humanity by his selfish behaviour.

But Mill's views remained closer to British tastes. And, in light of the crimes of the twentieth century, safer for mankind. Hobhouse may be right in that we can be liberated by accepting restraints: obviously it is better to give up smoking, drinking, over-eating and so on. Few, however, would *feel* more free if these benefits were imposed by wise moral guardians. I may become a better person, to be sure, liberated from my noxious vices; I may truly be a freer person as a result; but I would cease to consider myself a responsible, autonomous agent – feelings of self-worth which Mill put at the centre of his view on liberty. But most importantly I would lose the right to resist: that would be a selfish, immoral act, a crime against the family of mankind.

Maintaining freedom in society meant keeping up a habit of mind which, while accepting the necessity for central authority, always retained an inherent prejudice against state power except in the last resort. All good things could not come at once; the pursuit of social justice conflicted with some people's liberty, but at the same time freedom meant occasionally turning down things which might bring great benefits. 'The jealousy which prevails in this country of any extension of the coercive and compulsory powers of the general government', wrote Mill back in 1851, 'I conceive to be, though not always wisely directed and often acting the most strongly in the wrong places, yet, on the whole, a most salutary sentiment.'[37]

Mill's arguments can be picked to pieces: he does not propose specific solutions in all cases. What he does argue for is a society which places liberty at the centre of its sense of identity. The dangers of democracy could be offset if everyone saw value in complete freedom of expression, for when freedom of speech was held to be sacred the majority was powerless to interfere in the lives and thoughts of minorities, oddball eccentrics and unpopular progressive thinkers, even if this went against the instincts of a democracy where the collective will is all-powerful. Absolute freedom of speech was the first step in defending the individual from the coercive power of the majority in other matters: for at some point free speech is translated into action and, if censorship is tabooed, you cannot very well censure that behaviour if it is not destructive. The inviolability of these basic rights would imbue society with habits of liberty which were often counter-intuitive: toleration of offensive words, for the arguments of your country's enemies and for outrageous behaviour. That is to say liberty is impossible without this toleration and toleration is impossible without a cultural belief that liberty is a positive good in itself.

The key point of Mill's life and work is that there is no one form of society or politics or economic system or lifestyle which brings us liberty. The road proposed by the Liberty and Property Defence League would bring class conflict and permanent inequality; Stephen's world was one of moral authority and strong leadership; Green's utopia demanded permanent tutelage to a mystical entity called *The State*. Yet all these arguments were valuable to society. The League helped alert people to the dangers of hasty legalisation for the sake of legislation; but it did not halt progressive legislation. Green taught that liberty was useless if people had all the right in the world to speak their mind, worship whatever gods they chose, march down the street, set up political parties, but had no power to translate this freedom into positive benefits. Mill's arguments do not appeal to people with tidy minds. The line between the individual and society cannot be drawn with any precision. Green would do away with negative liberty entirely; Spencer would make it so large and so inviolable as to paralyse virtually all government action. The line that defends the sanctity of the individual is so porous that the state can invade it upon a plea of necessity. It can therefore seem like a nebulous concept without an absolute rule.

The lesson of Mill's writing is that liberty is best defended within a liberal society. It exists in the clash of real events, not the realm of an unassailable philosophy. Liberty should be the test of every piece of legislation: a gold standard which stays the government's hand more than it prompts it to act. It can only exist when people want it to exist – when it is prized as the most valuable thing within democracy. If it is an ideal, it should be an ideal which is believed in by leaders as much as the public. There can be no perfect resolution between the claims of society and the individual, between outcomes which are determined by the state and by the market, between complete freedom and a level of compulsion. In this light liberty might begin to look patchy and inconsistent and they who profess it hypocritical. So be it, Mill would say; life is messy and complex and the best that can be hoped is that conflicts can be resolved within a society which holds the individual to be a responsible agent whose free judgement is of high value.

In the epigraph which begins this chapter 'A.E.' (G. W. Russell) wrote that the melancholy choice facing modern society was between a free-for-all anarchy where the strongest subdued the weak and 'the grim mechanic state'. This was not necessarily so. A mature society should have within itself the power to combine a free market with state intervention, democratic solutions with personal autonomy, without endangering liberty. Maintaining individual freedom and securing social justice is a perpetual struggle, and one which will never satisfy everyone. But liberalism recognises that as a strength, not a weakness. The road to unfreedom is one which follows one route dogmatically – that is the lesson Mill teaches. It is a philosophy which realises that in real life we all have to live with compromises and best-fits; that to agree on everything is to abdicate the struggle which makes life interesting and to lose that clash of opinion which gives freedom a living rather than theoretic existence.

Karl Popper would write in the 1940s that it is often thought that when a theory of liberty hits a contradiction, or when it is limited for some other benefit, then the theory *in toto* hits the buffers. But this is wrong, he said. It is the borderline cases which give liberty its vitality in a democratic state: 'for without the stimulus of political struggles of this kind, the citizen's readiness to fight for their freedom would soon disappear, and with it, their freedom'.[38] This is true for a socialist and a member of the Liberty and Property Defence League.

By the beginning of the twentieth century Britain was taking its first tentative steps in social welfare. The change in the function of government had been partly the result of greater information about the lives of citizens. The recruitment drive at the time of the Boer War had shown that the young working-class male population was underdeveloped and undereducated. Such information increased concern for the masses of poor. It also showed that the line between state intervention and personal privacy was harder to draw than anyone had assumed. The magic circle in which people were exempt from the claims of the state was shrinking – not for ideological reasons but simply because social problems were more readily apparent and at the same time government had greater technological and bureaucratic means to solve them. David Lloyd George's 'People's Budget' taxed landed property in order to create welfare and pension provision for the deserving poor. For those bred in the notions of the nineteenth century it was an act of vengeance on the upper classes which marked the beginning of socialism; for others it was another stage in the progress of civilisation.

Yet it remained undoubtedly a free society where the claims of business and private endeavour were respected and, for all the reforms, people still had the sense of living in a laissez-faire economy. As so often, this was so because throughout the world the other great powers had gone further than Britain in different ways: cartelisation, protected industry and social welfare in Germany, repression in Russia, and even in the US rationalisation of industry placed the worker in a micromanaged, soulless production line. If the market was less free than it had been in Britain, it was freer than anywhere else. That 'aristocratic' sense of liberty remained, where the first instinct of people of all classes was to distrust the state and its employees and prefer self-reliance to collective action. The liberty of a mill owner was less than in the 1830s to be sure; but the freedom, working conditions and quality of life of the majority had improved since then. Diehard members of the Liberty League would see it as collectivism in all its hateful self, a step towards socialism; socialists saw it as a world where capitalist individualism trumped social reform. Most people saw it as the practical outcome of politics. Common sense said there could be no absolute division between the individual and the state; complete independence was, and always had been, an illusion. 'No man can be a collectivist alone or an individualist alone,' said Winston Churchill in Glasgow in 1906.

He must be both . . . The nature of man is a dual nature. The character of the organisation of human society is dual. Man is at once a unique being and a gregarious animal. For some purposes he must be a collectivist, for others he is, and will for all time remain, an individualist.[39]

V

THE NEW JERUSALEM AND THE
NEW DESPOTISM

1914–1951

CHAPTER 9

A Half Revolution

—ɯ—

'The inevitability of gradualism' is passing out of our political thinking, and the 'inevitability of dictatorship' is becoming the common stock of socialist discussion, while Fascist machine guns are openly boasted of on public platforms.

LORD ALLEN OF HUNTWOOD, 1934[1]

Looking back from the miserable days of post-war Britain in 1949, the libertarian publisher Ernest Benn remarked that his countrymen had learnt a lamentable custom in the course of the twentieth century. Before August 1914 'we had not . . . acquired the German habit of queuing'. No one born since then, he wrote, could know what freedom meant. Queues are a totemic image of these years, and for Benn they symbolised state control and sheepish docility; in war and peace, the British had accustomed themselves to the dictates of remote authority; the once robust, risk-taking and proudly bloody-minded people did not now ask whether an action was right or wrong but tamely enquired, 'Is it permitted? Can a licence be obtained?'[2]

If the British of the nineteenth century instinctively despised officialdom and regulations and if the conflict between individualism and collectivism was resolving into a compromise, the First World War marked the beginning of a revolution. For some August 1914 was the moment when the history of liberty came to an end.[3] But for others out of the carnage of total war came a new way of living. One firm Tory of the Herbert Spencer school of individualism told the House of Commons that he had abandoned his lifelong creed and favoured the reorganisation of society and the economy along 'social-istic lines'. The old world of nineteenth-century laissez-faire was dead, and Britain would be reborn, the people and the economy united to face challenges as a collective whole.[4] Winston Churchill said that the achievements of the central co-ordination of production to meet the demands of total war 'constitute the greatest argument for State Socialism that has ever been produced'.[5]

Out of the Great War came votes for women, greater educational opportunities and an expansion of welfare. It accelerated develop-ments that were already trundling along. But the attitudes that lay behind them had been transformed. Individualism, it was felt, had been a casualty of war. 'Life seems wider and more impersonal,' Alfred Zimmern wrote at the end of hostilities.

Our fellow-country men seem nearer to us. Rank and class seem to count for less. All have suffered alike and all have served alike, and all have the same world to live in and repair . . . Men who have breathed the larger air of common sacrifice are reluctant to return to the stuffy air of self-seeking.[6]

Herbert Spencer had written that only a war would resolve the battles of his generation between individualism and collectivism.[7] People on all sides knew that the Great War had changed everything. Marxists saw the war as bringing 'the second phase of capitalism' to Britain, just as German unification had supposedly led to Imperial Socialism. This meant that, in spite of themselves, aristocrats and plu-tocrats had introduced the rudiments of a socialist state: social secur-ity, rationalised industry, nationalised institutions and collectivism. Such policies were intended for nationalistic purposes, but they undermined the foundations which capitalism rested upon by replac-ing naked individualism with a national or collective consciousness. Self-interest would gradually be taken over by self-sacrifice. And socialism would inevitably step into the spiritual vacuum created by this transformation of mentality when capitalism was finally shown to be a defunct and spiritless phase in history. Britain was following Germany, under the pressure of emergency, to dismantle laissez-faire and bring the whole economy under central direction. Most impor-tantly, the British government was compelling the people, whether big businessmen and industrialists or humble workers, to sacrifice themselves to the wider interests of the state.

Left-wing writers talked of the withering away of subjective rights, and the birth of a new kind of liberty. The old conception of negative liberties, which imprisoned everyone in their own private concerns, was giving way to the supremacy of the common good and self-sacrifice to the nation. The war was really a world revolution, the only force strong enough to raze the foundations of liberal society, from the ruins of which would be built the new society of man. Britain represented the 'counter-revolutionary' force, that of 'anarchic capitalism' and barbaric individualism. But in the quest for discipline, efficiency and patriotism the British had unconsciously joined the revolution. It pointed to a new kind of freedom, where the interests of the individual and the state merged into a glorious whole – it marked the end of selfish commercial values, which separated men and countries into mutually antagonistic units. For what was the war but the outcome of naked greed, violent competition and imperialism – in other words, individualism writ large?[8]

For all for its halting steps in social reform, compared to the rest of Europe Britain was seen as the playground of unrestrained capitalism and extreme individual liberty. When war was declared in August 1914 politicians were forced to confront this difference. They were painfully conscious – sometimes to an exaggerated degree – that an economy geared towards free competition and personal independence in peacetime was totally incapable of fighting total war. This was especially true when the enemy was seen as having an economy directed towards militarism and a people accustomed to discipline and regimentation. The medicine must therefore be quick-working, even if it was bitter.

On 7 August 1914 the Defence of the Realm Act (DORA) passed both Houses of Parliament, giving the military authorities control over communications and transport. On 12 August martial law was declared and on the 26th DORA (number 2) was passed, extending to the military authorities power over the trade of the country. The Defence of the Realm (Consolidation) Act in November gave a competent military authority (that is to say, an officer above the rank of captain) the power to try and even pass sentence of death over a civilian for breaching wartime regulations. The Defence Acts were general in their wording, delegating legislative functions to the executive to make whatever regulations it deemed expedient for defending the realm and prosecuting and winning the war. Lord Halsbury called it 'the most unconstitutional thing that has ever happened in this country'.[9]

Within a few weeks of war every aspect of civilian life was brought under central control; arbitrary powers that would have made the Stuarts blush were handed to the government and the army; in short every hard-won liberty was surrendered or placed at the mercy of the executive. And on what terms was the capitulation made? The report of the first and second readings, the committee stage, the third reading and the royal assent merits just two columns of Hansard both times the defence bills were brought to parliament.[10] In other words, a measure of extraordinary dictatorial power was rushed through a panicked parliament in minutes. Later, MPs would realise that DORA meant 'the formal abdication of parliament' and its replacement with 'an autocracy disguised as Constitutional Government'.[11] But no one complained at the time, not even at the indecent haste.[12]

As David Lloyd George, successively Chancellor of the Exchequer, Minister of Munitions and Prime Minister from December 1916, never ceased to remind the public, this was more a war of materiel than of men; the country which reached and retained the highest output of shells and ships would eventually out-power the other.[13] And as ministers were eager to inform the public, Germany had highly centralised industry, a disciplined labour force and a tariff wall which protected its domestic economy. In contrast, British individualism and competition could not readily supply the War Office. In past wars, the military had bargained for supplies and munitions on the open market. At the start of hostilities in 1914, the City speculated on every business which was engaged in competitive tendering for war contracts, everything from shell to sock manufactures. But in the age of total war, the profit motive could bankrupt the country and ruin the war effort.

The problem can be illustrated by one of the melancholy icons of the war. Sandbags were a priority for the army as they dug in on the Western Front. By the end of the war 1,186 million bags had been supplied to the Allies. The problems of the free market immediately became apparent when at the start of the war a clever speculator purchased the entire stock of bags then on the market and offered to sell it back to the military at a profit of one hundred per cent.[14] In another case it was suspected that the Dundee jute manufacturers (the bags were made from jute), by sticking to their free-trade principles and the obligations of contract, were indirectly supplying the German army. All this was perfectly legal and expected of businessmen. In response military officers requisitioned all the sandbags in Liverpool and all the jute in Dundee. The officers, acting under DORA, were supposed to recompense the manufacturers at the market rate and take into account previous contracts which would now be impossible to honour. But what was the market rate when the War Office was ordering sandbags in the millions each month? High demand and high prices were entirely caused by war conditions and the government refused to pay at the top of this skewed market. The speculators were deprived of their fundamental liberties; their property had been requisitioned by the state; their contracts had been invalidated; their right to make a profit was completely taken away.

Jute and sandbags may seem like the most mundane of mundane examples. But the government's inept handling of contracts revealed that the War Office and the market were bad bedfellows. It was one of the first major crises of the war and taught the government the lesson that the ordinary rules no longer applied. What was true of jute was true also of a plethora of products: jerseys, tents, munitions, ships and foodstuffs. The community had been promised 'business as usual', but it was clear that industry and agriculture had to be directed towards the needs of the war economy. Inexperienced, cautious and initially unaware of the magnitude of the task, the government made early mistakes. In time banks, shipyards, factories, agriculture, mines, the import trade and railways would come under direct or indirect government control in an unprecedented feat of economic organisation. Munitions, ships and submarines had to be built on a vast scale; food and clothing had to be allocated to servicemen, munitions workers, children and unconscripted civilians. And in this topsy-turvy situation, the government had to regulate prices and wages. Once the government became, for the first time, the biggest player on the market, the principal importer and major employer, it was inevitable that the economy must needs be planned – the practical realisation of state socialism by politicians whose instincts were to combat socialism.[15]

And as the nation's chief employer and provider, the government also felt it had to become the nation's moral guardian and disciplinarian. Lloyd George tended to believe that heavy drinking would incapacitate production. Heavy taxes were placed on alcohol to reduce consumption, and pub opening hours were restricted nation-wide and cut to almost nothing in areas of munitions production. The army was also allowed to break up public dances. As Minister of Munitions Lloyd George was aware that traditional freedoms in the workplace could also retard the national effort. His Munitions Acts put millions of men and women under strict government supervision. They were deprived of the right to strike and, more annoying to the average worker, factories, workshops and mines were placed under military and ministerial supervision, so that minor infractions of discipline were punished by government officials or soldiers. Even more offensive to the independent worker was a regulation which prevented people leaving one job and taking another without a certificate from the authorities. Again, this was a drastic measure to limit the free market, this time the free market in labour. The normal situation where workers could leave their employment for better wages elsewhere was considered to be a freedom too far when essential war work needed to be done.

'The whole of the working men of this country have been brought up under the old Manchester School of the ideal of individual liberty,' an MP told the house, and the habits of personal and industrial liberty would be hard to overcome.[16] But some believed that the scales would fall from the eyes of the proletariat; the war was the self-immolation of capitalism. When the Chief Inspector of Mines said, 'The present system of individual ownership of collieries is extravagant and wasteful, whether viewed from the point of view of the coalmining industry as a whole or from the national point of view,' it was clear to some that the ruling classes were speaking the language of socialism. The same was true when the interests of the railway companies were subordinated to the needs of the country. The British government also took measures to limit war profits being made by companies and abrogated in many cases the right of contract. Left-wing pamphleteers tried to convince workers to put up with DORA: there could be no going back to pre-war individualism. However unpleasant were working conditions in the short-term the consequence would be beneficial: the capitalist class was planning the economy and collectivising factories and transport systems; it had been forced to lay the foundations for a socialist state. One day this would be in the hands of the proletariat.[17]

The British working class were having nothing of this. DORA and the Munitions Act did not represent the death-throes of capitalism but of servility. The veneration of individual liberty and independence went very deep indeed – far deeper than the apostles of international socialism and the British government assumed. Indeed, it was Labour MPs who were now speaking the language of individualism, while their Conservative opponents were talking of the necessity of socialist organisation.[18] Many working men and women came to believe that the periodical bursts of liberty-denying ordinances had nothing to do with raising efficiency, but were ways in which the ministry shifted the blame for shortages from themselves to the drunken, lazy, disloyal workers. The government, it seemed, was prepared to sacrifice liberty for political advantage.

One of the most famous rebels from this time was the Glasgow engineer and trade unionist David Kirkwood. According to his autobiography, *My Life of Revolt*, generations of Kirkwoods had been imbued with a 'mania for self-reliance', nurtured in the Presbyterian Kirk, and reinforced with tales of the Highland chieftains, Covenanters and Jacobites.[19] In the war, David Kirkwood was a highly skilled engineer at Beardmore's Forge, a workshop at Parkhead in Glasgow. This was the key area in the country for the production of munitions and ships; ministers believed that the war would be won or lost on the Clyde.

Kirkwood used his influence with the workers and management to foster a harmonious atmosphere and keep up production. 'Fellow engineers,' he told a meeting at City Hall, 'the country is at war. The country must win. In order to win, we must throw our whole soul into the production of munitions.' He put up with the high demand for production, the strict calls for discipline and overtime and even the dilution of skilled labour with inexperienced engineers (which most unions were resisting). Kirkwood achieved extraordinary power at Beardmore's, settling disputes between workers and foremen, foremen and managers, managers and the owner. Thanks to his position, he was able to keep the Forge in high production without disputes. The managers, however, hated him for bypassing the conventional structure of the company.[20]

'I was happy in Beardmore's as a free man,' he wrote of the Munitions Act. 'I resented being in Beardmore's as a slave. I was part of the Forge by nature and by inclination. I would not be part of it by compulsion.' He felt that the engineers had complied with all orders and all diminution of their rights. The government was exploiting their patriotism and replacing co-operation with compulsion. As the press and parliament argued, the munitions crisis was not a want of patriotism, drunkenness or industrial unrest, but the failure of Asquith's government to implement central control. The view Kirkwood maintained throughout the war was that engineers knew best how to raise production. Surrendering their autonomy to inexpert military officers and civil servants was both counterproductive and insulting. All workers would now be tied to their current jobs for the rest of the war, unable to barter for better conditions or even leave for another job. It was a slap in the face for the whole labour movement.[21]

Kirkwood and other labour leaders on the Clyde decided to resist. They were put in an impossible situation. They were determined to retain the rights of labour, not just for themselves but for their colleagues when they returned from the trenches. They were being asked to sacrifice their liberty and their right to improve working conditions without any guarantees for the future. But they also opened themselves to accusations of treachery, which they received in excessive measure. The Clydeside rebels were compared to the men in the trenches who had cheerfully submitted to discipline and never thought of challenging their officers about military strategy or conditions in the dugout. One MP defended them, saying that a soldier had a clear sense of duty. A factory or a mine was quite different. The skilled engineers on the Clyde were not allowed to leave their specialised work and join the army. The worker and the soldier made sacrifices. Who benefited? The soldier or sailor knew that he was fighting for his country. The worker, subjected to a code of stifling, petty rules dictated by bureaucrats, knew that all the sacrifices he made to raise efficiency would ultimately benefit the owners when they resumed control of their factories after the war, happily modernised at others' expense. The worker, whether he was kept at work or fighting in Flanders, would return to peacetime work not a whit better off, and perhaps deprived of his accustomed rights. In other words, the labourer was working not just for his country, but for the profit of another. The government talked of 'equality of sacrifice' but it was apparent to everyone, including Conservatives, that this was not so clear-cut. Conflict was inevitable.[22] Whether the Clydesiders were right or deeply misguided, they stood for a matter of principle: 'These trade rights are not ours to surrender,' said Kirkwood. 'They are ours to defend. Our fathers fought for them. It is our duty to guard them.'[23]

In Christmas 1915 Lloyd George went to Glasgow to pacify the situation. One of his visits was to Beardmore's, where Kirkwood and some of his colleagues were pulled off the floor to meet him. The minister was forty-five minutes late, which infuriated Kirkwood. When the politicians and management deigned to appear, he was enraged by their look of plump good health and superciliousness. 'Here's a fine cairry-on,' he exploded. 'Does he no' ken there's a war on? We're here to produce munitions, no' to staun' idly by waitin' on him.' There followed a stormy meeting where Lloyd George, with his famous charm, tried to persuade the engineers to join the common sacrifice. Kirkwood replied that they only wanted to co-operate with the government and manage the changes themselves. Lloyd George agreed to address a meeting at City Hall on Christmas Day.[24]

The Christmas meeting would become infamous. To Kirkwood's horror, the Clyde workers were in an ugly mood, which was not helped by the stage-managed show of patriotism – Union Jacks, girl workers in khaki uniforms and Lloyd George's arrival to 'See the Conquering Hero Comes'. The crowd drowned out the hymn with 'The Red Flag' and shouted out 'Get your hair cut' (and worse) to the minister. The meeting proceeded as it had started. In a further insult to liberties, the press was forbidden to report Lloyd George's discomfort, and when *Forward*, a Glasgow workers' paper, gave an unflattering account it was immediately suppressed.[25]

Unrest continued in Glasgow, and David Kirkwood found himself in the unenviable position of trying to satisfy the government and the militant workers. Soon after the tempestuous meeting with Lloyd George the management of Beardmore's lost patience with his unusual power. When the Women's Welfare Superintendent complained of Kirkwood's unlimited access to all parts of the works the management was happy to restrict his movements. Kirkwood said he could not do his work of greasing the wheels of worker–employer relations if his access was curtailed. To the secret delight of the authorities, the workers came out on strike. It was an opportunity for Beardmore to regain control and the dangerous experiment in co-operation to be stopped. Kirkwood was arrested at dawn under DORA and transferred to the competent military authority. He was tried in absentia, deported with his fellow labour leaders the next day from the Clyde Munitions Area, and restricted to a five-mile radius of Edinburgh city centre.

Unbeknown to Kirkwood, Sir Edward Carson, believing that the Clydeside trade unionists were working with German spies, called for their execution, and that might have happened had not the Procurator Fiscal decided there was not enough evidence for a capital trial. The accusations were ridiculous, and soon found to be so. Yet loud voices called for them to be hanged, German spies or not. Some of the other deportees were on the hard left and actively opposed to the war. David Kirkwood was a moderate who had tried to act constructively. Nonetheless the government had acted decisively against the uncooperative part of the labour movement. Strikes were stamped out for the duration of the war.[26]

The Clydesiders were offered high-paying engineering work in England, and only Kirkwood refused. He was interrogated by the military authorities on suspicion of sedition and offered the choice of gaol or work. Kirkwood would only make a decision as a free man, and that was to go back to his family and to Beardmore's Forge. For months he was shadowed by the military and offered the chance to go home if he signed an oath that he would not impede the production of munitions. He replied that he had only ever speeded up the supply, and would never concede that he had done otherwise. Instead he went back to Glasgow, where he was re-arrested by the military police and imprisoned in terrible conditions with German and Austrian prisoners of war in Edinburgh Castle for fourteen days. Again he refused to sign anything, again he returned to Glasgow and again he was deported. Eventually the military authorities revoked the exclusion order, and Kirkwood returned to his family. But he was still not happy. He would only work at the place of his choice. After more months of conflict he secured a meeting with Winston Churchill, by then Minister of Munitions in Lloyd George's coalition government. They began a curiously warm association. At the time, Churchill thought that Kirkwood was mad to make such demands, but agreed to have him reinstated as a manager at Beardmore's. He returned and within six weeks the Forge beat the record for output in Britain.[27]

Churchill later wrote that David Kirkwood represented the 'sturdy independence', the 'super-developed sense of injustice' and inherent suspicion towards the state of the radical working class. And he was an old-fashioned radical, not a revolutionary Marxist. Like so many on the left at the time, he believed strongly in individual rights and saw the state as an overbearing Leviathan which working people should stave off at all costs. As such he spoke for many members of the working class who felt deprived and degraded by DORA. He made a stand not against wartime demands, but against the draconian spirit in which they were enforced. Many would agree that working life had become impossibly stifling. The woman who was disciplined because she turned up late to the factory after she received a telegram announcing her husband's death at the front (sadly not an isolated incident) would have agreed.[28] All those who were dismissed without good reason and without a government certificate would have supported him. The men and women punished for grumbling or untoward words would have seen something of their problems reflected in Kirkwood's plight. William Pringle, a truculent Scottish Liberal MP, told the government: 'If you are going to out-Prussianise the Prussians, out-Prussianise them in efficiency and not in tyranny.'[29]

'Prussianisation' had become the word to describe what was happening in Britain. In March 1917 many of Kirkwood's views were heard in parliament when the government introduced its National Service Bill, which created a new department, led by a director general who would manage the whole of British industry and direct labour to whatever part of the country he chose. If the DG believed that too many people were employed in, say, the hosiery business, he could requisition the labour for martial ends. Asquith's government fell because it was believed that it had failed to prosecute the war with the requisite elan. The new Prime Minister, Lloyd George, reformed the coalition government, creating a five-man War Cabinet made up of ministers who had no departmental responsibility so that they could dedicate their energies to the one end of pulling national efficiency to a hundred per cent. Parliament had been a rubber stamp since 1914; now the cabinet itself was forced into the same undignified role. The real business was done by the Prime Minister and his inner cabinet, aided by their civilian and military appointees.

The bill before parliament was, like DORA, a skeleton act, the details of which could be filled in by the new ministry. The proposed Director General, Neville Chamberlain, was not an MP or peer, and therefore not accountable to parliament. Many MPs complained that they were creating an economic Napoleon in the person of Chamberlain, who had been given 'a blank cheque upon the vast bank of the Defence of the Realm Act'. If working men like David Kirkwood had complained that the Munitions Act tied people indefinitely to their place of work, the new act put everyone at the mercy of Neville Chamberlain, who could compel people to up sticks and move to some distant part of the country to do whatever work was chosen for them by an official. Critics called it the conversion of British life to Prussian military autocracy, or least a centralised bureaucratic state. There was a strong feeling that parliament was being asked to surrender even more of its legislative functions, this time to bureaucrats.[30] The ranks of officialdom had swelled during the war, transforming Britain in the process from a country inherently suspicious of government inspectors to one teeming with them. The figures speak for themselves. In July 1914 the Army Contracts Department meandered along quite happily with a staff of twenty clerks; by November 1918 it employed 65,142.[31]

An MP talked of 'officialdom gone bad'. There was a growing discontent in the country that even the simplest action had to be monitored by a gang of officials; that everything was centrally organised: 'We were to have a margarine controller, and everything was to be controlled. The thing now seems to be arriving at a state where for every act we do we must have a special controller in a special palace, with special staff to look after it.'[32]

The result of the war in terms of administration and economic management was to show that comprehensive planning and nationalisation could work. It was socialism in practice, conducted by Liberals and Conservatives. Yet it was not the self-immolation of capitalism, but capitalism marshalling its resources in self-defence. The actual experience of state control was a painful one for workers and ordinary citizens: it was coercive on a large-scale and draconian in petty matters. It was big on promises for the future, but, when Germany was defeated, impotent. During the war, the government had promised 'homes for heroes' and hinted at the concentration of national effort in peacetime to solve social injustice. After a short boom peace brought economic depression, industrial unrest, shortages and mass unemployment, which was between one and three million until 1940. Successive governments were chary of reviving wartime planning, constrained by the principle of liberty and by the reality of politics. Even mining, an industry crying out for nationalisation, was allowed to ruin itself.

But the country would never be the same. The way that governments governed, the procedures of parliament and the experience of the citizen were fundamentally altered by the war. Faced with the reality of mass unemployment for the first time and worldwide economic ills the government was called upon to take greater powers, powers which had previously been considered arbitrary. Many grumbled that the modern state was overpowering the individual. Others argued that the government was not doing enough; that it was constrained by constitutional propriety and hamstrung by a misplaced and outdated concern for the individual.

'The new despotism' was the term adopted by Lord Chief Justice Hewart in his book of that title in 1929. More and more power, he alleged, was being given to state departments who made their own rules to govern the citizen, enforced by their own 'quasi-judicial' decisions which could not be challenged in the courts. Parliament was passing 'skeleton acts', so called because they gave ministers and their departments the power to make up their own regulations when situations not covered by the act arose; such a mechanism is more usually known as secondary or delegated legislation. It gave them, as *The Times* commented, the arbitrary authority of Henry VIII to make laws by decree, combined with the dispensing powers enjoyed by the Stuarts.[33] It meant that the individual was ruled by regulations made by the bureaucracy, which Hewart characterised as 'organized lawlessness'. It was a kick in the teeth to the traditional relationship between the state and the individual.

In the past judicial oversight had sided with individuals when they had come into conflict with local improvement schemes which might have interfered with their unfettered right of private property or economic freedom. This was well and good, modern bureaucrats reasoned, but it put private interest above the public good. Delegated legislation was designed to break a rigid rule of law in matters when the public need demanded it. In many ways it reversed assumptions about the common law and administrative procedure; as Maitland had written in 1908: 'the attempt, characteristic of modern times, to protect the economically weaker classes has given rise to statutes which bristle with powers'.[34]

Some foresaw economic dictatorship, the first steps towards totalitarianism. Others saw it as the continuation of a state of emergency which had begun in August 1914 and showed no signs of ending. Between October and December 1931 the National Government – itself an emergency expedient – passed a series of emergency measures to combat the economic disaster of the Great Depression. The laws tore up contracts between the state and its employees by reducing official salaries; ministers were given discretionary powers to make orders altering the exchange rate or suspending the Gold Standard; ministers could make good shortages of food or limit prices of foodstuffs; and they could act immediately to prevent large-scale imports or exports by imposing duties of up to a hundred per cent.[35] As unemployment remained a pressing social problem the provision of labour exchanges and public welfare increased. The government acted as a guiding force in the economy, rationalising banks and sectors of industry, such as transport and mining. In the 1930s the government provided loans for industries and incentives to direct the location of industry to depressed areas, put in place trade tariffs, stimulated the economy with public works and managed the currency. Since the First World War, governments had intervened in town planning, using compulsory purchase orders and other coercive policies.

Ramsay MacDonald, the Prime Minister, said that these were emergency powers, necessary because the normal parliamentary and legal procedures were too slow.[36] Dingle Foot, a young Liberal MP, complained that the Commons had been transformed into 'a machine for registering the decrees of an omnipotent executive'.[37] The barriers put up by law and parliamentary scrutiny had been knocked down. Upon what security did individual liberty now rest? 'In the eternal dispute between government and liberty,' wrote Sir Cecil Carr, 'crisis means more government and less liberty.'[38]

Since the First World War it was apparent that there had been a revolution in government and the constitution. In response the government set up a committee under Lord Donoughmore, which reported on delegated powers in 1932.[39] It acknowledged that the 'new policy' involved bypassing parliamentary and juridical safeguards built up over ages. But the complexity of modern life and the pressure of emergencies meant that the government must have the power to act expeditiously. In its daily operation, government needed the advice of experts and technicians more than the citizen required six hundred MPs to debate issues the complexities of which were far above their heads.

Another committee said that the function of government in the twentieth century had become 'the management of the life of the people'. But liberty in the twentieth century had changed as well. Liberty expanded when the conditions of people's lives improved, and this needed a strong government. Yet at the same time the new state Leviathan 'should not in its zeal for interference deprive [the people] of their initiative and independence which are the nation's most valuable assets'. Quite how this was to be done was left unclear.[40] The Donoughmore Report recommended continual debate about the evolution of governmental power in relation to individual liberty. It was nicknamed the 'Do-no-more Report': every year the government promised debate and did nothing except pass acts which gave the executive more power at the expense of the citizen.[41] Finally in 1937 Dingle Foot proposed the motion 'That, in the opinion of this House, the power of the Executive has increased, is increasing, and ought to be diminished'. As if to underscore his point that the Commons had given up on its role as watchdog of the country's liberties the house adjourned its sitting because there was not a quorum in the chamber.[42]

Such issues did not worry public opinion. There were bigger dangers about. This was the age of rapidly expanding government, legions of inspectors, form-filling, permits, traffic lights – to name just a few of the increasing mountain of regulations and rules. For those who had memories which went further back than 1914 it was clear that the country had changed beyond recognition; that old assumptions of liberty had been crushed by a state which had accrued to itself powers in the course of decades of emergency.* But at the same

* 'Until August 1914 a sensible, law-abiding Englishman could pass through life and hardly notice the existence of the State, beyond the post office and the policeman,' wrote A. J. P. Taylor. 'He could live where he liked and as he liked. He had no official number or identity card. He could travel abroad or leave his country for ever without a passport or any sort of official permission. He could exchange his money for any other currency without restriction or limit. He could buy goods from any country in the world on the same terms as he bought goods at home.'

time dependence on the state *had* increased. Some would have said that this dependence was shameful for a country once populated by manly individuals. Yet it was surely the case that the problems confronting the individual in the 1930s were so great that they could only be overcome by economic reform.

Liberty had grown in nineteenth-century Britain because the country was strong so the government could be weak in its relationship with the people. Now the individual was vulnerable to global economic problems. Added to this, threats to the individual's autonomy had grown with rapid technological progress. These included environmental factors such as pollution and industrial effluents, not to mention roads, traffic and urbanisation. The citizen, if he wasn't overmastered by the state or society, could be by multinational companies, a powerful media, the ill winds of global economics or a slum landlord. The worker or the long-term unemployed man or woman felt far more powerless than the working class of the previous generation. And the middle classes were as beset by insecurities. Nearly everyone could see that at work he or she had less independence and was under more control. In a democratic country (which Britain could finally claim to be) the citizen should demand services from his government without fear that it would become tyrannical. Where else could he or she look? The cry in the 1930s everywhere was for stronger governments.

Unless the democracies became more efficient at fulfilling the desires of its citizens then, said many on left and right, the panaceas offered by Mussolini, Hitler, Franco or Stalin would attract miserable people. The barriers which had safeguarded liberty throughout history might indeed become the enemy of liberty. This would be so if the rules which governed individuals and the state were seen as being too rigid to adapt. Confronted with unprecedented problems at home and the rise of totalitarianism throughout the world the democracies failed to articulate how freedom and progress were compatible. Britain, stubbornly conservative as she was in these years, appeared to be drifting. Occasionally politicians and bureaucrats would take more power in response to a crisis; sometimes they would forbear to do anything so radical. It was a time of half-hearted debate, partial reform and dreary reports.

The American Herbert Agar called it the 'sickness of the West': 'Mr Hoover was as inadequate as Stanley Baldwin or Georges Bonnet or the Social Democrats in Germany. They were all inadequate for the same reasons: they had forgotten how to think in terms of the moral purpose of our culture.'[43] And this moral purpose was not just the robust defence of liberty but the courage to think creatively – enlarging it to cope with man's here-and-now problems. Throughout the ages people had sought ways to defend themselves from political coercion; in the 1930s the threat came from other forms of power, principally economic. Faith in liberal-democratic solutions was on the wane everywhere; the state of Europe was a horrific portent for the future if the public lost confidence in its traditions. In countries racked by mass unemployment and perpetual uncertainty, liberty became a dead and hollow thing. In countries without a deep attachment to liberties people were prepared to subordinate their individuality to what they saw as the greater good – and they did it in the name of the liberation of their selves, their nation or their race. What did the legions of unemployed in Britain or America have left to lose? Harold Laski wrote that

those who know the normal life of the poor, its perpetual fear of the morrow, its haunting sense of impending disaster, its fitful search for a beauty which perpetually eludes, will realize well enough that, without economic security, liberty is not worth having. Men may well be free and yet remain unable to realize the purposes of freedom.[44]

CHAPTER 10

A Very British Revolution

—❧—

A revolutionary moment in the world's history is a time for revolutions, not for patching . . . The scheme proposed here is in some ways a revolution, but in more important ways it is a natural development from the past. It is a British Revolution.

THE BEVERIDGE REPORT, 1942[1]

Liberty for liberty's sake is clearly a meaningless notion: it must be liberty to do and enjoy something. If more people are buying automobiles and taking vacations, there is more liberty.

DWIGHT WALDO, 1948[2]

There was a sense of irreversible decline in the 1930s; a feeling that educational achievements, hard work, self-sacrifice and freedom itself availed one little. It was seen by some thinkers as psychologically dangerous: a state of mind which endangered liberty and democracy through unresolved anguish and generalised dissatisfaction: a feeling that freedom was worthless. It was what Erich Fromm characterised as 'anomie', the fear of freedom first identified by Emile Durkheim which came from surveying the modern world and acknowledging your utter insignificance and powerlessness in it. Feeling such helplessness would make absolute security, made to seem possible by the bluster of a dictator, a comforting proposition and one well worth the price of a delusive liberty. Fromm wrote that

the lag between 'freedom from' and 'freedom to' has grown . . . The result of this disproportion between freedom *from* any tie and the lack of possibilities for the positive realisation of freedom and individuality has led, in Europe, to a panicky flight from freedom into new ties or at least into complete indifference.[3]*

The realisation that classic negative liberty left people with a sense of alienation and helplessness was preoccupying thinkers in Britain as well. People were becoming dangerously apathetic. 'We are our own kingdoms and make for ourselves, in large measure, the world in which we live,' wrote the intellectual and future Labour MP Evan Durbin in 1940.

We may be rich, and healthy, and liberal; but unless we are free from secret guilt, the agonies of inferiority and frustration, and the fire of unexpressed aggression, all other things are added to lives in vain. The cruelty and irrationality of human society spring from these secret sources. The savagery of Hitler, the brutality of Stalin, the ruthless and refined bestiality that is rampant in the world today – persecution, cruelty and war – are nothing but the external expression, the institutional and rationalized form, of these dark forces in the human heart.[5]

Horrific as it was, the Second World War offered the chance for renovation. Democracies could provide what totalitarian regimes only promised. The participation of the people in rebuilding their states and the traditions of freedom inherent in their political systems would bring social justice while avoiding the evils of fascism and communism. It was a war for freedom; and there were many who believed that that war was being fought on the home front too – against the selfish spirit of laissez-faire competition which had riven society with insurmountable class divisions. Aneurin Bevan expressed this vision of peacetime society: 'It will reconcile the needs of an ordered economic life with the fullest efflorescence of personal liberty. Without an ordered economic life the individual frustrates

---

* Cf. Karl Popper: 'It is part of the strain that we are becoming more and more painfully aware of the gross imperfections in our life, of personal as well as institutional imperfection; of waste and unnecessary ugliness; and at the same time of the fact that it is not impossible for us to do something about all this, but that such improvements would be just as hard to achieve as they are important. This awareness increases the strain of personal responsibility, of carrying the cross of being human.'[4]

himself in a morass of fears and insecurities. Without personal liberty an ordered economic life is like the plant that never flowers.'[6]

The Atlantic Charter signed by the united nations fighting the Axis powers promised war aims of 'improved standards, economic advancement, and social security' for all. Franklin D. Roosevelt's 'Four Freedoms' were freedom of speech, freedom of worship, freedom from fear and freedom from want. The first two are familiar from the history of Anglo-American liberties; the second two are freedoms *from* a menace – liberation from constraints – which only the state could guarantee. As FDR's Second Bill of Rights put it, 'true individual freedom cannot exist without economic security and independence'.

If some reformers assumed in 1914 that social change would naturally come from world war those in the 1940s knew that the revolutionary conditions of total war must be exploited by men and women who desired change. After the First World War, a Labour Party manifesto of 1942 said, the sacrifices of the people had produced little for them. From 1919 government controls of the economy had given way to an 'ugly scramble for profit' and the working class had to put up with high unemployment and low standards of living. The same must not happen after WWII. Only economic security guaranteed by state planning and augmented by state provision of essential services could provide the conditions for true freedom.[7]

Following the Atlantic Charter the government commissioned the Beveridge Report, which promised the people that when peace came full employment would be the reward for wartime sacrifices. William Beveridge stressed that a planned economy could only work within free, democratic institutions:

Freedom from want cannot be forced on a democracy or given to a democracy. It must be won by them. Winning it needs courage and faith and sense of national unity; courage to face facts and difficulties and overcome; faith in our future and in the ideals of fair play and freedom, for which, century after century, our forefathers were prepared to die; a sense of national unity overriding the interests of any class or section.[8]

It was a bold statement of modern freedoms. 'The British stimulation of and response to the Beveridge Report', wrote Herman Finer, 'inspired the whole world.'[9] The Report was a powerful message of how an Allied victory would give civilisation new freedoms, the first definite promise of the fulfilment of the Atlantic Charter. It was read by millions, supported by ninety per cent of the British population, translated into many languages and read throughout the world; one MP said the government needed to back it up with 'a new British declaration of the rights of man'.[10]

The Report was an important statement of a future of economic security within the framework of democratic liberty at a time when Britain was using fire to fight fire. An expert on government planning in the First World War said that any future world war would mean 'a sort of military communism'.[11] Certainly the government in 1939 was better prepared for total war than Asquith's in 1914. Whereas Asquith and Lloyd George passed various acts consolidating their economic and labour regulations throughout the war, Neville Chamberlain's government asked for, and got, the most skeletal of skeleton acts *before* war was declared – the Emergency Powers (Defence) Act.[12] Parliament gave the ministry unlimited power to fill in the provisions of the act with whatever regulations they thought necessary; there was no need to seek fresh legislation, as all legislative functions were delegated to the executive. By February 1943 there were some 2,100 regulations covering every aspect of life from civil liberties to the running of the economy. There was little chance of appeal to the courts over anything the government chose to do thanks to the clause of the Emergency Powers Act which said that people might be called upon to place 'themselves, their services, and their property' at the disposal of His Majesty's Government. And, by delegating legislative powers to the government, parliament had rendered itself virtually powerless to check executive action. The only power it retained was that of withdrawing its confidence in the government, something it did once to unseat Chamberlain. That it would do the same to Winston Churchill's administration was an unlikely scenario to say the least.

As in the First World War, many of the regulations were irksome and civilian life became highly regimented. One Conservative MP told the Commons:

Today we live under a system of permits . . . So far from an Englishman's home being his castle, he cannot even mend a leak in his roof without a permit. A man without an identity card or a ration book is an outlaw. This conception of permits is fatally easy to take root. It must be eradicated. Tyranny can so easily be clamped on a people by such simple measures.[13]

The plan followed from the beginning of the war was to place all the resources of the country under central direction, leaving no room for waste, misapplication or duplication. There was danger in dither; instead the government had to show 'decision, drive and direction' to wage economic war and satisfy public expectation. There was near unanimity in accepting these dictatorial powers, even if many saw it as totalitarian. When Chamberlain fell in May 1940 it was because parliament lost confidence in his government's grip upon foreign and defence policies but also upon the manpower and industry of the country. When the elderly Lloyd George – the victor of the First World War – told the Commons that Chamberlain's preparation for war was all 'leisureliness and inefficiency' the Prime Minister's time was up. In short he was not delivering joined-up government, and, as Clement Attlee said, only a government which directed everything towards the goal of victory would satisfy parliament and people.[14]

The demand was for more, not less control, and there was high tolerance for the unrestrained authority which came with it. One of the reasons for this was that everyone felt they were contributing to a common end, and there was a feeling of solidarity. 'Equality of sacrifice' was a vague generality in the First World War; in the 1940s it was an explicit statement which implied equality of reward upon victory. Excess Profit Tax was set at a hundred per cent so that no one would profit from the war, a stringent luxury tax was imposed and a Fair Wages Council would protect workers' rights.[15] As the war went on the process of rationalisation sped up: decisions were centralised, monopolies were created, the direction of labour became more efficient and small, uneconomic companies were wound down. What was clear was that after the war things could not return to the status quo, after such a revolution. One Labour MP called it 'the death-knell of the small man'. The choice would be between monopoly capitalism and the corporate state; private enterprise by individual entrepreneurs could not return when the work of reconstruction began. War called upon conformity, obedience and regimentation; it stifled individuality, initiative and insubordination. The state's victory was total; and in the mess of peace the same national effort would have to be maintained.[16] 'We are not a totalitarian state', Churchill told the Commons in 1941, 'but we are steadily, and I believe as far as possible, working ourselves into a total war organisation.'[17]

Many felt that going back to the status quo ante bellum would be impossible. The longer the war continued the further industry went down the road towards complete state control; dismantling this entirely would be impossible. But more importantly the people would not continue to make sacrifices until they were assured that the postwar world would be better than that of 1939. Indeed, many working people experienced a greater standard of living during the war; thanks to state-provided milk their children were more robust and free health care benefited all. The Labour Party was pledged to full employment and public welfare after the war, in other words the continuation of wartime economic solutions in peace. A government White Paper in 1944 made full employment the promise of the British state, whatever party was in power. One MP said it 'means the end of one chapter and the opening of a new one. It means the end of *laissez faire* and of the Free Trade century . . . [I]t represents the definite adoption of a planned economy.'[18] In fact, it only pledged future governments to Keynesian economic solutions rather than state socialism, but it possessed symbolic value, especially as 1944 fell two years short of the centenary of the repeal of the Corn Laws and the advent of free trade. (But some might have said that the previous hundred years had marked not the triumph of free trade but the advent of social improvement – for another centenary was nigh, that of the 1844 Factory Act.)

If parliament had been happy to hand entire control of the country to the government in 1939–40, two events provoked ideological splits. The first was the entry of the USSR into the war; the second was the victory at El Alamein. Churchill had been lukewarm about social reform during the war, and privately believed the Beveridge

Report to be utopian. But there was a group of Conservative back-benchers who trumpeted the danger of state control. Alliance with Soviet Russia added a new dimension to British economic policies: it was all very well to make a temporary sacrifice to defeat totalitarian Germany, but military alliance with another totalitarian power tarnished domestic policies. It seemed that the war might not be simply freedom versus totalitarianism, but the conflict of two different brands of tyranny. After Britain's first major victory the Tory malcontents began pressing the government to give an undertaking that all regulations would be rescinded upon peace. At the same time a group of dissident Labour backbenchers grouped around Nye Bevan started pressing their leaders in the coalition government to hold Churchill to active policies of social justice while the war was still in progress.

The chorus of Tory rebels represented the last shout of laissez-faire individualists for a generation. They warned that wartime regulations would become a permanent feature of civilian life. Full employment could not be guaranteed unless the economy was planned by central government. And a planned economy could only be maintained by coercive policies, interference with private property and the replacement of individual effort with bureaucratic control. And such a society would have to retain wartime censorship and restrictions on civil liberties. The warning voices had their prophet, Friedrich von Hayek, whose *Road to Serfdom* (1944) argued that the British were so besotted with social justice that they would follow Germany and Russia into despotism. Equipped with an intellectual justification, the MPs now talked of the coming serfdom and believed that peace would bring a socialist dictatorship in which individual liberty would die.[19] The totalitarianism of the war would continue, except it would be a war against want, disease, squalor, ignorance and idleness in which the ordinary rules of justice and parliamentary government would be suspended in the name of victory.

Hayek believed that Britain was moving away from the principles that underpinned civilisation, principles it had given the world. Only with economic freedom was personal and political freedom possible. That is to say, the independence which property and wealth brought gave the individual the private space within which liberty was possible. The sacredness of the individual and the inviolability of property had allowed society to progress. Security of property, above all, meant that owners exerted every ounce of ingenuity and entrepreneurial energy to wring the last drop of profit out of their property. Public ownership would destroy this incentive, which had over the years spurred improvement, innovation and progress. But progress was taken for granted, and people felt that they could dispense with the liberties that lay behind it. The very act of planning an economy undermined the spontaneity of the individual acting in the market, instead subjecting life to predetermined policies. Whereas in the past independent producers and consumers had, by the coincidence of ends, reached collective solutions, planners would demand conformity. A planned economy would sweep away the variety which gave free societies their vitality.

Not only was this unfriendly to economic progress, but it was the opposite of democracy. Democracy was messy and led to dispute and compromise, never to unanimous agreement. Collective solutions must be determined by experts who would cut through the bluster of competing interests and legislate away poverty, disease, ignorance and misery. And as the utopia of a fair society becomes more desirable, encumbrances such as law and justice become less valuable and more easily disposable. The outcome would be coercion as government herded people toward the common good and the monotony of regimented life. Without economic inducements, without the experience of ingenuity, without the vitalising feeling of risk, the people's only solace would be the glory of the country – that is to say nationalism, the natural-born child of collectivism.

And as the value of the individual sank in comparison to the collective will, actual individuals would become disposable: that was the road to concentration camps and gulags. Dissent, in such a society, would be an obstacle to the One Big Goal. In short, Britain would kick down the barriers which had prevented – and promote the economic and political conditions which had allowed – the rise of fascism and communism. 'British strength, British character, and British achievements', wrote Hayek, 'are to a great extent the cultivation of the spontaneous.'[20] And a free economy depended on the spontaneous – in the sense that in a completely free market needs and desires were satisfied by a free exchange of information. A planned economy would need to evaluate these needs and desires by statistical measurement, which was bound to be artificial as these things were unquantifiable by any kind of analysis. Planning would, according to Hayek, interrupt the pure flow of information and provide one-size-fits-all solutions, which would satisfy a generalised perception of a collective need but could take no account of individuality, diversity and human peculiarities, which would be seen as anomalous to the prescribed 'system'.

Planning may be bad for society but it was, said the classical economists, suicide for an economy. A free economy, Hayek would later argue, was like the human brain: individual neurons fulfilled their particular function, but in doing so facilitated a complex two-way flow of information; they were also adaptable to new, fast-changing stimuli.* A planned economy, by contrast, was like a clunky robot with fewer, more contrived operating parts which moved to rule and could not brook unexpected changes. In conditions of freedom, information flowed freely from worker to employer, from consumer to producer; thus waste was eliminated, processes were refined, resources were allocated according to need and prices were set fairly. As the Soviet Union showed, according to Hayek's intellectual guide Ludwig von Mises, excessive centralisation and a rigid top-to-bottom hierarchy were good at setting targets, but bad at transmitting knowledge back up the hierarchy. Thus artificially set targets put a burden on the workers, who falsified their figures to meet the expectations of their bosses; the feedback loops were badly deranged and the loser was the humble consumer who would have to put up with shortages in some

---

* Hayek saw consumers and neurons alike as independent operators, the first condition of their success being absolute freedom. 'In both cases we have complex phenomena in which there is a need for utilizing widely dispersed knowledge. The essential point is that each member (neuron, or buyer, or seller), is induced to do what in the total circumstances benefits the system. Each member can be used to serve needs of which it doesn't know anything at all . . . [K]nowledge is utilized that is not planned or centralized or even conscious.'[21]

areas and overproduction in others. As for the worker and bureaucrat, their experience would be one of constantly scrambling to meet impossible targets and a sense of frustration that their frontline experience was not being transmitted to their distant bosses. The operators of this system would become automata themselves, toiling and trudging, trudging and toiling like the enslaved workers in Fritz Lang's masterpiece of cinema, *Metropolis*.

In 1944 the British were scared of a return to poverty and put value on immediate solutions to the wreckage of war. They should remember, however, that the shortcuts to prosperity led to tyranny. It was better to be like a neuron – an independent and unconscious facilitator of an unplanned process – than a repetitive cog in a programmed machine. Renovation would come, as it always had done, from the cumulative effect of the exertion of individual effort – and if it was gradual then that was the price societies had to pay for freedom.

The left in Britain were just as strong defenders of individualism. It is a mark of how central liberty was to all political discussions at this time, and it was motivated by a strong reaction against the experience of so many people in Europe who had surrendered their individuality to what they deluded themselves to believe a higher cause than the individual. But the terrible lessons of totalitarianism should not call upon what was supposed to be the opposite – economic individualism. Indeed the left called upon an alternative history to the Whig property-based story of gradualism. Progress had come as middle-class and working people had stormed the citadels of power. Freedom had been obtained by the dispossessed and disadvantaged by their own efforts.[22]

Liberty was not a plant of spontaneous growth; it was not the by-product of any form of economic arrangement. Indeed the advances made by the lower classes had been as a direct result of changing the basis of property ownership. Whereas freedom of speech, of worship, of assembly and choice of occupation were essential liberties, property ownership was only an 'economic device' according to Beveridge. If it was an 'essential liberty' it was one which belonged only to a very few and it had been used to coerce others.[23] Look back to

Harrington, Hume and the Founding Fathers and the same phrase was used again and again: *property is power*. Once this might have been a rival power to kings, priests and cabinets; but it was power nonetheless, one enjoyed by a minority and wielded like any other sort of power – unaccountably and selfishly. For the millions of workers and their families who had experienced unemployment and/or grinding poverty in the interwar years their liberty had actually declined compared to that of their grandparents. The modern state had failed them.

The process of 'feedback' which Hayek talked about was just as deranged in a 'free' economy: the massive accumulation of property in a few lucky hands had skewed the economy, producing benefits for one class and shortages, high prices, unemployment, inequality and social immobility for less fortunate classes. William Beveridge and others stressed that the proposals for postwar development were radical, but they fitted into a history of British liberty whereby the people themselves had demanded and won freedom. Public education, welfare, fair wages, universal suffrage and the like had only come after intense struggle against groups who enlisted 'inviolable' liberties on their side. In the twentieth century liberty could only exist when people were free from fear and insecurity, free from artificial obstacles to develop their characters and struggle in pursuit of their goals. The modern state should not only safeguard liberty, but it should enrich that basic standard of liberty. Above all the advocates of the new economic order were mindful of the British love of privacy and hostility to regulation and officialdom. Change must conform to these traditions. The challenge was to show that a planned economy and public ownership (or public monopoly as some on the left, including Laski and Bevan, wanted) could co-exist with individual effort.

The war showed that when people co-operated and pulled together they could achieve great things. And a planned state, Harold Laski argued, would be compatible with a free society if certain safeguards were respected. Laski was professor of politics at the London School of Economics, a journalist, the author of widely read Pelican paperbacks and, in the last years of the war, Chairman of the Labour Party. He was an important exponent of liberty in the modern state for the public and, most importantly, for the left. By harnessing the talents of the people, he argued, and calling upon their innate love of privacy and individuality an all-powerful bureaucracy would be placed under scrutiny and kept away from presumptuous authoritarianism. Laski talked of 'the three planes of British historical experience'. These were local self-government, which prevented centralised uniformity; local voluntary institutions, primarily the chapel and charities; and co-operative movements such as the trade unions which encouraged participation. These would be the bulwarks against central authority and the nurseries of active involvement. They would allow people to exercise their ingenuity and inventiveness; they would also protect the idiosyncrasies which were a hallmark of Britishness. By harnessing the latent power of the British people the new state would unlock the individual's potential. By giving them welfare and security against illness and unemployment, it would not be giving the people freedom, but the conditions in which freedom could be enjoyed, conditions which did not thrive when wealth, opportunity and security were unfairly divided.[24]

The ideas represented by Hayek and Laski were motivated by similar assumptions. Both put individuality at the heart of their concept of freedom. Laski envisaged a society and economy worked by individuals making decisions independent of central direction. He argued, like most on the left in Britain, that the citizen must have the courage and legal right to resist authority and that the state should never overwhelm individuals in their daily concerns, including their work. Most of all he believed that uniformity, wherever it came from, was the enemy of freedom. The crucial difference between the two concepts of liberty was not over the role of the state, but over the connection of property and liberty.

Those on the left believed that inequality of property ownership made liberty impossible because it fostered barriers which the individual alone could not overcome. Even Hayek's kind of freedom could not be fulfilled because of artificial hindrances to the free flow of the market. And like all restraints on liberty, the sacredness of private property prevented the individual from developing his or her personality. He or she would be wrapped up in the frustration of thwarted ambition, the painful awareness that life was inherently unfair and shameful feelings of envy for others, hardly the best way to form character. Inequality, and the abiding knowledge that some people automatically prospered and others unjustly remained stagnant, caused those psychological barriers to liberty identified by Evan Durbin. Property represented power – economic, social and political – and an argument which based liberty primarily on property rights was making an excuse for an economic device which constrained the majority. Public ownership would redistribute economic power to wider groups in society. The real issue was over-centralisation. If power was delegated down the scale, liberty would be retained – even enlarged. Collective ownership need not mean central co-ordination of every aspect of life. British socialists did not want to banish one form of power to set up a rival. State power was necessary to protect the individual against the horrors of economic insecurity. But no one should be under any illusions; it would always be dangerous whoever held it.[25]

What is noteworthy about all arguments about the future of society when the war was won is the centrality of liberty and the concern for the individual. The intellectual roots of the left went back not to T. H. Green or Hegel or even (in matters of individual liberty) Marx but to nonconformist religion, urban radicalism and John Stuart Mill. Like Mill British socialists put the development of character at the centre of their concept of liberty, and they were committed to the principle of free discussion as the bedrock of individuality and liberty. Most importantly they were concerned to apply the Millite test to all new proposals. Laski pointed out that interest in liberty in a democracy dwindled except when temporarily awakened by exceptional and extraordinary events:

Tyranny flows easily from the accumulation of petty restrictions. It is important that each should have to prove its undeniable social necessity before it is admitted within the fabric of the law. No conduct should be inhibited unless it can be definitely shown that its practice in a reasonable way can have no other result than to stunt the development of personality. No opportunity should be offered for the exercise of power unless by its application men are released from trammels of which it is the necessary price of purchase.

Social renewal did not come without dangers. Those who desired it the most should be the most vigilant for liberty-denying tendencies on the road to social justice. 'We ought', said Laski, '. . . to be critical of every proposal that asks for a surrender of liberty.'[26]

This was to set a high test for social renovation. And there could be no other way to limit power and meddlesome policies in the modern bureaucratic state than the attitude of citizens. The constitutional and legal mechanisms for liberty had never worked of themselves; 'They depend for their creativeness upon the presence in any given society of a determination to make them work.'[27] The love of liberty must be woven into the fabric of society, and the intolerance of interference or compulsion to conform must run high. Whatever the economic system, it was believed that the British would be able to prize liberty and design institutions to safeguard it in accordance with their historical experience. Hayek argued that a departure from nineteenth-century liberal economic models would lead to serfdom, because the alternatives fostered habits of mind and techniques of control which were incompatible with civil liberties. Just look at Nazi Germany and the impact which state economic control had on all aspects of private life. The liberal left, on the contrary, believed individuality would transcend economic systems of any sort.

What made British freedom so valuable would be the maintenance of historic negative liberties. That was up to the people to defend and augment. Government there would be; its strength and freedom would be proportional to the level of participation, control and scrutiny on the part of active citizens, who would work from the inside for the first time. 'The freedom of our time cannot possibly be an entire freedom from government,' wrote Herman Finer in reply to Hayek, 'it can only be freedom within government.'[28] The idea of complete independence in modern society was fantastical; the question must be how to shape a system in which the individual could find freedom in the midst of the tangled relationships of the twentieth century. What politicians and academics such as Bevan and Laski were clear upon was that liberty could exist within a radically altered economic system as long as the habits of tolerance, discussion, dissent and individual responsibility were continually relearnt and tested in practice. This had only been speculated on before. The 1940s were a time when the problem of combining a powerful, creative state with historic liberty could not have been more urgent. It tested the theoretical questions raised by Mill to the limit. A planned economy and social welfare, the left argued, need not lead to the drudge of regimentation, still less gulags, as long as they were accompanied by laws and habits which protected the individual. The experiences of fighting war, and the task of rebuilding after it, gave the British a unique opportunity to put these ideas into practice.

But there were those who argued that far from involving the people in the war the government had shut them out. Politicians such as Bevan argued that planning had a bad name because it had been guided by Tory authoritarians and had not been ameliorated by democratic socialism. The people had to suffer the very worst of a collective state, with none of the benefits of control or participation. They were stultified by propaganda and restricted by censorship. The most notorious case was the miners. They had been allocated to the pits by ballot, and served their country in that unglamorous way. And, like Kirkwood and the Clydesiders in the First World War, they were conscious that they were working for the profit of the mine owners whilst their union privileges were cancelled. Working in bad conditions for low pay, the so-called 'Bevin Boys' (named after Ernest Bevin, Minister of Labour) were conscripts who had no choice but to accept their lot. Churchill was determined to stave off calls for nationalisation – which would at least have satisfied the Bevin Boys that they were not the slaves of pit owners and wealthy shareholders but contributing to a national endeavour. The Labour ministers in the coalition did not stand up for the miners, whose grievances were growing. The Labour left on the backbenches used the issue to show that they were committed to individual liberty and to put pressure on the leaders of their party. By late 1943 discontent in the mines was brewing, and the government imposed Regulation 1AA, which banned incitement to strike.

'I represent the people at the bottom, the individual men and women,' Nye Bevan told the Commons in a pugnacious speech attacking 1AA, 'and I say that this Regulation is the enfranchisement of the corporate society and the disenfranchisement of the individual.' The regulation effectively banned the expression of dissatisfaction in mines. Bevan attacked the trade union officials who were still allowed to agitate for concessions: they had 'a licence to be free', but they had pledged their loyalty to the government, betraying their obligation to the workers. The regulation had been imposed to stifle the wave of unofficial strikes. Half a million miners walked out. They did so despite official ban, union disapproval, hostile public opinion and a lack of political support from Labour ministers. And they suffered: the government and the press blamed them for delaying D-Day. They were labelled anti-war Trotskyites. Bevan was furious at the slander of half a million working men and teenage boys who had suffered up to five years of low pay, bad conditions and no choice: 'Do we expect men to be lions on the battlefield and sheep at home?' The regulation was offensive because it pointed the finger of blame at the miners, who had a legitimate grievance and who were fiercely pro-war. Bevan also accused the government of deploying 1AA as a way of deflecting accusations that it had mismanaged the mines and mistreated the miners: obviously, as he said with sarcasm, hundreds of thousands of miners had been duped by a handful of Trotskyites or Nazis or whoever and did not have genuine grounds for complaint. It was a government whose instincts were increasingly authoritarian.[29]

The mine dispute went to show that, even in war and even when the weight of public opinion was against them, individuals would resist authority when it became overbearing. The 'corporate society' had many guises; it could be overbearing or benign depending on how it was managed. In the 1945 general election campaign Labour put full employment, national health care and national insurance at the forefront of its campaign. Churchill made a fatal blunder when, in the manner of Hayek, he accused his erstwhile cabinet colleagues of seeking to impose 'Gestapo' methods on the country – the corollary of their economic policies. Churchill had given his backing to the Beveridge proposals; but he assumed that a national government, under his premiership, would regenerate the country in peacetime. But the people were sick of wartime authoritarianism. The mine dispute revealed something like Gestapo tactics where men were treated like sheep and officially banned from muttering complaints;

this had happened under an administration made up of people on the right as much as the left. For years the parliamentary system had been mothballed, not least because the three major parties were locked in the stupefying embrace of coalition. Another parliamentary term of coalition government would have been a continuation of the controls and regimentation of the war, the individual left without the protection of a parliamentary opposition. Labour promised social justice and renewal within a democratic state. The people trusted that socialist government would not impose these benefits by using Gestapo tactics.

Beveridge had said that the new order after the war would be a 'British revolution'. This was not so. The utopia of a planned economy run by decentralised groups of eager participants who gloried in their individuality never happened. Although Clement Attlee's government abandoned wartime restrictions on civil liberty, its instincts were still to govern by regulations in economic matters. It was not partial to independence on the part of workers, and used war regulations to suppress strikes and direct labour. The vague notion bruited about from the left of worker control in the newly nationalised industries was never countenanced, and the unions and their rank-and-file members evinced scant enthusiasm for such an experiment. Their role was to do the work and stand up to managerial heavy-handedness, whether management was private or public.

Conservative MPs throughout the war had always said schemes for economic planning would falter simply because the British people hated jobsworth officials, form-filling and bureaucracy. And there was truth in this. They welcomed the NHS and all the other benefits of social democracy; they were resistant to regimentation and interference, and did not see them as the price to pay for social progress. The New Liberty, consisting of active participation in the country's collective effort of regeneration, did not catch on – partly because there was scant encouragement to do so and mainly because it wasn't in people's natures. Planners of all sorts, and especially in the realm of town planning, did not welcome the input of ordinary people, who preferred homes with private gardens to communally centred blocks of flats, traditional high streets to shopping centres and old-fashioned architecture to utopian designs. Planners were brimming with idealism which had been thwarted in the conservative interwar years; they did not want the humdrum desires of normal people to get in the way of the Brave New World they were creating for normal people. Politicians and administrators likewise preferred to command from the centre rather than delegate responsibility. They were about the important task of rebuilding the country, and private needs and wants should not stand in the way of the overriding priorities of housing, stabilising the economy, getting industry on its feet and feeding the people.[30]

In his book *Austerity Britain* David Kynaston has a wonderfully emblematic instance of this attitude. The government met serious opposition in siting new satellite towns on old market towns and greenfield areas. The people of Stevenage, one such proposed 'new town', put up a fight. The responsible minister, Lewis Silkin, tried to win over a meeting of three thousand residents, explaining that he was embarking upon a bold experiment in modern planning and communal living. To jeers and laughter he said that Stevenage would be world famous. He left the hall to shouts of 'Gestapo' and 'Dictator' to find that the tyres of his car had been let down and the petrol tank filled with sand by the youths of Stevenage. Silkin lost a local referendum but won appeals to the High Court and the House of Lords. 'Silkingrad', as the indigenous people called their soon-to-be-world-renowned town, went ahead. This kind of encounter of the state was common – when ministers considered an overriding need existed local or individual feeling could be steamrolled.[31]

Overall, however, the experience of planning was mixed. Some people felt the sharp end of compulsion as they received planning orders or saw their towns and villages change beyond recognition. But the City got off lightly, as did Oxbridge, the public schools and agriculture. The government could bully in one area and be hesitantly conservative in another. There were to be few bold attempts to revolutionise society. The ideals of Laski et al. in constructing a new theory of freedom were not considered by the Attlee administration. What was readily apparent to everyone, from a resident of Stevenage to a City banker to a middle-class housewife, was that socialism meant controls which crisscrossed society. 'Were there to be no fruits of victory?' asked the editor John Lehmann. 'The rationing cards and coupons that still had to be presented for almost everything from eggs to minute pieces of scraggy Argentine meat, from petrol to bed-linen and "economy" suits, seemed far more squalid and unjust than during the war.' Labour MPs, he said, seemed to take puritanical pleasure in decreeing drab clothes and making austerity a virtue.[32]

It was a land of samey clothes, decrepit buildings, partial pleasures, permits and queues, queues, queues. 'We realised we had become shabby and rather careless of appearances in our battered surround-ings,' wrote Lehmann. 'That we had become crushed as civilians to accept the ordering about of officialdom. That we had become obses-sively queue-forming, and were priggishly proud of it.'[33] Individuality was harder to achieve once choice had been whittled down to a restricted range of rationed clothes and food, a limited choice of mass-produced goods (which made everything and everyone look identical) and a limited cultural life. Harder too when so much time and effort had to go into getting the basics of life – food, shelter, work and warmth.

British writers on liberty from the left had, since Mill, said that the evils of collectivism and planning would be mitigated by encouraging participation and rousing the liberty-loving sentiments of the people. But the war-weary population were more inclined to despise official-dom as a result of daily encounters with the state. They were, as ever, better at resisting than participating. The state and its officials were, at first hand, rationers and controllers, not fast friends. During the war the government had become rather good at propaganda, espe-cially of the kind aimed at educating, warning, nagging and scolding about a host of day-to-day activities. Peace did not halt this desire to monitor and advise.

And the British people did not welcome the idea of co-operating in the collective march towards the New Jerusalem. The war had not given them a taste for solidarity but rather a longing for privacy after years of collective life in barracks, camps, temporary housing and air-raid shelters or working with others on centrally directed projects. Those who fondly imagined that the people would pull together, take a lead in initiating improvement, participate in regeneration, share their pleasures with the neighbours or elevate themselves by listening to the high-minded Third Programme on the BBC and taking adult education courses had misread the British. The devastation of war had made people eager for a return to normality, or what they nostalgically perceived as the normality of the 1930s.

Peacetime reconstruction and the burdens it required were very different from the sacrifices of war and the obligations of service demanded then. People were quite simply bored – bored of drabness, rationing, sub-Churchillian calls for resolve in the face of ever-accumulating sources of danger. For ordinary people liberty meant what it always had – being left alone. It did not mean acting up to the expectations of left-wing intellectuals by embarking upon a journey of citizenship and self-improvement. Ministers and academics expressed disappointment that working people preferred the dog-track, Hollywood films and the pub to the Third Programme, the *Listener* and the meetings of the local council. But why would people give up their rare pleasures when there was so little to gain?

The exhaustion and poverty of postwar Britain did not make for a revolutionary atmosphere. It was a time of limited ambition, apathy and conservatism. These were also years of fear and insecurity, which are the enemies of experimental liberty. It made people happy to conform to prevailing expectations of morality and behaviour, grateful for small benefits. The late 1940s and 50s were hardly times of bold experiments in living. When that did happen, in the 1960s, the social revolution was not accompanied by a political revolution. By then the hunger for a new politics awoken during the war had lapsed. Two revolutions – or attempted revolutions – which did not click together.

In the First and Second World Wars the British state had been ruthless in planning, co-ordinating, marshalling and directing its resources; also in feeding, healing, housing, informing and educating its population – far better than its totalitarian enemies or democratic allies. It was capable of great things when its back was to the wall. But this very success left a deep and abiding distaste for the corporate state precisely because it was so uncompromisingly efficient. People could see how good the country was at collective action. But they were clever and/or cynical enough to perceive that it did not enrich life; that the state had gone as far as it could. To expect more when the state had already exerted its utmost energies was, clearly to most people, a hope too far.

At the same time war aroused hopes of a new future, when the heaped-up abuses of ages could be swept away. But then war left the population exhausted, depressed and suspicious of bureaucracy. The least unpropitious time for social and political reforms in Britain coincided with despondency. The people welcomed the NHS, universal education, welfare provisions, nationalisation of key industries and other postwar boons; they just did not get idealistic about it.

In accordance with the British historical experience a sort of compromise had been forged. Economic life could not be said to be laissez-faire, but nor was it fully planned. State efforts to make people better and give them 'positive liberty' to realise their talents were only ever indirectly attempted; the old tradition of 'negative liberty' and 'mind your own business' remained the predominating sentiment. Britain was marked by traces of all these traditions and forms of liberty, none of them predominating. This was at once a strength – even Labour radicals were afraid of invading the accustomed liberties of the people – but also a cause of timidity. There would be no British Declaration of Rights for the mid-twentieth century. But then there would be no British Big Brother. The benefits delivered by the Labour government of 1945–51 were just that – benefits. The reference to liberty was more a limiting factor than an ideal to be pursued for the good of individuals.

Instead government shouldered the burden of planning and control. And it did so by delegated legislation. That which had been a temporary expedient to cope with emergencies had become a regular part of government. Government had increasingly become a matter of crisis management, which was to be resolved at the centre, be it war of defence, war on alien economic forces or war on unemployment. Parliament had delegated legislation in the 1920s and 30s, at first happily unaware of the constitutional implications; the war revealed how limited were the parliamentary safeguards; and the postwar period showed that government by way of secondary legislation was a permanent feature. The Cold War and the acceptance by the Labour and Conservative administrations that they were responsible for the commanding heights of the economy meant that these mechanisms were kept in place. As a writer on the constitution noted in 1957:

Given a continuance of an unstable world order, a precarious domestic economic situation, and continual demands for Government action in the realm of social and economic welfare, it is difficult to foresee much of a departure from the 'exceptional' type of matters of principle and a generally broad discretion left to the executive.[34]

The world had changed, and Whiggish liberty and parliamentary procedures were out of date. The state had necessarily expanded; but new formal constitutional procedures had not kept pace with the revolution in governance. The citizen was left with fewer safeguards. In 1955 the Labour MP Richard Crossman wrote that the cause of liberty, and the traditional radical/Whig/libertarian instinct to limit arbitrary power, had not kept up with 'the Leviathan that now dominates our lives' – which had been built up by Labour and the Conservatives, grabbing power by Orders in Council, cabinet dictatorship and, after 1945, unprecedented control over the economy and industry.[35]

It was little wonder that ideas of liberty dropped away from political discussion. They were replaced with social justice, choice and a kind of contractual relationship between state and citizen. Decades of war and emergencies of one sort or another had been accompanied by idealism and hopes that destruction would be followed by revolutionary change. They were also accompanied by anomie. It was clear that the assumptions of the liberal phase of British history were shaken beyond repair. Through these years of pain and suffering liberty had lost its magic. If in the past liberals had made distinctions between interference by the state and individual liberty this was harder in the twentieth century. No one but a handful resisted the welfare state, the NHS and nationalisation on the grounds of liberty, but welcomed them as solutions to real problems.

Governments were restrained by what they judged to be the prevailing standard of liberty which existed in the mood of the press and public opinion, but it would be truer to talk of *liberties* than *liberty* in the modern world. There was no standard which ran through all levels of government, but rather a sliding scale. An emergency might require an indefinite and unspecified sacrifice of liberty; if your land obstructed a housing development, a road, a hospital or a leisure centre it might be purchased compulsorily; parliamentary procedures might be gradually altered from the historical standard; bureaucrats could enforce rules and require permits; the autonomy of those engaged in providing public services might fall victim to onerous central control; a private business was subject to health and safety regulations, government set controls and other bits and pieces of legislation. And so on. Any one liberty might fall to the needs of the state or the community. Or you might be allowed to continue in your own way, independent of external intervention. The degree of compulsion on one side, and liberty on the other, depended upon the gravity of the situation and the implication for the community. There was no rule. Instead there was a tacit agreement on what was and what was not permissible, a vague consensus which could change over time. In some areas of life there was considerable freedom; in others you might be subject to controls, permits and management.

When society engaged in self-examination various freedoms could be ticked off: fair and free elections, the rule of law, an independent judiciary, a free press and so on. That there could be crosses against other boxes – greater state surveillance, the growth of officialdom, top-down governmental control through ministerial powers and delegated legislation, compulsory purchase orders, censorship of the stage and so on – was not considered by political scientists and public opinion, as it was in previous generations, to be a denial of general liberty, but simply a feature of all modern societies. In the twentieth century wars and emergencies combined with the greater complexity of life had made the lines that separated liberty and authority harder to distinguish, if not impossible. The state was no longer regarded as a friend *or* an enemy, but a friend *and* an enemy. What was left was a general sense of liberty, something which existed in minds as the historic condition of Britain, the norm; something which might be infringed upon in the pursuit of benefits but with which governments meddled at their peril.

The idealism that had accompanied theories of liberty drained away, even from the polemics of intellectuals and politicians. The government was to guarantee economic prosperity, and the people were to make the best of the resulting wealth in their own way: that was modern liberty, a world of refrigerators, cars and televisions; a world of choice within the 'affluent society' backed by the safety net of welfare and the provision of basic services. And to be honest, people in the age of austerity wanted their small luxuries more than they felt a desire to participate in the management of their factory, have a say in the planning of their town or attend an improving lecture. 'Responsibility is an acquired taste', wrote Crossman, 'and the majority will always be far more concerned with material benefits and social security – at least until, in some particular case, their own personal freedom is threatened.' He wanted Labour to reconnect with its radical roots, and politicians to design new constitutional ways in which the individual could be protected against an expanding state.[36]

It did not catch on as a party or a popular cause. What people now had was the confidence to plan their own lives, take risks, enjoy goods and services which had previously been considered impossible luxuries, and rise up the social scale as never before. By the mid-point of the 1950s productivity exceeded pre-war levels, and this had been done despite maintaining full employment and economic security. A free capitalist society survived the devastation of the twentieth century precisely because the state had stepped in to guarantee health, education and welfare, to provide the foundations for economic recovery which the free market, on its own, would never have been able to achieve.

VI

THE TWILIGHT WORLD

1914–1951

CHAPTER 11

Playing by the Rules

—⁂—

It is the nature of power to be ever encroaching, and converting every extraordinary power, granted at particular times, and upon particular occasions, into an ordinary power, to be used at all times.

TRENCHARD AND GORDON, 'CATO'S LETTERS',
9 FEBRUARY 1723

Once lead this people into war, and they'll forget there ever was such a thing as tolerance. To fight, you must be brutal and ruthless, and the spirit of ruthless brutality will enter into the very fibre of our national life, infecting Congress, the courts, the policeman on the beat, the man on the street . . .

WOODROW WILSON[1]

Governments in the twentieth century faced a bleak prospect. Confronted by the challenges of total war, economic disaster and a precarious world order British governments felt that not only did they have to go against their instincts by mobilising the resources of the nation, but they had also to mobilise public opinion and sacrifice normal civilian legal protection. The desire for uniformity in production was mirrored by a desire for unity in opinion. And the longing for security and order came at a high price for normal civilian rights. In 1914 and 1939 accustomed liberties were surrendered by panicked parliaments with extraordinary speed. And it was an experience not confined to wartime. There was a sense that nothing was normal any more; modern democracies had to keep adapting themselves in response to succeeding threats.

Modern war, in Harold Laski's words, led to a 'twilight world' in which secrecy and censorship, preventative justice and restrictive laws, fear and insecurity trapped governments and citizens in a situation where injustice and blunders became inevitable.[2] The world took a step away from freedom and democracy in these decades. In Britain and America commitment to these ran deep, far deeper than in countries where these were recent developments. But even in Britain the tide was running in one direction. Respect for liberty and belief in democracy wore thin. Sacrifices had to be made to protect even a glimmer of freedom and defend the constitution from annihilation; successive governments had to make this decision with varying degrees of success. What was clear in these years was that the ideal of liberty had been tarnished by its repeated suspension. The fear was that a desire for order in a dangerous world would sap instincts of liberty and justice on the part of the people.

What these years provided was a lesson in why civil liberties had come into being in the first place: the abuses committed in wartime and in moments of national panic had the effect of reawakening a commitment to traditional liberty. They also demonstrate harder truths, not least the melancholy inevitability that expedients intended to meet an immediate and specific crisis drift into normal administrative procedure. 'In Germany democracy died by the headman's axe,' Nye Bevan wrote at the start of the Second World War. 'In Britain it can be by pernicious anaemia.'[3] The 'world of twilight' is a situation which repeats itself in human history. Britain's experience of it between 1914 and 1945 is a stark vision of what happens when civil liberties are disregarded.

Herbert Asquith's government was preoccupied with several immediate problems in August 1914, as we have seen. Not the least was that after a century of peace the British state, unlike continental countries which had experienced war, invasion and revolution, had no mechanism for dealing with a modern crisis. Legal decisions that went back to the seventeenth century stressed that the executive could not use the plea of necessity to abrogate a citizen's rights or dispense with laws; if it did, it would be accountable in the ordinary courts. The common law remained in force even in war. The sovereign might proclaim martial law, setting up special courts and delegating discretionary authority to officials, but this could only happen in a state of actual war or rebellion on British soil. If the courts could function, then martial law could not be applied.[4]

It was a set of laws appropriate to ages when wars were decided by great battles and to an island defended from incursion by the sea and the Royal Navy. If the law in peacetime punishes after an offence has been proved, DORA reversed this assumption. It was preventative in character. In three major areas the government used the act to eliminate dangers *before* they could endanger the life of the nation. First there was a danger that 'aliens of hostile origin' or nationals of 'hostile association' might spy or commit acts of sabotage. Orders in Council gave the government the right to hold, without trial and without the right of habeas corpus, those whom the Home Secretary considered to be a risk to national security. The consolidated DORA of November 1914, which permitted the military to try and execute civilians, was considered a necessary measure because the speedy operation of martial law was unavailable until the German hordes mastered the Channel and swept across the South Downs.

The government claimed that the common law did not take account of modern war. Small bands of spies and saboteurs, whether German or British-born, could wreak havoc on the nation's infrastructure without a state of outright, conventional war existing. DORA was intended to act as a deterrent to underground enemies and disloyal British subjects who knew that they could no longer rely upon the cumbersome machinery of justice, with its prohibition of general warrants, limited powers of arrest, inconvenient rules of evidence, juries, appeals procedure and so on. But it was also a mechanism for dealing with ordinary Britons who offended against the regulations, however petty they might be – and, as we shall see, many were very petty.[5]

Another immediate danger was that the freedom of the press threatened the war effort on three fronts. First, skilled reportage from Fleet Street's finest might impress readers, but such investigative derring-do would also feed the Kaiser's High Command with useful information. Second, the traditional freedom of opinion enjoyed by the fourth estate could prejudice conscription if young males read about the horrors of the trenches or followed a skilled polemicist who artfully exposed the futility of war. And third, unrestrained rights of comment provided the enemy with juicy propaganda and frustrated British diplomacy. Regulations made under DORA reversed all the achievements of eighteenth- and nineteenth-century journalists, making it a crime to spread reports that might cause alarm (even if they were true), might help the enemy (even if it was in the public's interest to hear them) or might undermine the recruitment effort (that is to say, almost any fact or opinion that was uncongenial to the military). The legal protection given to a peacetime press was seen as a potential danger to a nation struggling for its survival. Any newspaper or publisher could be raided and suppressed at a moment's notice by the fiat of the Home Secretary. And thanks to the wording of the regulations – particularly the liberal use of the word *might* – the powers were left deliberately vague so that the government could stop the presses on any pretext.

Within months of the beginning of hostilities DORA spread her tentacles to embrace with loving intensity every aspect of British life. 'The civilian's duty in time of war', it was written, 'was a fluctuating code of negative rather than positive injunctions.'[6] If the citizen was prohibited from doing things which were perfectly legal in times of peace, the government was given positive powers to carry tasks that would have been ridiculous prior to 1914. DORA was felt most by businessmen, pacifists, journalists and workers in war industries, but the regulations touched every aspect of daily life. Where and when you might get a pint of beer was placed under strict limitation. A dance could be broken up or forbidden by the military. It was illegal to feed wild animals (because it wasted food) and to fly a kite (in case it attracted Zeppelins). The laws protecting birds of prey were suspended in order to protect carrier pigeons. How you earned, saved and spent your money was a matter directed from above. Your land could be requisitioned or your house commandeered as a billet. The nature and even location of your job would come under central control.

Most in the country believed that the government was right to do everything it needed to win the war. Patriotism rode high, as did suspicion of defeatism or disloyalty. MPs granted every power the government asked for and gave it great latitude in the exercise of those powers, and the public felt that the sacrifice was worthwhile. It was the sheer scale of the war that contributed to this support. There was a widespread fear in the early period of the war that the German army would soon be mounting an invasion of British shores. But what played on people's minds most was a sense of inferiority to Germany. The enemy's industrial and military machine had been perfected over years; compared to free Britain, it was believed, the Germans were ruthlessly disciplined and meticulously prepared for the new conditions of total war. Pre-war freedom, in hindsight, seemed like a fool's paradise. New rules applied in this fight for national survival. Those who pleaded for civil liberties were branded 'sentimental' at best, or, as one MP said, 'If anything is done either here [in parliament] or in the country [including the courts] which prevents the government taking the steps necessary to carry the War to a successful conclusion, that action is the action of traitors.'[7]

But the reaction against the full implications of dictatorial power came soon. A group in the House of Lords threatened to derail the Defence of the Realm (Consolidation) Bill in November 1914 by introducing an amendment guaranteeing full civil trials for British citizens who offended against the regulations. Early the next year the government capitulated and restored jury trials. In the Commons many MPs were shocked that the government should deliberately weaken itself, and lashed out at those who indulged in 'general heroics about the liberty of the subject' at a time of peril. Other members were humiliated that British liberties were salvaged thanks to a bunch of crusty old peers and no thanks to a supine and panicky House of Commons. The government amended DORA, allowing jury trials but crucially reserving the right to restrict them by decree if ministers felt it was necessary. It was at once a victory for defenders of liberty and a terrible reminder that any minor concession was the gift of the executive – a gift that could be recalled at will. After seven months of war, parliament had at last woken to the fact that it had surrendered all its powers and all MPs could raise in defence of the rights of the people was a feeble whimper.[8]

It took something as catastrophic as the First World War to show the interconnectedness of civil, economic and political liberties. Fighting total war, the government came to see how interwoven were all aspects of British life. The complete mobilisation of every national resource – mental and physical – called upon new rules. In every case the liberty of the individual was secondary to the needs of the collective whole. For example freedom of speech had a bearing on the economic war. By the last year of the war over two million men and women were engaged one way or another in producing munitions. Soldiers have always been protected from dangerous propaganda, but the new industrial army should be treated no differently. Indeed, servicemen on leave – who had a sense of comradeship with the ordinary soldiers in the opposing trenches – were amazed at civilians' murderous hatred of the raping, pillaging, savage 'Huns'. This spirit was fostered because, it was believed, more anger equalled more shells.

The press went along with this partly because it considered itself part of the war effort, and because it laboured under fear of government reprisals and the lash of public opinion. Dissenting voices were not welcome. In 1916, a panicky general prevented Bertrand Russell from lecturing on 'Social Reconstruction' in protected industrial areas lest his philosophical opinions and gentle pacifism drain angry passions and bring a stop to war work.[9] It was a high-profile case, but there were daily examples of vindictive action against expressions of opinion in factories and workshops. One worker was arrested when he allegedly called the army 'scum' and said 'he would rather be ruled by a dog than by the King' in the Bradford workshop where he was employed. He denied it but was sentenced to two months' hard labour for prejudicing recruiting, although two of his colleagues subsequently enlisted.[10]

The government's attitude was that fighting a major war was particularly hard for a free country. Sir John Simon, Attorney General at the beginning of the war, and later Home Secretary, encapsulated this view: 'We shall be forgiven by posterity if the steps we take are more than adequate, but we shall never be forgiven if the steps we are taking are not sufficient.'[11] Conscious of the depth of the passion for liberty, the government clearly felt that it had to overcompensate if it was to win. That explains the draconian attitude to the press and the feeling that the people could not be trusted to hear adverse criticism. It also explains its concern to maintain a high level of discipline.[12]

Contemporaries would judge that Lloyd George's pared-down, ruthless war cabinet and its administrative energy broke the lethargy and pushed the country to victory. Much of the anxiety that had preoccupied people was simply forgotten. At the time, and after, the attitude was that no price was too high to pay for victory. But the problem which parliament wrestled with and could not resolve was to find a course that reconciled liberty, security and national efficiency.

Some would have liked to separate matters of civil liberty and industrial rights from broader issues of national security. In practice the sad truth was that this was impossible. In the case of David Kirkwood civil liberty, labour rights and freedom of speech collided with national security and national efficiency. In more extreme cases the country discovered that there was no limit to what the government could do. The Home Secretary took the power to intern without trial people he considered to be a threat to national security. Some legal experts assumed that the emergency powers the executive had taken ran the risk of being struck down by the courts as *ultra vires*. That is to say, they would be found to be incompatible with constitutional principle. But the courts did not reach that interpretation; legal decisions stated that the government was entitled to do anything within the limits of the powers that parliament had given to it. As DORA stipulated that everything necessary should be done to defend the nation and win the war, the powers were unchallengeable unless parliament repealed the act. Those who argued that they were being imprisoned contrary to a constitutional principle of liberty were brushed away. The courts of appeal were reluctant to subject DORA to judicial scrutiny, lest loopholes start to appear which would weaken the war effort.

Some MPs complained that parliament had never intended that DORA would entail de facto suspension of habeas corpus. Under regulation 14b the Home Secretary could arrest and hold a suspect indefinitely without trial. The only right of appeal an internee could have was to an advisory committee appointed by the Home Secretary. There could be nothing more contrary to the deepest notions of British liberty. It made the Secretary of State prosecutor, judge and jury in his own cause. It removed all the safeguards that had been built into the system through years of experience. Was this a violation of a fundamental principle? MPs asked whether internees could be tried in front of independent judges, in camera if necessary. These brooding issues became the focus of a debate in March 1916, when the whole nature of civil liberty in wartime came under serious discussion.

The Home Secretary, Herbert Samuel, told the house that sixty-nine people of hostile origin or association were being held. Of these eight were British-born subjects, most of whom were born in Britain to German parents and a few who were born of British parents but had connections with German spies. None of these people could be tried for treason or espionage in the ordinary way, because, it was candidly admitted, there was not enough evidence to satisfy a court. The government was faced with a dilemma. It could either suspend habeas corpus completely, as governments had done in the last comparable crisis (between the 1790s and the 1810s); it could declare martial law and try whoever it liked by secret military tribunal; or it could wait until each of the sixty-nine suspects committed a crime. But the government approached the matter in a new way. Regulation 14b was a preventative measure, necessary because the kind of crimes that the suspects might commit were of such gravity that the state itself might be in danger. To involve the courts would be a further assault on liberties. It would compromise the independent judiciary because the Home Secretary would have to ask judges to sit in private and evaluate secret information that would not satisfy an ordinary court. It would draw them into the realm of policy, not justice.

The Home Secretary had to make a policy decision about protecting the public. And this was necessary, he said, to preserve liberty in the long term. By acting under DORA regulations, it remained clear that this was a wartime measure. To drag the courts in would be to enshrine the decision in law. This would have long-term implications. The decision to intern a citizen must be an executive one made under emergency powers. The decision to punish must be a legal one made in court and based on strict interpretation of evidence. The distinction between prevention and punishment was a crucial one to maintain: the former was for the unforeseeable exigencies of war only; the latter was eternal and based on strict rules designed for moments of calm and reflection. When the emergency ended, the Home Secretary's powers lapsed. Unless the fact that this *was* temporary was kept firmly in mind there was a danger that courts could be used to rubberstamp executive decisions. Judges must not be made responsible for assessing the unknowable quantities of risk, something only a cabinet minister, armed with reports from MI5 and mindful of the overall war situation, should do. Were the courts asked to judge whether one of the sixty-nine suspects was a threat to the public, the judges would have to balance national security with natural justice. If they came down on the side of national security, which any reasonable person would in time of peril, they would be ruling unjustly, albeit for good motives. This was intolerable. If the Home Secretary made a mistake or acted beyond his powers he should be judged politically, on the floor of the house and in the press.[13]

No one pretended this was satisfactory. No one claimed that injustice would not be done. Voices of liberty were silenced in the face of compelling reasons. An extraordinary situation required extraordinary measures unless the whole of English law was to be permanently changed. However, another problem lurked behind this. For lesser threats to national security, the courts *were* asked to exercise discretion and act under the regulations decreed by DORA. This meant that every JP and policeman in the country was dragged into the business of defending the realm. Some responded with somewhat indecent enthusiasm. Many such men, who had sons and friends serving on the front line, were little inclined to defend the constitutional rights of pacifists, conscientious objectors, Quakers, suffragettes, shop stewards or socialists.

The trial in camera of an elderly travelling salesman for words said in a railway carriage which were likely to prejudice recruiting was an example of hysteria; what state secret could he possibly have divulged which would have halted the war effort?[14] A man who, observing military exercises in Hyde Park, remarked that the horses were treated better than the men spent six months in prison as a result.[15] Secret trials in such footling cases were worryingly common. The editor and publishers of the *Labour Leader* were prosecuted in camera for saying that Britain shared responsibility for the war and criticising the government's policies. *The Times* and *Daily Mail* got away with saying similar things and worse – Asquith's government was brought down thanks to the unrestrained criticism of respectable Fleet Street. Even if the prosecution of the *Labour Leader* served some national interest, the authoritarian actions of the magistracy made it seem politically motivated. Indeed, rights were placed in the hands of the military and local judiciary, people most likely to see political dissent as treacherous.[16]

The Military Service Act of 1916 did the unthinkable for liberals and individualists by introducing conscription for the first time. It was another sacrifice of liberty in the interests of victory. A clause of the act exempted genuine conscientious objectors from conscription. These objectors faced the opprobrium of public opinion and the insults of military tribunals who were eager to dismiss pleas for exemption as bogus. Many saw the exemption clause as an extravagant loophole nonetheless. Magistrates cracked down on pamphlets written by conscientious objectors, believing that they were actively trying to encourage young men to 'acquire a conscience' they did not have before. The charge against the small groups of conscientious objectors was that, in cahoots with Berlin, they would convert men en masse to their way of thinking.[17]

It was farfetched to say the least. That these principles could be manufactured overnight to a degree that would win over a sceptical tribunal was, in the circumstances, ludicrous. But it did not stop widespread persecution of those who were suspected of dissentient opinions. A regulation of 1917 allowed the police to search premises without a warrant and use unpublished notes as evidence in a prosecution.

(It was a regulation clearly written to bypass the onerous restrictions on executive action imposed by *Entick* v. *Carrington*.) A man was tried for handwriting an essay on Tolstoy and pacifism for his personal enjoyment.[18]

Some magistrates were enthusiastic suppressors. In one area a pamphlet written before the war urging women to campaign for baby clinics was banned because it supposedly sapped national unity by inciting political protest. In Northampton two ladies were fined £50 for distributing leaflets of dangerous tendency: the literature consisted of reprints of an article by Sydney Smith written in 1813, a speech made by Cobden in the Commons in 1854 and an extract from a book called *Liberalism* published in 1902 – the dangerous pacifist author in this case being none other than Herbert Samuel, Home Secretary. Some Conservative JPs began to threaten or punish their local socialist opponents. There were instances where a magistrate in one part of the country, sitting in camera, would ban a pamphlet or paper while another magistrate elsewhere would sanction it. Shielded by emergency powers, the police acted with considerable brutality against political protesters. And so the catalogue of suppression went on.[19]

After the Russian Revolution, the government became convinced that something similar would happen in Britain unless action was taken against pamphleteers. Regulation 27c was made so that all new publications had to be submitted to the official censor – the first time this had happened since 1694. At the same time police raids against pacifists, the left and even the National Council of Civil Liberties increased. In the Commons Ramsay MacDonald had nothing but contempt for Lloyd George's attempts to shape the nation into a war-winning machine:

That at the beginning of the twentieth century a British government should imagine that it is going to suppress opinion, and that it is going to keep together the semblance of a united nation by the force of the policeman and the judge, is such an absurd thing that if it were not so serious one would meet it with a loud guffaw.[20]

This, not the legally controversial issue of internees, is the true heart of DORA. The longer the war went on, the more inclined the government and its supporters were to identify the interests of the state with the interests of the men in power. Led from the very top, the respect for liberty (supposedly the epitome of the national character, after all) fell to a low ebb. It was a question of attitude – liberty could only depend on the commitment of politicians, magistrates and the public. As it was, it became a minority pursuit. In the Upper House, Lord Desart said that the government could ask for 'literally any powers' and they would be granted. Many MPs in the other place agreed wholeheartedly.[21] It was a dangerous attitude to hold in a democracy.

At the beginning of the war Lord Parmoor said that in the strains and fears of war it was incumbent more than ever upon men in positions of responsibility to protect the unpopular minority from the storms of public opinion.[22] This duty had not been fulfilled. Despite repeated pleas from the Lords and the Commons that men in high office keep a close eye on their subordinates the situation got worse.[23] 'What can we say during the war?' Ramsay MacDonald asked. What guarantee was there that if he wrote a pamphlet critical of the cabinet 'I am not going to get a court which will try me in such a way that I shall get a real, legal, decision from a constitutionally minded man who is not mixed up in the passions, fears, hates, and hopes which are so prevalent at the present moment?' The chance was small, when politically motivated magistrates doled out summary justice without the right of appeal to a more sober tribunal.[24]

Most of Fleet Street got off lightly, partly due to their self-restraint and partly because the government was selective in the fights it picked. The *Mail*, *Times*, *Post*, *Express* and other venerable organs were generally left alone. There were exceptions. The *Globe* was banned for two weeks in 1915 when it claimed that Lord Kitchener, Secretary of State for War, had offered his resignation to the king.[25] In 1917 the *Nation*'s foreign edition was banned when it reported that a German retreat had been tactically sensible and had taken the British General Staff by surprise.[26] Such high-profile acts of censorship were authorised by the four Home Secretaries of the war, who personally risked the ire of Fleet Street and had to face an angry house. The suppression of provincial pamphleteers, however, was not subject to this kind of political control. The Home Office did not direct censorship at a lower level, but left it to its minions. The result was bullying and intimidation throughout the country, away from the glare of publicity.

No one denied that restraints were necessary at the height of war, but no effort was made to distinguish between words that would hinder the prosecution of the war and words that might have a distant tendency to do so. The government put morale at the centre of the war effort, and in doing so overestimated the power of words on the fortunes of war. The tendency was to assume that hostile opinion would contribute to retarding the war effort and drawing workers and soldiers from their duty. And any criticism of war policies by the British press would be read abroad and would whip up the German people into a fever of national rejoicing and war-winning energy. Ministers came to believe that any kind of criticism of them, even in a political capacity, was an act of disloyalty and defeatism. 'It is the cheapest kind of argument,' Winston Churchill said in one of the brief intervals he was out of the office, 'and, pushed to its logical extreme, it would lead to a universal harmonious chorus of adulation from morning to night until some frightful disaster took place.'[27]

The governments of Asquith and Lloyd George made a mistake common to politicians in this situation. They began to accept one version of the truth and to doubt the people's capacity to hear anything else without losing their sense of duty. It took a voice as powerful as Woodrow Wilson's to criticise the Allies' war aims with any effect (in his Fourteen Points). And monotone war propaganda led the peoples of the victorious nations to demand vicious sanctions against Germany in 1919 without any reflection: they had heard one voice urging them to fight for so long, the voice of hatred and vengeance. When Charles Trevelyan tried to give a lecture on 'A People's Peace' he was suppressed by the magistracy for attempting to infect the people with such milksop attitudes towards the reckoning of victory.[28] The catalogue of follies of the authorities in the war was an object lesson in why liberties existed in the first place. Hysteria, fear and a lapse into an isolated, official mindset set the struggle for liberties back for decades. Habits of liberty were dulled;

intolerance and bossiness increased; and, when it was illegal to even discuss the military situation in public, the citizen's duty to highlight abuses and express dissent in order to warn governments of potential dangers was not just discouraged but made to seem immoral.

The message was that the more liberties were curtailed, the safer the country would be. It was a dangerous lesson to teach. It was this contempt for traditional freedom which echoed down Whitehall to the subordinate officers of state, people less constrained by living in the political limelight or by a sense of propriety. As one advocate of freedom put it, the government had used every effort to distort news for 'a people of traditionally tough and notoriously cross-grained temper, a people who flourish on contradiction and opposition'. What was obvious, however, was that in the face of danger all these sacred principles vanished instantly; it was a salutary lesson.[29]

And they were avoidable follies; a look at history would have shown the futility of censoring opinion, the discredit it brings on governments and the fatal effects of treating the public like particularly dim children. In sweeping away the restraints built up over centuries of experience the cabinets of Asquith and Lloyd George made mistakes which were entirely predictable. They made themselves look vindictive and unduly nervous; they relegated the people to passive spectators with little choice but to cheer, even when in their hearts they despised what they saw. They forgot that to silence others is to stop one's own ears.

Many people wondered why so much attention was paid to conscientious objectors when their sons were dying in the trenches. In the catalogue of horrors of 1914–18 two elderly ladies unfairly fined £50 in Northampton rate pretty low. The feeling that something greater was at stake tended to relegate these concerns. But there were still those who believed that principles fundamental to the constitution were being eroded. Some MPs said that the climate of fear and secrecy was putting people off the war, people who had been taught that the war was in defence of liberty. 'We have got to protect frontiers at home,' said one, 'so that men when they come back from the war shall return to an England which is not worse than that which they left.'[30]

But just as the state got the taste of managing swathes of economic affairs, it also developed nasty habits of authoritarianism. It was as if the spell had been broken; all those taboos which had stayed the executive's hand in the nineteenth century had been transgressed, and, having broken the fundamental (unwritten) laws of constitutional propriety no deviation from principle would ever seem so bad. The country *had* changed during the war. Not least was the feeling that the government was entitled to override the law when it felt that circumstances demanded. It was a profound shift.

Armistice might have been signed on 11 November 1918, but in a legal sense the war continued until 1921. This allowed the government to keep in place wartime regulations. It believed that it had to manage the transition to peace. In practice old habits died hard. A postwar boom quickly burst, to be replaced by inflation and mass unemployment. Glasgow, which had bristled with armaments factories and shipyards during the war, suffered considerably when the demand for munitions dried up. David Kirkwood was arrested in 1919 for inciting violence among unemployed engineers on the Clyde. In reality he had been trying to pacify an angry crowd, but the bench was more inclined to believe the hostile police witnesses until a photograph was offered in evidence showing a submissive Kirkwood being batoned by policemen.[31]

The threat to the country was now considered to be industrial unrest and, stalking behind it, communist revolution. Special Branch and MI5, both healthily fattened thanks to their war work, transferred their attention from German spies, pacifists and other internal enemies to the Communist Party of Great Britain. It was not until the General Strike of 1926 that the country saw the extent of the government's peacetime powers. In 1921 Lloyd George's coalition government had introduced the Emergency Powers Bill, which allowed the king to proclaim a state of emergency in peacetime and make such regulations needed to supply the essentials of life and, controversially, to 'preserve the peace' of the nation.[32] Most MPs agreed that the government needed predefined powers to meet a threat to the life of the nation. The supply of essentials was well and good, but 'the preservation of peace' affected civil liberties. It gave governments in the future unlimited powers to restore what they, and they alone, deemed to be the public peace. It sanctioned any number of measures, including the suppression of opinion or the detention of political opponents. It was passed over a few days when a coal strike was brewing and many MPs thought that the government was once again blackmailing them into a surrender of powers. They managed to get several concessions, most importantly that regulations made by virtue of a state of emergency would be valid for only seven days unless parliament met and agreed to them. After that they could only continue in force for one month, at the end of which time parliament would have the chance to debate whether a state of emergency still existed and whether any of the regulations should be annulled.

By giving in the government was reassuring critics who said that since the war the government had acquired the taste for ruling 'swiftly and expeditiously' by issuing Orders in Council, thus bypassing such longwinded institutions as parliament and the common law.[33] Under the amended bill parliament retained control in an emergency. It was a crucial safeguard, but if the government of the day had a large majority it could wield extreme powers without serious challenge. The Conservative William Joynson-Hicks said that 'this Bill in effect rivets for all time [the] provisions of the Defence of the Realm regulations on this country'.[34]

At the end of April 1926 the TUC called out all its members – forty per cent of the workforce – in a General Strike, to put pressure on the government which had withdrawn its subsidy from the coal industry. MI5 had intelligence that such a move on the part of the unions would be a prelude for revolution. For a year the government had been planning to combat this threat, building up a civilian defence force and influencing middle-class public opinion with scare stories about communist activities. Revolutionaries stalked the land, the press hinted darkly, and had infiltrated the army. Russia was brewing discord. David Kirkwood (now a Labour MP) and his fellow Red Clydeside MPs were planning to capture parliament and proclaim a soviet.[35] And so on – a stream of misleading or preposterous stories. In December leading members of the Communist Party were tried and found guilty of the long-forgotten crime of sedition, thus ensuring that when the crunch came Russia's puppets would be behind bars.[36]

So in the spring of 1926 the government had a strategy to deal with a general strike, a large parliamentary majority, a panicky middle England and, crucially, the political will to crush any threat to the state. And this is how they saw the crisis – the hawks in the cabinet believed it to be a serious constitutional issue in which the unions were trying to dictate terms to parliament. The government had to win and win completely. They had, deliberately or not, misread the situation. Few of the union leaders had any intention of foisting socialism on the country, let alone proclaiming a communist state. Moreover, the unions were disorganised, divisive and timid. That did not put off Baldwin's ministers. Months of fearmongering about a communist uprising, sedition trials and rumblings from the Conservative backbenches had done their work. Public opinion was ready for a showdown. Many in the middle class were in the mood of 1914; this was a time to pull together and confront another challenge to the British way of life. Businessmen, shopkeepers and undergraduates gleefully enrolled as special constables and armed themselves with batons, or, in some cases, old service revolvers and cavalry swords. Whatever the political sympathies, there was a realisation that normality was suspended.

There was a feeling in some quarters that no measure was too strong to combat a threat to the constitution, even if those measures were in themselves unconstitutional. It was a mark of how far things had changed. In the event the General Strike itself was short-lived. After eight days the strikers were demoralised, conscious that most of the country would not tolerate paralysis of normal life. The government was ruthless in maintaining supplies and defending blacklegs with police and troops. The ports were guarded with warships, food convoys were escorted by troops, tanks trundled down the streets of London and middle-class volunteers rallied to the government. Unlike the TUC, the government was meticulously organised and armed to the teeth. The General Strike came to an abrupt end. Only the miners remained out.

All parties in parliament agreed that the government was right to use emergency powers to prevent chaos and maintain the supply of essentials. Conservative backbenchers and most of the cabinet were happy to see the government take literally any measure to stamp out the revolutionary menace. More sober voices pointed out that the regulations made under the Emergency Powers Act were perhaps unconstitutional and certainly very far from the spirit of English law. Lloyd George, the grand master of emergency authority, warned the government that the powers they now had were dictatorial; the only practical limit was 'the spirit and way in which they were carried out'. A declaration of emergency opened up a chasm in the British constitution; it meant the existence of arbitrary government and executive lawlessness for a time determined by men in power. It was incumbent upon the Home Secretary to act with discretion and accept a self-denying ordinance to act in a non-partisan manner.[37]

The Home Secretary in 1926 was Sir William Joynson-Hicks, known to his colleagues as 'Jix' or 'Mussolini-Minor'. He looked like an avuncular Anglican gentleman from a novel by Dickens, with a frock coat, high collar and cravat.[38] But when in power he was an old-fashioned authoritarian Tory who was determined to stamp out communism, hardly the self-restrained Cincinnatus-like Home Secretary of Lloyd George's imagination. The state of emergency was declared by Baldwin on behalf of the king on 30 April and parliament returned a Humble Address to the king (in effect, agreeing that an emergency existed) by 308 votes to 109 on 3 May; two days later Jix brought his regulations before parliament. The Commons was then asked to pass them lock, stock and barrel, rather than discussing them regulation by regulation. MPs could table amendments saying that such and such a regulation should be left out. The first time the regulations were brought before parliament, Labour MPs introduced amendments which would distinguish regulations which provided essentials to the community from those which allowed the police to invade civil liberties.[39]

Jix's attitude throughout the crisis was to see the regulations as crucial for speeding up the business of saving the country. Law courts were too slow when the country was in chaos. But the regulations did more than that. They made illegal things which were normally permissible and gave the authorities powers which were unknown in more tranquil times. Regulation 21, for example, made sedition a crime punishable in a summary way before a magistrate, rather than by indictment in a higher court. Regulation 22 abolished the right of public assembly; number 33 allowed the police to raid printing presses; number 18 empowered the Postmaster General to control the transmission of telegraphic messages. These were among the most hated measures – those which gave the authorities sweeping powers over expressions of opinion. These were powers which a government might need in the event of a full-scale civil war. Many thought they were excessive for the eight-day General Strike; when they were still in force seven months after things returned to normal Jix's reputation as the English Mussolini became fixed in the public mind.

The redoubtable David Kirkwood was on hand at the very beginning of the crisis to remind fellow MPs of the inevitable consequences of governing the country under regulations. Kirkwood described the way in which he had been dealt summary justice with no right of appeal during the war: 'I do not want anyone to be treated by his fellow countrymen as I was treated. I want the great tradition of the British race to remain unimpaired, even during this terrible crisis.' He told Jix that the measures were doomed to failure. The tradition of British liberty was firmly ingrained in the working people and any injustice would be resisted – in the spirit of fair play rather than rebellion. 'You have never crushed the spirit I represent, because the spirit I represent is the spirit of liberty.'

'For whom?' a Tory MP cried out. (Throughout the debates, Conservatives had said that socialists were hypocritical when they complained about the loss of civil liberties because the strike was, as they saw it, an attempt by a minority to coerce the majority and also because the print unions had suppressed the publication of newspapers.)

'Liberty for all,' replied Kirkwood, 'not liberty for a few to dictate terms.'[40]

When Jix brought the regulations before parliament again in June, two weeks after the TUC called off the strike, he lost the support of the Labour Party and some Liberals. An MP said that the pretext for emergency powers had been the threat to constitutional government presented by the General Strike; now only the miners were out in a dispute over pay and conditions. Was a strike in one industry to be considered unconstitutional by the government? The government had taken the powers in exceptional circumstances; the circumstances had now changed, but the powers appropriate for one threat were being used for an entirely different one.[41]

Jix and other ministers still claimed that the regulations were needed – in recent weeks to ensure the supply of coal and prevent violent protests in the coalfields – and that they were being administered fairly. 'I am a rather amiable kind of person,' Jix reassured those who saw him as a budding tinpot tyrant.[42] Unfortunately the regulations were being administered in many cases by men who were still in a state of counter-revolutionary enthusiasm or blind panic. Herbert Buck, a miner from South Derbyshire, to pick one of many such examples, was given a fine of £55 or sixty-one days in prison for 'using words calculated to impede the distribution of coal'. He had shouted, 'Stop the pits.'[43] A Welsh Congregationalist minister was bound over and fined £20 for saying, 'I've turned rebel.'[44] Throughout the country miners and their relations were gaoled for violence on picket lines, throwing stones at cars and for intimidation. But more commonly they were punished for careless words said in the heat of the moment, for annoying their neighbours who crossed the picket lines or for being cheeky to policemen (one man got three months' hard labour for telling a policeman that he would be better employed elsewhere[45]). At the same time accounts of police brutality, particularly baton charges, were reaching parliament.[46]

When the Emergency Powers Bill was being discussed in 1920 the then government promised that a measure of such enormous power would never be used to break a legal strike or suppress political opinion. But under Jix it was being used for just that. Miners' pickets were worn down by constant intimidation, their non-violent meetings were being broken up, their pamphlets were seized and many were arrested on trumped-up charges. David Kirkwood clocked up another arrest in November when he toured Derbyshire and Yorkshire addressing miners' meetings. In the Commons he had said that if he were a miner he would wish the whole rotten edifice of the state swept away; Jix accused him of hiding behind parliamentary privilege and said he would never utter those words in public. Kirkwood accepted the challenge. Whenever he arrived at a pit village he found the police had already banned him. At last he found a village in which he had not yet been banned; he was promptly arrested for sedition and tried by the local magistracy. He was found guilty and fined £25 for two extraordinarily vague offences – impeding the supply of coal and causing disaffection among the civil population. The magistrate told the MP that his words 'were of the gravest nature and have been fraught with the gravest danger'. It was clear that it was impossible to even express support for the miners in public. No one knew how the regulations would be administered from one district to another and miners were in a 'state of exasperation' as to what they might or might not say, let alone do.[47]

This was a wholesale abuse of civil liberties – and it was not confined to sensitive industrial areas. A naval veteran living in Portsmouth was punished for encouraging people to lose confidence in the police when he said that starving miners in Nottinghamshire had been baton-charged. His bad character was proved in court when the prosecution presented written evidence found in a police raid on his home which showed that he supported republicanism and deplored the regulations. This would have been impossible to do in normal trials, but a regulation allowed character to be considered in evidence. The gains of *Entick* and the 1794 London Corresponding Society trials, which stopped governments charging people with constructive treason by building up their treasonable nature through masses of unconnected jottings, were forgotten. The farce also gave the impression that there was something sinister afoot. Portsmouth was a long way from a mining district, so the danger that this man was single-handedly depriving the country of coal was remote; the regulations were not confined, as many assumed, to pit villages but to the whole country.[48] There was a growing suspicion that the regulations were being kept in force for so long because they gave the magistracy the opportunity to target dangerous types who were normally shielded by the law. In all some one thousand members of the Communist Party were punished. In some areas members of the CP were disenfranchised because, by being held in prison, they were disqualified by non-residence.[49]

Ramsay MacDonald complained to the house of an 'extraordinary drift of the State towards the type and mentality of a police state'. Something had changed in British politics, he said, and it was a growing contempt for fair play and the ordinary process of the law.[50] 'It is not cricket,' other MPs said. The fabric of liberty had been constructed over centuries, but now that the lower classes had finally clawed their way to equal political rights the ruling class violated their sacred rule of law. On 30 July Jix wearily announced the fourth successive proclamation of a state of national emergency as if it was the most boring and repetitive thing in the world. He hardly bothered to justify the regulations any more, and introduced them to the Commons in the middle of the night so that the discussion would be as short as possible. Throughout the whole time the act was in force only a handful of Conservative backbenchers bothered to justify their decision to troop, en masse, into the government lobby to vote for the most stringent abuse of civil liberties in peacetime. Their contempt for liberty is breathtaking. MacDonald warned Jix that his perfunctory treatment of parliamentary forms was bad, but far worse was the effect it had on the country. Unhampered by normal law the police scorned popular rights and the attitude of ministers and the majority of parliament fostered a lax attitude among the bench of magistrates. The political authorities had spoken – or not spoken – and the message was loud and clear.[51]

What were the working classes to make of constitutional government? 'There is the freedom you boast about –' Kirkwood fumed in the house, 'freedom as long as you do not operate it, but, the moment you operate it, you are banned and threatened . . . That is how the miner sees it.'[52] When an MP from a mining district was describing the harassment suffered by his constituents he did so over the hoots of laughter and catcalls of Conservatives who seemed amused at the pettiness of it all. The MP looked across at his barrackers and told them that they were setting a fine lesson in civil liberties and justice to the working classes; they would not laugh so heartily when a socialist government came to power shorn of its respect for British freedom. Others said that miners were not afraid of being tried in open court where the rules were known and fair. They objected to summary justice in front of politically biased magistrates, whose decision they could not appeal. It certainly was not cricket. Membership of the Communist Party of Great Britain soared as communists were unfairly treated. In attempting to close the lid on radicalism, the government only served to discredit the country's freedoms and turn people towards extremism, both in a left and rightwards direction.[53]

On 26 November Jix asked parliament to renew the regulations for the eighth time, which the Conservative majority dutifully did. Six days later they were revoked by Orders in Council. Until the last the government had used parliament as a rubber stamp. No one had noticed in those six days that the country had suddenly been pulled back from the brink of self-destruction and ruin to order and sanity. The truth was that the emergency had ended long before, but the government, confident with its massive majority, would dispense with its powers as and when it felt like it and pointedly without parliament's advice.[54]

Charles Trevelyan argued that civil liberties were even more essential in emergencies because threats to the individual, which were only theoretical in peacetime, became realities: these were the only times when the majority really did coerce the minority and when the state's authority became absolute. Yet this was the very time when safeguards were dispensed with.[55]

This casual attitude showed that freedom was a dangerous quantity, something which was fine in balmy days but which was incapable of serious challenges or difficult questions. If freedoms were dispensable in rough times were they therefore an illusion in 'normal' times? That is to say, free speech is permitted until your free speech offends the majority; opposition is permissible until the time when it *really* matters – when you are fulfilling the moral obligation to urge your leaders to change their disastrous but popular policies in time of war. And it was not just true of war; the experience in Britain and America since 1919 was that no constitutional guarantee was enough to defend those who deviated from the paths of political orthodoxy in a leftwards direction. Communists in the 1920s came under surveillance, their opinions were censored and they were punished by draconian laws. During the General Strike and its aftermath opposition MPs pointed out that the danger in wielding emergency powers in peace-time was that it alienated people who bore the brunt of the sacrifice of liberties and who increasingly saw the state as opposed to them and historical rights as the hypocrisy of the privileged. Indeed, the younger generation of all classes had lived through years when the usual laws and liberties of Britain were the exception not the rule. Old men and venerable books might talk of them with reverence, but were they really a sham which were not robust enough to stand the test of real life? Would they continue to see value in something which was patently disposable and suspended at the first hint of danger?

The Baldwin government managed to turn the country against the use of emergency powers, even people who had rushed to its support in April. As the coal dispute went on they saw manifest breaches of traditional liberties and an authoritarian spirit in government. It meant a retreat from the routine use of extraordinary powers. But it did not mean that the government decided it was futile to prevent dissatisfaction. During the Depression the mood turned ugly. Confronting the legions of hungry and idle, the state found that old laws could be more effective than new ones.

As the constitutional expert Ivor Jennings wrote, there were many laws the government could deploy which were 'relics of feudal anar-chy and of anti-revolutionary reaction'; the liberties which the British people enjoyed did not come from the law but from the government's reluctance to enforce certain laws. Britain's reputation as a free coun-try was thanks to a long period of tranquillity in the nineteenth century and the circumstances which had made political prosecutions counterproductive. That these laws had been so long silent did not mean that they were dead. They were made at a time when it was illegal for the disenfranchised millions to demand constitutional change; they were made with mass meetings and statements of radi-cal opinion in mind, and they had never been repealed or modified to take account of democracy.[56]

Throughout the 1920s the ancient law of sedition had been brought back from the grave to imprison and censor communists. The leading communists were charged with professing an ideology that could only be accomplished by overthrowing the constitution. The antiquated laws of sedition made it illegal to bring the constitution and public authorities into contempt or advocate revolutionary change. In theory, any politician's election address could be prosecuted; in practice, it was used to prosecute those who deviated from political orthodoxy. In the United States, Judge Holmes famously said that such opinions should only be silenced if they presented a clear and present danger to the state; this was not the case with the British communists, who were professing an ideology, not actively soliciting political violence.

In the thirties the oldest of all laws, those dealing with the public peace, had new life blown into them. When the National Unemployed Workers' Movement (NUWM) marched on parliament in November 1932 to present a petition signed by a million unemployed people, Parliament Square was blocked by police, people caught distributing leaflets were arrested and the petition itself was confiscated. 'Breaching the peace' was a catch-all phrase that could be applied to virtually any kind of public act, but which could be used selectively. The leaders were arrested for breaking a number of statutes, including the Seditious Meetings Act (1817) and the Six Acts of 1819. One of the organisers was arrested for incitement to 'cause discontent, dissatisfaction and ill-will between different classes of His Majesty's subjects and to create public disturbance' – in other words, sedition. Moreover, a meeting was illegal if it blocked the streets, if it infringed bylaws, if a policeman considered a breach of the peace was likely, if a person of 'reasonable firmness and courage' was alarmed, or, according to a law of 1816, if it was held within one mile of parliament.[57]

The actions of the government and the courts in the 1930s showed just how fragile political and civil liberties could be in Britain. A slew of books and articles were published on the leaching away of liberties and the National Council of Civil Liberties was formed to keep close watch on the situation.* In one notorious case, Katherine Duncan, a

---

* An earlier organisation of the same name had existed in the First World War, closely associated with the pacifist and anti-conscription movements. The new incarnation, formed by liberal and leftish lawyers in response to the indifference to civil liberties in the 1930s, did not have the radical political agenda of its predecessor.

well-known south London activist, was arrested for addressing crowds outside a Test and Task Centre for the unemployed in Deptford. She had previously been banned from speaking on the grounds that she would impede the public highway, so she chose a spot in a nearby alley where no pedestrians or motorists would be inconvenienced. Mrs Duncan was arrested before she could speak and was fined £2 with five guineas costs; she appealed to the Quarter Sessions and then the Divisional Court, arguing that her meeting was orderly and in no way obstructive. The conviction was upheld on the grounds that if she spoke it might lead to a breach of the peace. According to the Metropolitan Police Act 1839 a policeman could arrest anyone for words or behaviour which could lead to a breach of the peace.

This act was immensely popular with the police, who called it 'the Breathing Act' because a constable could interpret its general wording in order to make an arrest for any kind of public nuisance, including breathing. In practice it allowed the police to ban any political meeting of any sort. They could also stop people who were inciting violence in public. But Duncan had not opened her mouth. The courts said that on a previous occasion a disturbance had occurred after she addressed the unemployed, but there had been no evidence that her speech and the offence were connected. The logic was that Mrs Duncan's views would self-evidently make the unemployed unhappy, and an unhappy unemployed person might at some later date commit a breach of the peace. The effect of the judgement by Lord Chief Justice Hewart – the critic of *The New Despotism* himself – made the police arbiters of freedom of speech and public assembly; judges in the age of Jeffreys or Eldon had not dared go so far. The case set a precedent in common law which would not be overturned until 1999. The *Police Journal* said that 'the police are better served by the common law – with all its elasticity and adaptability – than they would by a rigid statutory code'.[58]

The Duncan case joined many others in the 1920s and 30s whereby political dissenters were kept in check by old laws and new interpretations. Courts gave retrospective support to police when they cracked down on unemployed or communist protestors. The sacred judgement of *Entick* v. *Carrington* was undone by a judge who ruled in favour of the police when they raided NUWM offices. It revived the eighteenth-century power of general warrants and trawls for evidence. This attitude came from a sense of fear, inherited from the First World War, that secret forces were working to undermine the country. Even in the 1930s this was widely believed to come from the far left, not the right. The National Council of Civil Liberties pointed out that Oswald Mosley and the British Union of Fascists got off lightly. The far right was allowed to hold huge meetings, which often turned to violence, but the police did not do much to intervene. There was one law, it seemed, if you were Katherine Duncan on a soapbox in a Deptford alley and another if you were Sir Oswald Mosley addressing thousands of uniformed thugs. Members of the NUWM were routinely bound over to keep the peace before Hunger Marches and the like; no such condition was placed on Mosley at the time of the massive BUF march that culminated in the Battle of Cable Street. The Home Secretary said he was powerless to prevent a provocative demonstration, even though the police had regularly banned or redirected processions under the act of 1839 or the Town Police Clauses Act (1847), which made provoking violence an offence and clearly applied to the BUF's decision to march through the Jewish areas of the East End.[59]

When the government bestirred itself and passed the Public Order Act in 1936 the effect was to stifle all political demonstrations, not just fascist thuggery. BUF violence in the East End was enough to make the authorities ban *all* protests there: 'Fascist provocation has had the effect of suppressing this popular form of public expression in the very quarter where it was most frequently used.'[60] The elasticity of the common law in dealing with demonstrations had given way to a severe statute because discretionary powers had been so clearly abused by the authorities.

Worse was to come in this violent decade. In 1939 English cities came under severe bombing. The public had an early lesson in living with acts of random terror. Between January and August the IRA were responsible for three hundred bombs left on the underground, in stations, hotels, cinemas and power stations, which led to seven deaths and ninety-six injuries. On one raid the police uncovered fifteen hundred sticks of gelignite and a thousand detonators, suggesting that the campaign was in its infancy.[61] In response the government passed the Prevention of Violence (Temporary Provisions) Act, which extended the time a suspect might spend in police custody without charge to five days and gave the Home Secretary the power to deport Irishmen he thought dangerous.[62]

This was seen as yet another departure from British standards of liberty. The government went out of its way to stress its reluctance to take these powers and accepted opposition amendments in the spirit of compromise. It was done with calm even though the committee stage took place on a day when bombs went off at King's Cross and Victoria stations and as Britain was poised on the brink of war with Germany. *The Times* called it a 'drastic measure, running contrary to cherished principles of the common law', but one which was necessary, subject to two conditions. The first was that it was a temporary measure that expired after a year, and the second that parliament retained control over executive actions.[63] The Commons and the Lords debated the issue thoroughly and all sides of the political divide worked to reach a compromise. Winding up the debate one MP said that the concern for the liberties of suspected terrorists in Britain and the level of parliamentary scrutiny involved in passing an exceptional measure was a rare thing in the world of 1939.[64]

But this sobriety masked executive skulduggery. The Home Secretary told parliament that the IRA's 'S-Plan' for war in Britain had just come into his possession, and that it said that the IRA had the support of a foreign power, which he could not, for security reasons, name. Anyone with half a brain assumed this meant Nazi Germany. It was later found that the foreign funding came from Irish Americans. It was also discovered that the government had known of the S-Plan for months. So they manipulated fears of Hitler and waited until bombs were actually going off before they asked for this sacrifice of liberty.

As these years showed, British liberty existed by the grace of dormant laws. There were precious few positive rights granted by statute or the courts that could not be undone. As people on the political margins were reminded, the government was very good at maintaining order in a variety of ways, be it by emergency legislation or by reviving long-forgotten statutes dating from the age of reaction. The country was reminded that there were as many laws suppressing liberty as those which enlarged it, and those legal decisions which supported liberty could be reversed by a politically minded judge. Faced with the turmoil of continental Europe the establishment was sensitive to political movements welling up from the streets, particularly the legions of unemployed who might be hurled to the extremes of left or right. Political extremism was not confronted head-on and argued out in public; instead passions were contained by manipulating the common law dealing with public order, binding over soapbox orators and deploying antiquated bylaws; it was all very low-key, but for this reason more effective in dampening political involvement than invoking dramatic new laws.

The same flexibility which had made the constitution and allowed civil liberties to flourish – decisions reached in individual court cases, the parliamentary safeguard and the self-restraint of the authorities in exercising draconian laws – could undo those privileges. The period seemed like history in reverse; great revolutions meant less liberty, not more; and the threat of political disorder meant rolling back the liberties that had been tolerated in more tranquil times. The ease with which this was done, and the forbearance of the public, is deeply significant. The legal expert Cecil Carr wrote that Britain had two legal traditions, one prerogative – which gave the Crown flexibility to deal with crises – and the other common law, which had built up precedents to protect the subject. It was also one where no court could challenge the sovereignty of parliament in making draconian emergency laws, unlike America where the Supreme Court could strike down legislation as *ultra vires*. It meant that Britain was 'better equipped to extemporize statutory measures in a crisis', but less good at protecting the rights of citizens.[65]

It should be noted that the same people who fretted about the draining away of individualism and the growth of executive government were less squeamish about the loss of civil liberties. Indeed,

Lord Hewart saw no contradiction between decrying the 'new despotism' – when it came to progressive policies – and handing down legal judgements unfavourable to political dissent. The Hayekian view that individual liberties could only function in a society where economic freedoms, property rights and the unrestrained play of the market were sacrosanct was under considerable doubt. On the contrary, the needs of economic individualism were often incompatible with the kinds of liberty enjoyed by ordinary citizens. Faced with threats to the economic order, property and the status quo, the state was clearly prepared to make sacrifices, the first of which were the rights of ordinary people, especially if they expressed discontent. An industrial dispute could be turned into a revolutionary threat which justified deploying the full resources of the state, and the delivery of coal was put above freedom of speech. In this way the state gave the very strong impression that it would always subordinate individual liberty to economic interests (in 1926 and 1984, for example) and it almost put the entire left off the very notion of civil liberties. That the left retained its faith is testament to the moral capital built up over the years, which one government could not on its own undermine.

The interwar years were not friendly to freedom anywhere. In the United States there were similar attacks on political protest. Europe was convulsed by totalitarianism. Why worry about a few truculent miners or outspoken socialists? In a decade when the lights of liberty were being dimmed there needed to be a beacon of liberty somewhere. By acting in the ways that they did the governments in Britain and the US signalled that old-fashioned liberty and democracy might be incompatible. And, more significantly, that liberty was expendable: it was the luxury of tranquillity, not an essential requirement of humanity. Whatever the scale and wherever it took place in the world, the drift was in one direction.

Above all it exhibited alarming weakness on the part of Western leaders. They could not trust their own people and had to resort to panicky methods of control at home. The violation of essential liberties in Britain and America eerily mirrored the collapse of the rule of law in international affairs. The West was failing to honour its beliefs, and the casual treatment of domestic liberties symbolised the wider problem of the grievous failure to articulate that Western civilisation had the inner strength to defeat the horrors of the century. Herbert Agar wrote:

The essence of civilization is a restraint, imposed either by divine law or by reason, upon the instincts of man. Civilization means rules and promises which are kept . . . Without such discipline and standards, victories over the forces of nature may be more disastrous than defeats. We now know that a people can be heir to all the technics and the knowledge of the ages and still behave pathologically like hordes of vicious and sadistic children.[66]

The language of liberty belonged to outsiders like David Kirkwood, pit village orators and people on the left. They believed themselves to be part of the radical inheritance which protected civil liberties while the ruling class were backing away from those rights in response to the challenges of democracy. In the 1930s, as in the 1790s, as in the twenty-first century, the battles have to be refought by each generation.

CHAPTER 12

The Blackout

—ᴍ—

I have never known normal times, and I never expect to know them.
FLIGHT LIEUTENANT VICTOR RAIKES MP,
HOUSE OF COMMONS, 17 FEBRUARY 1943[1]

[British liberty] is in Burke's words a regulated freedom . . . [I]n this constitution there are no guaranteed or absolute rights. The safeguard of British liberty is in the good sense of the people and in the system of representative and responsible government.
LORD WRIGHT, *LIVERSIDGE* v. *ANDERSON*,
HOUSE OF LORDS, 1942

For all the attacks on established liberties Britain remained a free state. After the Second World War the American scholar Clinton Rossiter looked at the experience of France, Germany, Britain and the USA in emergency situations. Whereas nations throughout Europe succumbed to crises, sacrificing liberties, constitutions and democracy in the process, Britain and America possessed the capacity to do everything to defend themselves – including breaking constitutional law and suppressing all normal liberties – whilst retaining their essential freedoms. Britain had the flexibility to give its politicians unlimited dictatorial power, but her politicians had the self-restraint and constitutional propriety to refrain from becoming dictators. Not least among the reasons this was so was a long historical tradition of freedom and individual liberty, which, in the end, proved a greater bulwark than laws and constitutions.[2]

There was something in the waters which furthered a respect among politicians for liberty, an intolerance among the people for Great Men who presumed to solve all problems, and a general commitment to constitutional forms which meant that emergency laws did not become permanent. In the Second World War this spirit had to be upheld. At the beginning of his premiership Winston Churchill gave an undertaking in a wireless broadcast:

Immense surrender of their hard-won liberties have been voluntarily made by the British people, in order, in time of war, to preserve better the cause of freedom and fair play. Parliament stands custodian to their surrendered liberties, and its most sacred duty will be to restore them when victory crowns their exertions.[3]

This was said at a time when the executive took great powers to manage every aspect of life and all political and civil liberties were in suspension. Much later Albert Speer said that the reason Britain prevailed over Germany was because it was able to act like a totalitarian power when it had to. And upon peace the state could dismantle these powers and things could go back to normal.

It was an impressive achievement. But it should not mask the reality. Churchill promised liberty as the outcome of a war for freedom. By making such a promise he received a blank cheque from the people, from which no exaction was too much. An immediate and indefinite loss of liberty was an appropriate price to pay to live in freedom and security one day. If in the First World War people believed that a war against Germany would mean adopting German economic and social controls, many in the Second believed that a war against totalitarianism would mean the permanent replacement of civil liberties with totalitarian techniques. It was quite possible that measures taken to defend liberty could stifle the very spirit of liberty and dull the habits of freedom so that they could never be restored even in victory.[4]

Could civil liberties be simply mothballed for the duration of the war? And most importantly, for that age and ours, how can the state take liberties whilst retaining a commitment to freedom, so that the people have confidence that the essentials of their political society will be preserved through an indefinite period of crisis? In this situation the formal commitment to the ideal of liberty – however tarnished and hypocritical it begins to sound – becomes important, even when those in power have to resort to extreme measures. For the hypocrisy of politicians at least holds them to a sense of morality; it is the hostage they give to public opinion. And political opposition takes on an extraordinary value, because this voice of vanished idealism will always go against the grain of patriotism, the desire for safety at any price and the instincts of self-defence. Both these things help to retain a sense of normality, even in the worst of times. As Harold Laski wrote in the war, retaining freedom in time of national defence is one of the hardest tasks. 'A war-world, by its very nature, tends under modern conditions, to be a twilight world. The physical blackout is the supreme index to the character it assumes.'⁵ Facing these emergencies and sacrificing liberty for security, the first duty of a government should be to acknowledge that it *is* a twilight world; that the sacrifice is productive of evil as well as defence.

The problem of seeking security by dimming liberty is that not only does the citizen suffer, but the government exposes itself to danger. Censorship and propaganda, for example, prevents the citizen from airing views, dangerous and benignant, but it also cuts the government off from hearing truths and answering lies. The surrender of civil liberties was far more drastic than in the First World War. By 1940 the government had not only effectively nationalised everything, but voices of political protest or criticism had been silenced and the executive had the power to imprison or intern anybody it chose.

As the Ministry of Information sloganised, 'If you must talk, talk victory'. People began to suspect that the compilers of Mass Observation surveys were spies sent to delve into their private thoughts – so called 'Cooper's Snoopers', named after Duff Cooper, Minister of Information. The press was more heavily and ruthlessly censored than in the First World War, and techniques of propaganda were carefully refined. The media was saturated with 'positive censorship' – doctored 'facts', misinformation, simplistic arguments and gung-ho propaganda. 'Immediately on the outbreak of war', wrote Bevan,

England was given over to the mental level of the *Boy's Own Paper* and the *Magnet*. The Children's Hour has been extended to cover the whole of

British broadcasting and the editors of the national dailies use treacle instead of ink. If one can speak of a general mind in Britain at all just now, it is sodden and limp with the ceaseless drip of adolescent propaganda.[6]

His views were widely shared. The government was deeply worried about morale – and believed that even a stray paragraph of criticism would 'shake the British people to their core'. 'Cooper's Snoopers' actually found that morale was high; it dipped when the public felt that it was being kept in the dark and treated like a baby.[7]

The diminution of liberty in these years awoke a desire for liberty. The people wanted to know that they were fighting for something worthwhile and that things would not be worse when the war was won. They wanted to hear reassurances that liberty was prized. They did not always get them from the government. Indeed, by talking tough, by being cruel to be kind and by weeping crocodile tears as it assumed absolute power over the individual the ministry under-mined confidence. The voice of liberty became the voice of oppos-ition and those who spoke out were branded disruptive nuisances. In December 1940 MPs raised the question of eighteen hundred people held under detention orders, Oswald Mosley and other members of the BUF included in the number. Herbert Morrison, Labour Home Secretary in Churchill's coalition government, rounded on the hand-ful of MPs who had criticised the curtailment of liberties. He was absolutely furious that people dared uphold rights for enemies of the state. It was the kind of airy-fairy liberalism that had allowed Hitler to come to power.

In situations of war, and situations of revolution, if you are to be soft and preserve meticulously liberal doctrines and principles which may be, and are, ordinarily right and defensible, and if that is the line ministers are to follow, I would only say to hon. members: Take my advice, do not be a min-ister in these circumstances because it will be exceedingly dangerous for the security of the state and the success of the cause.[8]

He was right in essence: if there was no other in this country's history 1940 was certainly one year when liberty did need to be sacrificed for security. Britain had seen the Netherlands, Belgium, Norway and France fall to Nazi aggression and thanks to the actions of traitors.

Britain was under attack. There were pressing reasons for interning foreign nationals and detaining suspicious people when the German army, air force and navy were about to launch an invasion. Most MPs did not dispute that, but they wanted safeguards against government despotism. And when ministers are sold on this tough-talking, tough-acting attitude all perspective is lost: the tendency is to go too far – far beyond what is necessary. It is a dangerous moment for a state – the arrival of twilight indeed. Security trumps all other argument, the accustomed barriers fall, and injustice multiplies.

And when the accustomed checks against executive tyranny are silenced the danger is magnified. After the formation of the coalition government Churchill had the support of all but three MPs – the one and only Communist MP and two Independent Labour MPs. The number of ministers expanded to meet the expansion of government functions, curtailing the independence of the brightest members of all parties; some two hundred of the youngest MPs were on active service; and few wanted to hold up the war by being difficult. A group of seasoned parliamentarians (the so-called 'ginger group') took on the formal functions of a frontbench opposition without the teeth of a committed political opposition. Every time this loyal parliament appeared to get tough – or at least showed signs of not being supine – Churchill blackmailed them into silence by holding or threatening to hold a vote of confidence. The press was shackled by emergency regulations and its own sense of loyalty.[9]

On one extraordinary occasion the cause of liberty was held up against the trump card of security. And it happened when German bombers were menacing the coastal towns, the Luftwaffe was about to extend its raids to London and provincial cities and a full-scale invasion was believed to be weeks or days away. Faced with this the government wanted powers to declare parts of the country under invasion to be War Zones in which the military had full jurisdiction without appeal to civilian courts. It was a lamentably realistic scenario. The Germans might, for example, blitz and then land on the Norfolk coast. The defending British forces would need to secure the area, provide essential services to the civilian population, commandeer land, round up pro-Nazi traitors and arrest saboteurs and looters. The Home Secretary, Sir John Anderson, wanted the bill passed on the day he introduced it.[10]

But a group of MPs were less than happy that the military would have powers to try and execute a person without judicial review. Anderson and loyal MPs expressed bemusement and then anger that liberally minded MPs should make panegyrics on liberty at the moment of the country's greatest peril. 'It is time that hon. members spoke in a forthright fashion,' said Bevan.[11] And some did. Anderson did not get his bill passed that day, and had to come back to the house to hear his policies savaged. On the second day he capitulated and agreed to an amendment which allowed convicted traitors to appeal to non-military judges. The bill then went to the Lords, and when it came back to the Commons a week later Anderson had to accept an amendment which said that if a traitor was sentenced to death by a military court the sentence would *automatically* be reviewed by three men of high judicial office. It was a complete defeat for the government for it made their plan of emergency trials in the heat of invasion redundant.[12]

In the acrimonious debates over military justice Sir Richard Acland MP said that few would weep if a traitor was hanged. What every citizen should fear was a government that became so strong that it weakened itself: 'We have seen that happen in several countries in the last few months, precisely because the executives have taken to themselves too much power over the liberty of the subject.'[13] It was believed that one of the reasons why France had fallen was because public morale collapsed when the government assumed total powers and then kept the people in the dark with stringent censorship. Governments could become so brittle that they rendered themselves unable to lead. As one MP said, 'there is a growing feeling that we are not quite prepared at every point to trust the executive,' and in saying this MPs were expressing the silent views of many of their constituents.[14]

Between 23 July and 1 August 1940 the government faced day after day of criticism from the house in these debates. In the end Sir John Anderson resigned and was replaced by a tougher Home Secretary, Herbert Morrison, who, as we have seen, took a zero-tolerance approach to arguments on liberty. Significantly he was a leading member of the Labour Party, not an authoritarian Tory.

Churchill faced hostile questions about oppressive regulations during this week. He also faced the Blitz and the threat of invasion. Were the MPs dangerously indulgent, as many on the government benches claimed? As the parliamentary rebels admitted, quislings and saboteurs and spies would be shot in a ditch anyway when it came to it by soldiers and civilians who would not fret about civil liberties.[15] What was crucial, however, was that parliament should not cave in to government pressure every time they were bullied with accusations that they were endangering the war effort. And it was just as important that the laws should continue to offer fairness even in war and even if such pristine notions of justice could never be fulfilled in the bloody chaos of battle. The proposal was fraught with the danger of abuse, both by the government and individual soldiers; parliament should not pass badly drafted and vague laws for the sake of patriotism, for then it would be a rubber stamp. The proposed measure was an instance of the government demanding (not requesting) powers that were clearly excessive – one which were intended to be token expressions of toughness, not absolutely necessary for national defence. Nye Bevan told parliament that he had received letters from members of the public containing 'evidence that we are now slowly degenerating into a police state'. Those people needed reassurance that someone spoke for them because they could no longer speak for themselves.[16]

Parliament would never limit the government in this way again. Morrison and Churchill would play nasty cop/nice cop: the former blasting MPs with icy disdain for liberal bleating and the Prime Minister offering rhetorical flourishes about the value of liberty. And MPs found that they were powerless. They had delegated all legislative functions to the government. Ministers passed regulations, and MPs then had twenty-eight days to vote them down (provided they could find out which regulations had been passed – they were not automatically told). In reality a vote against a government measure would bring down Churchill, so only token resistance was ever offered, if at all.

One of the most notorious issues of government abuse was over the thousands of foreign nationals who had been interned in 1939 and 1940. Twenty-seven thousand people of foreign birth were interned in appalling conditions and eighteen hundred imprisoned under detention orders. Amongst these thousands of people were very dangerous characters. But thanks to the government's zeal and the lack of independent oversight there were many innocent prisoners. Of the detainees, some eight hundred were former members of the BUF; the other thousand included suspected spies, communist shop stewards, pacifists and others held for various reasons.[17] A mother of young children was interned for five months when the authorities found a diary entry which read 'Destroy British Queen. Install Italian Queen.' She was later discovered to be a beekeeper.[18] There were other such frivolous cases, but no one could judge how many because the Home Secretary released scant information about the detainees. At a time when civil liberties were considered a luxury or a hindrance, and when fears ran high, it was to be expected that abuses would abound. Churchill himself said that to detain a person 'without the judgement of his peers is in the highest degree odious and the foundation of all totalitarian government, whether Nazi or communist'.[19]

Parliamentary control was weakened by the utmost confidence that MPs had in the government. The courts were not prepared to rock the boat either. In the famous case of *Liversidge* v. *Anderson* a prisoner under detention order took his case to the courts saying that the Home Secretary had given no reason for his decision. What is significant about *Liversidge* is not so much the legal principle as the attitude of the law lords. The wording of the Emergency Powers Act said that the Home Secretary could detain a person if he had 'reasonable cause to believe' that person was dangerous. The House of Lords decided that the courts did not have to be supplied with evidence of the Home Secretary's decision-making process. In other words the Home Secretary did not have to prove that he had acted reasonably: the court had to take his word for it. In his dissent from the law lords' judgement Lord Atkins said that the phrase 'if the Secretary of State has reasonable cause to believe' had been stretched to mean 'if the Secretary of State *thinks* he has reasonable cause to believe'. And if the Home Secretary thought he was right to imprison a man no other authority could question those private thoughts. Sir Cecil Carr wrote that the decision showed the 'elasticity of British freedom' – and not just during the war but generally. There was no absolute right of liberty, no constitutional principle that overrode parliamentary sovereignty.[20]

The law lords took the view that in a national emergency they should put a favourable construction on laws such as these to give effect to the will of parliament that the executive should not be hampered in its efforts to defend the realm. But was that what parliament had intended when it delegated power to ministers? Atkins said that the judges, far from being the check on executive power, were 'more executive-minded than the executive', especially in their generous construction of the words of the statute. Indeed they were more generous than the many MPs who, in 1939, had forced the government to compromise and add the 'reasonable cause' proviso for the very reason that this would allow for judicial scrutiny.[21] But judges did not take into account the intent of parliament, only the words of the statute. Carr said that the Emergency Powers Act was so general an enabling statute and so lacking in *any* check on executive power that it was 'the highwater mark of the voluntary surrender of liberty'.[22] The law lords had given a judgement similar to that of the Five Knights' Case in 1627: the executive alone judged necessity. The difference in the 1940s was that parliament could repeal the statute. But the price would be decapitating in one blow the political leadership of the country in its gravest days.

The decision caused great anxiety on the benches of the Commons. There were regular debates on the liberty of the subject in wartime. They followed a pattern: MPs would lament the loss of the basic principles of British freedom and ministers would ask them to suggest a better alternative that would permit liberty but prevent spies and saboteurs seeping back into society along with the less dangerous or innocent people. These debates became almost a ritual in which MPs rehearsed the history of liberty and parliamentary democracy. As Laski noted, these occasions were like shadow-boxing matches, where the outcome was known in advance. MPs could criticise draconian policies because they knew that their heroism came cheap: the government would never change its policies of locking up potential quislings (thank goodness, they no doubt secretly thought) but their consciences were salved, the forms of parliamentary democracy were upheld, and

Britain's reputation for liberty and free discussion was broadcast to the world.[23] There was evidence that public opinion had sympathy for people held by the authorities, but also evidence that they did not want to give advantage to the enemy by sticking to peacetime standards. Backbench interest in the subject might have contributed to the government's decision to release people held without charge as soon as the immediate danger of invasion receded after 1941, but there was no hard evidence that it did. At the very least MPs' speeches and questions to ministers elicited a theoretical commitment to liberty which could not be forsaken when circumstances changed.

Churchill's government was highly centralised, with most operational decisions channelled through Downing Street. The Prime Minister shouldered a heavy burden – too heavy to be fully effective, many in administrative, military and political circles believed. Whether it helped or hindered is not the question here. What it engendered, however, were feelings of sensitivity to criticism and a peculiar sense of vulnerability common to many autocratic administrations. Churchill had criticised the emergence of an official mindset in the last war; when in power he fell into that same trap. The problem came from identifying the government's interests with the national interest, and seeing criticism of ministers as criticism of the whole war effort – or even as opposition to the war itself.

But this sensitivity was due to the fact that almost all viable outlets for opposition had been cut off and none put in their place. People learnt to bite their lips and conceal their thoughts; not hearing these thoughts, the men in power began to have terrible nightmares about what they might be. When adverse feelings did find expression they were loaded with significance they did not deserve. There was a kind of downward spiral. Taking liberty from the people caused anxiety, which justified taking more liberty, closing ranks and becoming more authoritarian.

Everyone agreed that the press should be censored in wartime. This was done by extracting promises from editors that sensitive military information would not be leaked. Matters of opinion, however, remained a grey area. The cabinet and its legal advisers were eager to avoid conflicts over civil liberties with Fleet Street, and their preferred method was to warn rather than prevent or punish. The anti-war *Daily Worker* was the only paper which was banned. In general the regulations dealing with the press existed as a sanction hanging over editors, not a regularly enforced weapon. And the press was eager to be on the government's side.

Two Mirror Group titles however annoyed the government – the *Daily Mirror* and the *Sunday Pictorial*, both popular with troops and workers. They were less than respectful to the ministry; the columnist 'Cassandra' was venomous, and the papers did not veil criticism as the rest of Fleet Street did.[24] In December 1940 Churchill wrote to Cecil King, executive director, warning him to rein in his papers. In autumn 1941 the Group was threatened with prosecution under the regulations, but nothing happened. At the beginning of 1942 however things changed. The danger of invasion was over, but Churchill was unpopular and people believed that the war effort was being bungled. The *Mirror* expressed these views: 'The same old faces talking the same old bluff,' it depicted ministers, who had, after all, been elected in 1935. 'The same old raddled intellects unalterably engraved with the same old prejudices and stupidities. Where is the new broom to sweep out this dusty mausoleum of dead minds?' Churchill, whose new broom status had lapsed, was incandescent and wanted immediate suppression. He was warned against it.[25]

In March the *Mirror* published a cartoon showing a sailor clinging to the wreckage of his ship in a stormy sea; the caption read 'The price of petrol has been raised by a penny (official)'. Churchill and Morrison believed that it was a slur on the government, accusing them of risking sailors' lives so that the oil industry would profit. The paper said it was a warning to people that wasting petrol meant that the merchant navy was required to risk its ships and men by importing more fuel. The cartoon coincided with a leader criticising the snobbish, blinkered, Blimpish old boys' network which it claimed ran the military. Morrison privately told the editor, Guy Bartholomew, 'If you go on, we can suppress you at a speed that will surprise you.' The *Mirror*, Morrison told the Commons, intended to undermine national discipline and confidence in the government and that 'the general line of this newspaper is consistent with the Fascist propaganda policy'.[26]

Bartholomew was threatened with regulation 2D, which gave the Home Secretary power to ban a newspaper without trial. This regulation had passed through the Commons with great difficulty, and only when Clement Attlee said it was necessary when the country faced invasion and promised it would be reserved for extraordinary circumstances involving national defence.[27] But now it was being used when the government was under political pressure. At the same time, Brendan Bracken, Churchill's boon companion and Cooper's successor as Minister of Information, announced tougher restrictions on cables sent to foreign news agencies. He said that some criticism was giving a false impression of feeling in Britain, thus undermining diplomatic efforts by broadcasting opinions which have 'been pre-eminently useful to Dr Goebbels'.[28]

Morrison faced an angry house. MPs said that it was typical of the drift of policy: regulations had been passed in a moment of nervous strain and enormous danger for specific reasons of national defence. Over time they had been converted from emergency measures to methods of routine administration. And worse still the government had blurred the line between national defence and politics. The *Mirror* incident was emblematic of all wartime control. At the moment of real crisis, the government had not dared to exercise its new powers; two years later it found that its considerable powers were useful for other reasons. It also showed how powerless parliament had become. The reasoning behind regulation 2D was that if the case of a subversive or pro-Nazi paper came to court, the court would have to sit in camera so that the Home Secretary could present secret information; parliamentary debate on it would be cut off because the matter would be *sub judice*. When he used 2D, the minister was acting in his executive capacity, and MPs were then free to censure his actions. But as MPs pointed out, the government insulated itself against all criticism by treating major and minor issues alike as matters of confidence. Defeat for the Home Secretary on a relatively trivial matter would bring down the government as surely as if the house voted against a vital war measure.

Nye Bevan said that the government's partisan attitude was harmful to morale. 'Whenever a British statesman makes a speech that says that Great Britain is fighting for the rights of ordinary people, what is the response in the minds of millions of people? The *Daily Mirror* and the *Daily Worker*.'[29] Perhaps it was a minor matter compared with the loss of freedoms throughout the world. But it meant something to people, and it showed an alarming tendency in British politics. It should be a principle of a democracy that it is measures not men that are important, even in war. Bevan remained a persistent and powerful critic of the government. His oratory was second only to Churchill's (although the gap between them was still wide). During the war he dared to be Churchill's greatest critic, maintaining that 'in a democracy, idolatry is the first sin'.[30] He reminded people – and Churchill – that there was a democratic choice, even in war. Such outspokenness made him unpopular with the public.

As Michael Foot wrote, Churchill should have been grateful that there was one man of ability to joust with, if only to show the people and the world that he was leading a parliamentary democracy, not a dictatorship.[31] But Churchill called Bevan 'the squalid nuisance in war'. When Bevan came to Downing Street the Prime Minister made sure he was seated in a way which made shaking hands impossible.[32] For all his strengths Churchill was often averse to checks and criticism. He believed that parliament was an obstacle to strong government in war. Bevan, on the contrary, believed that MPs acted like 'docile sheep', and they needed to be occasionally awoken from the Churchillian spell, if only for the sake of parliamentary form.[33] He genuinely believed that the war was being mismanaged by cautious old politicians – the 'guilty men' of the days of appeasement who were instinctively defeatist – and that the cause of the people was being betrayed by Labour ministers who failed to extract concessions from the Tories. The people should not be lulled into thinking that *their* successes in the war were due to one man. Otherwise bad habits would creep in. They also needed to know that the ruling class was not hugger-mugger in some cliquey establishment embrace. Ministers themselves needed the bracing experience of opposition or they would doze at their posts. As he told the house, in the presence of Herbert Morrison: 'The Home Secretary has become irresponsible because he has not been sufficiently kicked in this House. If he had been restrained more he could have been a better man.'[34]

It was in the middle and end parts of the war that the government became more authoritarian. Churchill had been a close observer in 1916 when Asquith fell because he was accused of leading a weak cabinet which was failing to marshal the resources of the country. He faced similar accusations in 1942, when Britain was doing badly in the Far East, North Africa and the Atlantic and questions were being raised about the productivity of industry. He faced a motion of censure in July 1942, which he furiously countered with accusations that a handful of MPs were abusing their liberty, sowing discord in the country and undermining his position of strength in negotiations with foreign powers, mainly the USA and the USSR. He survived the motion by 475 votes to twenty-five.

In March 1944 he received the first defeat of his premiership, when MPs broke ranks and undermined the authority of their leader. The issue was of crucial importance to his authority and the prosecution of the war: equalisation of pay for female teachers. Churchill came to the house and threatened the resignation of the government over the issue on the eve of the invasion of Europe unless the Commons reversed its vote. Parliament retreated immediately from its coy flirtation with independence and it was left to Bevan to point out the 'megalomania of totalitarianism'. Alec Cunningham-Reid MP, who had been expelled from the Conservative Party for his maverick behaviour, criticised the government's increasing authoritarianism from a different point of the political divide: 'The majority are either too old, too stale, too mesmerised, too honours-seeking or just too, too Tory, to do anything else but be a drab chorus chanting a shrill subservient "Yes, yes, yes"'.[35]

Whether the government's hard line on conventional liberties helped win the war cannot be known. But that is the point. As the years from 1914 to 1945 showed – in peace as in war – the suspension of liberty for reasons of security did lead to a twilight world. In all these situations the government took a step into the dark in which they felt, understandably, that to do too much was more forgivable than too little. Was it necessary to intern thousands of men and women? To keep the newspapers under perpetual threat of suppression, deluge the country with propaganda and monitor private conversation? To disempower and mute parliament? We can never know.

What the two wars and the intervening crises demonstrate is that a departure from normal civil liberties means an unavoidable period of pain and injustice. The twilight brings long shadows and dark glades which might contain real monsters or phantoms of the imagination. It engenders fear and insecurity, and an official mindset which holds that it is better to be safe than sorry. The value of the individual's rights sinks as the sense of danger increases. Britain was by no means alone among democracies when it came to this kind of reaction. America had seen German spy panics in the First World War and communist witch-hunts in the 1920s, and during the Second World War great and unnecessary harm was caused by interning the Japanese-American community. As Justice William Brennan of the US Supreme Court said,

There is considerably less to be proud about, and a good deal to be embarrassed about, when one reflects on the shabby treatment civil liberties have received in the United States during times of war and perceived threats to national security . . . After each perceived security crisis ended, the United States has remorsefully realized that the abrogation of civil liberties was unnecessary. But it has proven unable to prevent itself from repeating the error when the next crisis came along.[36]

The same goes for Britain: fear makes it impossible to judge the balance between liberty and security. It is a sad and seemingly unavoidable fact.

Civil liberties were created for a reason – to protect the individual for sure, but also to insure public authorities against their own blunders. The greater the discretionary power given to these authorities the more chance there is of injustice and mistakes, and the greater the risk that the government will incur public disapproval and charges of partiality. This is multiplied when apprehensions run high and people are in a state of nervous strain. No one can be sure if they are doing too much or too little. Should the governments of 1914–18 and 1939–45 have been harder or softer? Did they go too far and make avoidable mistakes? In a way those kinds of question are irrelevant. Mistakes are inevitable in periods of emergency. As William Pitt said long before in another period of crisis (the 1790s), necessity makes its own law; and this is often wrong, reactionary and foolish. It is a brave government that faces up to this honestly. The only protection the citizen retains is a hope that politicians and agents of the state exercise their great powers responsibly and in a spirit of self-denial.

In any case, it might be said that the emergency powers were only temporary. After VE Day all the regulations involving civil liberties were revoked and parliamentary government was soon restored. The fears that the war would destroy these things proved to be incorrect. No politician gained a taste for dictatorial powers to the extent that they were reluctant to give them back. As there was no constitutional guarantee for liberty this was not a given. But was there any possibility that British liberties would be fundamentally altered? Respect for civil liberties ran to a very low level during the war. The government showed that it was not averse to covert and overt suppression of opinion and arrest of political dissidents, even while it talked about the sacredness of freedom. Some have seen this as hypocritical and indicative of a political system which has never had many qualms about sacrificing liberties when under threat. It was a regular theme of British history whereby politicians came to identify themselves personally with the fortunes of the state and mistook criticism for treason.[37]

But the very hypocrisy of the country's leaders meant that power could not be usurped permanently after the war. By talking of liberty so much they ensured that the political class and the public kept in their minds a sense of what normality was, after so many years of emergency rule. This is vital in the British system where, because there are no absolute rights, liberties are defended in the last resort by public opinion. Churchill might have thought them nuisances who tied up busy ministers in futile and repetitive debate but the back-bench MPs who spoke up for liberty played a part. It would be too much to say that they alone kept alight the beacon of liberty, but in their questions and speeches they helped fertilise the soil in which liberty thrives: dissent, especially when dissent is out of fashion.

The public never lost sight of the ideal of civil liberty, even when it seemed like an impossible luxury. The British people would not tolerate suspension of their liberties for a moment longer than was necessary. This was symbolised by the reaction against ID cards. In 1950 Harry Willcock, a dry-cleaning manager, when asked by a policeman for his card refused on the grounds that he was a liberal. He was found guilty in the magistrates' court, which was upheld in the Court of Appeal. Lord Chief Justice Goddard however had considerable sympathy, on moral grounds, for Willcock: 'To use Acts of Parliament passed for particular purposes in wartime when the war is a thing of the past tends to turn law-abiding citizens into lawbreakers. In this country we have always prided ourselves on the good feeling which exists between the police and the public.' But the conversion of an emergency measure into a routine tool of convenience by the police tended 'to make people resentful of the acts of the police and inclines them to obstruct the police instead of assisting them'.[38] In 1951 the British Housewives' League set out to burn their cards outside parliament but were thwarted by rain. Mrs Irene Lovelock was, according to *The Times*, 'partly successful with a frying-pan'. This was the revolt of middle England against restraints with which they had put up for years and which they had been told were for emergencies. The cards were withdrawn in 1952. The government's promise that suppression of liberty would be temporary was finally made good by the direct action of bloody-minded individuals.

In Britain there was no automatic safeguard for liberty under the constitution. Under English and Scottish law it was possible for the executive to take supreme power by legal means. The constitutional writer Ivor Jennings looked at the supremacy of parliament and tried to find 'fundamental' liberties. On the basis of parliamentary action since 1914,

parliament may remodel the British constitution, may prolong its own life, may legislate *ex post facto*, may legalise illegalities, may provide for individual cases, may interfere with contracts and authorise the seizure of property, may give dictatorial powers to the government, may dissolve the United Kingdom or the British Empire, may introduce communism or socialism or fascism, entirely without legal restrictions.[39]

These years also showed that there was a barrier. As Cecil Carr wrote, the legal road to dictatorship was not confined to Britain and its unwritten constitution. 'The most successful dictator is he who gains his power without forsaking that road . . . Yet laws and constitutions are but the paper safeguards of liberty. A people must have the will to be free.'[40]

The British people were genuinely affronted by wartime controls, from the regimenting and docketing of the bureaucratic state to censorship and internment. The majority of people may not have read history particularly deeply; but they had a sense of history and nationhood. Liberty was at the heart of this self-identification. Like at other times in British history this freedom may have been imperfect, slightly battered and subject to a thousand objections and contradictions. But belief in it in the abstract was of more importance than anything tangible. It set the tone for politics; it made people feel free, or at the least see freedom as the normal state of affairs and any move away from ideals of historic liberty as the ultimate political betrayal. In *The Lion and the Unicorn*, George Orwell wrote:

In England such concepts as justice, liberty, and objective truth are still believed in. They may be illusions but they are very powerful illusions. The belief in them influences conduct, national life is different because of them . . . Even hypocrisy is a powerful safeguard. The hanging judge, that evil old man in scarlet robe and horsehair wig, whom nothing short of dynamite will ever teach what century he is living in, but who will in no circumstances take a money bribe, is one of the symbolic figures of England.* He is a symbol of the strange mixture of reality and illusion, democracy and privilege, humbug and decency, the subtle network of compromises, by which the nation keeps itself in its familiar shape.[41]

---

* To illustrate this point, Goddard LCJ, quoted above, was a 'hanging judge' with a fine scruple for civil liberties.

VII

THE TRIUMPH OF THE INDIVIDUAL

1951 ONWARDS

CHAPTER 13

Risk

—ᴍᴍ—

... let each individual decide what is essential to his or her self-constitution and act accordingly ... who is to decide what is essential to the constitution of the self other than the self?

KENNETH ARROW[1]

... the same riches that make us timidly conservative in politics make us bravely liberal in morals ... it is the same soul that hungers for the license of liberty and the security of order; the same mind that hovers, in its fluctuating strength and fear, between pride in its freedom and admiration for the police.

WILL DURANT[2]

There was a revolution still to be made, but too few revolutionaries.

MARGARET THATCHER[3]

The gains for individual liberty since 1945 have been considerable. The principle of Anglo-American liberty that individuals should be free in their private sphere took on a new meaning, almost unimaginable to thinkers of another age. The intrusive force of the state and society over sexuality and sexual behaviour was diminished when consenting homosexual sex was decriminalised, contraception became widely available, abortions were permitted, and society tolerated relationships between unmarried couples. The rights of women were gradually conceded, and those oppressive bonds of home life, recognised by John Stuart Mill, were weakened by the availability alike of meaningful careers and divorce without legal restriction or social stigma. The opening up of higher education gave the lower middle and working classes the possibility, for the first time, of upward social mobility. Old racial prejudices were overcome, slowly and incompletely, by laws and the evolution of social attitudes.

Society became more permissive than it had been since the late eighteenth century, tolerating and welcoming highly individualised forms of behaviour. And from the late 1970s people gained freedom in the marketplace, as entrepreneurs and consumers. Old and new institutions, which had been accused of locking up the full range of individual action – such as ancient academic institutions, the City of London, the unions, public sector monopolies, professional bodies – were reformed beyond recognition. By the end of the century more people than ever before owned their homes, making real the traditional conception of freedom residing in the Englishman's castle. It was, in new and often surprising ways, a golden age for liberty.

It was no wonder that respect for – and belief in – the ideals of justice and liberty peaked in the 1980s according to surveys of social attitudes. The generation which grew up in the wake of the Second World War experienced an unprecedented expansion of freedom and opportunity. The fall of communism from 1989 seemed to vindicate a certain conception of liberty based on the free market and what is called 'negative liberty' – the right to privacy and personal choice. The availability of computers, and a future of supranational electronic communication and trading, offered further, unlimited, possibilities of autonomy and choice independent of state, society and multinationals. The 'knowledge economy' would transform the traditional pattern of work from a hierarchical, disciplined model to one of creative independence and co-operation.

Above all this economy represented the ultimate victory of the individual over the state. In 1992 Walter Wriston, chairman of Citicorp from 1967 to 1984 and chairman of Ronald Reagan's Economic Policy Advisory Board between 1982 and 1989, prophesied the sunset of the state of sovereignty and the destruction of ageing power structures, including the workplace; an 'international democracy' was being worked out in the new electronic markets and media.

One new rule which is becoming more and more manifest is that technology has begun, in many instances, to bypass politics. As we have seen, the global financial markets have become the transmission belt for conveying the world's judgements about national economic policies. In a similar manner, the information technology that touches all of us each day has become the conduit for the myriad demands of citizens and consumers made to corporations and governments . . . We are witness to a true revolution; power really is moving to the people.[4]

The confidence in liberty reached its peak in the early 1990s. Social surveys in the early twenty-first century show among the overwhelming majority a diminished faith in freedom, a willingness to trade civil liberties for security and, most worryingly, a growing number of people who would sanction torture in some circumstances.[5] The present century has also seen the first sustained questioning of the absolute commitment to free speech on the part of governments as well as by members of the public for centuries. They are trends which are deeply concerning for supporters of liberty. Governments have become unmoored from old liberal assumptions just as their electorates have, on one hand, demanded more controls and, on the other, lost the appetite for resistance and bloody-mindedness. Where once liberty was held to be an unqualified human good in liberal societies its very value has been questioned by politicians, who sometimes are honest enough to verbalise the belief common to administrators in all ages that individual freedom and the rule of law are hindrances to good government. At the same time society has backed away from the idea that there is anything, least of all a formal commitment to liberty, which remains as a national value. The terrorist attacks on New York, Washington, Madrid, Bali and London and the possibility of further attacks have augmented this climate of pessimism.

But the changes predate 2001. Western states have used the technological revolution to become more controlling. Former faith in the possibilities of liberty has been overtaken by cynicism, mistrust and above all the defining characteristic of our age, fear. Just as the possibility of more freedom became a reality the desire for security, re-assurance and control gripped the peoples of the countries who had scored so many gains for freedom. That these things should coincide is perhaps not so surprising or unrelated. Unprecedented freedoms can lead to fear of freedom, fear of the sudden disappearance of traditional centres of authority and morality, fear that social freedom will be abused by our antisocial neighbours and murderous enemies.

This is a time which Popper would define as one of the perennial flights from freedom in human history. It has stemmed in great part from the diminution of the first condition of liberty: courage. It has in turn led to a breakdown in public trust and an atmosphere of surveillance, control and violation of liberties: an atmosphere which diminishes the feeling of freedom which gives immeasurable value to society and the individual.

Sir Isaiah Berlin, in his famous lecture on 'Two Concepts of Liberty', made famous the distinction between 'positive' and 'negative' liberties. He traced the ideological distinction back to Benjamin Constant, Alexis de Tocqueville and John Stuart Mill. They defined liberty as the absence of interference from others, be it the state, a church or society as a whole. At the heart of Western civilisation was the idea of privacy. Not only should the individual have an absolute and sacrosanct sphere in which he was independent, but it should be as large as was compatible with the needs of society. The state had a duty to intervene to educate, inform and protect its citizens, but it should take as its starting point the conception of the individual as an autonomous moral agent. It should seek always to enlarge liberty. The first needs of mankind, as Berlin said, were food and safety. But history taught, by a series of painful and tragic lessons, that the interests of the individual were bound up with liberty. 'Freedom for an Oxford don . . . is a very different thing from freedom for an Egyptian peasant,' said Berlin, paraphrasing his opponents. He answered them in this way:

The Egyptian peasant needs clothes or medicine before, and more than, personal liberty, but the minimum freedom that he needs today, and the greater degree of freedom that he may need tomorrow, is not some species of freedom peculiar to him, but identical with that of professors, artists and millionaires.[6]

Whether people called this liberty 'the universal rights of man', 'civil liberties', 'justice', 'liberal democracy', or whatever else, it boiled down to the same eternal fact. Unless the individual had an absolute freedom to pursue his own goals, experiment with different ways of life, live in privacy and make his own moral judgements he did not enjoy liberty. And unless a society was free to debate, discuss and make bold trials in the alternative roads to the future it would atrophy.

Very few people in history, or in the modern world, had ever experienced this liberty. The desire to perfect and liberate people through religion, a common morality, an economic system or a national endeavour had preoccupied wise and virtuous men. They presumed to know better than the herd of mankind who were either enslaved by some outside force or dehumanised by their ignorance – and the ends they sought Berlin called 'positive liberty'. In its mildest form it meant depriving people of personal autonomy by a paternalist and benevolent government which interfered with its citizens in small matters and hedged them in with pre-emptive controls.

But such an attitude commonly led to something much worse. People did not know their own interests, the advocates of positive liberty would argue; they had to be led towards freedom, self-realisation, independence, enlightenment, salvation – call it what you will. The individual could only seek fulfilment in such a society if he subsumed his will into that of the collective whole, because only the collective whole, not an isolated thinker, can determine the truth; if he accepted every piece of dogma with blind faith. Above all he must believe that the collective endeavour is bigger than his weak will and divergent opinions; that something greater than him is at stake; that any personal sacrifice for his God, his country, his cause, for generations yet unborn, for whatever the ultimate end of life is deemed to be, is worth it. Mankind had been subjected to this since men and women had formed societies. And it had crushed creativity and subjected whole peoples to a stagnant social, economic and political existence when they were deprived of the freedom to choose between competing routes to different ends of life – what is called pluralism. In the twentieth century such regimes had seduced supposedly enlightened nations and reached murderous proportions.

The example of the culmination of this in the USSR and Eastern Europe and the living memory of oppression made many in the West define themselves against such dangerous ideas. There was coming to be an absolute difference between the two civilisations which had weapons of mass destruction pointed at each other: 'One finds the essence of freedom in spontaneity and the absence of coercion,' said one academic, 'the other believes it to be realized only in the pursuit and attainment of an absolute collective purpose.'[7] The tendency was to polarise the debate – to make absolute and irreconcilable the difference between negative and positive liberties; indeed, between collectivism and freedom.

Berlin's arguments were gladly accepted in the West, but they were often distorted for partisan ends. His distinction between the two liberties is better understood as the difference between an open society and a closed one. An open, or liberal, society can, and has, adopted so-called 'positive liberties' (any number of paternalistic policies) without much harm to its people; such polities have been able to make experiments without becoming tyrannies. What they have retained is the liberal ethos which puts the dignity of the individual first, places freedom of thought and action at the centre of its moral code and does not see opposition as a threat. It is the closed society – such as the Soviet bloc – which eradicates these. Yet the age of cold war was more at ease with sharp polarities than nuanced arguments. Neoconservatives recast John Stuart Mill as the warning prophet of twentieth-century totalitarianism and the advocate of complete independence from the state. And it was not just that the individual should be free from the state; the state should, as far as possible, be free from its people. What had the century taught but that democracy was imbued with dangers?

The concept of the 'New Right' – 'small state, big individual' – could be made possible when the individual diverted his or her talents into activities far removed from participatory politics – or, put another way, from things which necessarily involved imposing values on another. Society needed more entrepreneurs, money-makers and risk-takers, motivated by profit, and far fewer civil servants, administrators, local councillors, public-service broadcasters, scholars, and others motivated by a sense of duty – people who thought that *they knew best*. Mill's *On Liberty* was taken to be a manifesto for the complete autonomy of the individual within modern society – and not just as a right but an obligation on the part of the citizen to mind his own business. Those parts of his thinking which enjoined people to participate in their communities to preserve and enlarge liberty were brushed aside.

The good of the individual, and society, was best served when he or she pursued selfish interests, which at least did not raise the Leviathan of the state or awaken the sleeping giant of social prejudices. If Friedrich von Hayek had been a solitary voice in the Second World War, arguing for a forgotten principle of individualism, the cold war threw his arguments into sharp relief. The language of laissez-faire and economic individualism, presumed as dead as Queen Victoria, was revived. Economists and academics, many of whom had actual and painful experience of the European tragedy, argued that the state and brutish mankind herded together in its collective capacity were the sources of all misery and persecution. The sense of social duty – which lived in a generation brought up in the Depression and the war – however laudable it was, was misplaced and possibly dangerous. The argument that any increase in state power, even in welfare provision, would inevitably lead to totalitarianism had been scoffed at. But as the cold war intensified and memories of the Great Depression receded, it became ever more widely accepted.

It also chimed with the ongoing social revolution. People were encouraged to seek independence from irksome social ties, to see themselves as individuals free to shape their own destinies and pursue their own interests, to revel in their new freedoms. Hayek's widely read *Constitution of Liberty* (1960) marshalled the liberal inheritance. It was written in fine and accessible liberal language making the case for the West to build on its libertarian heritage to construct a robust and viable ideology to match communism. Hayek called upon the British and American experience which had subdued arbitrary government and empowered the individual. There was something in it for everyone: for the historically minded as much as the convention-defying rebel of the 1960s. It is a paean to liberty in the tradition of radicals from the seventeenth century onwards, a treasure trove of examples and quotations from the heroes of Anglo-American history and the thinkers of modern civilisation. Hayek saw the expansion of the state in the twentieth century as a temporary deviation from historical standards of liberty. Democracy had made a mistake by listening to politicians – both well-intentioned and demagogic – who held up the state as the source of social justice and progress.

Democracy had learnt its lesson, and the future would be one where the individual was sovereign. And to do this democracy must build up barriers against itself. 'The individual has little reason to fear any general laws which the majority may pass,' Hayek wrote to a generation experiencing greater freedoms than ever before and seeking new ones.

. . . It is not the powers which democratic assemblies can effectively wield but the powers which they hand over to the administrators charged with the achievement of particular goals that constitute the danger to individual freedom today. Having agreed that the majority should prescribe rules which we will obey in the pursuit of our individual aims, we find ourselves more and more subjected to the orders and the arbitrary will of its agents.[8]

There is much to agree with in Hayek's generalities about the worth of liberty; what lay behind them, however, was the single idea that there was a straightforward connection between economic liberty and Mill's negative liberty. In other words, if the ends of human life were plural and not guided by a single ideology it followed that this was possible only where men and women had absolute freedom to dispose of their property, labour and talents independent of any outside intervention.

Those who had been brought up in the war and the postwar age of austerity had mixed views about the state. It had, after all, provided the conditions for prosperity and affluence. But for the citizen state provision continued to be one of palpable drabness, a brittleness which meant inadaptability to individual circumstances, and recurrent public-sector strikes. A host of services, from hospitals to schools, were still marked by the austerity which gave birth to them. Monopoly public industries were combined with monopoly trade unions. Few were eager to make the state the fountainhead of everything; fewer still wanted to abolish things which gave them advantages through the life cycle. But many contrasted the choice and quality of the private sector unfavourably with the public. Most people believed, despite the arguments of prolific economists such as Hayek and Milton Friedman, that freedom was possible, and perhaps more valuable, in a mixed economy. But they were coming to realise that when restraints were removed from the market, as they had been in society more generally, consumer choice increased and personal ambitions were more easily satisfied.

The desires which drove – and which were awoken by – the social revolution of the 1960s, therefore, also led to demands for reform of impediments to the realisation of economic goals. There was a heightened desire for the good things in life, exacerbated by greater availability of mass-marketed goods and more subtle techniques of marketing. Greater choice meant, above all, a richer experience of life. The explosion of youth culture, and the search for self-identity in a consumer society, was indeed anti-authoritarian. But student protest and pop culture were wholly new types of anti-authoritarianism. Apart from a vague and fluctuating deference to leftist sentiments there was little in the way of ideology; there was, however high desire for personal autonomy, self-expression, self-exploration and individualised preferences which combined with plummeting deference for authorities of all sorts, including that of tradition. Freedom for many became freedom from internal repression, societal brainwashing and such like; liberty was seen less in terms of politics or wider society. Liberation – for the individual and society – would come from within.

The rebels of the sixties saw the failure of *their* revolution. It left a generation disillusioned about politics and sadly aware of the inability of hopeful and zealous people to change the world. The alternative was to cultivate one's own garden; to retain that part of their youth which was most seductive, which gave a comforting feeling of virtue, and which was the most easily fulfilled: the individualised culture of bohemianism, personal liberation and anti-authoritarianism.

These brooding desires and frustrations were resolved in a radical way by the governments of Margaret Thatcher. She was a far cry from the student rebels of the sixties, but there was much in her politics which brought out this generation to vote for her. Mrs Thatcher was imbued in the traditions of lower-middle-class, nonconformist Victorian values: a culture in which rewards should naturally accrue to the thrifty and hard-working who deferred instant gratification for future pleasures. It was a set of values which held that nature rewarded the virtuous and punished the feckless; one which despised state-organised welfare because it bred a class of workshy parasites, and despaired of officialdom because it was untouched by the energising effects of the profit motive. Society and the state should conform more to these values. In the 1970s disillusionment with social democracy thanks to adverse economic conditions combined with growing discontent as the social revolution of the sixties turned sour. Alfred Sherman, one of Mrs Thatcher's most important advisers, told the *Guardian* in 1985 that 'Ideas from Hayek and Friedman . . . were assimilated precisely because experience had already created a place for them by convincing people that neo-Keynesian economics, trade union hegemony and the permissive society had failed.'[9]

In the view of many budding Thatcherites Britain's decline in the twentieth century could be put down to the shrivelling of the spirit of enterprise and the liberating experience of risk-taking, the result of the dulling of competition thanks to the growth of the state, the coddling of industry, monopolies, and the provision of welfare. Britons of all kinds, in short, were suffocated by a cultural malaise which tabooed the unseemly accumulation of lucre – a state of mind which had infected a generation scarred by the Great Depression and which reached maturity during the war.[10] Mrs Thatcher claimed to carry Hayek's *The Road to Serfdom* in her handbag. When in the 1970s the Conservative research department was agonising about the politics of consensus (a dread word for Mrs T.), she took out Hayek's *Constitution of Liberty* and slammed it on the desk: 'This is what we believe.' (When she visited Hayek at the Institute of Economic Affairs the staff asked the aged professor what he thought of the aspirant prime minister. 'She's so beautiful,' he replied after a long, dreamy pause.[11])

In the view of the 'new right' the state should roll back, empowering self-reliant citizens to be risk-takers and entrepreneurs, to have their preferences answered by the dynamic market rather than by the stagnant state. Sir Keith Joseph, Thatcher's key ideological guru, claimed to have been converted to 'true' Conservatism only in 1974 – that is to say, to dogmatic liberal economics. The postwar consensus was a delusion which had crippled Britain, he came to realise. 'What Britain needs is more millionaires and more bankrupts,' said Joseph; in other words more risk – a return to the buccaneering spirit of the Elizabethans and the entrepreneurial zeal and self-help ethos of the Victorians.[12] Some libertarian thinkers held that democracy was its own worst friend: great parts of the economy should be taken out of political control and tested on the uncompromising free market. Democracy – when it entailed voting every five years – was inefficient; far better, surely, to express your preferences every day as a consumer.

The two revolutions – those of the sixties and the eighties – bear more than a resemblance. They came from mistrust of traditional politics and institutions, and from a desire for autonomy and self-reliance. They were also connected with a concern for the inner self which had boomed since the 1970s (what Francis Fukuyama calls 'extreme individualism') and more than ever before challenged the notion of community or society existing beyond individuated or family experiences. Thatcher's language was about empowering individuals, making them responsible for driving the economy by their creativity and enterprise. It appealed powerfully to the desire for individuality which, independent of politics or economics, had been growing in the West. Politicians, much as advertisers had done, played to feelings of the liberated self. And it worked, even for people who despised the political reality. The idea was to liberate the people and cut back the state, to make politics and society fairer and freer and more dynamic. It followed the libertarian idea, now brought to sudden prominence, that full social and political freedom was only possible in a free economy.

Thatcher bought into the Hayekian view of history, which argued that economic liberty and personal liberty were one and the same. It was a view which ignored or downplayed other aspects of liberty and institutions within civil society, notably the liberating possibilities which are bound up in *some* of the activities of the state. The notion that people could find and enjoy liberty not only as economic players but also as participants in the democratic process and as engaged citizens, or that they took pride and comfort in collective and national endeavours and institutions, or even that individuals sometimes needed protection against big business, dropped out of politics. It was a view which forgot that not all people are naturally acquisitive and that the profit motive does not work equally across all aspects of life, particularly for those engaged in public service.

Stridently and seductively, not to say simplistically, Thatcher made an absolute distinction between the free market and socialism centred on the principle of freedom. Her speech to the Conservative Party conference in 1975 is one such example:

Some socialists seem to believe that people should be numbers in a state computer. We believe they should be individuals. We're all unequal. No one – thank heavens – is quite like anyone else however much the socialists might pretend otherwise. And we believe everyone has the right to be unequal. But to us every human being is equally important.

It was as if the right had a monopoly on individuality. She went on to say that the basic right to earn and spend as you liked independent of the state, to own and have unfettered enjoyment of private property and to rise through the social scale through competition was 'the essence of a free economy, and on that freedom all our other freedoms depend'.[13]

Independent of ideological concerns however, as politicians of all sides acknowledged, things were changing. What James Callaghan called the 'cosy world which we were told would go on forever' – the postwar consensus of welfarism and Keynesianism – was in a mess; the country was riven by mass unemployment (which had risen to over a million for the first time since 1940), strikes and inflation. Ministers seemed at the mercy of international markets and militant unions rather than masters of the economy. Economic stagnation entailed a retreat from progressive policies and a growing intolerance for statist solutions; the luxury of altruism and experimentation drained away as insecurity mounted. The mood was for change, but perhaps not the millennial change envisaged in the minds of radical economists and politicians.

For the new right, which emerged in opposition in the 1970s and entered power with Thatcher in 1979, the Conservative Party was returning Britain to its true course after decades of aberrant social-ism, welfarism and statism (introduced by Conservatives as well as the Labour Party). But for other, more traditional Tories, the

Conservative Party existed to defend institutions and traditions; it was not a doctrinaire free-market party; it had successfully maintained conservative Britain by allying the free market with state activity and collectivism. It had recognised the strength of institutions which were wholly or partially insulated from the full heat of the market, including the civil service, the professions, academia, charities, the Church and the BBC. Thatcher's reforms represented a revolution in the governance of the realm and the complexion of the state; whatever it was it was not conservative. 'The preservation of freedom is a complex business,' wrote Sir Ian Gilmour, one of Mrs T.'s more intelligent critics.

But if people are not to be seduced by other attractions, they must at least feel loyalty to the state. Their loyalty will not be deep unless they gain from the state protection and other benefits. Homilies to cherish competition and warnings against interference with market forces will not engender loyalty. People will not tolerantly sit back and wait for impersonal forces to overcome disaster. They expect and demand action, and if they do not get it they are likely to look elsewhere and take action themselves. If the state is not interested in them, why should they be interested in the state? Complete economic freedom is not therefore an insurance of political freedom; indeed it can undermine political freedom.[14]

But the state was still interested in the individual, very interested. Gilmour was right that people, used to the traditions of politics and leadership, would not easily come to terms with a vacuum of power. They would be confused if government became inactive and laissez-faire. And politicians were not minded to give up control. As the state rolled back in some areas so it rolled inexorably on in others. And as it increased it took on greater powers and became ever more centralised. Similarly as it dispensed liberties on the market it snatched away others in the civil sphere. The process of freeing the market was accompanied by authoritarianism. And some of this augmented power came from the very process of liberation. Showdown with the miners in 1984 springs to mind, and so too does the undermining of local centres of authority, which were perceived to be stubbornly stuck in a collectivist past, by marshalling power at the centre. It was quickly found that revolutionising society by consent and compromise was a doomed exercise; only the state, strengthened beyond precedent, could prise out limpet-like socialistic tendencies, destroy the 'enemy within', and banish them beyond recall. For Tories who believed in healing tensions and divisions, piloting the state through choppy waters whatever policies were required, this was no less than an ideological crusade in which the state descended from the Olympian heights to scrap it out in an unseemly partisan manner.

Conservatism was pulling in contradictory directions. While the state was mistrusted in some aspects it was needed for the great tasks of rebuilding post-socialist Britain (as the new right would have put it). It was required to enforce social disciplines, guard against external and internal enemies, take a moral lead and provide a bulwark against pesky lefties in subordinate offices, particularly schools and local government. It was also needed to impose discipline on all servants of the state – as well as parts of the private economy – in order to retain the tight grip on finance which could ensure tax cuts and control over inflation. It was a paradox that the small state (small in the sense of tax and spend) needed big government to manage the economic life of the country with a rod of iron. Conservatives could simultaneously be pleased and displeased at this turn of events.

There were plenty of paradoxes to contend with. Tories were in favour of the market, but they were not in favour of some of the by-products of a fully free market: a sensationalist, scandal-loving, licentious entertainment/news industry; family breakdown and a corresponding breakdown in family values; rampant greed and profiteering; a decline in civic virtue; the influx of foreign capital and immigrant labour. The free market also required eradicating barriers to an equal playing field: affirmative action and anti-discriminatory laws – things which did not sit easy with rank-and-file party members and the columnists they read. Conservatives did like giving greater powers to the police in the name of law and order, and augmenting the powers of the state in defence and security terms, however at odds with libertarian rhetoric this might have been.

Resolving these tensions required strong leaders, leaders who could crush internal dissent and who did not appear to baulk when they encountered ideological inconsistencies. Whatever else Thatcher's rule did to the country it undeniably shook up the constitution, concentrating power in the hands of the Prime Minister and closely supervised Westminster departments, breaking down loci of authority which had traditionally put a brake on centralisation.

The Thatcher revolution would never have gone so far had not circumstances, in the person of General Leopoldo Galtieri, intervened. War against Argentina gave Mrs T. the victory, the popularity and the hard edge to carry out policies which were vain dreams before 1982, and which garnered scant support from within her party let alone the country. If the libertarian philosophy of 'small state, big individual' was still trumpeted as the essence of the new Conservatism, the headrush of military and electoral triumph confounded it with a new phenomenon in British politics – that of a presidential premiership. Just as military forces could be co-ordinated from Downing Street, so could economic matters; the tide of criminality could be turned from the private office; social affairs, industrial unrest, education policy and everything else was taken to be a matter for the personal attention of the Prime Minister.

The war was also an occasion for an outpouring of pronouncements upon liberty. It went wider than the self-determination of Britons in the South Atlantic, however, and encompassed the spirit of people in the North Atlantic. The conflict had awakened the British spirit, so long imprisoned by defeatism and faint-hearted liberalism. 'Doubts and hesitations were replaced by confidence and pride that our younger generation too could write a glorious chapter in the history of liberty,' Thatcher said. It was a spirit of confidence, she also said, which was revived thanks to the economic struggle which had defeated socialism and prised open the dead hand of the state.[15] Throughout the 1980s the word liberty was heard a lot, and it was, predominantly, an assertive, government-approved version of liberty made all the more insistent by the collapse of effective opposition from Labour, from the liberal left, from within the Conservative party and even the press.

In the Thatcher view economic liberalism and individual liberty were yoked together; the experiments of the postwar years (which had contributed to liberty) were aberrations. Her view of liberty was one-sided and highly political. The danger was that wider notions of liberty – discussed throughout this book – were being buried under a mountain of dogma. Liberty was being narrowed, in the public mind, to mean private, economic freedom rather than citizenship. The public still cared about inequality and social justice, as polls revealed. But what was hardened in this time was a cynicism towards idealism and public service.

Thatcher believed passionately in the liberation of the individual, but this consisted in the freedom of private enterprise. 'Such expansion of business freedom,' wrote Hugo Young, '. . . was not matched by a growth of political freedom – of the individual, or anyone else below the level of central government itself.'[16] When communism fell throughout the world from 1989 one idea of liberty seemed to have triumphed. Confidence in it was evinced by the way neo-liberalism was fostered on countries which had won independence and freedom. But it was apparent that there was a radical disjunction in the dogmatic view of negative liberty. The central argument of Mill and Berlin – that of independence from the state – had been appropriated by people who used the language of liberalism selectively. If the freedom trumpeted by Hayek, Friedman, Reagan and Thatcher had any validity it had to be more than just the right to make a profit and spend it as you wished; it had to serve a higher purpose than money-making. And indeed Milton Friedman had explicitly said that free-market capitalism naturally and automatically created and promoted other basic freedoms, such as liberty of speech and of worship.

Trusting to such a pleasant outcome is like relying upon your gods to protect you against a hurricane. The private sector is interested in profits; if civil liberties and political freedom aid this then it is a happy accident, but one not worth waiting for. The leading thinkers of liberalism, from Constant and Mill to Isaiah Berlin, argued that the kind of liberty which gave value to personal life could be endangered by political passivity.[17] If the sanctity of the individual lay at the heart of Western civilisation, other rights were – and must always be – deployed in its defence. For it is certain that negative liberty, taken to an extreme, turns into its opposite. If you do not take care of public business, then someone else will, and you will be powerless against the interfering and prescriptive activities of other people who *do* have power. And it is impossible, even for those who shelter behind the Maginot Line of negative liberty, to avoid the fact that the more passive a citizenry becomes the more government has to act. Liberty, by definition, consists in self-government and autonomy. The governments of Margaret Thatcher and her successors talked of empowering the individual by cutting back the state. Yet in the name of liberty – of, it has to be said, economic liberty dressed up as liberty *tout court* – Britons were diverted away from meaningful participation and public service. The result has not left individuals more powerful: they are more controlled than ever.

State control from the 1980s came to mean something quite different from what had been previously understood or experienced. The lower and middle tiers of government were gutted, taking political power and the chance of participation away from self-motivated citizens. In the 1980s the administration of urban renewal was taken away from city government and given to centrally controlled Urban Development Corporations. After successive reforms Britain has the lowest numbers of elected officials per head in the democratic world, and anyone who suggests reform to encourage participation is greeted with ridicule or cynicism. In any case, most of the functions of local administration have been put out to competitive tender or transferred to Westminster, making the job rather less attractive than it might be.

Why does this matter if we are left in freedom to pursue our individual aims? The history of the later twentieth and early twenty-first century supplies the answer. In this time old solidarities and concepts of citizenship declined, replaced in many cases by single-issue campaigns, identity politics, multiculturalism and other rights-based claims which put personal interests above the idea of civic virtue and fellow-feeling. Those who saw the outcome of economic freedom as – for good or ill – extreme individualism failed to realise that people would recreate new forms of association. In most cases this is harmless, but bundles of competing groups, often claiming rights at the expense of others, have the potential to cause great harm. Those who call upon the state to give special protection to their culture, their customs, their religion, their preferences or their sense of decency are motivated by something very different from the ideals of citizenship when these rights are claimed without regard to the impact on others. The emergence of this type of politics, even these habits of mind, constitutes a grave danger to liberty in the modern state.

If the supreme value of liberty consists of learning to live in a tolerant, plural society in which all are treated equally it can only be made real when people have experience of the needs of others. Autarky, in any form, cuts one off from other groups and turns the state into a forum of conflict rather than of compromise. Participation is not a privilege of liberty, but its foundation. Mill wrote that the only way to teach the habits of liberty is to give a person a role in public affairs: 'He is called upon, while so engaged, to weigh interests not his own; to be guided, in case of conflicting claims, by another rule than his private partialities.'[18] If there is confusion about what liberty means it is because a group mentality has trumped one of citizenship. The remaining chapters of this book follow this development.

This process was speeded up as politics was transformed. As the state grew the business of public affairs was remorselessly dragged to the centre. Attempts at liberation often led to an outcome appreciably different from the stated aim. Deregulation and swathes of privatisation transformed Britain, often for the good – especially the impetus it gave to a stalling economy. But policies of economic liberation, including privatisation of publicly owned utilities, industries and transport systems, meant a greater role for central government through regulation, target-setting and strict Treasury supervision. That which could not be sold off was brought under tight, not to say stifling, central control.

In the areas of national life still under public ownership the move was away from local autonomy. The NHS had been a series of services, often run under the aegis of local government. In the 1980s it was pulled into the remit of direct ministerial control. Schools were subjected to a national curriculum and competition through league tables. The Education Reform Act of 1988 revolutionised British education by requisitioning ninety per cent of teaching time for the state. A further act in 1993, when John Major was in power, imposed even more control over schools and how they were funded. The autonomy of higher educational establishments was stripped away in a process which was compared to the dissolution of the monasteries. Police forces had, since their creation, been locally accountable. The Police Act of 1964 had reduced their number from 123 county, borough and city forces to forty-seven; throughout the 1980s the Home Office began to take responsibility over many aspects of policing, including the size of forces and the type of equipment they had used. In the 1984 miners' strike they experienced a high degree of central co-ordination and political pressure. An act of 1994 detached the forces even more from their regional bases, subjected them to targets and brought them under the control of the Home Office. And over these years the Treasury extended its tentacles into a vast array of life, public and private, subjecting even ministerial autonomy to targets, restraints, incentives and disincentives. It had the power to audit and manage all those aspects of public and private activity which had been remorselessly dragged under central control.

Eric Hobsbawm wrote: 'Central power and command are not diminishing but growing, since "freedom" cannot be achieved except by bureaucratic decision.'[19] And as Major himself was ruefully to concede Britain got the worst of both worlds: the attempt to free society of clutter had led to *more* government and *more* regulation in areas where the government had never trod before, combined with the imposition of a virtual market in public services. The outcome of both was to cede power to bureaucrats and officials to set targets and obsessively design ways to monitor and measure. The result for British politics and public life has been corrosive.

The reforms in government have been corrosive not least because they have sapped liberties from various areas of life which once stood between the individual and the state. It has certainly sapped creativity and autonomy from people who did still prefer public service to private profit and whose participation was most valuable – teachers, academics, public-service broadcasters, doctors and civil servants.

The concentration of power at the centre has made ministers CEOs of national life. There is a marked dependence on government generally. If something is wrong the complaint goes straight to the top. *Something must be done*, the cry goes up from individuals, lobby groups and tabloids however trivial the issue; and the responsible person is a minister. Something wrong with your local hospital, school, policing? Blame the relevant minister and ask him or her to intervene. Litter on the street? Unruly neighbours? City fatcats getting paid too much? You know who to blame.

Gilmour was right that the public would not tolerate the kind of government Hayek imagined – one that was a neutral and distant umpire overseeing the managed anarchy of capitalist life. Increasingly political leaders descended into the minutiae of the country's life, promising to resolve problems which had previously been left to less exalted officials closer to the people who demanded these services. John Major personally intervened to end the scourge of redundant traffic cones; Downing Street under Tony Blair investigated and pronounced upon a bewildering array of apparently strictly personal concerns; every day the newspapers are full of ministerial promises to change our eating habits, curb how much we drink, adjudge what children should learn in school. The tendency has been to encourage this by demanding more, and when cabinet ministers intervene in local and operational matters they are vulnerable to small flurries which blow up into political hurricanes. They inflate hopes and, when they fail, look even more powerless and untrustworthy. In acting this way politicians were attempting to legitimise themselves, but also rebuild faith in the political system. Small things mattered to people, they said, and central government could and should respond to them. It was, if you like, a change from macro to micro.

A beneficiary of and witness to the upheavals of society and greater freedoms of the late twentieth century, Tony Blair understood and articulated the curious mixture of fear and faded confidence which he and his generation were beginning to feel. The men and women behind New Labour were acute observers of the new economy and the fears and frustrations it generated. In particular they paid close attention to the confusions and recurrent moral panics of the 1990s. People were losing faith in politics and the institutions of the state; they were disengaged from their communities and there was a sense of fear of social breakdown. New Labour believed in renegotiating the relationship between the state and the individual. The results have changed Britain dramatically. The thinking which lay behind this renegotiation, and the assumptions it was built upon, must be understood in order to make an assessment of liberty in the modern state.

In 2004 Blair amazed the remnant of liberal Britain with a speech which while praising the benefits of greater freedom expressed frustration and anger at the consequence of these benefits. He articulated just how unsettling many people found the new society. In the 1960s and 70s, he said, crime policy 'focused on the offender's rights, protecting the innocent, understanding the social causes of their criminality'. At the same time, governments and courts were concerned to prevent miscarriages of justice. 'Here, now, today, people have had enough of the 1960s consensus,' Blair said. 'People do not want a return to old prejudices and ugly discrimination. But they do want rules, order and proper behaviour . . . For me this has always been something of a personal crusade.'[20]

Margaret Thatcher had often talked of Victorian values, but she did little actively to restore them, presumably because she expected that rolling back socialism was enough to reawaken inner control and strength of character. Blair, by contrast, believed along with many voters that what he called the culture of respect would only return by compulsion. The self-restraint of past times had been blown away; some people could deal with rampant consumerism, lifestyle choices, moral relativism, social freedom; they could behave even when old forms of discipline had been taken away; but others could not, and the state must deal with the consequences of too much freedom. The empowerment of the individual and the related destruction of communities through economic and social change had disempowered the moral force of society. Blair wholeheartedly supported the economic reforms of the Thatcher years. But he could see that they had brought social breakdown, a new, well-publicised underclass and, above all, a sense of fear and uncertainty in the general public. The individual had triumphed, and people did not like what they saw.

Tony Blair and his New Labour colleagues bridled at the word liberal. It had become a dirty word in their political lexicon. New Labour analysed the radically different economy of the 1990s. If liberalism was a product of the Industrial Revolution the information revolution required a new ideology. It would also demand a new form of freedom (liberty was as tabooed a word as liberalism) – a freedom different from the old assumptions of liberalism. I will describe New Labour policies in the next chapter. What need to be described first are the social changes which accompanied the economic and political transformation in the last two decades of the twentieth century. It was this revolution in society which set the terms for political reforms after 1997.

Society and economy in the late twentieth century had been revolutionised by electronic technology. From the 1950s economists had predicted a wholly new social system as the electronic media took over from old forms of communications, entertainment and economic relations. It awoke hopes on the left that centralisation and resource allocation could become fully automated and all but invisible: the dockets and files associated with bureaucratic states would be replaced by non-intrusive computers which could amass information and target it towards those most in need.[21] Thatcher's disparaging remarks about a socialist state computer quoted earlier reflect this.

But the possibilities of a computer economy also had much to please those on the right – or neo-liberals as they were becoming known – such as Hayek and Friedman. The old metaphor of a free economy running like a human brain could be turned into reality. Fast-as-light communications would transmit information between consumer and producer in real time. The old problem of over-production would be eradicated as business analysts monitored demand, keeping up with sudden changes in consumer preferences. Resources could be allocated to the most profitable parts of the market; waste would be eliminated the more producers knew about their customers. And the customers themselves would in turn benefit as prices were driven down. Choice would increase.

In the past, when communication was ponderous and information hard to come by, the market could only supply a limited range of goods which satisfied a generalised perception of public taste. Computerisation made those feedback loops talked about by economists not only instantaneous but the products themselves, to some degree, bespoke. In the past the economy had not been geared towards demand. It was impossible to fully know and uneconomical in any case to tailor products to individual need; it was better to supply mass-produced goods. Now producers could see that catering to the eccentric and personalised choices of a diverse population could be profitable, so long as they were forearmed with the right information. In the globalised, connected economy there was something for everyone, whether they wanted this season's fashion, an obscure book on Amazon, that Christmas's mass produced toy, or a typewriter spool on eBay. And in all these purchases they could find the cheapest price in the whole world from the choices displayed on their computer screen.

This economy made real and immediate the politicians' promise of choice and freedom. It also allowed the extraordinary consumer boom which has brought wealth and new kinds of jobs. The deregulation of markets and the availability of credit had made possible this two-way exchange of information. For the information-gathering potential of credit cards beat the path for what was to come. They laid bare consumer spending habits; they hinted at a model whereby the instantaneous two-way flow of knowledge could be translated into business success. Store loyalty cards followed as a way of measuring demand and responding to it. In the past your local grocer would get to know your family's habits and buy more of what you habitually wanted at a given period; in the highly competitive supermarket age this response was replicated by the data you provided every time you made your purchases. The Oyster card on London's transport networks similarly offered participants a significant discount in return for laying bare their travel habits, thus allowing planners to analyse bus, train and tube networks and passenger flow with precision. Shopping on the internet took this to new lengths. The data a consumer provides in his or her online habits are now used to tailor advertisements and special offers for that particular consumer, revealing a world of unknown choices to the buyer and a wealth of information for the producer.

The chief virtue of these kinds of relationship, economists from Hayek and Friedman to their modern successors would say, is that they are depersonalised.[22]* For a start, the problem of prejudiced, inefficient human agency is removed as computers allow for greater automation. And intrusion is kept to a minimum. The information accrued is extracted in an invisible way and it is anonymous: *they* aren't interested in *you*, they are interested in breaking down consumer demand into disembodied data. In the words of the National Consumer Council, we are all 'glass consumers' who willingly make available most of our personal information because transparency suits us.[24] But the people who are interested in our habits make no moral judgements. We are watched, but we are not conscious of being watched by a disapproving judge, merely by invisible profit-driven organisations.

The defining characteristic of this kind of economy is risk. As consumers and producers become distanced from each other, when there is no such thing as face-to-face interaction, and when capital is pooled from investors around the world, conventional forms of trust become impossible. The risk of providing financial services therefore becomes greater as the potential for larger profits presents itself. The new technologies which made this possible also provide the solution: risk can be managed. Information is accrued on a vast scale (in 2001 the average Briton's details were on seven hundred databases[25]) and has a high value (the list industry is worth in excess of £2 billion[26]). The range of information is formidable in its depth and extent; records may include information extracted from the following: credit, loyalty and travel cards; insurance, mortgage and job applications; credit rating; online shopping, the harvesting of search terms people use on the internet and their habits on social networking websites; drug tests at work, educational history,

---

* Philip Mirowski argues that many of the influential economists, social scientists and systems operators of the cold war years were scarred by their experiences of the European nightmare: 'It was a foregone conclusion that each of them would be infatuated with the vision of an "institution-free" economics, a virtual reality extracted from the disappointments of their own histories. In operations research they discovered a full-blown virtual reality: war as a problem in logic; politics as a problem in logic; machines as the best embodiment of logic. In statistics they thought they had found a way of conjuring order out of chaos. And then they were already predisposed to believe in the self-sufficiency of the asocial generic individual, for how else had they themselves persevered [against Nazi and Communist persecution]?'[23]

criminal records and welfare entitlements; charitable gifts and membership of political parties. In 2008 an online database was made available
for employers which would detail when someone had been sacked – even
if the police had not been involved, even if it had been a malicious allega-
tion which had led to the person resigning rather than having to deal with
it, and even if it had happened long before.[27]

Having so much information has had two significant results.
Accurate information has allowed people to be judged worthy of credit
who otherwise might have been condemned by human prejudice – a
whole new industry was invented to provide specialist credit, insurance
and mortgage services to the sub-prime market thanks to the sophisticated (as it was thought) statistical analysis of consumers at all levels
of the market. But it has also revealed people to be 'at risk' if the
data relating to them shows them to be likely to default or, simply, if
their data footprint is incomplete. It has been called 'actuarial justice'
whereby data reveals where you lie on a line which goes from 'low
risk/innocent' to 'high risk/guilty'. It has allowed businesses to assess
who is worthy of credit and other services and who is not: a virtual
mapping of the community and the country.[28]

This so called 'dataveillance' allowed the private sector to police
risk to a very high degree. Justice on this model has little to do with
legality: it is concerned with the harm you are likely to do, the costs
you are likely to incur to creditors, insurers and the rest of the community who have to foot the bill for other people's risky economic
behaviour. There has been a shift in risk in modern society from
the state – and hence the taxpayer – to the private sector – and hence
everyone who invests and buys insurance. That is to say the private
sector provides that which used to be provided by the state – loans,
mutual assurance, housing and, increasingly, protection. But the
availability of these benefits is dependent not on justice (in a conventional sense) but upon 'actuarial justice'. If you are in a situation where
you are an otherwise blameless and respectable citizen – say a writer
who does not drive, own a home or have a credit card – you are something of a closed book to the private sector and consequently a risk. If
your credit and loyalty cards reveal that your shopping trolley is
brimming with gin, cigarettes and foie gras then insurance providers

may penalise you. Worse still, if you had a youth chequered by petty crime, debt and poor education in an at-risk postcode, but you have subsequently reformed your ways, then you may face permanent exclusion – for the statistics all point to risk, and the computer does not forget. The paradox of privacy in the connected world is that remote transactions demand that you provide a high degree of information to establish your trustworthiness. The greater your virtual profile, the more you can be trusted to remain anonymous.[29]

The consequences have been extraordinary, and have escaped from the depersonalised computer to the physical world. In the realm of data there are three essential facts: everything is calculable, everything is a risk and everybody has a stake in reducing risk because everyone pays. The ability to monitor the world has revealed risks which, in some cases, people did not realise existed before and, in others, were not problems before. The risk economy obliges everyone to take responsibility for their own risk – and it also has ways of enforcing discipline and shaping personal behaviour.[30] Insurance companies are adept at regulating the risk society. The industry is naturally averse to spontaneity and unpredictability – things which give richness to a normal life but which add cost to society as a whole.

Many of the controls in modern society are put there by insurers, who indirectly force the private and public sector to comply. There is an architecture of pre-emptive security: from nightclub bouncers and private security guards, to alarm systems, gated communities and CCTV, from urgent warnings on food packets and public transport to rules and regulations in the shopping centre. The last time you took part in a sporting or entertainment activity, however seemingly risk-free, you probably noticed that even the most minor thing was hedged in with rules and requirements – the penalty for dissension is exclusion. The same is probably true at your work: a veritable library of negative injunctions and positive requirements. Economists sometimes talk of a theory of 'spontaneous order' arising not out of human plans but economic and social need: this kind of policing is one example. There is no theory, however, of 'spontaneous liberty', apart from the long and winding history of building up restraints against authority.

Until now I have used liberty and freedom interchangeably, not just for stylistic reasons but because they were always bound up. Now I want to make a distinction. Just as we are authors of our own surveillance so are we authors of the controls we experience through the daily round. There is no such thing as a self-regarding act when we are conscious of being connected to each other in these complex relations of modern society. I just stopped writing to smoke a cigarette: who pays? Not just me, but the community when I need to be treated for the consequence of my vices. My neighbour has driven to a supermarket: who should be responsible for the environmental costs she incurs? In the past it was only when the consequences of our actions became apparent that they were liable to punishment, after strict standards of justice were applied. This kind of liberty required discipline, whether it came from self-responsibility or from an informal code of morality. So long as these disciplines existed we were accountable for our own private behaviour: we were told what we could not do, but we were free to do anything where the law was silent.

Our new freedoms are different. We are regulated not by discipline but by control. And control acts pre-emptively. We revel in our new freedoms, but we know that others have like rights, freedoms which may conflict with ours, entailing a cost to our quality of life and our pockets. What is noteworthy is how readily we have accepted controls in society. For our recent freedoms are closely bound up with the controls which suffuse modern society.

We are safe *and* sorry: our liberties have been sacrificed not to state tyranny but to our own profound sense of unease. The French academic A.-G. Slama prophesied the rise of an apolitical future where we are ruled over by 'the angels' – experts, inspectors and evaluators who work on the basis that the 'entire population [should be] considered irresponsible in advance'.[31] There is nothing malevolent in this; it is a soft or benevolent form of power – a kind of health-and-safety utopia – but one which limits human agency nonetheless. Slama holds that it is a moral theory. Safety, hygiene, risk management and so on are good things, but the thought behind them is non-ideological and apolitical; they are preventative not positive, protective not liberating. Unfortunately the regime this theory supports and the culture it engenders is one that necessarily relies on fear. It warns of specific and non-specific threats, and in doing so draws attention to lurking dangers which we might have been blithely unaware of before. For how else would people act unless fear was involved? It relies upon stirring emotions, and as is clear from our own experience and scientific study, humans are particularly ill-equipped to adjudge the proportionality of danger. In most circumstances we err on the side of caution. And the more information there is the more we are inclined to err.

Risk-aversion and what is called the 'precautionary principle' takes over from experimental liberty.[32] It is a peculiarly modern form of anomie, the vertiginous fear of freedom. We mistrust our neighbours; anxiety about crime, sexual deviancy, suspicious strangers, plausible fraudsters or terrorism becomes acute; we do not trust what is put into our food or the safety of the products we buy and the leisure activities we enjoy; and, in the end, no sacrifice is too great to defend our children, families and selves. When it comes to assessing danger we, more than any other generation, tend towards caution; we look for stable doors to bolt or others to blame. In Milton's distinction, 'bondage with ease' trumps 'strenuous liberty' every time. We are caught in a dilemma: as Hans Boutellier argued, 'More freedom is accompanied by more uncertainty, and more certainty goes at the expense of individual freedom.'[33]

But what we might get is more uncertainty and less freedom. For the very act of patching up a problem draws attention to it, increases the feeling of fear, and puts more pressure on the authorities to do something about it. The high demand for health and safety is a consequence of freedom. As Boutellier and others have argued greater social and market freedoms in the modern world exacerbate a sense of danger. It is a kind of post-liberty environment: groups who have won freedom and enjoy the fruits of it (in terms of opportunity, wealth, leisure, social interaction and the thousands of possibilities in the twenty-first century) want a managed freedom, one purged of the downsides of personal independence – social breakdown, offensiveness, accidents, cheating and so on. Put this way the greater the range of freedom of action the greater the risk because you are exposing yourself to danger in your myriad activities. People quite sensibly want to enjoy their new opportunities, and they can be more fulfilling if we know they entail minimal dangers. It can be called managed freedom and managed risk – we enjoy the exhilaration of both *up to a limit*.

Boutellier calls it 'safe freedom'. The cover of his book *Safety Utopia* shows a bungee jumper. It is a symbol for the twenty-first century. We enjoy the thrills and spills of our self-governing lives – but only once a qualified inspector has come and checked things through, the government has passed laws, and a nice gentleman makes us wear a hard helmet despite our feigned protests of bravado. We therefore enjoy the sensations of unlimited freedom – even the illusion of it – but it is carefully managed; like the bungee jumper we have the feeling of flying through the air, but we are safely anchored. As I say this is very sensible. In many ways it is the culmination of our tradition of negative liberty. We are left to enjoy the benefits of whatever freedom we can carve out for ourselves. People increasingly see liberty primarily as existing in personal 'values and lifestyle' rather than in politics. Lives which are already free and full of opportunity need only to be defended against risk and exploitation by outsiders. It does not matter how this is done externally, by any means of government authority, private security, CCTV, new rules; just so long as we retain what we have got, to be enjoyed in the sanctity of our own homes or our favourite leisure spots.

And the consequence is that the *style* of power changes. New authorities are created in response to the myriad activities of social and business life. The consequence is that the external world takes on a new look – that of a society under siege.[34] It breeds a new form of authoritarianism and the attitudes which go with it. It is the authoritarianism which slaps down individuals who endanger the community, only in this case these are people who dissent from the great goal of prevention and protection. The great sadness of managed freedom is that it, in the end, reduces freedom, because we no longer feel fully independent and trusted. It is hard to complain about in general, because in specific situations we are reliant on health and safety. But taken in a collective capacity it creates agencies whose job it is to hunt out, identify and eradicate risk. It is a crusade that has no end, can have no end. And the authority that is required for this infinite task can only grow. One illustrative example is the idea of Situational Crime Prevention (SCP), which has had a large impact on Home Office thinking and, more importantly, private security.[35]

SCP is posited as being entirely fair and democratic. It comes from the starting point, like that of the Hayekian economists, that, left in freedom, we make rational choices on the market. It is based on the 'Economic Model of Man', and is called Rational Actor Theory (RAT). We are all RATs now. Whereas in the past criminology identified particular groups and classes as prone to crime, RAT posits that we are all equally potential criminals, a mixture of good and bad. It is the quintessence of individualism. The theory 'views all individuals, regardless of their social background, as capable of crime, and approaches its preventative measures without identifying any such crime-prone group'.[36] For we are all consumers who make choices. Most often, nice people buy things as the law dictates rather than steal them. This is for a variety of reasons (social expectations, upbringing, a belief in morality, etc.) but mostly because of lack of opportunity and a rationally made decision that the detrimental consequences of theft (losing your job, losing respect, etc.) outweigh the beneficial. In many ways it is like our decisions as consumers: we are exposed to numerous temptations on the high street or online and we choose which ones to give in to. It is a pessimistic view of the individual. If it was easy to steal you would do so routinely, once you had overcome your inner repressions. A criminal makes such choices; the decision to steal or not steal is based on a rational calculation. The language of SCP reads like a manual on advertising: RAT 'portrays offenders as active decision-makers who undertake cost-benefit analysis of presenting crime opportunities'. The way to prevent crime is to reduce 'immediate environment eliciting stimuli'.[37] SCP, like health and safety regulations, is designed to eliminate risk before bad things happen by changing the physical environment.

The impact that SCP has had in the UK can be seen every day. Even if you have never heard of the theory, it has an effect on your daily life and it dominates the landscape. SCP holds that everyone is a potential criminal and the world is a crime scene waiting to happen. That includes you. And likewise you are responsible for the petty crime that dominates modern society. If the thief takes your mobile phone it is because you have failed to pay for a remote immobilisation device. Your failure has presented another person with temptation and a realistic chance of gain. If the thief goes on to rob an outlet in a shopping centre then there are plenty of people we can add to the list of criminals: the centre's management who did not fill the precinct with CCTV and private security guards; the architect who did not think in terms of 'defensible space architecture'; the shopkeeper for putting up an enticing window display; the insurance company who did not insist that the vendor install his wares with electronic chips which could be traced to the criminal; the company who fitted the alarms and advised on security. We are simultaneously victims and accomplices. SCP spreads blame, but it also spreads responsibility. It can be enforced on society by direct and indirect means. The ubiquity of CCTV is a direct means; making insurance companies insist on remote immobilisation devices for cars is indirect. Crime happens when we fail to take precautions, according to the advocates of the theory. A Home Office document in 2000 advising on crime reduction advocated a 'design strategy' for businesses, product designers and individuals protecting their homes. 'View offenders as illicit entrepreneurs', it said, 'and price them out of the market through systematically raising the cost and risks and lowering the rewards of offending.'[38] In other words it was up to us to outpace criminal development by building up our defences through new technology. Blair said that it was the citizen's duty to 'design out crime'.[39]

Situational Crime Prevention has been around as a concept since the 1960s, and as common sense since we lived in caves. But as technology improved and tolerance for petty crime has decreased so have the techniques of SCP. The implications are enormous. Like health and safety policies SCP makes risk reduction a never-ending process. It makes precaution a non-ideological moral issue, something at the heart of our relations with other humans. Am I being unethical, not just unwise, if I dress smartly in a poor area, thus giving someone the temptation and the opportunity to risk arrest by mugging me? Am I turning my neighbours' children into criminals if I have a vintage car (or even an old banger) without state-of-the-art security? Does society make itself culpable if it refuses to guard every public and private space with security guards, CCTV, anti-climb paint? Is the demand for privacy in public places merely selfish? The effect is, in the words of an advocate of SCP, to build a 'fortress society'.

The thinking behind SCP illuminates the age we live in. We are all consumers in the great mart of life. We are offered an array of choices; some people make the wrong choice, and they should be nudged towards choosing the right one through a series of negatives woven into the architecture of daily life. SCP also symbolises the decline of civil society. As individuals alone in a societyless world, we have to live not amongst but against other individuals. It means constructing a system of defence so that we can enjoy our private freedom. It also requires modifying human behaviour through the design of public spaces and products.

Liberty ceases to be political, something we share in common, but something we have in private if we are lucky; if less fortunate we're left bearing the brunt of the 'fortress society' and the 'risk economy'. Individualism has, by a paradox, not made us independent but has made us interconnected as never before to the wider world. Economic liberation has not made us feel freer in every department of life, it has made us fearful and defensive. The courage which brought liberty into being in the first place has drowned in a sea of anxieties and suspicions.

CHAPTER 14

The Transparent Citizen

—ɯ—

> Subjection in minor affairs breaks out every day, and is felt by the whole
> community indiscriminately. It does not drive men to resistance, but it
> crosses them at every turn, till they are led to surrender the exercise
> of their will. Thus the spirit is gradually broken and their character
> enervated.
>
> ALEXIS DE TOCQUEVILLE[1]

When it came to power in 1997 the New Labour government
had analysed the consequences of a radically changed society
described in the preceding chapter. Tony Blair, his ministers and his
advisers were concerned at the consequences of the new economy:
the breakdown of community; the generalised sense of fear and
moral panic; the uncertainty many people felt; and the erosion of
trust – or 'social capital' as they called it – in society. They were also
close readers of the knowledge economy. New patterns of employment, the destruction of old-fashioned hierarchies at work, the
disappearance of heavy industry, and an economy which func-
tioned by producing intangibles had made people dynamic, creative
and innovative. They had no intention of taking power back from
the globalised market. There was a convergence of neo-liberalism
and the left: new technologies flattened hierarchies, destroyed flabby
institutions, democratised culture and gave people what they
wanted.[2]

Britain had a future as a leader in the intangible knowledge
economy – in the fields of financial services, high-tech electronics,

biotech, genetic research, entertainment, computing and so on. Such an economy *generated* freedoms by unlocking human potential from traditional work, which was authoritarian, routine, mechanical and specialised to a high degree. New Labour believed that these developments had revolutionised society and individual consciousness. What was lacking, however, was a politics to complement the knowledge revolution.[3]

Trust had evaporated, New Labour believed, because of the failure of traditional parties to keep up with the revolution. What had happened was that the private sector had broken free into a new realm of possibilities while the state was stuck somewhere in the past. In its provision of services, its administration of justice and its relationship with the citizen, the state was old-fashioned and inefficient. No wonder people had lost confidence – the gap between the public and private was glaring. The solution was to extend the knowledge economy into the field of government. The private sector had mapped out the country with detailed statistical analysis. But who should know most about citizens if it wasn't the state with its vaults of files and forms? Business had used this information to determine need and allocate resources – were these not priorities for the welfare state? The private sector had also influenced human behaviour with positive and negative inducements; could not this be a model for politics?[4] The new companies had done this with maximum effectiveness and minimum visible interference. The paradox, which had bedevilled the left, of utilising the state for good without interfering in private and business life seemed to be at last soluble through technology.* It was not about whether the state was big or small these days, the new government said: it was about effectiveness. At the heart of the New

---

* Hayek had argued that central planning would always founder for the simple reason that it required information, and information in a pure and universal form was, by the nature of things, unavailable: 'The economic problem of society is . . . not merely a problem of how to allocate "given" resources . . . it is a problem of the utilization of knowledge which is not given to anyone in its totality.' Was this true, in the information revolution, in the twenty-first century?[5]

Labour project was the mission to make the state 'strategic and enabling'.[6]

The interesting thing about the government was how many were human rights and criminal barristers and how many had been involved in civil liberties campaigns. Perhaps for this very reason they had much to say about liberty in the modern age. In the past the left had associated liberty with progressive politics: the triumph of socialism would liberate the individual. But the people had achieved an unprecedented amount of liberty by other means. They had also abused it. In the late twentieth century, New Labour believed, traditional liberties, which were, as they put it, vertical – running up from citizen to state – had broken down. These liberties enjoined participation, self-control and active citizenship. They reached perfection when beliefs and assumptions were held in common and when there were a host of tacit arrangements in society which regulated behaviour. But could these stand up in a radically different Britain of competing lifestyle choices, waning democratic participation, identity politics and multiculturalism? Now in an age of excessive individualism they believed the relationship should be horizontal – in other words a relationship between people's individual rights and their responsibilities to each other. These things had once been tacitly accepted; now they had to be enforced.[7]

The European Human Rights Commissioner Alvaro Gil-Robles, who visited the UK in 2004, commented,

The United Kingdom has not been immune . . . to a tendency increasingly discernible across Europe to consider human rights as excessively restricting the effective administration of justice and the protection of the public interest . . . I was struck by the frequency with which I heard calls for the need to rebalance rights protection, which, it was argued, had shifted too far in favour of the individual to the detriment of the community.[8]

This was a new language of communitarianism and responsibility incompatible with the liberal model under which traditional liberties had developed. The individual had been put at the centre of politics for centuries; the radical implications of New Labour's ideas were that in a multicultural society communities had to be protected as individuals had once been.[9]

The left had also associated liberty with protection from the blunders and selfishness of a capitalist ruling class. They were the product of the Industrial Revolution; but a new economic and social revolution, and the collapse of both progressive politics and democratic elan, demanded a rethink of liberty. In a way New Labour probably knew too much about liberty, and this very knowledge of its internal flaws left its leading lights disillusioned. Governments in the modern world had surrendered much of their power over the economy; decisions on the grand sweep of policy were increasingly being taken out of their hands. But if they could not make big changes to the lives of the country modern governments could make strategic interventions in the minutiae of national life. If in the past ministers had been responsible for setting the general terms of policy based on principles, and delegated the task of implementation to officials, they now switched to a hands-on operational function. When ministers pulled levers but the vehicle did not respond their promises to be all-round problem-solvers were somewhat exposed. Civil liberties seemed to be a hindrance to this new style of politics.

In this flurry of modernisation, the government believed that it could answer one of the fundamental anxieties in modern society. People had become intolerant of antisocial behaviour and petty crime; worse than that they feared disorder, and governments had a duty to reduce fear even if it was a feeling and not based on an accurate reading of crime statistics. This hardening of attitudes was related to the belief that state welfare led to dependence, and hence nurtured the vices which grew to become actual crimes. In other words the new creative, dynamic age was being poisoned by fear, hatred and animosity. The benefits of the economic revolution (which New Labour celebrated) had not been shared equally. As one minister told Tory MPs: 'Does anyone really doubt that mass unemployment juxtaposed with yuppie culture in the 1980s, with some young people living high-octane lifestyles and others with nothing to look forward to but the giro, did nothing but breed resentment, anger, criminality and antisocial behaviour?'[10]

It was an erosion of social capital, and the new economy – with its emphasis on co-operation, innovation and entrepreneurial risk – depended upon trust. The state had a very big role in this economy, but a very different one from past notions. Its primary job was to make neighbourhoods safe, raise the educational standards of the nation's future entrepreneurs and skilled workers and heal the tensions which economic dislocation had fostered.[11] In the words of one of the government's advisers, a society and economy which was fluid needed a fluid, flexible, strategic state to mirror it. There should be a move from 'social spending to social investment, passive to active welfare'. Government should be joined up, delivering 'holistic, integrated solutions'.[12] In other words, it should, like a modern fighter plane, combine intensive firepower with zero radar profile.

Joined-up government meant integrating the data that the state held on its citizens. Like private-sector dataveillance the state could use social statistics to map the country, finding out where need was the greatest. Governments have always wanted to predict behaviour and measure the resources of the country in order to lighten the burden of government, limit waste and increase efficiency; information technology was making this easier. By joining up the vast databases of the state – with each other as much as with data procured by private companies – a more complete picture would emerge. Suddenly new problems began to appear as the information flowed in. By data-matching across the separate welfare services, and with the aid of privately garnered records, the state could detect fraud, allocate resources effectively and, most importantly, identify 'at risk' children, the vulnerable and people who were on the border of legitimate and illegitimate activities. Problems that would develop later in life could be predicted from a sophisticated reading of the data which flowed into government departments, based on analysing the records of adults who had subsequently developed character flaws.[13] As Blair said, dysfunctional individuals could be predicted from their families' pattern of behaviour: 'In truth we can identify such families virtually as their children are born.'[14] Data-mining was a key part of pre-emptive child protection, and a national database of patient records was intended to allow the NHS to pre-empt diseases, set targets and direct resources. These were techniques, ideas and a language which the government admitted came from private commerce. The aim was to develop 'consumer-focused services'.[15]

The great advantage was that politics was taken out of state involvement in the lives of its citizens. Technology meant government at a distance: there would be less form-filling, interrogation and direct involvement with officials. And armed with this information the state could intervene with precision in the lives of people who needed it – like a rapier rather than a blunderbuss. As in other things, the government was eager to follow the business model, in this case embedding (to use the Prime Minister's Strategy Unit's phrase) a culture of risk-orientation in government departments based on statistical analysis of audited data.[16] The convergence of the data gathered from health, police, social services, Inland Revenue, DVLA, national insurance and welfare services would highlight who was defrauding the public and who was at risk of being abused or developing criminal behaviour.[17]

It was almost as if information was creating its own policies. For example speedy intervention could not work if people were shielded by privacy. Proving your identity was a prerequisite of utilising private services (in the sense of identifying that you were who you said you were when you used electronic methods of payment with PINs, etc.). This was of great use to the private sector which cut down on fraud and used the information to refine services. The same should be the case when utilising public services. A Smart Card or Entitlement Card or ID card, or whatever it happened to be called at any given moment in the early 2000s, would establish identity and feed desirable information back to the government. The essence of the case was that people were happy to do this in their private dealings, so why not in their encounters with the state? Privacy was a significant barrier to data-sharing, strategic pre-emption and resource allocation, something which the government felt made it less powerful than private business.

In many cases joining up data across government departments was a success, identifying and helping people in genuine need. But the refined techniques of statistical analysis raised a moral dilemma. Could the state continue to sit back and wait for crimes to be committed once the risk was flagged in their reams of data? This problem predated New Labour. It is called a change from the old penology to 'risk-based' penology. The old model consisted of preventing, detecting and punishing crimes and rehabilitating criminals; it was one which the public would acknowledge as the hallmark of the criminal justice system. However the new model has become dominant. It is a risk-based penology which is dependent upon 'actuarial justice', the product of the information revolution and data-sharing. Unlike the old model, which targets individuals, it uses its comprehensive information to target dangerous groups and put them under surveillance; and, like the actuarial techniques of the insurance industry, it is pre-emptive in character.[18]

The government seemed impressed at the kind of community policing which was emerging, and which I discussed earlier. A great deal of the burden of preventing crime was transferred to individuals, businesses and service providers indirectly. And the methods of shaping human behaviour by holding out incentives and disincentives (such as the extra-legal punishment of giving a bad credit rating) were also deeply impressive for ministers and officials.

New Labour liked the idea of public/private initiatives, and here was such a mutually beneficial scheme in operation. At a time when the criminal justice system was building in greater protections for suspects – by subjecting the police to strict supervision with the automatic right to a lawyer, taped interviews and an increase in the burden of proof necessary for a conviction – private security offered help in the fight against crime and a model for reform. Zero tolerance in, for example, a shopping centre of antisocial behaviour of all kinds – busking, begging, noise, groups of youths, political protest and so on – made respectable shoppers feel more secure and it seemed to prevent bad behaviour developing into crimes. The development of SCP techniques by private business (including CCTV) helped in the war on crime and showed the public that the government was getting tough. Data-sharing between private companies and the police offered a new frontier in the fight. At Stansted airport people who rented cars were required to give fingerprints to complete their transaction; the information was made available to Essex police. Similarly, Kent police worked with the Bluewater shopping centre in a scheme of fingerprinting customers, ostensibly to prevent credit card fraud. Identification and payment by biometrics and thumbprints were becoming more common in shops and pubs in the early 2000s.[19] Private CCTV footage and travel records from the

Oyster database provided police with other tools in the fight against crime.[20]

Ministers took very seriously the idea that the state was losing its monopoly on force. Their aim was to remodel state welfare so that it replicated the incentives and disincentives of the free market. The citizen had rights, they said, and he or she must have responsibilities as well. The state should enforce reciprocation. The MP Frank Field, who had a deep personal interest in the consequences of antisocial behaviour, told the Home Affairs Committee in 2003 that there had been a 'movement from class politics to the politics of behaviour'. Throughout modern history, he said, governments had left character development to other forces, to tacit agreements within civil society about what was acceptable. The highly individualised nature of modern society had ruined this. In the absence of this common morality and informal structures of authority the state now had to intervene when parents and teachers failed to teach young people the difference between right and wrong.[21] This represented a revolution in the relationship between state and individual.

John Reid, Blair's fourth and final Home Secretary, spelt out this changed relationship: 'There can be no rights without commensurate responsibilities, and we ought to be talking more about responsibility rather than concentrating on rights . . . The safety and security of the individual must be weighed in the balance with the safety of the public.' This was a powerful statement. The idea of individual liberties, which had underpinned thinking in Britain and America for centuries, was being seriously challenged. Now, it seemed, our liberties were enjoyed collectively; the security of 'the public' came above individual freedom. The war against antisocial behaviour, and its wide acceptance by public opinion, made it clear that tolerance had a limit, and society was entitled to enforce its collective opinion upon the minority.[22]

To the great frustration of ministers the old system seemed stacked against their crusade. It was common sense, they said, that the law enforcement agencies should have power to pre-empt antisocial behaviour because this kind of activity had a detrimental effect on communities and led to greater crime. It was common sense to intervene early to nip criminal tendencies in the bud. It was not common sense to hedge in the police with rules and procedures. It was nonsense to an ordinary person when criminals walked free for lack of evidence or on a technicality.[23] Protecting suspects and preventing miscarriages of justice was like fiddling as Rome burned. Jack Straw, Home Secretary from 1997 to 2001, and David Blunkett, his successor until December 2004, both believed that the working class would lose confidence in the criminal justice system, and politics generally, because they bore the brunt of antisocial behaviour and petty crime.[24] These people, Blunkett alleged, saw the justice system as alien to their interests, the plaything of what he amusingly called the 'liberati' – metropolitan liberals who made money and salved their conscience by supporting the anarchic system. The 'biggest miscarriage of justice in today's system', said Blair, 'is when the guilty walk away unpunished'.[25]

The criminal justice system, the government said, had been designed for a distant age of inequality when the individual stood in need of protection against forces which were corrupt, incompetent and partial. Sympathy was with the suspect and miscarriages of justice were held to be a moral affront to society; the victim was largely left out of considerations in this impersonal system, which was a moral affront to common sense and sympathy. Modernity, however, required rebalancing the justice system towards the victim and to society at large – everyone was collectively a victim when an alleged criminal got off on a technicality, the policeman's hands were tied and when courts were slow, ponderously procedural and pre-occupied by the old saw that it was better that a guilty person was acquitted than an innocent person be unjustly punished. From 1997 the government set about reforming the criminal justice system, cutting back on the right of trial by jury, ending the double jeopardy rule, toughening sentences, changing sentencing rules and allowing for more summary justice. Most worryingly legal aid was brutally slashed and the damages which might be paid to victims (if they could now be so called) of miscarriages of justice were limited by statute, so curtailing the workings of justice. It got more draconian at a time when crime was falling. What the government was doing, it admitted frankly, was improving the image of the justice system, democratising it so that it accorded to a human desire for punishment and natural justice. It was responding to the general frustration with the 'I know my rights' attitude of criminals which periodically worked tabloids into a lather.

And as violent and property crime fell people became more intolerant of petty misdemeanours and antisocial behaviour. Antisocial behaviour was, said Blunkett, a scourge and for Blair eradicating it was a personal crusade. They had firsthand experiences of how people's lives had been blighted by social breakdown. And once again the relationship between data and risk management became clear: computational modelling and data analysis showed that there was a 'hardcore' group of persistent offenders and an equally identifiable group of victims. Risk assessment identified these people; they were the group which Blair referred to as the beneficiaries of a suspect-orientated criminal justice system.[26] An act of 1998 created Anti-Social Behaviour Orders (ASBOs) which could be used to control an individual for particular offences. Antisocial behaviour was henceforth treated as a civil offence (judged by a balance of probabilities) rather than a criminal offence (judged by the more exacting 'beyond all reasonable doubt').

Police, local authorities, communities and even aggrieved individuals could respond speedily to public concern at local nuisances, placing an ASBO on repeat offenders and scourges of the community. A magistrate had to decide, on a balance of probabilities, whether an individual was engaged in 'behaviour which causes or is likely to cause harassment, alarm, or distress to one or more people who are not in the same household as the perpetrator'. The penalty for breaching the terms of an ASBO was five years in prison. In other words non-criminal behaviour could become criminal behaviour very easily and without exacting standards of justice. ASBOs were easily obtainable, and the system allowed the community to take matters into their own hands. They were backed by other powers once considered shocking, such as curfews and dispersal orders. It was a considerable innovation for a country which pioneered individual liberty. The European Human Rights Commissioner commented that ASBOs were novel in that they did not protect an individual against another individual but were a community punishment against an individual. 'This inevitably results in a very broad, and occasionally, excessive range of behaviour falling within their scope as the determination of what constitutes antisocial behaviour becomes conditional on the views of any given collective.'[27]

It was a new penalty for what was considered a modern kind of offence. Whereas crime was sporadic, antisocial behaviour was constant. It was typically perpetrated by young people against the vulnerable and defenceless. And it led to the development of more serious traits later on – antisocial disorders and violent crime. Therefore it had to be stopped by sterner methods than were available to conventional law (which treated individual crimes in isolation, not with regard to wider societal concerns) and it had to be integrated into a wider strategy of co-ordinating all agencies of the state to identify and prevent future crimes. 'It is very tough. It is intrusive,' said Blair of his policies. 'Naturally, people will complain about the "nanny state", but, for some of these families and their children, a nanny state is what they need – for their sake as much as for ours.'[28]

The draconian nature of ASBOs chimed with the government's overall policy in regard to problem groups. If parents could not, the state should teach the country's youth the difference between right and wrong. The value of ASBOs was that they were a short, sharp shock, which denied people access to places and enjoyment of activities they had previously regarded as normal. The aim was to deny freedom, because unbridled freedom was the problem. ASBOs were early interventions at a crucial stage of life, designed to show the consequences of actions and that society was not completely powerless. The government could act in many ways, nudging people in the right direction by banning advertising on smoking, forbidding smoking in public places or increasing tax on alcohol; ASBOs were a shove towards the good. Acceptable Behaviour Contracts, a further refinement to the system, were made between young people and local housing offices and the police. Similar contracts were made between children and schools, and others made youths promise not to commit acts of vandalism or become nuisances on pain of the forfeiture of privileges. Parenting orders and compulsory compensation payments made by parents of unruly children were supposed to mould adult behaviour and responsibility as well. This was an active welfare state, not the old-fashioned passive one. 'Policy should not simply proclaim personal responsibility or blame,' said a Strategy Unit report, 'but needs to be shaped around the ways in which people actually think and feel, and the social and psychological forces that influence behaviour.'[29]

It is an inescapable fact that these polices were popular. The invention of ASBOs was welcomed by all political parties and the public and the introduction of 'common sense' into criminal justice satisfied tabloid editors and thousands of people who called in to radio debates. Shifting policing to take account of social breakdown in the deprived areas of the country was badly needed and widely accepted. The government was prepared to take a hard line. It marked the end of the liberal consensus which had ruled politics for over a century. It helped entrench a feeling that different groups should be treated in particular ways. Where once the general belief was that citizens should be treated equally, politicians were articulating the idea that some people deserved liberty while others had to *earn* their rights. Liberty, justice, concern for the social disadvantages of a criminal were fine things, Blair said: 'But our first duty is to the law-abiding citizen. They are our boss. It's time to put them at the centre of the criminal justice system. That is the new consensus on law and order for our times.'[30]

But it is an equally inescapable fact that the war against antisocial behaviour was concentrated down the social scale, targeted at pre-defined groups. Ministers claimed that this was because antisocial behaviour was disproportionately committed and experienced by people in the poorest neighbourhoods. But antisocial behaviour simply is not a lower-class phenomenon. ASBOs and other interventions (such as on obesity) are aimed at behaviour and habits which have run far out of control; they do not get to the root of the problems. The state was powerless to curb the sources of antisocial behaviour: the high degree of individualism which permeates society; an outrageous media which glories in disrespect, offensiveness and consumer-driven desire; the consensus which makes a virtue out of moral relativism.

The government would not think to interfere with these aspects of liberal society. It could not afford to prevent middle-class anti-social behaviour. There were few votes in compelling people to set a good example, to police themselves. The consequence would be an unthinkable curtailment of social freedoms. Therefore we have one half of liberalism, the commitment to unrestrained freedom of speech and action with which the state dares not interfere.[31]

As Will Durant argued long ago we are brave in morals but cowards in the face of social disorder. Popular culture can say what it likes, and the sensible majority can take offensiveness, outrageous experiments, outspoken words without it affecting their behaviour. But others cannot; they translate art into action. There is a sense that life is out of control, that media, culture, social life and economy are in a state of constant flux. This is bracing and exciting for most; for others it is scary or an opportunity to slack off traditional commitments to the life of the community. We cannot deal with the consequence, and the demand is for more controls. The end of a liberal criminal justice system is tolerated because it restores controls for the weak-minded without affecting *us*, the law-abiding majority who can continue to enjoy the freedom of consumerism, personal independence and a taboo-busting culture. We are liberals in manners but illiberal in politics. 'Our forefathers were free in politics, and stoically stern in morals,' wrote Durant; 'they respected the Decalogue, and defied the State. But we deify the State and riddle the Decalogue.'[32]

The consequence is a multiplicity of rules and regulations, the construction of the 'fortress society'. Governments from the 1980s until the present date have responded to demands for a stronger state to fill the gaps of a weaker society. These demands have welled up from society, and they were woven into the New Labour ideology. What we have found is that we are caught between the pincers of a more controlling private sector and a more authoritarian state. And there is an unholy alliance between the two. The boundary between public and private has blurred. They are complementary in the fight against crime and disorder, and each borrows from the other. As the Information Commission said in 2006, 'more tasks of government are carried out through a sometimes complex combination of public, private,

voluntary sector and market mechanisms'.[33] The government has gleefully jumped at this opportunity. Informal controls adopted by business
are integrated into the state's policing functions and responsibility is
more and more shared between state, business and citizen.

Blair believed that civil liberties were 'invented for another age'.
They were needed when the individual faced state oppression, and
needed protection. But now the state was a benign presence. Why
would you oppose such a friend? And why would you throw road-
blocks in front of its mission to impose order? Old-fashioned liberties
made the task of governing far too hard. In any case, by merging
policing functions across the public, private and voluntary sectors the
government was merely conforming to public desires. 'For me', said
Blair, musing on the challenges of fighting terrorism and crime, 'this is
not an issue of liberty but of modernity.'[34] What was forgotten, in this
rush towards integration, was that the private and public have different functions. It is the state's duty to protect us from unwarranted
intrusions of all sorts. By adopting a business model in its approach to
government New Labour obscured this difference and betrayed its
role. It was taking politics out of the task of government. It assumed
that we welcomed the controls appearing throughout society because
we had voted with our credit cards, or that we liked surveillance
because so many people appeared so keen to unburden their souls and
confess their vices in blogs and on social networking websites. This
was, however, no excuse for the state conscripting people who still
enjoyed their privacy or lamented the controls of the private sector.

What was required more than ever in this time of growing authoritarianism were leaders who had the creativity and vision to articulate
a new form of liberalism. Society very frequently needs to be saved
from a headlong rush towards things it may later regret – the history
of liberty is, without a doubt, the constructions of restraints which are
counterintuitive and very often go against the instincts of human
nature. In the late twentieth and early twenty-first centuries the threat
to liberty came from fear and an overriding desire for security. Rather
than turn these instincts towards constructive ends, governments
have marshalled support around the politics of fear and made the
promise of absolute security their *raison d'être*. As society became

more intolerant and crime and disorder became prevalent what was needed was a politician who could reconcile greater security with the best of the liberal tradition.

Instead ministers queued up to ridicule liberty. The language of the Blair governments was to denigrate 'airy-fairy' civil liberties, in the words of Blunkett. Perhaps they believed that too much freedom was at the root of the problems they were dealing with; that freedom was making the people ungovernable. Perhaps they believed that the new economy produced liberty of its own accord, in terms of choice, individualism and creativity. Whatever they assumed they downplayed the value of classical liberty, treating it as incompatible with the new way of governing – joined-up, streamlined and targeted. They believed that as government became more remote thanks to technology it would cease to be irksome and interfering.

For a government which came to power promising to restore trust the ten years of Blair's premiership were a distinct let-down. The invasion of Iraq in 2003 certainly played a large part in this. But the attitude of the government certainly helped in this lamentable process. Withdrawing from liberalism and liberty did not reassure people that the government was modern, but made many suspicious that the state was becoming repressive. Greater controls and regulations did not make people feel safer, but highlighted reasons to be fearful. The language of breakdown and behavioural blights helped fuel the very process of degradation, making 'ASBO' an everyday expression, and ideas of Britain being an 'ASBO Nation' were repeated in the press with salacious glee. The government had acted firmly, stripping liberties. But it had no vision to put in its place. There was no theory of how the citizen could be protected from forces beyond his or her control because the new leaders could not see the state or big business as anything but benign.

And as society and the architecture of daily life became more controlling and surveillance of all kinds became ubiquitous people felt less free. People faced surveillance and tracking at work, fewer freedoms and more remote supervision. Shopping and leisure became fraught with checks and rules. This was bad enough, but it could not be resisted. When the government not only promoted these ideas but seamlessly integrated with the process the citizen could feel doubly cheated. The state, business and large parts of the media put safety first in all circumstances. Now no one knew who had information on them and how it was being used; how often and to what level they were being watched. Attempts at regulation and transparency, such as the Data Protection Act and the Freedom of Information Act, failed to keep up with technological advances. Britons experienced the highest level of surveillance in the free world. In 2008 it was discovered that the government's Chief Whip was being bugged by the security services without any minister being aware. In 2006, the last recorded year before the bugging incident, eight hundred government agencies made 253,000 remote intrusions into the lives of citizens. Surveillance had become routine, a reflexive habit on the part of law enforcers and government agencies; a person could be bugged if they were suspected of fly-tipping. One million innocent people had their DNA on police databases and the logging of fingerprints and DNA of schoolchildren was becoming routine. The blanket justification was that it was effective and justified by national security. At least at first. In April 2008 it was revealed that Poole Borough Council had been using surveillance techniques passed under the Regulation of Investigatory Powers Act, intended for terrorism and serious crime, to check whether a couple had told the truth about their circumstances when applying for a school place for their three-year-old daughter.[35]

Some have called this the Big Brother State. But it is, I think, wrong to say that all this is being used for malign purposes. It is certainly true that politicians and bureaucrats want to make life easier for themselves, and a quest for efficiency which is not tempered by an instinct of self-restraint or a strong opinion about freedom can become, of its own, stifling and oppressive. The intent certainly is not political; ministers profess to be 'ideologically neutral'[36] and mere technicians in a process of law enforcement and the administration of public services. But this professed neutrality is part of the problem; it means a drift towards a purely managerial ethos unbothered either way with ideological or moral scruples. The effect is to sap liberty from society because people *feel* less free. We feel like potential criminals, or at least passive members of the fortress society. 'All of today's surveillance processes bespeak a world where we know we're not really trusted,' said a report for the Information Commission in 2006. 'Social relationships depend on trust and permitting ourselves to undermine it in this way seems like slow social suicide.'[37]

New Labour's programme depended almost entirely on trust. But people have come to trust it less as it appears swept along by technological solutions without an ideology of liberty to modify it. People do still get treated unjustly by government departments just as they are judged harshly by business. The police – in common with other mere human beings – have not risen above blunders and prejudices to the extent that the protections the courts offered can be watered down. Blair heaped praises on ASBOs, rightly in some cases where people had been saved from vicious bullying, but he refused to mention that the ease of procuring an ASBO and the difficulty of gaining redress meant that many people were unfairly punished, or punished for laughably trivial forms of behaviour or, as the EU Human Rights Commissioner put it, turned from pesky nuisances into pariahs at a worryingly early age. When ASBOs worked they worked well, but that was no excuse for a system riddled with flaws. For many people at the sharp end – those who experience ASBOs, curfews and fixed penalty notices or who are labelled 'at risk' thanks to trial by data – the state does seem remote and unjust and they feel powerless against it.[38] The bus stops in the council estate near my home have threatening posters telling me I'm being watched; a harsh, monotone computerised voice on radio advertisements tells me that if I don't pay my car tax the police computer will find me. The effect of this tough love is to make people see the state not as a paternalistic guide but as authoritarian and intrusive. The natural response, I suppose, is to kick back at it. I would. Petty authoritarianism gets petty rebels, and so much the worse for society.

In removing the old protections against injustice in the name of efficiency the government has exposed itself to accusations of incompetence and vindictiveness. The government was rocked in 2007 and 2008 by a series of data leaks, the most serious being the loss of the records, including the bank details, of twenty-five million people. This was at a time when people were increasingly unsure about what happened to personal information and concerned about identity theft.[39] Whatever trust there was that 'database Britain' was slick, seamless and safe went out of the window.

That same old anti-authoritarianism which this book has high-lighted is still there. Unfortunately it manifests itself as hostility towards power and a deepening mistrust of the state in all its guises. The drive for bureaucratic efficiency, the desire for security, the common sense of risk-orientated policy-making and the ambition to eliminate waste and fraud – all features of our age in politics and in business and in private life – have produced great successes. But progress in these areas has not been matched by progressive politics. People have been left feeling alienated and disempowered, more controlled and less and less the agents of their lives. Efficiency simply does not translate into loyalty or a sense of involvement. Government is perceived less as a human institution and more as a self-acting machine. And a society which makes precaution and prevention a priority – 'safety first' – is hardly one which breathes the pure air of liberty. As the state becomes more effective yet at the same time more remote and bossier it becomes almost impossible to resist and harder to see how it can be changed by normal citizens.[40] Why participate in politics when you are so obviously powerless?

'You have zero privacy anyway – get over it,' said Scott McNealy, CEO of Sun Microsystems.[41] You don't have to be a paranoid reader of Orwell to find this, or other developments, alarming; the merest knowledge of the transparency of our lives produces feelings of discomfort, at least. It is hard to frame valid objections as technology burgeons. The mining of data to find patterns of child abuse surely cannot be resisted on grounds of privacy. But failures and inconsistencies can give us valid grounds for complaint. People who objected to CCTV cameras as they sprouted in profusion in the early 1990s on civil liberties grounds were soon muted when it was realised that they were being watched by an inert and passive piece of machinery. They looked, but they did not react. They did not make a moral judgement which modified our behaviour.[42] Sometimes they worked well, but often they were installed thanks to a misplaced belief that they would prevent crime. In fact they helped *solve* some crimes and

they prevented traffic offences, but, after spending £500 million on
4.5 million cameras (the ramparts of the fortress society), the Home
Office admitted that 'the CCTV schemes that have been assessed
had little overall effect on crime levels'.[43]

CCTV cameras are a daily symbol of our age: the useful and the
redundant bunged together; the unconquerable faith in technological
solutions; the 'safety first' state of mind; above all the outrageous
cost. Answering a question from Nick Clegg in the Commons in
2008 about the gargantuan expansion of the surveillance society
Gordon Brown countered the leader of the Liberal Democrats by
saying that everyone accepted CCTV, so why not DNA databases
and the like? That is how things work; accept one knick-knack and
the case for *more* CCTV, *more* databases, *more* intrusions becomes
irresistible. Once you have embarked on the route of technological
assistance there is no going back.

Overriding confidence in predicting behaviour from data-profiling
produces a state of mind which places the citizen at considerable danger of being enmeshed in a mysterious process. Creating a virtual
profile of some disembodied person is to read a 3D world, with all
its aberrations and unpredictability, in 2D. The profusion of data
makes risk assessment possible and the increasing sense of risk makes
data collection more frenzied. It also tends to elevate the value of data
beyond human judgement. But data are only as good as the information available, the algorithms used in the process and the person who
reads or misreads the output. It is a danger to which no one is
immune. In 2006 computer blunders meant that two thousand
people were wrongly labelled as criminals. In December 2003 and
January 2004 the FBI computer highlighted dangerous passengers
on Air France and British Airways flights, which were grounded or
escorted by fighter jets. They comprised a Welsh businessman, an
eminent Egyptian scientist, a Chinese woman and a five-year-old
child. Remote identification procedures resulted in considerable
disruption, resolved only by actual, face-to-face checks.[44] There are
plenty of other examples. More serious than the minor inconvenience of flawed data-profiling was the case of Maher Arar, a
Canadian who suffered eleven months' torture in Syria (where he

was extraordinarily rendered by the American authorities) after the information held on him and shared between governments was wrongly interpreted.[45]

There has been no politician who has articulated a politics which keeps pace with this change. There is no vision of liberty in the twenty-first century except a desire that the state retreat and stop meddling and monitoring. That is not likely to happen; the computer cannot be switched off and data cannot be ignored. It is futile to see technology as a problem of itself: it has been the retreat of ideology and the belief that politics can master the negative and positive results of technological change which has been truly corrosive. 'Citizens are asked to accept the gathering of greater levels of information and intelligence in the knowledge that this will facilitate improvements in public safety and law,' the government said in 2007 – following years of botched IT projects and well-publicised mistakes.[46]

This marked a reversal in the relationship between state and citizen – and between citizens. We are obliged to be transparent. And it is ever more the case that we are governed by the false assumption that if we have nothing to hide we have nothing to fear. We are all conscripts in the war against insecurity. We are all transparent, not just to a state computer but to everyone who has the wherewithal to plunder the vast mines of data. What does this do to people? It is hard to tell. More and more people gain a thrill out of making themselves transparent, putting their trivial lives on permanent public record. But this seems to me to be the liberation felt by the nudist rather than a new and valid form of consciousness. It may very well be that people will come to value privacy again and will seek ways of rebuilding protections. The ability of all kinds of people to construct virtual doppelgängers calls into question Mill's idea of our private, sanctified inner sphere, and makes us victims of neighbourhood prying and gossip, albeit often willing victims. The whole experiment in social sharing websites shows that we have within us a longing for the village or tribe which often gets the better of our longing for anonymity. This is the dilemma of modern man, and has been long before the computer was invented. We oscillate between the extremes of complete transparency and lonely anonymity, and neither really satisfies.

At the moment we are enjoying a revival in community life. But it makes us more conformist and less capable of original thought. Pity he or she who gets involved in a transient cause célèbre which is besotting the press; the price to pay for sticking your neck out, or even being in the wrong place at the wrong time, is for salacious muckrakers to pore over your life. It encourages passivity. What brave soul, for instance, would enter public life when he or she knows that every blameless but titillating habit and every tiny personal mistake is there to be discovered? The choice is to conform or to retreat into a kind of lifestyle where no one really cares what you do. It is little wonder that debate has in a sense been revivified by internet forums (such as those run by national newspapers and the broadcast media) in which participants can chose to be pseudonymous in vigorous discussions about topical issues (most do). It has revived something like old-fashioned townhall debate, but the very anonymity which gives participants freedom to vent their anger or express unpopular views with confidence devalues the discussion and makes it marginal to policy-makers.

The character of such public discussion bespeaks a world where courage is dissipated because we are so easily traceable. In a rule-bound and transparent world, where someone has the ability to monitor your petty infractions of minor rules, there are no such things as privacy or a self-regarding act unless you make pains to construct defences. An ID card which joins together all our information on a national database makes us live even more with the sense of being watched; whether it is well intentioned and well administered does not matter.

The problem with justifying everything on the grounds of utility or national security is that we quickly lose sense of the idea that freedom is made up of many intangible factors, privacy being key. There are advantages from maximum efficiency, but also great dangers, the first being the feeling of being less free and more regimented. This is the problem of technocratic government which downplays ideology: all those intangible things which augment purely formal freedoms begin to disappear. The innocent do have something to fear – and that is the loss of privacy which is at the heart of individuality and liberty itself.

CHAPTER 15

The Sunset World

—〰—

> ... the secret of true liberty remains courage. We acquiesce in the loss
> of freedom every time we are silent in the face of injustice. The more
> we insist that it is not our concern, the easier we make the demagogue's
> task. For it is of the essence of liberty that it should depend for its main-
> tenance upon the respect it can arouse in humble men.
>
> HAROLD LASKI[1]

A government which was disarming the state of old ideologies found
that it had to take up arms again in the new millennium. The attack
on the United States in September 2001 revealed a dark and pathological totalitarianism alive in the world which was capable of
destruction on a vast scale. If liberty had been a somewhat beleaguered idea in the late twentieth century the war on terror would put
it to an extreme test. Following the carnage the first rush of energy
on both sides of the Atlantic was to tighten up security and look for
ways to prevent such violence recurring. There was a sense that
things would never be the same again; that new methods would be
needed for the wholly unprecedented threat of suicide bombers with
whom there could be no negotiating.

Islamists had said that Western democracy was effete; liberalism was
riddled with ideological contradictions and vacillating principles; its
leaders, like its people, were cowards and hypocrites. It was therefore
an easy target. At the first sight of danger the mask would be stripped
away and democratic values would be exposed as contingent – the luxury of peace and prosperity rather than anything real. The work of

revolution would be done by manipulating the West's chief vulnerability, its pervading sense of fear, through sporadic iconic acts of terrorism and by maintaining a continual threat of terrorism; but the real work of destruction would be done from inside, by collective suicide and a flight from freedom.

This analysis is superficially attractive but it ignores the resilience of a free society. The perceived weaknesses are in fact advantages: the permissiveness and tolerance of liberal society unifies disparate groups better than a single ideology. And it underestimated the determination of people in the West. Leaders in 2001 were determined to show their strength in defeating terrorism. And they were very good at using force and marshalling its physical resources, from the use of arms to the brutal efficacy of covert operations; from modifying its technologies of control to persuading its own people to accept irksome restraints.

The attacks coincided with a time when politics had become markedly less ideological. As the last chapters have described the New Labour government did not believe in liberal solutions; it saw the principles of liberty as outdated, and it projected an image of hard-edged efficiency. This approach was translated into combating terrorism. It reassured many in the dark days of 2001. In time this very success would prove to be the Achilles heel of the anti-terrorism system. Not fully convinced of what, if anything, it believed in, the government had difficulty articulating an ideology. Indeed it seemed not to consider that one was needed. Terrorism needed to be toughed out; bin Laden's manic glare from the TV screen needed to be out-stared. But what politicians in Britain and America forgot was that this was not just a competition of toughness but a vital ideological struggle.

Politicians liked to talk of balancing liberty and security. The psychopathic ideology thrived in Britain, as they well knew, and urgent measures were needed to prevent a tragedy. The Home Secretary, David Blunkett, agonised about what posterity would have to say if the government did not do everything in its power to prevent outrages and fretted that large segments of the population would turn to extremist parties if the government was not seen as being tough.

Tony Blair tried to shift the debate, saying that the fundamental liberty is the right to life. If this is the starting point then it betrays the mindset in setting anti-terrorist legislation. It put security above all other considerations and replaced questions of principle with technical assessment of risk.

Alvaro Gil-Robles, the European Human Rights Commissioner, wrote of the situation in Britain in 2005: 'Against a background . . . in which human rights are frequently construed as at best formal commitments and at worst cumbersome obstructions, it is perhaps worth emphasising that human rights are not a pick-and-mix assortment of luxury entitlements but the very foundation of democratic societies.'[2] The mindset which sees that starting point as maximum security is ill equipped to see things in this way. What has been most damaging in recent years has not, in the first instance, been the instinct to protect but the political strategy. By taking emergency powers the government entered what I have called the 'twilight world', which was a familiar situation in the world wars of the twentieth century – one where the quality of information deteriorates, mutual understanding suffers and injustice becomes another price to pay for safety, regardless of the cost. In the risk-averse culture of the twenty-first century it becomes even murkier, because we are more fearful and make decisions based on that fear. In such a situation it is incumbent on the government to justify its policies to its people and especially to those who are most likely to suffer. This is only possible if politicians are prepared to state in clear terms what is sacred and integral to democracy; what it is, in fact, we are seeking to defend.

Blair and his ministers tried to take principle out of the equation and present their policies solely on the criteria of efficiency. In doing so they lost a large amount of political capital. Blair seemed in thrall to the security services, and he used their views to hammer legislation through parliament. Policy seemed dangerously unmoored from principle. The job of the security services is to prevent at all costs; the duty of statesmen is to negotiate between different groups and account for policy, especially to minority groups. But this was forgotten; it made debate confrontational rather than constructive. 'If we are forced to compromise,' Blair threatened MPs at a fraught moment in 2005, 'it will be a compromise with the nation's security.'[3]

This either/or attitude is a false one. But it had an effect on public opinion. Respect for civil liberties has declined over the last twenty years, but the real story is the massive increase in the numbers of people who *just don't know* any more. In the 1980s, asked whether extremist literature should be banned or whether dangerous suspects should have legal protection, most people had pretty clear ideas either way. The National Centre for Social Research asked people whether they thought it was better to convict an innocent person than let a guilty person go free. The results are as follows:

	1985	1990	2005
Worse to convict an innocent person	67%	62%	52%
Worse to let a guilty person go free	20%	19%	23%
Can't choose	12%	19%	23%

While there was a decrease in the number of people who supported civil liberty arguments, there was no significant increase in the number who would take a hard line. The 'don't know' category almost doubled. Interestingly the jump took place before 1990: during the liberty-loving, free-for-all 1980s ideas of classical civil liberties took a dive. Mark Johnson and Conor Gearty, who analysed the data, wrote that the British people were still generally in favour of civil liberties:

Like the secular grandchildren of devout church-going believers, they know they should care – and want to for the sake of their own offspring – but cannot for the life of them articulate why. Civil libertarians need to re-evangelise the British public if they want to turn the graph back.[4]

There has been without a doubt a collapse in confidence in the laws and institutions and states of mind which made us free – in the things which, after all, distinguish us from the people who want to destroy our way of life. Since 2001 anti-terrorist legislation has come thick and fast, and the issues have seemed so abstruse and the stakes so high that many have been left bewildered or indifferent. Over these years many taboos were broken. The Terrorism Act of 2001 gave the state power to intern foreign suspects. Further acts in 2005 and 2006 tinkered with free speech, made inciting and glorifying terrorism illegal, criminalised certain forms of religious hatred and restricted the right to protest. In 2005 the government introduced control orders, which allowed it to place suspects under house arrest, and extended the period of pre-charge detention to the extraordinary length of twenty-eight days. But among the controversial matters the acts also brought in worthwhile measures to combat terrorism. As the dissident Labour backbench MP Bob Marshall-Andrews put it, describing the 2001 legislation, 'This is a compendious, complex camel of a bill. In very large part, it is incontrovertible; in very large part, it is worthy. In juxtaposition, parts of it are draconian, dangerous and completely unacceptable and, unhappily, other parts of it are completely incomprehensible.'[5]

In that it resembled other anti-terrorism and criminal justice acts over the following years: parliament was asked to pass lock, stock and barrel a host of measures, some necessary and some highly contentious. And these crucial matters were rushed through parliament in very short measure. Douglas Hogg, a former Conservative minister and one of the most passionate supporters of civil liberties in parliament, said that when 'the electorate see that important measures are being introduced without discussion in this place, they will lose their understanding and respect for democracy'.[6] And for those who knew little of liberty and British history it could be perplexing. Ministers were extremely eager to be *seen* as being tough, to allay public concern and to send a 'strong signal' to terrorists that Britain was not a soft touch, hamstrung by legal procedures and liberal dogma. But in adopting this posture the government made itself seem authoritarian and illiberal to many, to others oppressive and hypocritical, and to many more casual and careless.

In its bursts of legislative activity the government gave the impression that it was in the grip of an emergency comparable to 1914 or 1939. At the same time it said the threat would last for generations. As a result the chance for mature and serious consideration of liberty in the face of the new horrors awaiting us in the twenty-first century was passed over. It was panicky legislation at a time when there was the luxury for reflection; it was short-term when the problems were generational. Laws were rushed through parliament with a speed which one member of the House of Lords said might have been appropriate for a minor reform of local government but was irresponsible when the issue was reversing eight hundred years of history.

For a government to respond to crisis with emergency legislation is not new, and the Labour government could be seen as following a pattern which was long established. In 1974 the IRA had begun a campaign of bombing on the British mainland, and in November twenty-one people were killed and 180 wounded in pub bombings in Birmingham. In immediate response the Labour Home Secretary, Roy Jenkins, introduced the Prevention of Terrorism (Temporary Provisions) Bill. It had its second reading, committee and report stages and third reading in the Commons and in the Lords in an exhausting (but not exhaustive) all-night sitting on 28 November 1974 and received Royal Assent first thing on the morning of the 29th. The Commons was in the mood for drastic measures, with proposals for a restitution of capital punishment, the introduction of stringent censorship and ID cards and wide freedom of executive action. They reflected public opinion. 'There are times when the emotional response to a public event is also the soundest one,' said *The Times.* 'The natural response to the murders in Birmingham is one of anger and determination. This is a healthier response than any attempt to rationalize what has happened or to pretend that any but the most effective counter measures will satisfy public opinion.'[7]

Jenkins's legislation was milder than many had hoped. He wanted laws which would satisfy public opinion, but which avoided falling into a 'panic reaction' to the carnage. Throughout the committee stage he turned down powers which backbenchers tried to foist on the government.

It cannot be without reluctance that we contemplate powers of the kind proposed in this Bill, involving as they must some encroachments – limited but real – on the liberties of individual citizens. Few things would provide a more gratifying victory to the terrorists than for this country to undermine its traditional freedoms in the very process of countering the enemies of those freedoms.[8]

His bill followed the anti-terrorist laws of 1939. The act banned the IRA, it gave the police powers to arrest and detain suspects for forty-eight hours – rising to a maximum of seven days on application to the Home Secretary – and introduced security checks on passengers entering and leaving Britain and Northern Ireland. The most controversial measure, however, was the power given to the Home Secretary to serve orders on terrorist suspects which would exclude Northern Irish people from entering and living in Great Britain. The exclusion orders would be made by the Secretary of State and they would not be subject to judicial review, although Jenkins appointed a panel to assess any objections to an order.

This part of the bill received the greatest opposition from back-benchers of all parties. The central objection, voiced by many including the young MP John Prescott, was that the inevitable injustice involved in making the order and the absence of independent scrutiny would alienate the Irish community. Irish Catholics would feel the injustice, and if they did not support the IRA they would cease to help what they saw as a vindictive government. As Prescott said, as the morning sun rose on Westminster, 'The IRA will argue that it alone can protect the Catholics in this country and that is the beginning of a very difficult road indeed.' The only protection a citizen had from an overzealous policeman or a malicious informer, argued Leo Abse, was 'the integrity and liberality' of the Home Secretary.[9]

Roy Jenkins had a reputation as an unusually liberal Home Secretary. In the 1960s he had given support to liberalising measures on a host of issues, and it was this moral capital he was able to exploit in the fraught days of 1974 in allaying fears that this was anything more than an emergency measure which was being introduced reluctantly and which would be administered fairly. Jenkins took great pains to express his displeasure at what he repeatedly called 'draconian' laws. 'We will use these powers as selectively as we can,' he said in a broadcast, 'but I do not pretend that they will not occasionally inconvenience, perhaps worse than inconvenience, a few people who do not deserve it.'[10] However what he did not say was that he engaged in some extensive liberal window-dressing. The laws were not drawn up in response to the pub bombs but had been in preparation for a long time. The ferocity of public and parliamentary opinion in November helped Jenkins because it made his proposals seem pleasingly liberal and proportionate in comparison. In fact the laws had been patiently waiting for an event irrespective of whether the Secretary of State was Labour or Conservative, instinctively liberal or naturally authoritarian.[11]

Writing two decades later, at a time when the laws were still in force, Jenkins said that 'It is a classic example of the truth of the adage that it is only the provisional which lasts. It should teach one to be careful about justifying something on the grounds that it is only for a short time.'[12] What was passed in the heat of the moment as an emergency stop-gap remained on the statute book and became the model for subsequent legislation. Indeed the PTA was something of a trap. It was temporary and it had to be renewed within six months (until 1976 when the period was extended to twelve months), but letting the law lapse would mean the return of all the men and women who had been excluded from the mainland by executive action – men and women whom the government believed to be active terrorists. So it was temporary in the sense that it would last as long as the crisis – or until parliament rebelled against the government.

When the act was up for renewal in 1975 the Labour MP Kevin McNamara said that such measures were 'the eternal dilemma of any liberal democracy'.[13] While the executive needs free action to prevent outrages it simultaneously weakens itself by making the police and the government seem hostile to minority groups. When emergency powers are in place the government and its dealings are obscured by secrecy and its own decision-making is led by imponderable considerations of risk; it becomes ever harder for the state to justify its actions and satisfy the aggrieved. Even the most liberal statesman would face accusations of double dealing, partiality and gross abuse from a community which develops an embattled self-image. Trust erodes. There were plenty of cases reported in parliament and the press – and circulated as rumour throughout the Irish community – of people arrested by the police, held in poor conditions for five days without being able to communicate with their families and at the last possible minute released without charge. People who were detained for a period of days suffered – perhaps losing a job – and their families and friends shared the sense of grievance. Fewer than five per cent of people held under the PTA were ever charged, and only a proportion of these were convicted or excluded. An unusually high number of those convicted confessed. When wide latitude is given to the police by emergency laws and when pre-charge detention is extended people are more likely to break down and give unsafe confessions. And when the police had the responsibility to prevent another massacre great abuses occurred in the name of safety, as the gross miscarriages in the Birmingham and Guildford cases proved.

Did these abuses make the country safer? Were terrorist attacks prevented at the price of the erosion of civil liberties? Did the PTA increase resentment and act as a 'recruiting sergeant' for the IRA while at the same time scaring off potential informers? It is impossible to say: that is the condition of the twilight world. What is certain, however, is that by the nature of its constitution and parliamentary procedures the country was stuck with the act which was rushed through parliament overnight in 1974. At the time of the annual renewal motions, under Labour and Conservative administrations, the debate became ever more perfunctory, often taking place late in the night in front of a thin house.

The problem was that whatever had been introduced in November 1974 could not subsequently be undone without the risk that it would unleash more violence or send out signals to the public that the government was soft on terrorism. Renewal debates were occasions when grievances could be aired but substantive policy changes were not debated: the choice was all or nothing. A sunset clause, which would mean that the act lapsed and had to be replaced from scratch, was unsatisfactory because only something more or less identical to the original model could ever be countenanced. Politicians, press and public were afraid of a step into the dark. By the 1980s emergency laws had become familiar and, by their long duration, were seen as necessary. As Roy Hattersley pointed out from the Labour opposition front bench in 1983 the paradox of anti-terror legislation is that if terrorism has decreased over the previous year the act is held up as a success and is therefore needed; if terrorism has increased it is needed more than ever. Therefore the failure of the laws can become the prime reason for their retention.[14]

Parliament was caught in a bind. Home Secretaries in modern times, from Jenkins to his New Labour successors, have resisted calls for judicial review in executive decisions on exclusion orders (for the IRA) or control orders (under the 2005 act). This was because they did not want judges dragged into executive actions, compromising their independence by making them scrutinise confidential security documents. Judicial review, by its nature, only allows judges to examine the procedure of the relevant minister – they do not make a decision based on facts but on whether the Home Secretary has followed the terms of the act. In the absence of independent scrutiny ministers have, like their predecessors in the World Wars, asked to be judged politically, on the floor of the house. But when debate is curtailed and information restricted by the needs of security the only assurance the members of the house can have is their trust in the government of the day. Leaving things to the arbitrary decision of politicians and being asked for absolute trust is anathema in a democracy and completely opposed to the tradition of British liberties. That is why open debate and consideration of new powers are of critical importance. But so too is the complexion of the government which exercises these powers.

None of the governments since 1974 can lay any great claim to being favourable to civil liberties yet no one law has completely removed those liberties. Rather, legislation has weakened liberties bit by bit; this has not been an ideological process but in response to various crises. That uncertainty on the part of the public has increased as reasons of necessity and security have trumped principles of liberty. The rise of the security state during the cold war when the country was threatened by nuclear missiles helped inure the public to exceptional measures. Sporadic terrorist attacks since the seventies have further worn down resistance to executive action. The price of liberty, it is wisely said, is eternal vigilance; and, as Marshall McLuhan wrote, the price of eternal vigilance is indifference. In the late seventies E. P. Thompson talked about the new phenomenon in Britain of 'the dulling of the nerve of resistance and of outrage' as the security state burgeoned and 'extraordinary' measures to prevent subversion from a range of groups – from foreign powers and terrorists to radicals, the far left and CND – were 'becoming part of the *normal* repertoire of power'.[15]

Thompson saw the state acting in ways it always had throughout history – gradually and naturally expanding its powers to suit administrative convenience. The sedation of the 'nerve of outrage' made this easier. Throughout the 1980s the process continued, and the common law – as K. D. Ewing and C. A. Gearty argued in their book *Freedom under Thatcher* – proved a feeble defender of liberty and in many cases sanctioned the growth of executive power. The government itself talked of freedom but restricted itself to the realm of economic choice – conventional civil liberties were often regarded as some sort of threat to those freedoms. Thatcher's government was determined to use the claim of 'national security' to retain a veil over the secret state – and sometimes to cover its own back in the realm of politics. It was draconian in its use of the Official Secrets Act to discipline civil servants and frighten journalists. In a number of high-profile cases the government used the plea of security to stifle debate and enforce a code of silence in the ranks of the secret state. At times the government looked vindictive in pursuit of minor infractions of its code, quite prepared to gaol civil servants for minor breaches or chase journalists around the country so it could serve injunctions and raid homes and offices.

In 1984 the landmark case of the government's ban on employees at Government Communications Headquarters (GCHQ) joining their trade union proved an important point. The government claimed it had acted for reasons of national security in forestalling unrest at a key part of the national defence system. The Lords ruled that the government could only change employment conditions if there was reliable *evidence* that it based its decision on the grounds of national security – but the courts could not question whether that decision was *necessary* for the maintenance of national security. Lord Fraser argued:

The decision whether the requirements of national security outweigh the duty of fairness in any particular case is for the government and not for the courts. The government alone has access to the necessary information, and in any event the judicial process is unsuitable for reaching decisions on national security.[16]

A few years later the Master of the Rolls ruled that it was necessary that sometimes security agencies should go beyond the law in the execution of their duty. In the trial of Clive Ponting – a civil servant who sent Tam Dalyell MP documents relating to the sinking of the *Belgrano* in the Falklands War – the judge blurred the distinction between transient politics and the eternal state, between national security and the interests of the government of the day: 'The policies of the state were the policies of the government then in power.' The jury was wise enough to acquit Ponting.[17]

These judgements and opinions went against the spirit of *Entick* v. *Carrington* which said that it was not up to the government to determine the scope of its own powers: national security trumped the rule of law. Throughout the eighties the government tried to enforce this; often it was successful but the result was bitter conflict with the press, which maintained that the public needed to hear what was happening beyond the veil, if no really sensitive secrets were leaked which would compromise safety. The government looked tough, but information always escaped. As the legal decisions stated, it was a matter of government to decide what constituted national security. What was the determining factor, therefore, was the government of the day's attitude to civil liberties. At the time it was clear that civil liberties were taking a back seat. Mrs Thatcher put it like this: 'Unfortunately, there seem to be people with more interest in trying to ferret out and reveal information of use to our enemies rather than preserving the defence interests of this country, and thus the freedom which we all enjoy.' Roy Jenkins put it like this: ministers were, in their relentless defence of the secret state, 'prepared to look as though they were running a second-rate police state, infused equally with illiberalism and incompetence'.[18]

The Official Secrets Act of 1989 removed the defence which had successfully been used in court that leaking sensitive information could be in the public's interest. In other matters the government made the expression of dissent harder. The Public Order Act of 1986 gave police constables the authority to prevent a demonstration which they believed might lead to the damage of property, disruption to the life of the community or the intimidation of others. As Ewing and Gearty argue, protests by their nature involve a clash of interests and annoyance to someone – be they shoppers or diplomats from a tyrannical nation. Protestors are also likely to represent the minority, and the act seems to oblige the police to defend the majority from inconvenience. In any case, as the authors argue, there were plenty of ways the police were able to pre-empt protests, most fundamentally the ancient law of breach of the peace (discussed earlier).[19] The expression of dissent was made harder throughout the 1980s – by law or by proactive policemen. It is noteworthy that in 1984, unlike in 1926, the government did not need to declare a state of emergency to deal with the miners' strike: new and old laws and greater refinements in police equipment, training and organisation proved good enough on their own – not to say the political will to use force.

Whatever one's feelings about the politics of the strike the actions of 1984 showed that the state could crush dissent in all areas with ruthless efficiency if it so wanted. Britons believed that their country was still one characterised by liberty, but thanks to the advance of the state in various areas many of these liberties had been whittled away – not all at once but piecemeal, by new laws and legal reinterpretation of old ones. As ever in British history the state had great flexibility, and there were few constitutional protections for civil liberties. It was little wonder that by 1990 people were increasingly unsure about the value of civil liberties given that their leaders regarded them as bothersome and, in any case, they proved to be easily circumvented. What protected liberty – as it always had – was the vitality of liberal values and what Roy Jenkins liked to call the instinct of ministers to impose 'self-denying ordinances'. Was this any longer the case? In 1988 the *Sunday Telegraph* commented that not only had Thatcher 'trampled on genuine ideals and deep roots in our national history' but that she had 'enjoyed doing so'.[20]

If the governments of Wilson, Callaghan, Thatcher and Major were prepared to grapple with civil liberties, no government relished conflict with civil libertarians more than that of Tony Blair. The erosion of these liberties had been going on for a long time; from 1997, however, the Prime Minister and his ministers were openly scornful of the tradition. In 2006 Blair complained that he had not managed to go far enough in protecting the country; every time he made progress his policies were diluted in parliament or the courts. Crime and Islamist terrorism had developed so fast and 'in a way that, frankly, mocks a system built not for another decade but another age'.[21] At the same time he said that reform of the criminal justice system in the age of antisocial behaviour, organised crime and terrorism could not be complete 'unless we change radically the political, even philosophical, context in which it operates'.[22]

In 2000 the government passed two very important pieces of legislation, the Human Rights Act and the Terrorism Act. The latter was supposed to supersede the old PTA by introducing a permanent anti-terrorist code which went beyond the old threat of Irish terrorism. Most of the act was unexceptional and reasonable. But as in subsequent acts badly drafted clauses were passed as well. Police were given stringent powers to arrest people they suspected of offences under the act. The definition of terrorism was expanded to include offences against property and it included supporting or advocating efforts to topple established governments. As opponents pointed out the act could be used to stop legitimate protest unrelated to terrorism and its definition of terrorism included supporting efforts to remove undemocratic dictators. It would have criminalised supporting Nelson Mandela in the era of apartheid. In the nineteenth century Palmerston's government fell when it tried to outlaw conspiracy against foreign governments. That was felt, by the grandees of politics in that faraway age, to be a sinister favour to foreign despots and, above all, an affront to the very idea of British liberty.

Jack Straw, the then Home Secretary, denied these criticisms as alarmist.[23] But over the following years the fears were found to be justified. Famously the laws were used against the elderly Labour activist Walter Wolfgang when he heckled Jack Straw, by then Foreign Secretary, at the party conference. It was also used to arrest protesters campaigning against an arms fair in London and against a woman walking along a cycle path – to name two other famous examples. The House of Lords upheld the parts of the act which criminalised supporting foreign groups which aimed to topple dictatorial regimes.

The act set a lamentable tradition of badly drafted anti-terror laws which were used well beyond the original intent of MPs. It also betrayed, early in the long rule of New Labour, casualness when it came to civil liberties. But the Human Rights Act, although it said little new about the liberties of freeborn Britons, had the effect of awakening the judiciary and restoring them to the long dormant role of defenders of liberties. It made a rod for the government's back, something ministers would bitterly regret as their anti-terror laws were savaged in the courts. In the past no law, including one as fundamental as habeas corpus, could be upheld in court if parliament had passed an act suspending or abolishing it. Now, for the first time, legislation passed in the sovereign parliament could be struck down as *ultra vires* if it was incompatible with the European Convention on Human Rights.

The HRA sparked into life judicial activism which came, in large part, from the nature of modern anti-terror law as rushed, panicky and devoid of parliamentary scrutiny. The 2001 act was, as we have seen, pushed through parliament at a time when fear was running high. In December 2004 the law lords struck down clause four of the act, which empowered the Home Secretary to intern foreign terrorist suspects without trial – a clear break with the ancient principle of habeas corpus. 'Indefinite imprisonment . . . on grounds not disclosed is the stuff of nightmares,' said Lord Scott in his judgement. Incompatibility with the HRA made this possible, not incompatibility with the British tradition of liberty. The judges struck down the clause for a number of reasons. One was that under the HRA laws should not discriminate between British and foreign nationals. They also had to decide whether the government could derogate from the European Convention on Human Rights. This meant that if a country faced a threat to its very existence it could, by agreement of parliament, derogate (or temporarily withdraw) from the relevant part of the ECHR. 'The real threat to the life of the nation', said Lord Hoffman in his judgement, '. . . comes not from terrorism but from laws such as these.'[24]

Hoffman's words won him howls of outrage from the government and the tabloid press who saw him as living in a judicial fairyland. The government was left in the damaging position of not only being in conflict with the judiciary but required to pass new laws if they were to keep their suspects in detention. Charles Clarke, Blunkett's successor as Home Secretary, announced emergency legislation to replace the illegal internment of the eleven foreign nationals in Belmarsh high-security prison. The government had only a small amount of parliamentary time to get new laws on the statute book before parliament was dissolved.

Clarke had to abide by the Lords' decision, and his proposal was not that the inmates be released, but that new laws, now applicable to British citizens as well as foreign nationals, should allow him to impose control orders on suspects, restricting their movements. This could range from tagging them and preventing them from using the internet (among other restrictions) to outright house arrest. Again, this was to be an executive decision based on intelligence reports and evidence obtained from abroad, even if it was extracted under torture. The judiciary was to be involved, but only after the order had been made. Those under a control order would have their case assessed by a judge, but they would not be told of the evidence or the charge against them and their court-appointed special advocate would be similarly restricted. The case would be held under the civil dispensation of a balance of probabilities rather than the exacting requirements of a criminal trial – beyond reasonable doubt. In sum, the presumption of innocence was to be removed, and for the first time in peace a citizen could be held under house arrest. The government believed that these 'restrictions' on a suspect's liberty would not involve derogation from the HRA – and hence challenge in the courts – because they were not 'depriving' people of liberty. It struck many as a creative use of the word liberty. In any case, this was a definitive move away from the ideals of English law. It reminded people of apartheid South Africa and its 'pass laws'. Britain, which oppressed people saw as a beacon of liberty, was adopting the very laws associated with oppressive regimes.[25]

The onus, therefore, was on the government to prove why this was necessary – to give a justification so rigorous as to preclude any doubt that this would lead to gross injustice. Critics asked why these suspects – after all they had been subject to rigorous intelligence surveillance over the years – could not be tried for some crime such as conspiracy to commit a serious offence or other terrorist-related crimes. The gold standard would remain a fair trial in open court. Since 2001 the anti-terrorist system had been in a mess. This represented a chance to develop a new approach, in partnership with people from all sides of the debate. It could have marked a return to the principles of justice – or at least a rational justification of unpopular polices. Instead the government asked people for trust that they would not abuse the power. But how much trust had the government earned?

Unfortunately yet another crucial piece of legislation was passed in a moment of chaos. The government were under considerable pressure to get the laws on the statute book: the law lords' ruling said that the Belmarsh detainees would be released on 14 March. Even so the resulting legislative process was a shameful farce. By the time the bill got to the Commons on 28 February the government had already introduced an extraordinary number of amendments to be discussed in an eight-hour timetable; that was, said one Tory MP, one hour for every century of British liberty. 'What we are being asked to do is scandalous,' said Dominic Grieve, the shadow Attorney General, reflecting the views of MPs from all sides of the house. 'You only need to look at the 260 amendments tabled to realise there is no possibility of doing justice to what must be one of the most important pieces of legislation this house has considered since the Second World War.'[26]

The government then backtracked. It would concede: control orders which meant a 'restriction' of liberty – those which involved electronic tagging, curfews, constraints on interaction with others and so on – would be tested by 'reasonable suspicion' of involvement in terrorist activity. Orders which meant a 'deprivation' of liberty – house arrest – would be tried in front of a judge under the only slightly stricter criterion of a balance of probabilities. These subtleties, so it was thought, would keep Britain within the terms of the ECHR. But the government would make these concessions in the Lords; it would not be seen to cave in to backbench and opposition pressure in the

Commons. MPs were therefore left discussing a bill which everyone knew would be changed beyond recognition in the upper chamber.[27]

There followed an extraordinary and embarrassing week in British politics. The Lords chewed over the revised bill for three days, and subjected it to serious – and hostile – scrutiny, the kind of which the Commons had been deprived. Clarke would not make any more compromises which would give the judges greater power over executive decisions. He refused the proposal that the act should have a sunset clause so that parliament could return to the issues and redesign another bill in less fraught days. Given that the government admitted this was an emergency measure this might have been a reasonable compromise, but Blair argued that a sunset clause would make the country unsafe – it would send out the wrong signal.[28] And so the battered, unpopular, rushed bill was passed into permanent legislation.

While the legislative juggernaut lumbered on, the language of politics degenerated. As the deadline for the release of the suspects approached, parliament was involved in a thirty-hour session of what is called parliamentary 'ping-pong', whereby amendments are batted back and forth from the Lords to the Commons in the dead of night. It was, said the *Guardian*, 'the politics of the bear pit'.[29] After its mauling by the Lords the bill said that control orders would be subject to greater judicial scrutiny, but the fact remained that a British citizen could have his or her liberty removed without hearing the evidence and without a fair trial. It was a partial compromise – a fig leaf for the greatest restriction yet of civil liberties in peacetime. Looming behind the debacle was the presence of two inescapable ghouls. Within days the detainees would have to be released and in May there was to be a general election. As Andrew Rawnsley of the *Observer* argued, 'There is only one thing worse than making complex, sensitive and unprecedented law in a rush of fear. That is doing it in a pre-election panic as well.'[30]

The judgement the government had to make was not whether injustice would happen but how tolerable the inevitable injustice would be. As in other realms of government they believed that miscarriages of justice were a risk worth taking, especially when dealing with suicide bombers. Lord Carlile, the statutory reviewer of control orders, concluded that the system was a proportionate response to the threat as long as it was administered correctly. The problem for the government was that in its legislative fumbles and tough-talking language it had sacrificed a lot of trust. As was clear the government took the view that any measure of prevention was worth it. They feared above all that an attack on the scale of those in New York or Madrid would mean that the public would turn on them for failing to take every conceivable measure.

In the context of the risk to society these kinds of nightmare penetrated deeply into ministerial consciousness. Kenneth Clarke, a former Conservative Home Secretary, made the point very forcefully in the Commons that advice given to a politician by an official whose job was to prevent outrages had to be treated appropriately.

I am tempted to say that, looking back over the years, some of the silliest pieces of advice that I was ever given urged me to do certain things on the grounds of security, protection of the national interest and prevention of terrorism. The second most silly have been on the grounds of health and safety: the blood is made to chill in the face of what might happen if one does not take some essential step.[31]

Refusing the demands of the secret services and the police took courage – and intellectual confidence. That is the essence of a democracy. However, the language of politicians made it clear that they *were* acting on such advice. They had ceased to act out of principle or to seek consensus: weight was placed almost entirely on the policy of prevention at any cost. When the courts found that it was legal for the police to use anti-terrorism laws against protesters at an international arms rally in London, David Blunkett said that 'The ruling reinforces our message that the protection of the public and national security is the responsibility of the government and the police and neither can take risks.'[32] Such an attitude of mind explains a lot – even protesters were to be considered a risk, and no risk was worth it.

It was the poorest advertisement for a democracy at a time when democracy was facing serious challenge throughout the world – from fanatics as much as a disillusioned public. As the Bishop of Worcester said in a punchy speech in the Lords, the passing of the 2005 act showed the 'the capacity of terrorists to undermine our own capacity for calm and considerate reflection'.[33]

'Let's be very, very clear: were there to be a serious terrorist act in this country and afterwards it was thought we had not taken the measures necessary, believe me no one would be talking about civil liberties,' said Blair in February 2005. 'They would be talking about why we had not done more to protect the security of this country.'[34] The nightmare did happen on 7 July of the same year when bombs were detonated on the London underground and bus services with great loss of life, serious casualties and an abiding sense of fear which lives with every commuter. Ever since there has been intermittent terrorist activity which has failed to inflict loss of life or has been pre-empted by the security services. But few people, in the media or on the streets, thought to blame the government for not having passed the right laws.

It was clear, however, that none of the laws passed or proposed would have prevented these attacks. Those plots which were successful came seemingly from nowhere, from groups below the radar, and the rest were foiled thanks to the initiative of the security services. In the aftermath of the horrific attacks of 7 July and the failed attacks two weeks later opinion polls showed that the public were prepared to make any sacrifice of liberty. It was a natural response, and the government began to draw up plans.

Once again it seemed as though the aim was to reassure public opinion rather than think seriously about how terrorism could be tackled in a liberal democracy. There was no attempt to put proposals in front of a parliamentary scrutiny committee of the kind which, in other cases, canvassed and interrogated a wide range of opinion before legislation was drawn up. Indeed, the opinion which was canvassed was loud and clear. The police wanted pre-charge detention of a maximum ninety days – up from the then limit of fourteen days, which many believed to be excessive enough. The feature of regular police lobbying in public now became common. In the past such advice was made in confidence to ministers who had to make the case to parliament and the public. But now the debate was biased when the security services broke out of discreet silence to make their case. It is their job to imagine the worst and the find ways to prevent it – but politics in a free country is surely more than straightforward risk assessment. Politicians need to seek consensus and allay fears that citizens may have. What else is the history of liberty but the reluctant conformity of authority to the demands of citizens? No one doing a risk assessment would design a habeas corpus act because he believed it would be a positive good; policemen are not charged with determining the health of society. Going public with their fears and practising the arts of lobbying was a breach of trust. Opponents found themselves arguing against the police, a rather unattractive proposition given the respect the public justly accords to senior police officers.

'If the police say they need this power to detain terrorist suspects for ninety days then they should have this power,' Blair said.[35] And much of the media was behind him. 'Britain is fighting al-Qaeda with one arm tied behind its back,' declared the *Sun*. 'In times of war, normal rules don't apply . . . it is time for the human rights laws which weaken us at every turn to be put on the back burner.'[36] And at the same time fifty-two per cent of the population did not believe that the courts should be able to strike down legislation.[37]

Questions were now being seriously asked in other quarters as to whether an imbalance had been reached – in other words whether laws which had been designed to protect us were actually making us more vulnerable. In November 2005 yet another anti-terrorism bill came before parliament, and Blair received his first ever defeat when the Commons only agreed to extend the pre-charge detention limit to twenty-eight days. The enforced compromise was not so much a compromise between liberty and security as a political manoeuvre. The principle of habeas corpus had already been violated two years before when the limit was raised to fourteen days; now it was just a question of timing. The police said they needed a long period to hold suspects because the evidence involved in modern plots was inordinately complex, involving a tangle of foreign connections and encrypted computer files. But such a case lay in the future; it was a matter of pre-empting all possibilities. No minister or policeman could come up with a situation where a long period of pre-charge detention was necessary beyond a list of hypothetical scenarios. Yet, on the criteria of risk management, it was worth assaulting civil liberties and altering the rights of citizens in advance.

As MPs and journalists argued, the purpose of limiting the police in this way was to protect them against blunders. Long periods of questioning often end in false allegations against others and unreliable confessions – from sheer exhaustion if nothing else. The unsound nature of this makes acquittal more likely in subsequent trials because the defence is given more grounds to exploit procedural irregularities. And furthermore a long period of detention (and twenty-eight days is very long) tends to mean early, pre-emptive arrests followed by an investigation, the reverse of the usual procedure. The consensus held that a long period of detention was counterproductive, in spite of the warnings of the government and the police. Parliament reluctantly accepted twenty-eight days, but it was based on nothing more than politics. Detecting principle in preferring twenty-eight days to ninety is just about possible – but we are a long way from the principle of justice. The Rubicon was crossed when MPs accepted fourteen days.

The experience of Irish terrorism was that supposedly emergency legislation could never be taken off the statute book without risk that it would backfire. In the 2000s, and particularly after the bombs of 2005, the problems MPs faced revolved around the fear that if they voted down a government proposal and a tragedy subsequently occurred they would face the lash of public opinion. Therefore the best they could do was to compromise with government proposals; and the government knew that in this situation they could get a large measure of what they proposed.

In light of these fears many people were turning against the government's strategy – the judiciary, the parliamentary Human Rights Committee and much of the press, left and right. But one of the most eloquent critics came from within Downing Street. 'It is all too easy for us to respond to terror in a way which undermines commitment to our most deeply held values and convictions, and which cheapens our right to call ourselves a civilised nation,' said Cherie Booth in July 2005.[38]

VIII

THE NEW ORTHODOXY

CHAPTER 16

Free Diversity

—∽—

If all mankind minus one were of one opinion, and only one person were of the contrary opinion, mankind would be no more justified in silencing that one person, than he . . . would be justified in silencing mankind.

JOHN STUART MILL, *ON LIBERTY*[1]

It has become hard to hold a simple and straightforward idea of liberty in the twenty-first century. The latter chapters of this book have described the entanglement of human relations in the modern world which render notions of personal autonomy – which might have seemed so clear-cut a few decades before – devilishly complex. Not only does liberty in its classic sense suffer daily and necessary violation, but it has become harder for everyone – from political theorists to the average citizen – to talk about liberty without being forced into caveats, self-contradiction and confusion.

Where the language of classic liberalism hits a ferocious storm is when it meets multiculturalism, which has become coupled with terrorism in recent years. Throughout its history in the modern West, liberty has been couched in terms of promoting social peace, tolerance, equality and individuality in relatively homogeneous nation states. As the Nobel Laureate Amartya Sen put it, the injunction 'Love thy neighbour' was a whole lot easier when your neighbour had the same faith, skin colour and cultural assumptions as you.[2] And it is a whole lot easier, one should say, to laugh at each other when a culture has been held in common for generations.

Deciding which rights should be accorded to groups whose values and practices are at odds with the dominant culture involves the state in wholly new territory. In many ways the interventionist hand of the state, particularly the need which it has to treat different groups in different ways, is seen as being totally at odds with liberty. Judging what words and imagery are permissible in discussion, debate and humour has become a matter for the state as well. The controversy over the publication (and non-publication) throughout the world in 2006 of cartoons which satirised Muhammad were seen at the time as a defining moment in modern liberalism, and the uncomfortable issues they forced us to confront will surely stand out in the history of our times.

Yet however queasy these issues make some people – not to say the despondency they generate in some liberals – the challenges of multiculturalism offer the chance for reviving the language of liberty. In an age when people question the purposes of government and ponder the moral basis of liberal democracies, the old-fashioned notion of liberty might usefully be dusted down.

The politics of multiculturalism certainly recalls the history of liberty. It involves, after all, the relations of individuals with each other and between the individual and the state. But, as with so many things, we tend to shy away from talking explicitly about liberty. This is a pity when we are confronting the moral deficit in modern liberal democracies. This book is about the value of history in explaining and defining liberty. It is about the contradictions and compromises which are bound up with freedom – and, most importantly, it is about the way in which a society accommodates itself to these contradictions, establishing a narrative of liberty. When we attempt to reconstruct civil society we have to look again at the process by which this kind of society has been built, and the glue which binds it together.

Multiculturalism offers a challenge to our society. It asks questions of the role of the state, the power of communities over individuals, the competing needs of minority groups. The following two chapters look at how the history of liberty might contribute to multiculturalism in Britain and Europe. In confronting the tensions of a diverse society, governments have taken a top-down, regulatory approach. And the various groups which make up the modern UK have been encouraged to demand and compete for rights and privileges. The debate has been impoverished in recent years because that process by which society was constructed has been downplayed, ignored and trivialised. Over issues such as free speech – for example, attempts to regulate offensive words – the impression has been given that there is no such thing as a fixed right and that serious things can be bargained away when the state sniffs the first whiff of troublesome conflict. The lesson which is being taught is that the state takes matters into its own hands, while the individual is relieved of the onus of taking responsibility. In the end it is the history of liberty which is our greatest asset and our best moral weapon.

We must be clear about the foundations of our society and the rights of individuals. Are our social freedoms the result of a gift from above or of a duty placed upon us all to make it work? The 'vital question of the future', wrote Mill in *On Liberty*, would be the 'nature and limits of the power which can be legitimately exercised by society over the individual'. The good society, in Mill's concept of liberalism, is one of diversity, where everyone has the freedom to make a plan of life which suits his or her character, even if others think that plan is 'foolish, perverse or wrong'. It puts individuality at the fore, but it does not preclude people making a rational (or not) choice to unite with others, as long as it is a genuine choice. Indeed, the liberty to unite, Mill explicitly says, is an extension of individual liberty. Note that the proviso of this is that the individual comes first in this relationship – a group is built upon the presumption of individuality and the group, organised as a faith or a culture, cannot claim a superior right or liberty over its member. From this it follows, crucially, that the individual who unites (in a culture, a faith or whatever) must not be coerced or defrauded and must have the freedom to renounce his or her choice and leave that group.[3]

The essence of liberty is that everyone should be, to the largest extent possible, independent of the pressure of society to conform to a set rule. One is free to worship as one pleases and express allegiance to whatever religious, political or cultural life one chooses. In Britain this pluralism is a very old idea. 'The great liberty and independency which every man enjoys', wrote David Hume back in the eighteenth century, 'allows him to display the manners peculiar to him. Hence the English, of any people in the universe, have the least of a national character, unless this very singularity may pass for such.'4 Mill's argument that a free society is defined by the room it gives for a diversity of lifestyles and experiments in living chimed with Hume's view, and in a multicultural society it is more relevant than ever. No one has to profess loyalty to any one thing enforced from above or from within society.

There is a price to pay for this. And that is acceptance of certain rules. Article 9 of the European Convention on Human Rights restates Mill: 'Freedom to manifest one's religion or beliefs shall be subject only to such limitations as are prescribed by law and are necessary in a democratic society . . . for the protection of the rights and freedoms of others.' A belief, however central it is to someone's identity, cannot conflict with the greater needs of society and it cannot trump the rights of others. Parents' right to educate a child in a way they deem to be absolutely essential to the demands of their faith is necessarily limited by the state, and furthermore the state claims a right to insist on a basic curriculum which covers all children. This is built upon the assumption that the child is not yet an autonomous individual, and the privilege of choice upon reaching adulthood would be rendered void by parental or community compulsion in the formative years. Of course it doesn't always work out like that in the complexities of family life, but it is an aspiration which should be insisted upon when the family comes into contact with state institutions.

Other benefits of diversity are similar extensions of individuality – and are subject to similar bargains with your fellow human beings. Freedom of speech, which makes possible freedom of religious and cultural observance, places everyone alike under the spotlight – and even the deepest attachment to a religion cannot defend that religion from insult or blasphemy, although the law rightly protects the individual from the manifestation of these views in bullying, threats or violence. If you want to be free from a stifling and conformist idea of a 'national identity' or a national character, then one thing does have to be accepted as inviolable. And that is a political morality which is shared by all and defended by all because it makes possible all the diverse modes of life which people demand for themselves.

Your right to live your life as you wish – however offensive and regrettable I find it – is bound up in this constitutional system. The freedom to do what you will is built upon a system of premises which derive from the idea of individuality and liberty buried deep in our culture. But Western governments have been spectacularly bad at articulating this basic precept to those who are new to the arguments; they have even backed away from these precepts in their policies. Just as worrying, the dominant culture in our society is losing sight of these things.

Multiculturalism has been seen as being in conflict with liberty. The idea of 'political correctness' and cultural sensitivity had been seen by some as an assault on absolute free speech. The tolerance and protection of illiberal practices which existed in some cultures was perceived as incompatible with feminism, gay rights, secularism and all the recent benefits Western liberals had wrested from traditional authorities. The desire for accommodation was, allegedly, stifling Western societies and forcing them to deny what was most sacred to them. And multiculturalism came under attack from some of those minorities as well, who claimed the right of secession from the dominant culture. The liberty which permitted them to live as they chose also seemed to undermine their faith. It made apostasy easy and attractive; it subjected them to what they saw as blasphemy; it forced them to lose authority over their children by sending them to secular and diverse schools. According to the Algerian filmmaker Karim Traida,

Muslims now have a big urge, a big need to show their Muslim identity – to show it obviously, even. So there is the risk of a clash. The clash is already in the mind. Muslims fear that, if they open up, they'll wind up like the Christians – very decadent. So when Islam looks at Christian history, it's worried by what goes with liberalism. They think of the decadence of European society.[5]

And it was the younger, second and third generations of immigrants – those caught up in the very modern urge to explore and assert identity – who were feeling the pressure and reacting against the consensus, which they believed the first generation of immigrants had accepted all too readily and at the expense of their Muslim identity. They could perceive how seductive Western secularism was, and they wanted protection from the corrupting influences which came with the fluidity of multiculturalism. Most of all, and in common with many other groups in the world post-1989, they were exploring alternatives to Western values and the injustices of globalisation – and doing so in ways which entailed re-examining their Muslim identity. The 1990s saw the rejection of the multicultural consensus of assimilation and passivity by young European Muslims and an upsurge in politicised Islam in response to the Soviet invasion of Afghanistan, *The Satanic Verses*, the Gulf War and events in Palestine and Bosnia. It was a way of engaging with Islam which had bypassed older generations of immigrants, who had experienced their faith as a private spiritual matter. The response from a motley coalition of European liberals, former leftists and conservatives was just as extreme.

In the wrong hands the idea of liberty was being perverted. In some cases the urge to retain habits of tolerance and plurality was leading to its opposite – the authoritarian imposition of lifestyles upon migrant groups. After 9/11 there was a hardening of identity. Muslims were, more than ever, regarded as Muslims before they were anything else, and throughout Europe there were calls for a restatement of Western values after what many regarded as doomed experiments in multiculturalism. Mathias Döpfner, head of the Axel Springer publishing group, wrote in *Die Welt* that the open nature of European civilisation had been undermined by misguided attempts at accommodation and toleration. Multiculturalism, predicated on freedom and human rights, bred the very things which would undermine human rights and freedom. Modern Europeans, brought up in cultural relativism and ashamed of their own misdeeds and hypocrisy, had not the moral authority or the will to confront the enemies in their midst. And what Europeans considered to be modern virtues were taken as weakness by 'an enemy which cannot be tamed by "tolerance" and "accommodation" but which is actually spurred on by such gestures'. It was a modern form of weakness which he compared to the appeasement of Hitler.[6]

The West, many others argued, was renouncing the values of the Enlightenment, imposing self-censorship and permitting groups to sub-jugate women, harass homosexuals and opt out of Western freedoms. These separatist groups were being left alone – sometimes encouraged – to entrench their authoritarian ways in the name of diversity; in this atmosphere extremist forms of Islam were being nurtured and the con-sequence was terrorism. Areas of European cities seemed to be stamped with an alien identity. Mental as well as physical 'no-go areas' were being created. In most countries with large immigrant minorities – and the Netherlands, in particular – there were loud and popular appeals for enforced integration and conformity to Western ideals. Restrictions should be put on Islamic dress codes; a more active pro-cess of secularisation should be pursued; and the heady experience of liberation, which had been going on since the Enlightenment, should be pushed on groups which resisted it.

This was done in the name of liberty – the intolerant must be made to be tolerant, and freedom must be defended from the illiberal. In the face of these pressures on their culture, Westerners should fight back with all the weapons they had – including the rights of free expression to shock people out of blind faith and unthinking conformism, just as Voltaire had done in the eighteenth century and popular culture had done in the 1960s. In particular, the filmmaker and broadcaster Theo van Gogh saw himself as the heir of the Dutch tradition of *scheldkritieken* – abusive criticism as literary art form. This he saw being buried by the platitudes of political correctness and by plain fear after 9/11. He was provocative and iconoclastic – and, it has to be said, even-handed – in his bombasts against everyone's sacred cows and cant.[7] In 2006 he made the film *Submission*, a com-mentary on the treatment of Muslim women, with Ayaan Hirsi Ali, a Somali-born Dutch MP who had outraged many Muslims with her beliefs that their religion was inherently at odds with democracy. Notoriously, Hirsi Ali was to find herself under twenty-four-hour protection and van Gogh would be assassinated. This violence forms the backdrop to the later discussion of these issues.

In light of these battle lines which were being thrown up in Europe, it is worth examining the thought of Amartya Sen. He saw the great civilising benefits (for all) of British multiculturalism, but he also saw its betrayal by the well-meaning. And, once again, its defence could best be understood in terms of liberty. He made a distinction between multiculturalism and what he called 'plural monoculturalism'. Multiculturalism is vague enough to allow for many interpretations, but in the liberal model, the state treats people first as individuals capable of making their own decisions before it makes predetermined assumptions about them based upon their cultural background. It is dependent upon the state remaining neutral – something which aggressive secularists and the isolationists alike were coming to reject as the atmosphere soured after 9/11. The acid test of the commitment of the state to individualism was education, for it gave people of all backgrounds an experience of different cultures and allowed them to make a choice. In a judgement in 2006, Lady Justice Hale made clear this assumption:

Like it or not, this is a society committed, in principle and in law, to equal freedom for men and women to choose how they will lead their lives within the law. Young girls from ethnic, cultural or religious minorities growing up here face particularly difficult choices: how far to adopt or to distance themselves from the dominant culture. A good school will enable and support them.[8]

This Sen calls 'cultural liberty' in which individuals are given as much knowledge, experience and opportunity as possible to choose from a range of cultures, religions, lifestyles and political attachments. 'Being born in a particular social background is not in itself an exercise of cultural liberty, since it is not an act of choice,' argues Sen.

In contrast, the decision to stay firmly within the traditional mode would be an exercise of freedom, if the choice were made after considering other alternatives. In the same way, a decision to move away – by a little or a lot – from the standard behaviour pattern, arrived at after reflection and reasoning, would also qualify as such an exercise.[9]

This is similar to the aims of Mill. His plea for individuality in *On Liberty* is sometimes taken to mean that you are most free when you break every shackle with which your upbringing and culture binds you, and rebuild your character on your own. This was, after all, what Mill had done with his own life, and why he remains an inspirational figure for migrants who are escaping suppression. Ayaan Hirsi Ali, for example, extols the Enlightenment because 'it strips away culture, and leaves only the human individual'. But modern cultural relativism had made a 'satanic pact' with Muslim groups, propping up their culture in the name of political correctness. 'This way,' she said, 'the cage will never be broken': people would be trapped in the culture of their birth, unable to 'remake' themselves as free individuals and have the liberating feeling – and human right – of cutting away the fetters forged by others.[10] But this is not an accurate reading. Mill is well aware that culture is unavoidable in a person's development – and not something which should be rejected automatically. And even if he did believe that nonconformity *is* liberty, it would be the weakest point in his argument – for human development is dependent upon at least some conformity to culture and society.* The state does not have a right to coerce people *away* from a given culture, only to present alternatives and make the choice to *leave* it a possibility.

Put another way, the cage need not be smashed (Hirsi Ali's 'hard' form of assimilation), but it should have clearly marked exit signs and protected exit routes. For compulsion – destroying the culture which people may very well choose having considered all the options – is itself a denial of liberty. This is not to underestimate the pressures which some people – mainly girls and women – are under to accept the authority of their elders. To understand, for example, the level of coercion a girl is under to wear a headscarf is impossible; she may have made the choice herself; she might be

---

* John Gray wrote of Mill's argument: 'if there is such a thing as an experiment in living, it is collective and not individual, it is conducted by social groups held together by common traditions and practices, and it is tried, not over a single lifetime, but across generations.' In similar vein Isaiah Berlin wrote: 'I am not disembodied reason. Nor am I Robinson Crusoe . . . I am what I am as a result of social forces . . . some, perhaps all, of my ideas about myself, in particular my sense of my own moral and social identity, are intelligible only in terms of the social network in which I am (the metaphor must not be pressed too far) an element.'[11]

wearing it as a political and social statement rather than in deference to paternal authority.[12] The state should not become a secular Inquisition, barging into private life. If it were to do so, society would have to reach agreement as to what the ends of life are. That is to say, it would have adopted a radical secularising agenda which put atheism above religion. That would be a big step, and not one consonant with liberty. However distressing one might regard the indoctrination of children into *any* system of thought or behaviour, a solution which went beyond confining the state's superior role *in loco parentis* to such things as the educational and the medical would completely undermine family life.[13]

But the notion that the state's duty is to maintain neutrality – never fully accomplished in any case – was being relegated by other concerns. Whereas the first decades of immigration had, in a way, united people of different ethnicities in a battle against racism, more recent political campaigns had stressed that culture was as important as skin colour, or more so. Multiculturalism was seen not so much as diversity of individuals within the nation but as a diversity of distinct groups. In 2000 the Runnymede Trust published the findings of a commission chaired by Lord Parekh on multi-ethnic Britain. The Parekh Report argued that the state could not simply treat individuals as straightforward equal 'rights bearers', but as people with distinct cultural identities which were as important as race or gender. It should not be 'colour blind'; rather it should equip itself with the knowledge and sensitivity to deal with a diverse population and provide the resources to maintain the integrity of distinct groups. The new language of multiculturalism talked of a 'federation of cultures' or a 'community of communities'.[14]

This, according to Sen, was an abandonment of multiculturalism based on 'cultural liberty' and the acceptance of 'plural monoculturalism'. This meant categorising individuals according to the communities from which they originated (which are unchosen), and giving that priority over other (chooseable) affiliations – for example to politics, gender, sexuality, literature and the many other things with which people can decide to identify in an advanced society. In an effort to be sensitive and not offend, the liberal consensus was forming a strange alliance with cultural conservatives. At the root of this policy was a desire to respect other cultures and, just as important, give people the freedom to live according to their values. The route to equality meant treating people unequally. As Lord Parekh wrote:

. . . since citizens have differing needs, equal treatment requires full account to be taken of their differences. When equality ignores relevant differences and insists on uniformity of treatment, it leads to injustice and inequality . . . Equality must be defined in a culturally sensitive way and applied in a discriminating but not discriminatory manner.[15]

No one, this orthodoxy held, had a right to barge in upon these cultures and make some sort of claim that another way of life was preferable. As Sen argued, 'despite the tyrannical implications of putting persons into rigid boxes of given "communities", that view is frequently interpreted, rather bafflingly, as an ally of individual freedom'.[16] This was not quite the 'satanic pact' Hirsi Ali denounced, but it was condemned as thoughtless by many. Minorities within minorities saw this attempt to deal with people on the basis of their culture as unhelpful: for who defined and represented their culture but self-appointed male elders? It was alleged that when confronted with a different culture, liberals put 'diversity' above what in other areas they deemed to be human rights. In many cases, social services and the police deferred to the definitions given by these 'community leaders', which were often at odds with those of more progressive but less assertive groups. As Women Against Fundamentalism and Southall Black Sisters wrote: 'Multiculturalism has provided the space for unelected community representatives, usually male and from religious groups, but also from the business classes, to determine the needs of the community and to mediate between the community and the state . . . this very rarely includes recognition of the individual rights of women or other sub groups within the community. Most have vested interests in representing only the dominant and often orthodox versions of culture and religion.'[17]

But it was seen as a form of freedom, for it allowed people to preserve their identity. People were encouraged to act politically through their communities. It bred a new, assertive expression of identity for some and for many others a greater need to conform to broad categories of identity as understood by the state. This was for the simple reason that the state was allocating resources (such as housing, regeneration schemes, business grants, artistic and sporting opportunities) and targeting social services and policing on the basis of community identity. In these circumstances it made sense to fall into line with the most recognisable cultural category.

These policies were motivated by the need to redress the balance in order to allow minorities to thrive within a plural society. Indeed, a monotone 'one size fits all' provision of state services might well have created unfairness if it tried to foster undeviating equality. That is to say, many people already felt cut off from the state because it refused to take account of their distinctive way of life and cultural taboos. Will Kymlicka argues that any multicultural society will be torn between the imperatives of individual rights and cultural sensitivity. Addressing the question of whether multiculturalism promotes illiberal tendencies, radicalisation and terrorism, Kymlicka points out that the problems of Muslim separatism, cultural conservatism and extremism are worldwide phenomena. Countries which design positive multicultural policies (such as Canada) and those which insist on assimilation (such as France) share the threats of terrorism.[18] Yet terrorism and radicalisation within Muslim countries has become the way in which multiculturalism as a whole is judged. Commentators from the right argue that Britain is 'sleepwalking into Islamisation' by appeasing Muslim sentiment. Melanie Phillips argued in 2008 that Britain 'is facing a pincer attack from both terrorism *and* cultural infiltration and usurpation'.[19]

No Western country has been forced to concede liberal territory to breakaway cultural groups by releasing them from the rule of law on, for example, arranged marriages or female circumcision. Yet these countries have taken very different approaches to assimilating immigrant groups. And as Kymlicka argues, the link between violence and multiculturalism was tenuous. The true test of whether multiculturalism was a success was, on the one hand, the ability and willingness of the state to make sure policies did not condone or ignore unacceptable practices, and, on the other, how much it increased the 'gravitational pull of liberal democracy' by allowing as many people as possible to participate in and benefit from the political process without alienating them. There would always be a tension between the two.[20] And in an age when the coherence of liberal democracy was being tested to the limit and becoming less attractive and explicable even to long-settled groups, this was an increasingly hard challenge.

In Britain serious questions were being asked about whether it had swung too far in one direction. The Parekh Report had called for the state to be flexible, and politics to be 'negotiable'. State and society should challenge themselves to rethink their history and culture, being tough on themselves for racism and cultural insensitivity. There was value in this, but the report had a conspicuous absence – it was not a shared obligation. While the majority culture was to search its soul and become malleable enough to adjust to the multifarious needs of marginalised groups, there was no call for this to be reciprocated. Minority cultures were not to be questioned or asked to justify themselves in public; they need not rethink their histories or myths; they were not encouraged to seek solidarity and share a sense of belonging centred on some aspects of British culture, for example the rule of law, individual liberty or freedom of speech. Indeed, one can quickly perceive what pressure this would bring on conventional liberties. In a competition between free speech and social inclusion, liberty may become one of those 'negotiable' political assets the report talked about. Indeed the report held up the violent protests against Salman Rushdie in 1989 as a defining moment in the postwar narrative because of the 'ensuing feelings of anger, isolation, solidarity and assertiveness' which united hitherto disparate groups of Muslims.[21]

The demand for cultural separateness was just an extreme example of developments in British society, as people of all kinds laid claim to privileges and exemptions while identifying less and less with wider society. And, as the Parekh Report seemed to admit when it discussed the Rushdie protests, identity was often shaped by shared grievances and experiences of unfairness and inequality – hardly the healthiest means of its formation one would have thought. And the tendency to see things in binary terms was intensified – negotiation

could be seen as capitulation to those superior to you. As one infor-
mant told the Parekh Commission: 'As Muslims in this country we
are being forced by the system to make a choice, either integrate,
therefore compromising ourselves, our cultures and our beliefs, or
separatism, whereby we create our own institutions and educational
system.'[22]

Ultimately it led to the demand for special treatment and for rights
to be awarded on the basis not of universality but of culture. It
fostered competitiveness between different groups for resources –
not to say the more worrying trend of a competitive attitude towards
identity itself. This was the fear that unless it was buttressed and
nurtured your identity would melt into the multicultural soup. In
other words there was a political discourse which encouraged and
institutionalised identities and compelled people to think primarily in
these terms and *use* them as means of self-assertion and political leverage. For Sen, faith schools, a particular enthusiasm of Tony Blair,
were a symbol of the rejection of the older model of multiculturalism
in favour of a communitarian one.[23] Faith schools, Blair said, brought
diversity; but this is true if you believe that a range of monolithic
institutions means diversity rather than that the institutions should
in themselves be diverse.

The trend in the first decade of the century was towards broad categories of 'identity'. Identity politics start when questions of ideology
collapse; it follows the solipsistic tendencies of people in the West. For
politics means transcending questions of identity and seeking solidarity with people who might be different from you; when the great
questions wither away you are left with nothing more than the personal. And when asked to define your identity in this way the danger
is that it becomes exaggerated and assertive. In twenty-first-century
Britain religion was impossible to ignore, and in many cases the government was treating the various faiths as political constituencies. It
was strengthening the idea in the minds not only of minority groups
but policy-makers that religion was at the heart of identity. This was,
argued Sen, a major threat to the kind of civil society which was the
primary bulwark of multiculturalism: 'A nation can hardly be seen as
a collection of sequestered segments, with citizens being assigned

places in predetermined segments.'[24] Faith schools were a signal from the state that different groups were to be treated differently. Such schools, although they had to follow the curriculum, tended to foster even more those feelings of separateness and teach, from the start, that the religion you were born with is your primary marker of identity.

Again, it is not the aim of religious education which is significant, but the role of the state in seeing this as a valuable contribution to society. And again, it doesn't matter so much that it was a Muslim school not a Christian, Hindu or whatever school: the government was following the trend towards assertive identity politics at exactly the same time as questions of identity and belonging were preying upon children of all kinds who were trying to negotiate between their faith and their position within society in the years following 9/11, the invasion of Afghanistan and Iraq, and the attacks in London on 7 July 2005. All these issues were pressing upon young people of all races and religions: promoting separatism in this context was not helping to build a more cohesive society with shared senses of belonging. It was another move away from the broad principles of liberty which had underpinned multiculturalism; from universalistic aspirations towards cultural relativism.

The state, by emphasising identity and culture in its official view, was in danger of transforming the development of a multicultural country from one where civil society possessed the self-acting energy and individuals the personal responsibility to reach accommodation, to one where the state drew the boundaries and set the rules. In other words, state regulation was becoming dominant while the meaning and purpose, not to say the imperative, of liberty was in eclipse. Some groups were acting as if the state dispensed all rights and owed them protection automatically, while they were by turns victims and claimants.

In the early twenty-first century this was presented by the media, the government and social commentators as most pertinent to Muslim communities and individuals. The reasons are not hard to determine: terrorism had raised concerns about the alienation and exclusion (primarily of young Muslims) from British social and political life (which was fragmenting in any case) and the concomitant hardening of Islamic identity across the world. But, in reality, it was an exaggerated example of what was happening throughout society. The failure was not in appeasing Muslims or tamely submitting to the Islamisation of society – as the right alleged – but a failure to think clearly about how a diverse society can live in harmony without the demand for rights being seen as competitive and mutually exclusive. The problem was not giving in to the demands of minority groups but the failure of the government to explain how social cohesion should be managed. As the rest of this chapter and the next explains, this failure led to dangerous conflict.

In essence what was being lost in the emotive discussions about modern Britain and the perilous efforts at compromise was the moral purpose of a pluralist society. Kenan Malik wrote:

The interesting thing about the multicultural argument is that it fails to understand what is good about diversity. Diversity isn't good in and of itself; diversity is good because it allows us to think beyond the tight box we often find ourselves in. It allows us to ask: should we change our way of life? Should they change their way? What's better? And therefore to create a political dialogue which, paradoxically, can help us form a more universal sense of citizenship.[25]

In an age of extremism and terrorism the government believed that the fabric of a multicultural society was easily rent. Part of the drive towards communitarian ideas came from a genuine desire to reassure Muslims that they were not being unfairly castigated after 9/11 by giving them the means to design their lives and find a place in British society. Policy-makers also feared that in such a sensitive environment the various communities co-existing in the country needed to be defended from each other's extremist elements if multiculturalism was to survive. They fretted that the precarious balance of communities was easily upset; that mutual tolerance could easily turn to mutual fear; that social peace was only superficial. As in other areas of policy, the government believed that it was responsible for shaping behaviour – setting the boundaries of what was and was not acceptable in this potentially flammable situation.

Before we get to the story of free speech in a multicultural society it is necessary to return to the Terrorism Act of 2006. The previous chapter ended with the government's attempt to get a pre-trial detention period of ninety days. But the act took a holistic view of terrorism. What the government wanted went far beyond the conventional remit of dealing with straightforward aspects of policing and prevention. Now it followed a growing trend in crime and terrorism legislation and strayed into the maze of free expression. There was a presumption in the thinking of ministers and the police that words and arguments – uttered by extremists and moderate commentators alike – were inflaming the situation. Words, therefore, needed policing. In dealing with religious hatred and radical language the government moved into areas which had previously been jealously guarded. It was without a doubt the most radical of the policies pursued at this time.

The 2006 act made the glorification and indirect incitement of terrorism a crime. This was introduced partly in response to offensive words spoken after the bomb attacks, but also because the police wanted the power to arrest people who were radicalising the community. The London bombers were believed to have been goaded into committing their crimes by hate-filled preachers operating in a shadowy culture which portrayed terrorism as a religious duty. The government's strategy – like its approach to antisocial behaviour and crime – was to pre-empt disaster by targeting those 'at risk'.

Public opinion was sick of outrageous preachers and the government believed that the police should have greater powers to prevent acts of terror by identifying the early stages of radicalisation. 'It is already an offence under our law to incite people directly to commit specific terrorist attacks,' Charles Clarke told the Commons. 'We now want to be able to deal with those who incite terrorism more obliquely, but who nevertheless contribute to the creation of a climate in which impressionable people might believe that terrorism was acceptable.'[26]

'Contribute . . . creation . . . climate': these were vague indeed when they were applied to the criminal law, especially regarding speech. The ancient principle of *mens rea* in English law – the stipulation that a guilty verdict was only possible if there was evidence that there was intention to commit an actual crime – was undone. The police only need show that someone was in favour of terrorism or owned or read material likely to be helpful to an act of terrorism to gain a conviction. In 2007 a rather pathetic young woman named Samina Malik – the self-styled 'lyrical terrorist' – was tried for possessing material likely to be useful in terrorism after she was discovered to own a veritable library of terrorist-related literature and poems she had written expressing her desire for martyrdom and her admiration for bin Laden. She was cleared of possessing articles for use in terrorism, but convicted for 'collecting information, without reasonable excuse, of a kind likely to be useful to a person committing or preparing an act of terrorism'. In other words, *mens rea* – the fundamental defence of the citizen to think and write – had no bearing. She was found guilty of reading horrible things: there was no evidence whether she would act on them. The trial judge described her as an 'enigma' and said that her case was 'on the margin of what this crime concerns'. As such, he sentenced her to community service, reflecting an uncertainty on the part of the judiciary when vague legislation compels them to deal with matters of opinion. And a few months later the uncertainty of the law was reinforced when Malik's conviction was quashed by the Court of Appeal.[27]

These measures were contrary to principles of British justice. Few considered reading extremist material anything but distasteful and worrying. Criminalising it, however, was a step towards censorship – and, as some pointed out, the thought police. In any case, it placed the police and the courts in the disagreeable and highly dangerous position of having to judge whether words were tantamount to crimes. It mirrored other, more worrying developments in the state's attitude to free speech. It was not hostile to this freedom, to be sure, but taken together its various laws and its general attitude were veering clearly towards putting safety above liberty. The Terrorism Acts of 2000 and 2006 should be read in the context of the Serious Organised Crime Prevention Bill (2005) and the Racial and Religious Hatred Act (2006). The former set a zone in central London in which it was illegal to protest without written notice. As a result of this and anti-terrorism laws, people were stopped and searched in the vicinity of parliament for wearing T-shirts with political slogans or even carrying newspapers of a left-leaning bias. An anti-war protestor was arrested for the crime of reading out at the Cenotaph a list of servicemen who had died in Iraq. Most notoriously Steven Jago, a management consultant, was charged under the act for carrying a banner bearing the words of George Orwell – 'In a time of universal deceit, telling the truth is a revolutionary act' – and having on his possession copies of *Vanity Fair* which bore an article entitled 'Blair's Big Brother Legacy'. Mr Jago said the police seemed to consider his reading material subversive and evidence of his desire to break the law.[28] When this liberty-denying part of the act was going through parliament, the minister justified such an important measure on the three trump cards of modern life: health, safety and security.

Since 2001 ministers had tried, and failed, to include clauses in various anti-terror bills which created offences involving stirring up hatred on religious grounds. While Christianity was, to some extent, covered by the common law of blasphemy (although it was, de facto, defunct) and Jews and Sikhs were protected by race laws, Muslims were not protected from insult on the grounds of their religion alone. Throughout Europe, as I described above, there was an alarming trend in liberalism to become more assertive. Part of this fightback was, to British eyes, unattractive, involving provocation and ridicule. I say unattractive, because in Britain most people saw no contradiction in reconciling free speech with the political imperative of integrating people into the traditions of freedom. There was little of what Theo van Gogh and others were doing in the Netherlands – an irreverent campaign to bust taboos and force the pill of reason (as they saw it) down with the cup of satire.

In November 2004 van Gogh fell victim to a nightmarish ritualised assassination for making *Submission* – he was shot and beheaded as he cycled through Amsterdam. (Ayaan Hirsi Ali had already accepted the protection of the state.) The intimidation and the murder intensified the already acrid conflicts in Dutch society. Politicians and commentators talked of war with a Muslim 'fifth column' – the enemies of freedom and democracy. If stories about reprisals on mosques were exaggerated and short-lived, there was a general fear that the Dutch were at the limit of their tolerance, Muslims were themselves intolerant of Dutch society, and violence would ensue.[29] The British government believed that a repetition of this across the North Sea was inevitable. There had been riots in the north of England in 2001 – and the fear was that if anti-Muslim feeling was accompanied by a literary, artistic or scholarly fig leaf then there would be a British Theo van Gogh.

But things were very different across the water. What in Britain might be called multicultural etiquette, or self-restraint in the name of the greater good of tolerance – maintained by consent rather than by coercion – was labelled 'appeasement' by a vocal alliance of voices in northern Europe. By this they meant that tolerance of radical Islam in the name of social peace was not putting off but intensifying the inevitable clash of civilisations.

In this view Britain was altogether too 'politically correct', or whatever pejorative was in vogue. Yet the Labour government seemed to believe that self-restraint was not something which could be trusted. The Racial and Religious Hatred Bill, as proposed by the government, shocked many because it seemed like a desire to stifle discussion of religion. It appeared to be another weapon in the armoury of national security – catch-all laws which were flexible enough to be deployed if circumstances demanded, yet which would not harm free speech because the powers that be would use them sparingly. There was also a somewhat less altruistic reason. The government wanted to assuage Muslim feeling by extending the law of blasphemy. As with faith schools, the policy seemed to be offering the very worst and most antiquated things enjoyed by the Church of England.

As legal scholars pointed out, the government, if it wanted to protect free speech, needed to make a distinction between an attack on a religious system of thought and an attack on people professing a religion. A recent law had created the concept of a religiously aggravated crime. If I doubt or ridicule belief in the Resurrection then, by this law, I am okay. But if I begin an intimidating campaign against individuals for no better reason than that I find those individuals' shared belief obnoxious, then I am straying into illegality. A member of the BNP had successfully been prosecuted for displaying a poster saying 'Islam Out of Britain' and blaming Muslims for 9/11. This the trial judge held to be an attack on *Muslims* not on Islam; it was as if the BNP were trying to make use of the gap in the law by substituting

'Islam' for their usual and more vicious racial categorisations.[30] This was clearly unacceptable. And indeed there had been many recent convictions on the basis of religious harassment between 2001 and the passage of the bill in 2005–6. As two legal scholars wrote of the BNP judgement (*Norwood* v. *DPP*):

This ruling cuts away much of the reasoning supporting the proposed incitement to religious hatred offence . . . The interpretation of the offence in *Norwood* appears, then, to make a further offence unnecessary – except for the purely symbolic purpose of enacting an alternative to blasphemy which applies to all religions.[31]

The new laws sowed confusion. They would make it possible to prosecute 'a person who uses threatening, abusive or insulting words or behaviour' towards another on grounds of religious belief. A person was free to debate or satirise religion 'unless he intends to stir up religious hatred or is reckless as to whether religious hatred would be stirred up thereby'. Note the word 'reckless'; artistic or academic discussion would be impossible under the law unless one watched and measured every word so that there was no possibility that another could, by these arguments, learn to hate a religion or – more vague still – be insulted.

Hate crimes involving gender, sexuality and race were already in place – and this was compatible with freedom of speech because attacking someone for an unalterable condition of their DNA was unacceptable in a civilised society. But religion is different. The historical development of liberty began when it was accepted that there was a crucial difference between criticising or ridiculing someone's opinions and attacking them personally. The law, according to its many critics, did not make this distinction clear. Now, it should not be underestimated how fundamentally some people connect religion to their identity; for many it transcends any other form of identity, including racial. The problem is not the sincerity of their belief but the way in which it is to be protected by the state. Confounding race and religion was a dangerous route to take, for religion, unlike race or gender or sexuality, is built upon ideas – and policing arguments is a world away from policing racist or sexist language. The Public

Order Act already made it an offence deliberately to stir up hatred against another through threatening words. The government's proposals added 'abuse' and 'insult' to the more plain meaning of 'threat'. To further confuse things for a policeman on the street, it also added religion as a component of someone's identity. There were cases of people claiming special treatment because they were devotees of Wicca – and if you add to the major religions all the myriad sects and variations of belief, then a policeman's lot would not be a happy one in determining someone's identity.

Ministers said that they would use the law sparingly. But like all discretionary law this led to serious problems. If the Attorney General was to be the judge of what was offensive, then his decision *not* to prosecute would offend the offended even more; and if he did prosecute the trial would be invested with political and moral significance. Worse than that, the vagueness of the law and its arbitrary nature would leave scholars, artists, novelists, performers and politicians permanently unsure as to the legality of what they were saying when it came to the discussion of religion. The law did not say to what extent identity and religion were intertwined, nor did it define what level of offence constituted a crime. Rowan Atkinson, who campaigned vociferously against the law, argued: 'All jokes and drama have to characterise a situation in human form. Knowing that there is a law that states that it is a crime to "threaten, abuse or insult a group of people defined by their religion" remains, I am afraid to say, very intimidating.'[32]

The government might very well exercise restraint when it came to this law. But Atkinson's point was well made. Writers and performers would be forced into self-censorship by the arbitrary deployment of the law. And worse still, the only measure of the law was if someone *felt* offended. There was nothing to stop them having recourse to this act and making a call to the police whenever they believed 'hatred' was being stirred up. And, although the person might never face a court, he or she would have to suffer investigation by the police and the lingering taint of possessing some phobia or other.

The new law was intended to protect individuals against violence and discrimination. It was not supposed to defend systems of religious belief from attack or offence. Yet this was how it was interpreted. A Christian group wanted to use the law to ban the sale of the Qur'an because they said it incited violence.[33] Many Muslims believed that such laws would protect Islam from insult, as if it was a revamped blasphemy law which would hermetically seal religion from outsiders and renegade insiders. Sir Iqbal Sacranie of the Muslim Council of Britain said the laws would stop people from traducing his religion in public and defaming the character of Muhammad.[34] These hopes were awoken in response to the act. In 2004 a group of Sikhs protested against a play in Birmingham which depicted sexual abuse at a temple. The violence forced the play off the stage and the writer into hiding. The government's response was not to defend free speech in word or deed, but to marvel at the interest shown in culture in modern Britain as if violent protest was as valid a critical response as open and peaceful debate.*

The Racial and Religious Hatred Bill was introduced for laudable reasons. Yet it awoke hopes that were impossible to fulfil without stringent censorship. It went to prove a fact known long before: that state intervention in free speech can never be targeted. It has to be painted with broad-brush strokes; the wording must be general in order to catch the particular. This was especially true when it came to religion (rather than race) where there are thousands of religions and sub-sects and labyrinths of interpretation. Such politics opened up ugly divisions in multicultural Britain. The test of the law would be whether anyone felt offended. And in modern Britain there were so many people claiming the right not to be offended that groups were being set against groups in a competition to entrench and protect taboos. The protection of one religion from 'blasphemy' would only work if all religions – including no doubt the esteemed faiths of Wicca and Jedi – were given like protection. All religions are in dispute to some extent, and there is even more vigorous dispute within a religion. Protection for one religion would also entail censorship for

---

* The minister Fiona Mactaggart said: 'Free speech of the protestors is as important as the free speech of the artist' – weaselly words indeed, especially when one considers the fate of anti-government protestors through the ages and into our own.[35]

that religion lest it offended a member of another faith. Religious hatred laws do the opposite, therefore, of defending multiculturalism; they replace peaceful co-existence with perpetual dispute in the police station and the court house. In the experience of Victoria, Australia, the law had led to a tit-for-tat conflict between religious groups: Christians were infiltrating Muslim meetings, and vice versa, with a view to bringing a prosecution against opinions expressed in a sermon; indeed some people were spying on their co-religionists for the same reason and for symbolic or political reasons. The former Attorney General of India, Soli Sorabjee, warned the Lords' select committee that a similar law in India had wrecked religious harmony and curtailed free expression.[36]

Given the new legal protections, self-censorship on the part of publishers, galleries, newspapers and theatre producers, eager not to give offence or provocation, and a government scared of confrontation, how could a genuine dissenter guarantee that he or she would get a fair hearing and protection from reprisals? The authorities were increasingly shy of wading into inter-community disputes, for fear of betraying racism or Islamophobia – leaving the noisy, intimidating and radical to impose orthodoxy on the weak and isolated. Ed Husain recalled his time as a member of a radical Islamic organisation within the student community in east London. His demands were always met, however at odds they were with the general freedom. University authorities, the police and every other institution were so afraid of the charge of discrimination that he had no trouble in pushing and pushing at an open door. 'Our magnetism and vitality drew people to us. A visible Muslim presence everywhere, women veiled, ubiquitous posters of Islam and the student population, almost without exception, under our control.'[37] And it wasn't just fundamentalists who made bids for leadership. There were many who gladly took the title of 'moderate' to solidify their power. Writing of the religious hatred law, Pragna Patel of the Southall Black Sisters organisation (which protects vulnerable women from abuse) said:

We have no doubt that it would be used as a weapon to suppress dissent within our communities, particularly those who are more vulnerable and powerless. Until we see greater equality and increased accountability from within, we can no more rely on religious leaders than we can on the state that often appeases them in the name of multiculturalism.[38]

Back in 1989 when Salman Rushdie and his publishers were rewarded with a fatwa for *The Satanic Verses*, the ensuing violence and book-burning hardened a sense of Muslim identity in Britain. Inayat Bunglawala of the Muslim Council of Britain recalled how the campaign against the novel gave British Muslims – 'a vulnerable minority' – the feeling that they were part of a global movement. There was strength in the consciousness of unity: 'If we were not treated with respect then we were capable of forcing others to respect us.'[39] Community leaders claimed to speak for an entire religion – and many of those who called for Rushdie's death in 1989 were, after September 2001, seen by the government as the spokesmen of moderate Islam. Sir Iqbal Sacranie, who had been active in trying to suppress *The Satanic Verses*, became secretary of the Muslim Council of Britain and led the way in demanding laws to protect Islam after 2001. The thought of what would happen when all the competing interests in a multicultural society and the issue of free speech reached the point of collision was put off.

But it could not be put off for ever. All this came to a head in the first two months of 2006. In January, Iqbal Sacranie – who had invested so much effort in getting laws put through which he believed would spare Islam from offence – was interviewed by the police after they received a complaint that he had caused offence when he said on Radio 4 that homosexuality was unacceptable. So if this was what he wanted – laws to protect the public sphere from religious offence – he got an early lesson in the kind of Britain he was helping to construct. He claimed his right to free speech, but when he had contributed to zero tolerance for insult he could, if he had wanted, have seen that he had made a trap for himself. Being part of a minority did not give you impunity to insult another minority. And if we all claim special status from the state and sacred areas of our life upon which others durst not trample with their muddy boots, then we will find our freedom of speech dwindle to the space reserved for the trite and the inconsequential. Here, perhaps, we could revive the words of Thomas Hobbes: every man (*sic*) must, if he is rational, 'be contented with so much liberty against other men, as he would allow other men against himself'.[40] If you don't, then the lesson of human history is that the laws you design to protect yourself have a nasty habit of affecting you in the end.

In the event, the police were proving extraordinarily keen to hunt out any sniff of racism, homophobia and anything which might involve hatred or insult. A couple in Lancashire asked the council if they could display Christian literature next to council posters promoting civil partnerships. They found themselves under police investigation. This was not an issue of political correctness but of liberty. The mere complaint of 'offence' was likely to bring the force of the police down upon a person who dissented from the new orthodoxy, even if there had not been any intimidation.

There is a twenty-first-century craving for prevention, which we see again and again in all areas of life. Whatever benefits it brings, it is certainly incongruous with liberty. The police seemed to claim the right to pre-empt the manifestation of nasty behaviour. It was not isolated: a young man in Oxford was arrested for joking that a police horse was gay; Tony Blair himself came under suspicion when a former aide recalled that the Prime Minister had said 'fucking Welsh' to his television when he was watching the results of the Welsh Assembly elections in 1999. The need for new laws began to seem bizarre given how proactive the police were without them. Speaking in the House of Commons, Ann Widdecombe said:

The society in which we now live is unrecognisable from the freedom that we knew only a few years ago. We are not in danger of being shanghaied off to the Lubyanka, but we are in danger of the police knocking on the door or ringing us up and starting an investigation against us not on the basis of what we have allegedly done, or of threats that we have allegedly uttered, but merely on the basis of a view that we have expressed.[41]

Shortly after the Sacranie incident, the Racial and Religious Hatred Bill was, as the government saw it, wrecked in the House of Lords by two amendments. The first made it an offence to use 'threatening' language in the context of someone's religion, but removed the words 'insult' and abuse'. The second introduced a clause guaranteeing that academic, artistic and political language would be protected. The government resented these revisions, but the Commons agreed with the Lords, by a margin of just one vote. It was a severe embarrassment for the government – and an accidental boon for free speech. It was a very strange month. The leader of the British National Party, on trial for racism and incitement for calling Islam 'a wicked, vicious faith' in private, was acquitted. The radical cleric Abu Hamza al-Masri was sentenced to seven years for soliciting murder and inciting racial hatred. David Irving, the British historian, was arrested in Austria for Holocaust-denying comments he had made more than a decade before. It also coincided with violent protests throughout the world against cartoons of Muhammad published in the Danish paper *Jyllands-Posten* some months before, and republished in European countries subsequently.

It seemed at the time as if the bluff had finally been called on the accommodation reached between different cultures and religious groups in European countries. Any previous restraint in the name of social peace seemed to be going out of the window; the gloves were off and the future promised to be one of competition for protection or impunity. If you wonder why some people despise our freedoms, then it is worth looking at how they should know in the first place what liberty means. Government policies seemed expedient and contradictory; the very idea of liberty had been removed from the debate in the first place.

CHAPTER 17

Taking Sides

—॥॥—

If liberty means anything, it means the right to tell people what they do
not want to hear.

GEORGE ORWELL, PREFACE TO *ANIMAL FARM* (1945)

'The Muslim face of Denmark has changed,' wrote Flemming Rose,
the cultural editor of *Jyllands-Posten*, 'and it is becoming clear that this
is not a debate between "them" and "us", but between those committed to democracy in Denmark and those who are not.' He went on
to say that the cartoons of the Prophet Muhammad which he had
commissioned for his paper had forced moderate Muslims either
to side with extremism or to show their commitment to the Danish
constitution. For this reason Ayaan Hirsi Ali said that the cartoons
had sped up Muslim integration by three hundred years; the bitter
draught of satire evidently worked.[1]

Those cartoons were commissioned in order to challenge self-
censorship in the European media, self-censorship which many
believed was a threat to Western liberties. An issue preoccupying
editors on the Continent was the determination not to cavil in the
face of intimidation. 'It's at the very core of our culture that the most
sacred things can be subjected to criticism, laughter and satire,' said
Roger Koeppel, editor-in-chief of *Die Welt* (though these things did
not, of course, include discussion of the Holocaust). Indeed, the
cartoons were invested with a high moral worth.[2]

No national newspaper in Britain republished the cartoons. They
held back because they said they did not want to cause needless

offence to British Muslims. There was also a wider context. Since the cartoons had first been published in Denmark, there had been a campaign throughout the Middle East – and, although many protesters had not seen the cartoons, they vowed to revenge an insult to Muhammad and attacked Danish embassies and other targets. This was nothing less than the manufacture of outrage. There was a widespread belief that Europe was doing what it had done throughout history, hypocritically using its 'freedoms' to insult and degrade weaker people.

As the cartoons were freely available on the internet, most British editors believed that they were not colluding in censorship. Rather, they were refusing to be made complicit in a political campaign. It seemed that the cartoons had been seized upon deliberately by extremists in the Middle East so that Europe would go into a paroxysm of self-doubt and moral confusion over some mediocre drawings. This was deliberate. As Rose said, the issue was forcing Muslims in Europe to take sides. But by February 2006 the issue had been manipulated to such an extent that 'taking sides' was fraught with complexity. To say to British Muslims that this was their last chance to sign up to freedom of expression and that they'd better choose their side now would have been a quixotic mission, perhaps shading into masochism. In the words of Flemming Rose: 'This is about the question of integration and how compatible is the religion of Islam with a modern secular society – how much does an immigrant have to give up and how much does the receiving culture have to compromise.'[3]

So it was no longer about the cartoons and freedom of expression, but issues of multiculturalism and immigration which were local to Denmark. These are vital questions, of course, but they did not have to be answered in Britain in the midst of a tangled web of Middle Eastern politics, simmering violence and northern European controversies.

The troublemakers wanted European journalists and politicians to stake their freedoms on these cartoons. And many were happy to oblige. Hirsi Ali and others had had direct experience of theocratic oppression; Flemming Rose had been shaken out of any vestiges of collectivist ardour when he reported from the Soviet Union.

Committed to multiculturalism, secularism and freedom, they believed the utopia of a diverse Europe was being betrayed from both sides. Rose said that his decision to satirise Muhammad was the very opposite of racism because he was treating Muslims as he would Christians, or any other religious group for that matter; he was treating them as Danes. 'It was', he said, 'an act of inclusion, not exclusion; an act of respect and recognition.'[4]

Now just what the connection is between free speech and the failings of Danish multiculturalism was not made clear. Nor was the value of baptism by insult. I may very well be free, just as Mr Rose was to publish the cartoons, but I do not need to prove it at every opportunity. It is said that a person's liberty ends where his fist comes into proximity with another person's flesh, but you don't have to swing your arms about to determine your freedom of movement unless you are a toddler – or unless you are deeply insecure about the extent of your liberty. It was not *illegal* to draw, publish or disseminate the cartoons; and if the journalists of Europe were combining to defeat liberty-denying religious hatred laws, they might have been able to speak in heroic terms.

Let's not get righteous about the satires; it was not about freedom of speech so much as the failure of some aspects of multicultural integration. It makes sense to encourage as many people as possible towards the principles of liberty. Doing it by picking a fight seems strange. If we are to serve the larger purposes of liberty for all in our countries (and around the world), then it cannot be by compulsion or by shock and awe. It was not coincidental that in countries which had unhappy experiences of multiculturalism and strong policies of assimilation (such as Denmark, France, Germany, the Netherlands, Norway and Spain) papers with high circulation published the cartoons, while in countries which were active in promoting multiculturalism (such as Australia, Canada, the UK and the USA) only relatively obscure and low-circulation magazines carried them. If an editor's self-restraint contributes to the gradual integration of others into the ideals of freedom, then I must find it somewhere in my heart to applaud, even if my instincts for liberty are offended. If an editor decides to exercise his freedom at all times and the consequence is that embittered minorities are sickened at the sound of liberty and retreat into isolation and hatred then I can see the larger purposes are not being served but being abused. There are things worth fighting for. If a cartoonist was *prevented* from drawing a satire then I would fight for his right. But this was not the case over the Danish cartoons. Not publishing the cartoons was not a denial of liberty. Those who wanted to make it a test case seemed to believe that freedom was worthless unless it was exercised at all times. But this is not so. What if the cartoons did not speed up integration, but retarded it? Whose liberties are being served thereby?

February 2006 was a strange time, and, in a way, curiously old-fashioned – it was if images only became important if they assumed physical form in newsprint. That was not a game that the newspapers were going to play with provocateurs. There was, in the twenty-first century, a resource of freedom far beyond the reach of any censor or thug – the internet. Until they had achieved notoriety – after the painstaking efforts of interested parties, it has to be said – there was no evidence that Muslims in any great number in Britain were genuinely offended by the cartoons. It is worth pointing out that the cartoons weren't aimed at individuals but at one of the most powerful religions in the world. Before the outrage was whipped up most Muslims, surely, were confident that the Prophet was strong enough to shrug off insult without much difficulty. The majority did not want to impose their religion's taboos upon others. The issue, as ultras on both sides willed it, was about how Muslims were treated in European countries in general; it was not about the theological implications. As it was, deferring readily to those who claimed that *all* Muslims were offended on religious grounds – as was the case as well over *The Satanic Verses* and, in 2007, over the decision to give Salman Rushdie a knighthood – was patronising to Muslims who were capable of making up their own minds as individuals.

The concept of 'Danish', or 'British', or 'European' Islam was invoked throughout these debates by imams in Denmark, by rabble-rousers in the Middle East, by journalists and politicians. That is the heart of the matter. People of all sides of the debate felt free to discourse upon Muslims – whether they were too easily offended, naturally anti-free speech, remarkably restrained or helpless victims in need of special protection. Who dared ventriloquise the multifarious opinions of millions of Muslims who came from diverse cultures from all around the world?

Islam is dependent on religious freedom – and the more freedom there has been in history the better Islam has fared. The *convivencia* of Muslim Spain in the Middle Ages is testament to this, when Jews, Christians and Muslims lived in relative harmony. Islam does not do authority like Christianity does; if it had it might have been much less successful. There are no bishops, no inquisition and no pope – it is decentralised and non-hierarchical, which has allowed its spread into geographically diverse lands and allowed it not just to survive but to thrive in multi-religious and multi-ethnic societies and at all times since Muhammad walked the earth. In Muslim Spain, Catholicism was the poor relation because, deprived of the mediating authority of ordained priests, it had nothing to offer its scattered flock in the Dar el-Islam. In the United States the multifarious and multiplying Protestant sects, competing in a free spiritual market, achieved things which the ossified *state* Church of England could only marvel at.

Take *away* state authority in religion and it is strengthened. As Paine argued long ago, the 'divine dignity of religion' is at its strongest when men and women come to it from free choice. Involve the state – as a promoter or protector of religion – and that religion 'presents itself to Man, like light intercepted from a cloudy medium, in which the source of it is obscured from his sight, and he sees nothing to reverence in the dusky ray'. Paine was writing here of Article 10 of the French Declaration of Rights, which allowed free speech, particularly religious expression, unless it disturbed public order.[5] In other words, the Article was like the proposed religious hatred laws in twenty-first-century Britain: it purported to leave a crack of acceptable regulation, but – by its plain and innocuous wording – it could be prised open to become full-blown censorship. How then could an individual claim to come to the divine truth unmediated and unsullied by other men's hands if certain topics were off limits? Ask for a religion to be taken under the wing of the state and you freeze it to a lesser or greater extent; but freeze it you certainly do to the detriment of its vitality.*

Who then sought to speak for Muslims in 2006? Given that Islam claims to be universal, it is impossible to offend Muhammad and Islam. An insult affects the living only; the contempt of an infidel cannot reach even the foot of the steps which ascend to the divine throne of God, if that is what you believe. But it is a feature of modern *political* Islamism that all the diverse and multi-ethnic votaries of Islam bridge these divides by the solidarity of the shared insult. Hans Magnus Enzensberger argues that the psychological process of radicalisation plays on all sorts of modern anxieties, particularly the pains and injustices of globalisation, which creates 'losers'. There is nothing unusual in this, but less common (though more common in the present century) is the 'radical loser' – a person whose very identity is wrapped up in his status as a powerless and humiliated loser. He (it is usually, but not exclusively, a he) at once seeks solace in his misery and yearns to humble his unknown humiliators in a one-off act of vengeance. History and literature are littered with such pathological human types. Usually they passively accept the slings and arrows, but sometimes they will massacre their schoolfellows or strap high explosives to their bodies.

The radical loser is harmless as a lost individual. But when he finds solidarity with similarly inclined allies he becomes dangerous. Amid the pains and scars of globalisation – and when no embracing ideology has come forward to offer an alternative – political Islam has stepped forward as *the* revolutionary opposition to exploitation, imperialism and war. The radical loser in the Islamic world has something upon which to fix his frustration. He masochistically feasts upon the pain and humiliation of marginalised groups, with which he is linked by shared religion, and identifies most strongly with the victimised members of the *umma*. It is a sense of inferiority which becomes unbearable;

* Here is Paine again: 'The first act of man, when he looked around and saw himself a creature which he did not make, and a world furnished for his reception, must have been devotion, and devotion must ever continue sacred to every individual man, *as it appears right to him*; and governments do mischief by interfering.'

it is pain felt vicariously – and all the stronger for it. It must mean the renunciation of all *other* ties that link humans in the immediate neighbourhood and, when it comes to the virtual community of brothers and sisters abstracted into a global community, the minimisation of all the differences that human beings are heir to.[6] Thomas Hegghammer pointed out that Muhammad Sidique Khan, one of the London tube bombers, turned to martyrdom to avenge the oppressed *umma* after he had subsumed himself into the 'imagined community' of worldwide Islam. 'He thus killed fellow British citizens to avenge brothers in faith he had never met. Such is the power of pan-Islamic nationalism.'[7]

Al-Qaeda and the many other Islamist groups, therefore, owe their considerable success to not just exploiting but creating these emotions. It is the same desire for respect and self-assertion experienced by the disaffected the world over, but pushed to grotesque lengths. There is, it seems, a desire for authority, for the charismatic dictator who will elide the complexities of worship, the realities of ethnic difference and the bitterness of sectarianism, and thereby unite believers. Belief is tied up with feelings of self-respect and the consolation that Islam will eventually triumph as a world force. Many believers feel like victims; the true destiny of Islam has been diverted by colonialism, the betrayal of Muslim leaders and, in modern times, globalisation and military action. Seeking an object of offence, therefore, with which to mobilise angry and alienated young men is a permanent objective, and the cartoon row was a golden opportunity. It was a fillip also to those in British Muslim communities who were demanding religious hatred laws – and who cynically pointed to the brewing violence among some Muslims as a reason for these laws, even as they preached peace.

The effort of the government and the press at the beginning of 2006 should have been to persuade those who would listen that this is a fundamental – and dangerous – error. Dangerous, it should be said, to Muslims. Freedom – and civilisation itself – progresses when people learn that criticism of their system of belief or their philosophical opinion or their society's cherished conventions is not a personal insult which has to be avenged. Intellectual arguments and matters of personal esteem have to be separated or there is no reasonable discourse. This is not easily learned, nor is it willingly accepted when your very being is bound up with your religion. When that religion is perceived to be at the mercy of others, words are not just brushed off. The response is to demand that thing which is the demand of the powerless everywhere – respect.

'What is being called for,' said Faiz Siddiqi, the leader of the Muslim Action Committee, 'is a change of culture. In any civilised society, if someone says, "Don't insult me," you do not, out of respect for them.'[8] This is how the context of the cartoon row must be judged. It revealed how many people were confused about the very idea of free speech. This was a demand for respect which was not reciprocal. Very quickly the debate turned to the victimisation of Muslims living in the West and renewed demands that special treatment be accorded by law. Claiming victim status seems to lead to a certain amount of selfishness: I must be respected but I need not show it to others for fear of exposing my weakness and subservience. It is the attempt to score a symbolic victory over those who are perceived as arrogant and supercilious.

And that brings us back to the government's multicultural policies which encouraged this kind of group identity: organisation on the basis of shared grievance. The trouble is that the grievance has to be maintained indefinitely for the community to be taken seriously. Countering the demand for unreciprocated respect could only have come from the top. It was the government, not the papers, which could rightly be accused of spinelessness. It was trying to enforce a culture of respect – to which free speech must take a poor second place. So Siddiqi wasn't too far out of step.

Neither the government nor Muslim campaigners seemed to trust self-restraint – even though that was exactly what the press was showing in 2006. Yet this instinct for social harmony in a multicultural society was being used *against* the press. Because they had refrained from publishing the cartoons, it looked as though Britain was in the grip of fear and people in authority were desperate to pay any price for safety. And in a way this was true. If the press did not publish because they were reluctant to follow an agenda set, in different ways, by free-speech radicals in Denmark and Islamist radicals in the Middle East, they at least had a duty to make an unequivocal case for free speech. In Britain some Muslim organisations were using the controversy to organise protest marches and demos against Islamophobia. This was how the 'change of culture' in Britain was to be effected: by the mobilisation of offended people with the spectre of terrorism hovering in the background. If the press would not publish the cartoons they should have asked the Muslim leaders who were demanding some sort of action to set out what sort of society they would like. If they wanted courtesy they could have been asked why the more offensive anti-Semitic, homophobic and violent material from the Muslim press was not banned as a matter of courtesy. There was no attempt to turn the lens on extremists within their own community or any measure of self-criticism beyond the perfunctory; so much for the new 'global civility' which was being called for by the Muslim Action Committee as veiled threats were made, embassies were stormed, journalists went into hiding and over a hundred people died in the violence worldwide.

A voice of reason was briefly heard: Jihad Momani, editor of the Jordanian paper *Al-Shihan*, asked the Muslims of the world what was the most harmful to Islam – the cartoons, or images of terrorism and violent protest? And the answer soon came: he was sacked and prosecuted for publishing some of the cartoons. Momani later said that Islamic groups and the government were using the controversy to present themselves as the defenders of Muhammad, to censor the press and to divert attention from corruption. The Egyptian judge Said al-Ashmawy asked what was happening to liberal sentiment in the Muslim world: 'How can we write? Who is going to protect me? . . . With the Islamization of society, the list of taboos has been increasing daily. You should not write about religion. You should not write about politics or women. Then what's left?'[9]

But where were the liberals in the West? If those advocating censorship or the voluntary silence of the media could have made their case and said what they wanted their proposals could have been scrutinised in detail and refuted; the trap they were making for themselves could have been patiently pointed out. What happened, however, was an embarrassingly equivocal response to the threats of violence and the shrill complaints of hurt feelings. Journalists and politicians of all sides excused the violent protests, saying implicitly or explicitly that mob reaction was a legitimate and reasonable response. Roger Scruton put it in the context of what he called the 'hooligan iconoclasm' of the West, and added that the problem was plunging respect for the sacred on one hand and, on the other, for the quiescence of Christians, who did not fight back but meekly shrugged their shoulders.[10] William Dalrymple put it in the context of international politics, implying that journalists and artists should be limited by realpolitik: 'It is not the moment to be throwing petrol on the flames.'[11] And so heavy and contradictory demands were not laughed out of court.

The consequence was what Nick Cohen called the 'politics of competitive grievance'. This incident, and the policies of the government, created a situation in which those who shouted loudest and expressed the most hurt feelings received attention. Following the protests of some fundamentalist Hindus – who threatened violence – the gallery Asia House withdrew an exhibition of work by Maqbool Fida Husain which depicted naked deities. After the cartoon row, Iqbal Sacranie demanded that the European press apologise, and a Hindu Human Rights organisation wanted the same symbolic gesture from Asia House, the Indian High Commission and everyone who was involved in the exhibition – what is tantamount to collective public mortification for a personal slight.[12] A group called Christian Voice tried to prosecute the BBC after it broadcast *Jerry Springer: The Opera*, which they regarded as blasphemous. Later in the year, a minority claiming to be community leaders protested against the filming of the book *Brick Lane* in Tower Hamlets because they felt it depicted the Bengali residents in a less than flattering light.

As was said, in echoes of all matters of this kind, the book was 'a most explicit, politically calculated violation of the human rights of the community'.[13] After the usual threats of violence, the film company moved elsewhere. Monica Ali, the author of *Brick Lane*, wrote on what she called the 'outrage economy' and the tendency of liberals to sympathise with those claiming victimhood whatever the case:

I can understand this liberal sentiment. But I fear it is taking us to a dangerous place, a marketplace of outrage at which more and more buyers and sellers are arriving, shouting their wares and inflating the prices. And now it is open for business it will not be possible to keep people out.[14]

The *Guardian* backed away from defending the right of artists to express themselves, saying that authors had a duty of responsibility in how they portrayed minority communities which had never been depicted before.[15] But it could not be compared to the cartoons; no one was claiming that books like *Brick Lane* were politically motivated attempts to mock people into liberal values. This was a genuine case of freedom of speech in a multicultural society. 'We are being taught to be circumspect,' responded Hari Kunzru. 'How long before it's suggested we should shut up altogether?'[16]

The price to pay in these cases is not fear of assassination – what happened to van Gogh, and the threat which the Danish cartoonists, Rushdie and Hirsi Ali face every day – but what Timothy Garton Ash called 'the creeping tyranny of the group veto'.[17] This is not confined to the religious, but to everyone who asserts identity politics; everyone who puts the validity of their emotions above rational debate. When it comes to political Islam, the hijacking of these kinds of issue gives the majority of Muslims a bad name. In most cases, writers have not sought out individuals to provoke, but opportunists have sought to be provoked. And their outrage has been deferred to.

The politics of offence crept into the mainstream after 2005. Artists and comedians believed that their freedom was being curtailed partly through fear and partly because society preferred the peace of a convenient silence to confrontation.[18] Indeed, in a few cases protest was not needed at all; John Latham's work *God Is Great* was removed from the Tate to pre-empt any possible offence.[19] Most alarmingly, the police used the new laws to investigate free debate and even opinion. They were taking very seriously any opinion which might tend towards hatred, discrimination or terrorism. Dominic Grieve told the Commons:

... the moment one orthodoxy disappears, a new orthodoxy starts to rear its head. I have no doubt ... that there is a danger of a new orthodoxy creeping in that prevents people from freely expressing their beliefs because the public good in some way requires it. Just as 150 years ago it was impossible to express one's beliefs on certain matters [concerning religion] . . . so we are suddenly moving, after what may turn out, if we are not careful, to be a very brief window of true freedom, into a new orthodoxy. That worries me very much.[20]

In 2007 the Channel 4 *Dispatches* team made a documentary film called *Undercover Mosque*. It showed that in a number of apparently moderate mosques there were some extreme preachers who were utterly opposed to multiculturalism and were advocating violence. The West Midlands Police requisitioned all the footage to see if a case could be made for a prosecution against the extremists. But it was the filmmakers who found themselves facing arrest. They were accused of stirring up racial hatred. The police and the Crown Prosecution Service believed that they had quoted one of the preachers out of context, and this was threatening the peace and cohesion of the community. Yet what kind of context would justify saying 'We love the people of Islam and we hate the people of kuffaar [non-Muslims]. We hate the kuffaar!'? Having reviewed the unbroadcast footage and decided there wasn't enough evidence to warrant a prosecution, the authorities saw fit to assess *Dispatches* on the same exacting standards. If a case cannot stand up in court, it is not fit for public discussion, the police and prosecutors seemed to be saying; and if it wasn't up to these standards it must therefore be racist.[21] Where the authorities lead, others will follow. John Ware of BBC's *Panorama* found himself under attack for Islamophobia by Muslim groups, while the Muslim Council of Britain called him a pro-Israeli polemicist, when the programme said that moderate Muslims were in denial about the extent of Islamic terrorism in the UK.[22] The charge of racism (against a religion) was becoming a convenient way of silencing inconvenient debate.

But in this world of 'competitive grievance', no one was safe from being prosecuted. It was soon found that what was most likely to be subject to prosecution was not the jokes and jibes of secularists and atheists, but the outrageous statements generated within religious disputes. Anyone engaged in proselytising or preaching or religious education could not be confident that their words did not offend or stir up hatred against other religions, or even against rival sects of their own faith. Between December 2001 and March 2003 eighteen cases of religious harassment were brought to court; of these ten involved Muslims, and of these six were actions brought by one Muslim against another. Many Muslims were left unsure if they were allowed to have political discussions at their mosque.[23] It was, I suppose, a rough lesson in liberty. If you demand censorship, then you cannot escape the fact that you set up another human being, as susceptible to prejudice, ignorance and fear as anyone else, to arbitrate. If you want to defend your private world from offensive outsiders, then it is best not to stray outside your little world lest those same laws are used against you.

There were some who were prepared to stand up for unconditional free speech. In January 2006, just as they were pushing for censorious laws, several senior imams and leaders of Muslim organisations wrote to *The Times*, without a jot of irony, complaining about the police investigation of Iqbal Sacranie's alleged homophobic comments: 'All Britons, whether they are in favour of homosexuality or not, should be allowed to freely express their views in an atmosphere free of intimidation or bullying. We cannot claim to be a truly free and open society while we are trying to silence dissenting views.'[24]

But then no discussion of free speech is immune from irony. During the cartoon protests, many claiming to be defending Islam from the accusation that it was inherently violent made a spectacle of themselves by wearing masks and camouflage (one person wore a suicide-bomb vest) and demanding that those who dared to satirise the Prophet be killed. Perhaps the protestors also felt their religious motivation gave them protection. But on this occasion the majority was rightly 'offended' by this intimidation – and there were some rather convenient new laws on hatred to deal stringently with these people. Several were arrested. In November 2006 the leader of the BNP was retried for his description of Islam as a 'vicious faith' and a North London web designer was tried for inciting violence during the cartoon demonstration by holding a banner saying 'Behead those who insult Islam' and advocating the deaths of British servicemen in Iraq and Afghanistan. And Islam had been insulted how? – by the accusation that it was inherently violent. The leader of the BNP was acquitted for a second time while the Muslim protestor was sent to gaol. It caused much anger in the Islamic community and ministers said they would think about changing the law – not to liberalise it, but so that it would be easier to prosecute offensive words.

How easy it is to shake the government! In truth neither deserved to be sent to prison. A few loose words, the consequence of which were not assessed, were enough to send a powerless Walter Mitty figure to gaol. In neither case had the people involved pointed to specific individuals and ordered other specific individuals to commit a crime against them. The web designer had no spiritual, moral or political authority to influence others to do his bidding with any degree of success. But did he deserve to be punished? Protest has never been particularly easy in Britain, and a plethora of laws have punished people for much less. Those who stir up violence and who make terrorism appear acceptable can be dealt with under many old and less dramatic laws dealing with incitement and breach of the peace. To equate offensive words with terrorism, racism and national security, however, is to raise the stakes far too high and to invest stupid protests with a significance which goes beyond the derision such behaviour merits. Tailoring special laws for special circumstances has one major effect – it makes martyrs of naïve boys or malicious nationalists by making them guilty of glamorous political offences rather than boring old charges of disorder or breach of the peace which can be dealt with by the unheroic penalty of community service.

A year after the 2006 Terrorism Act was passed by the Commons the police were publicly advising the government that the laws on incitement and religious hatred were not working. Islamic protestors had learnt to do what protestors had done throughout the centuries to avoid censorship: they learnt what language was and was not within the law, and broadcast the same messages in symbols or by implication. The police now wanted powers to proscribe words, phrases, images and chants, not just for Muslims but for animal rights and anti-globalisation activists. 'Is the sand shifting in our collective viewpoint around what constitutes "causing offence"?'

asked a report commissioned by the Assistant Commissioner of the Metropolitan Police, Tarique Ghaffur. 'Equally, we need to have a clearer determination of current community perceptions around what "public offence" actually means. We also need to think more laterally around how we police public demonstrations where "offence" could be caused, while still respecting the British position around freedom of speech.'[25] Here was evidence of where laws on glorification of terrorism, offence and hatred lead. The police were claiming a subjective power to determine what consequences various opinions might have.

There was in modern Britain, apparently, no robust ideal of free speech, only a 'position around' it – and no conception of what is likely to offend but what the police decide is offensive to a hypothetical thin-skinned person. It was as if extremism could be curtailed by banning the public utterance of offensive words, whether from Islamist radicals or white racists.

'One of the underlying assumptions of the debate about the cartoons is that in a plural society free speech must necessarily be less free,' said the writer Kenan Malik. 'I believe the opposite. In a plural society it is both inevitable and important that we do give offence. Important because any kind of major political, intellectual, artistic change has always offended deeply held beliefs.'[26] This is the essence of freedom. Thing have not changed by nice discussions but by intellectual revolutions which have torn up people's cherished beliefs much against their will. The privilege of living in freedom is that our lives are open to continual revision and the rejection of old verities. Most often that is a painful process – for you and those closest to you. Malik reminds us that offence is inevitable in an open society. Powerful ideas have a tendency to be offensive to the prevailing orthodoxy at first, and just as surely the freedom which nurtures them also gives crackpots and provocateurs the same right. The government got into an embarrassing mess in January 2006 because it failed to appreciate – or was brave enough to admit – that freedom and offence are inextricably linked. Mankind has not found a way to clean up noxious words in a way which would not cramp original minds or reinforce an orthodoxy, old or new. The New Labour government was no exception to this timeless rule.

Read Mill's *On Liberty* and decide whether we have reached a point where authority can discriminate nicely between the worthwhile and the incendiary. Who would set up someone to judge what opinion is true, or innocuous, or inoffensive, or conducive to the public safety? 'All silencing of discussion is an assumption of infallibility. Its condemnation may be allowed to rest on this common argument, not the worse for being common.'[27] Or, as Milton wrote long before, to silence someone is to stop your own ears. It is, above all, to strike right at the heart of their individuality, their very thoughts. And if you censor someone else, or desire that this be done to your enemy, you forfeit all right to your own freedom of speech.

This was put nowhere better than by Thomas Paine in the dedication of his *Age of Reason*: '. . . I have always strenuously supported the right of every man to his own opinion, however different that opinion might be to mine. He who denies to another this right, makes a slave of himself to his present opinion, because he precludes himself the right of changing it.' Who then assumes the right of fossilising your mind by calling upon the law to shield your tender sensibilities? No Muslim, surely, would gladly surrender this privilege in advance, even to another Muslim whom he does not know and whose doctrinal opinions might be alien to him. Is it that we have to track back over the experience of our civilisation and explain that which is the foundation of everything we hold dear? Perhaps. We would be better if every schoolchild knew this. But to see people with power and responsibility cheerfully elide these principles is distressing.

Mill's achievement, and value, was to demonstrate forensically how the liberties which are dear to us personally are interconnected with other liberties we would, perhaps, shrug off. It is like a house of cards; blow on one and the rest come tumbling down. It would be an important lesson to teach again. If you think that you can meddle with other people's rights and retain yours then think again. During the cartoons row – and at other times, such as in the wake of 9/11 and after the murder of Theo van Gogh – Muslims have been asked to sign up to Enlightenment values. But this is incompatible with liberty. People should live their lives as they choose without dogma being forced upon them. You cannot be forced to be free. And asking someone to choose between religion and liberty is discordant with the Enlightenment anyway. The Enlightenment did not happen overnight, and it did not come at the price of abandoning religious beliefs. In the modern climate, if you say that Islam is incompatible with freedom and offer Muslims a choice, then you might be disappointed with the answer. And if you ask someone to choose between satire and faith then you are asking him or her an impossible question – and one not worth it when serious issues are at stake. Rather you should ask yourself this question: How much is your religious freedom bound up with my freedom to say things which may strike at the heart of your faith? The answer must surely be, that without this embracing and equal liberty there is no freedom at all.

So the urgent problem does not include making Britons or Europeans out of Muslims by making them capitulate to Western values. What should be taught are the universal rules of freedom. What else can unite us? People are free to believe in whatever gods they choose and follow what lifestyle they will, but they should take as a matter of utmost seriousness that this is due to the constitution of freedom, liberty of speech and the rule of law. What binds a multicultural society is respect for laws which protect equally and a state which, in its dealings with matters of supreme importance, is neutral.

The danger of laws concerning offence, and glorification of terrorism for that matter, is that they pervert a genuine debate about freedom of speech. And if the state interposes itself in this way as a regulator of opinion, it prevents people seeing the larger picture of freedom: this is exactly what happened in 2006. Rather than try and patch things up with meddlesome laws, the government should have invested more time in explaining what freedom of speech entails. A look at history would have shown that no law could have protected Islam while allowing Muslims a claim to have their own potentially offensive opinions protected on the grounds of religion. It is nonsense to assume the government was forced into these laws. There was a choice, and the harder one would have been to lay down some basic lessons on freedom. But as I have argued, ministers had effectively disarmed themselves of that part of their political vocabulary.

Yet it was in keeping with a general policy of avoiding dangerous issues. That people assumed they could censor opinions offensive to them while retaining their right to be offensive suggested not that they didn't care about liberty so much as that they hadn't the first clue about it. This has much to do with policies, particularly in education, where the idea of teaching, let alone advocating, any values or assumptions of British culture is assiduously avoided. 'If we are going to create a Western Islam which is harmonious then . . . Muslims in the West need to understand how it is that . . . we got where we are,' Ed Husain said in a debate in 2007. 'Part of the reason why I walked the extremist path is that at secondary school . . . it wasn't explained to me what was the Reformation, the Civil War, the Enlightenment; how is it that Britain reached liberal democracy and government by consensus.'[28]

But then white British schoolchildren might not have had any better idea of liberty. The problem is cultural and political. It is the retreat from these once commonplace ideas of freedom. Liberty has the power to bind people in a diverse nation; it is the building block of multiculturalism. Everyone has a close interest in maintaining it because without it all those privileges of living in this country are debased. It is sad then that the principles of liberty have been downgraded. When the government violated habeas corpus and the rule of law and gave itself an active role in deciding which opinions were not permissible – and when it did this without a robust defence of the country's principles – it sacrificed this great advantage.

There are plenty of British Muslims who are caught on the margins of extremism, or who at least have sympathy for it. These are the people whom the security services need, and whom a healthy democracy needs, to win back. Sometimes they struggle to articulate why Britain is preferable to most other countries; why they get a chance to practise Islam as they choose here unlike in, say, Saudi Arabia. There are so many competing versions of Islam, and so many putative leaders, that if any were to predominate anywhere woe betide those whose conscience bids them dissent even in non-doctrinal matters. Pluralism, then, is the true friend of the devoted, even if the passage of life is beset by the Scylla of choice and the Charybdis of insult.

Those who advocate special treatment do so unthinkingly, or they are motivated by the less than generous or multicultural aim of entrenching their own power over their community. Religious hatred laws, followed to their letter, would be the death of the religious freedom of Muslims. Why was this not said in blunt terms?

Those who try and adumbrate the principles of liberty within their community find their task thwarted by the actions of the government. If the majority of people in Britain have lost touch with the tradition of liberties – and if they don't know and don't care – then it is hardly a surprise if immigrants find it puzzling. Campaigning for civil liberties and expressing dissent is the enthusiasm of the excluded, and it is a step in civic engagement for, by holding rulers to a better standard of justice, it is deeply satisfying. Most importantly, it can convert impotent rage into something constructive. You can see it in our own history; you can look at the struggle for civil rights in the 1960s.

This is to think in terms of an ideological struggle. Muslims want to live as Muslims in a free society. They may or may not be interested in homilies about the superiority of British liberty, but that is not to say that there are not universal truths about liberty which may be applied to Islam. The potential for reviving this kind of thinking is there. Inayat Bunglawala, who took part in the Rushdie demonstrations back in 1988/9, wrote in 2007 that it was only after travelling the world, particularly the Muslim world, that he saw how wrong he had been. 'Our detractors had been right. The freedom to offend is a necessary freedom. Moreover, Islam has flourished where there has been a free atmosphere. I continue to disagree strongly with the way Rushdie caricatured early Islamic heroes of mine, but banning the book was not the answer.'[29] Or as A. Sivanandan, Director of the Institute of Race Relations, put it:

When our rulers ask us old colonials, new refugees, desperate asylum seekers – the sub-homines – to live up to British values, they are not referring to the values that they themselves exhibit, but those of the Enlightenment which they have betrayed. We, the sub-homines, in our struggle for basic human rights, not only uphold basic human values, but challenge Britain to return to them.[30]

The complaint has been that there have been groups trying to 'Islamise' Britain. While it may be true that this is the aim of some organisations, I do not think it is something to which a majority of Muslims subscribe. It is true to say, however, that the government has created an environment in which rights are packaged up and accorded to various groups in different ways; in which those who complain loudest are often conceded to; in which competition is encouraged. When a premium is placed on respect and avoiding offence becomes a moral duty, it is clear the problem is not confined to minorities but is society-wide. In such circumstances it is sensible to make claims on the state, demand special privileges and play a game the rules of which have been set from above. Getting the best on offer is, after all, the goal of politics.

Yet it is poor training in citizenship; still worse is the effect on everyone's liberty. Freedom and mutual accord are rarely successful when they are forced on people; as we know by our own experience, it is by living and interacting with others that we learn to respect difference and to tolerate. And we certainly have history books which elaborate the cost to individuals and society when we are compelled to scrap it out for our rights. Accepting that our liberties rely on the like liberty given to all is without a doubt a crucial step in civilisation. The state's policies risk interfering with this process, making people more like selfish actors than part of a society.

Britain has shown a very poor example of liberty recently – partly out of fear of terrorism and partly out of guilt that it was imposing alien values upon people. Those lessons which should have been at the centre of society have been allowed to wither away – or be clouded by hazy thinking. There is another lesson from the cartoon row. A great deal of harm was done to the Danish economy by boycotts.[31] One of the reasons why liberal democratic values spread across the world was that – despite all their many flaws – British imperial power was succeeded by American hegemony. In the present century the relative power of America will decline, and the coming powers are less friendly to human rights, let alone freedom of expression. If you think the cartoon controversy was a one-off, then good luck to you.

Censorship works in all kinds of ways. In a future dispute involving a major economic player such as China or Russia, the reprisals would be more damaging. As Martin Jacques argued at the time of the cartoon crisis, Western values in the nineteenth and twentieth centuries were a feature of power, and they flourished at the expense of other cultures.[32] In an interconnected world, and in a modern Europe where other cultures are becoming more vocal, these assumptions cannot be taken for granted. In the relatively homogenised and very powerful nation states of the past, free speech was less problematic. Is it to be that the idea of freedom of speech being entirely permissive – where there are no taboos which cannot be ridiculed and no dogma which cannot be defied, which was such an important feature of postwar social freedom in Europe – cannot stand the test of the twenty-first century, of an interconnected world where we are dependent on the goodwill and economic partnership of cultures which are radically different from our own? 'By the end of this century', Jacques argued, 'Europe is likely to pale into insignificance alongside China and India. In such a world, Europe will be forced to observe and respect the sensibilities of others.'

That is a bleak prospect. Not because we will lose our right to be offensive but because liberty is essential for the progress of humanity, whatever abuses were committed in its name and under its cover in the past. If the rest of the world sees our liberty as chauvinistic and hypocritical and if they want, as Jacques argues, to settle the account, then we have only a few opportunities left to say why these freedoms are not just valuable but vital; not just a Western construct suitable to a time and a place but universal. There is no casual connection between scientific progress, artistic brilliance, feminism, multiculturalism and all the others we take for granted and the broad liberties which have grown up in the West. For all the horrors of Western hegemony – all the hypocrisies and acts of violence – I'm not sure that I'd rather have lived under another system. The basic liberties, discussed throughout this book, are universal and they are integral to civilisation. They are at risk. The choice is being provocative and assertive – using the shock tactics of liberty as in 2005/6 – or setting a moral example. That means getting serious about what liberty means and being prepared to justify it in words and deeds. We need a restatement of liberties, not more equivocations. We need to stress that multiculturalism and liberty are indivisible – and that is a message that Europe can transmit to the world if it wants to. Looked at in this light, restraining a traditional mode of liberty (in which unqualified liberty of speech is seen as the utmost expression of personal independence) serves the higher purpose of liberty if it presents this interconnected world with an attractive example of modern liberty.

As in other matters, the claims of expediency have obscured the fact that there is an important principle at stake. All other liberties are dependent on freedom of speech, and once you surrender that, you are in danger of impoverishing your society. Speaking at a debate in Toronto, when the Canadian government was passing religious hate laws similar to those proposed in Britain, Christopher Hitchens had this to say:

Where are your priorities . . .? You are giving away what is most precious in your own society without a fight. And you are even praising the people who want to deny you the right to resist it. Shame on you while you do this. Make the best use of the time you've got left.[33]

Epilogue

—∿—

We've given up far too many freedoms in order to be free.
GEORGE SMILEY, IN *THE SECRET PILGRIM* BY JOHN LE CARRÉ

'Laws are the scaffolding of human freedom,' wrote the intellectual G. D. H. Cole; 'but they are not part of the building.'[1] There has been a tendency for the debate on liberty to become fixed on changes to our legal freedoms. This is understandable given the assault in the last decade or so on habeas corpus and freedom of expression, not to say innovations such as control orders and ID cards. The erosion of these rights has made many uneasy about the direction that modern Britain is taking. Civil liberties are the measure of how much we prize freedom and how far we live up to a standard set in our past.

But any discussion of liberty should look far deeper. The value of history in this regard is more simple than a tale of the rise, decline and fall of liberties. Britain has been fortunate throughout her history. It was not just the development of legal protections and parliamentary forms which made the country free, but the will to be free evinced by all kinds of people. The emergence of history as a national passion helped in this. It was not a case of looking back with longing on a vanished past of freeborn Britons. Rather, history became a way of judging the present. It was a measure of how things should be, how people should react to overbearing authority, presumptuous politicians or unfairness in society. It gave examples of how other people wrestled liberties; how they sought *new* ways to be free in different historical circumstances.

Most importantly, history teaches that there is no such thing as liberty in an absolute sense. At no time did people not have to contend with injustice and inequality. At no time could someone wake up and say the business of liberty was finished. Those who seek a theory of freedom in a philosophically exact sense will be disappointed when the tectonic plates shift underfoot and personal freedoms are invaded for expediency's sake. This book has many examples of times when settled notions of liberty faced up to change. Hostility to state intervention, for example, seemed like a viable bid for liberty – as it still does to some people. Yet the state does have a positive role in extending freedom, just as it always strays perilously close to strangling liberty.

Negotiating this path is difficult and probably never satisfactory. It takes effort to make it work. How far should the state go? When should it restrain itself? This must be done as circumstances dictate – as example after example shows. Liberty is of value because, by giving free rein to as diverse a choice in life as possible, it shapes personality. Liberty is therefore equated with responsibility. That which hinders personal responsibility, curtails experimentation or places us under undue surveillance should be carefully watched. I do not oppose excessive interference because I fear the state is going to become tyrannical; I do so because I fear what effect it will have on the citizen. In an ideal free country, it should be instinctive to increase the space a citizen has to exercise his judgement and mental faculties. In this way, liberty is progressive; it has a positive end and a value. This is what I mean by dividing societies with a cultural attachment to liberty from those which are free only in a formal sense. There are degrees of freedom, and we should insist on the maximum. Living in a free society means exploring things which will make us more free as individuals. That takes courage and self-confidence.

What provides a guide is history, for in this way we can make sure we don't cede more than is commonly held to be the norm. It keeps society in health because it allows us to compare our liberty with what others enjoyed. It provides a set of basic assumptions – a heritage of freedom – which should command respect and thereby shape policies. It gives us the courage to resist when we feel the line has been crossed.

The theory of liberty suits best those who are attuned to the chaos of life: the need for compromise, bargains and continual revision. There is no formula which makes us free – no pristine constitution, philosophical theory or economic system which guarantees freedom more than any other. Taking a bird's-eye view of the historical development of liberty helps us understand this. For those who like certainty, the arrangements of society and the state look arbitrary and haphazard. Every encroachment made by the state looks like an exaction upon freedom. In order to comprehend this, and to understand why we have the liberties we have, it is necessary to look at history. And the contested notion of what sort of freedom we want must take account of the struggle which always exists within a liberal democracy. Otherwise, it sounds like nonsense when we have to justify the systems we have and the rights we want. Continually going back to first principles and repeating the journey of mistakes and injustice would be damaging. Explaining those principles from scratch every time we reach a crisis is frustrating; the past at least gives life to things which otherwise look archaic or irrational.

Liberty means, for all practical purposes, the ability to contend for political change in a society in which dissent is protected and encouraged, justice is done and seen to be done, the individual is the primary unit in the political system and redress is automatically conferred on the wronged. Britain may not, on paper, have been more free than other countries, but it had an appreciably freer atmosphere. Small infractions on customary rights were shouted from the rooftops. Officials restrained themselves rather than risk offending common notions of propriety. It was a country in which free thought, originality and a high degree of social harmony flourished. This happened not simply because Britain had the Habeas Corpus Act; it was because the national culture prized liberty.

This intangible freedom exists when people have confidence in the system. Civil liberties – the scaffolding of freedom – allow other liberties to breathe. Being spared even minor interferences makes our relations with the state less abrasive and the business of life easier. This is their value. And it is a pity that the defence of civil liberties in our own time does not stress their positive benefits for the health of society and the comfort of the individual. The historical development of liberty in Britain and America is without parallel in the history of civilisation. I have been hard on liberty throughout this book, choosing to question more than celebrate uncritically. It has been an imperfect liberty to be sure, often used to shield abuse and sanction privilege, but the history of wider groups – religious dissenters and trade unionists, feminists and minority ethnic communities – fighting for liberty within the system, adopting the language of justice, liberalism and liberty is one that has given Britain unique peace and stability. When liberty has been restricted in the past, in grave national emergencies such as the First and Second World Wars (and lesser ones such as the General Strike), various groups were identified as subversive and suppressed. The country had cause to regret the draconian action it took; in the light of history persecuting pacifists or communists was judged harshly. What the state had, and it might have used it unwisely sometimes, was great moral capital.

The legacy of liberty went deep. It meant that suppressed groups or people fighting for rights of their own had confidence in the state. Due process, the rule of law, the independence of the judiciary and other civil benefits have made Britain a good place to live in. It alleviated the social injustice of pre-democratic Britain and, later, made democracy worth having. Civil liberties may have been abused or bent in favour of the fortunate few, but they had a power which transcended politics. In the end, however, the greatest beneficiaries of civil liberties are those who have been most restricted by them. For the state, by being so bound, earned a reputation for fairness; it gained perhaps a greater legitimacy than it deserved. And living under a government which one believes to be free and fair is in itself a liberating experience and, in the history of the world, a rare privilege.

Where we differ in the early twenty-first century is in this cultural attachment to liberty. We have cut ourselves off from the historical tradition – the state of mind in which liberty was won. In ways I have touched upon, we are more inclined to demand personal rights than liberty in its wider social sense. We are more fearful. The modern tendency towards risk-aversion and safety at all cost puts us at odds with the history of our liberties. We have learnt to suppress our instinct for dissent – 'the nerve of outrage' – because we have become used to putting collective health, safety and security above individual liberty. This is beginning to extend even to free speech.

Health and safety are not bad things, of course; it is the government's responsibility to protect us. What has changed however is the attitude which lies behind the quest for these benefits. If the state is to have a positive role it can only be limited by its own concern for liberty or by its fear of opposition. We are not brought up to see things in terms of liberty any more. And officialdom has lost any instinct for self-restraint or 'constitutional propriety' as a result. It is important to be reminded that the Britain of the past did not have better laws and greater protection than we do. On the contrary, for every right in common law there can be found a liberty-denying law; on paper Britain bristled with potentially repressive laws and – compared to states constituted in periods of enlightenment – had only patchy guarantees of rights. Liberty was not owing to the liberalism of the law, but the liberalism of the people who enforced it and the strength of public opinion.

Nowadays there is a high demand for efficiency – and the techniques with which to achieve it. The state is called upon to provide more services, and it is not shy of finding new ways to extend its authority. In such a complex society it has to mediate between competing interests and ensure fairness for its citizens. The outcome is a more controlling society and a tendency to submit to the tidal wave of regulations. It has happened partly because the old-fashioned 'dissidence of dissent' has drained away. There will always be a tension between the necessary task of protection and the rights of individuals. One of the consequences of the loss of the spirit of liberty has been that the equation has become unbalanced. Power naturally grows, and therefore trenches on individual rights unless it is kept under control by the principles of liberty – that is to say, restrained by human beings who are motivated by ideas and who respect law and constitutional practice. If in the past the state limited its interference to what it could get away with in the face of public opinion, it now has less friction to push against. We are regulated and monitored more than ever. The question which should be asked is, what effect do such things have on the overall state of society?

What we have lost sight of in our political system is the connection between liberty and the health of society. There are few politicians who want to make this connection. And when the debate is about retaining old legal protections, it is hard to make liberty a popular cause. Simply to say that if the state restrained itself – bingo – things would be OK is wrong even if it is seductive. Liberty should be a constructive force, helping to shape policies in a way which frees the individual. But this is not the case. The liberal phase in our history seems to be coming to an end. Maybe we can recover the love of freedom and manage our modern rules and regulations in a spirit of permissiveness and liberality. As it is, however, policies are often developed without reference to the impact they might have on individual autonomy. But then politics has become the art of management and damage limitation. The ideological bankruptcy of politics is a problem which goes beyond the debate on liberty. Yet if we go on accepting interference and regulation, we may get to the point where we snap. Then questions may be asked about the legitimacy of the state, and it will be left with scant ideological or moral *raison d'être*.

Living in liberty meant the freedom to take certain things for granted. It was the benefit of knowing that liberty, however it was defined, was part of the constitutional furniture, and widely accepted. But while we complain less, we also trust less. Throughout modern history the British state attracted support, often grudging, from outsiders because it was admitted that it was at least fair and bound by its own conventions. Today we struggle to make our democracy look inviting. What we do have which is attractive and motivating is a vibrant tradition of liberty. In a time of plummeting respect for democracy and the growing allure for some people of radical alternatives, liberty may be our best weapon in winning people over.

If celebrating our liberty may perhaps gain friends, it is certain that eroding liberty creates enemies. Tony Blair said that extremist violence had to be confronted with every means at the state's disposal: anything less was to invite disaster. 'Tougher laws in themselves help,' he said, 'but just as crucial is the signal they send out: that Britain is an inhospitable place to practise this extremism.'[2] But the message they sent out was that any measure, however draconian and illiberal, was justified by necessity. In the fraught nerves and animosities in the first decade of the twenty-first century – after 9/11, the London bombings of July 2005, and wars in Iraq and Afghanistan – there needed to be reassurance that although tough measures were being taken, the loss of liberty was temporary and tempered by an administration which took these steps with reluctance and at the last resort. This was not the case. The government showed contempt for liberty and the 'liberati' who advocated civil protections. 'We have chosen as a society to put the civil liberties of the suspect, even if a foreign national, first,' said Blair. 'I happen to believe this is misguided and wrong.'[3]

And so when inevitable mistakes were made – the gaoling of innocent people, the shooting of suspects, miscarriages of justice – the government had only itself to blame if it was accused of incompetent authoritarianism. After embarrassing scenes when the government bulldozed its measures through parliament, conflicts with the courts and a series of miscarriages of justice, the state certainly looked panicky and repressive to many members of the public. 'I also say it is wrong to frame this debate simply in terms of the civil liberties of terrorist suspects,' said Blair '. . . Of course their liberties are important, but so are the liberties of the people who may be victims of a terrorist attack.'[4] The trouble with this approach is that it erodes confidence very quickly. Also, as examples throughout this book show, as soon as civil protections are played down at Westminster, it affects the way that officers of the state conduct their business.

There have been well-publicised cases of blunders made by the security services – and their mistakes have alienated members of Muslim communities precisely because the state seemed to be less bothered with finicky concerns about justice. 'People accept that it is the police and secret services' responsibility to establish law and order,' said Ghayasuddin Siddiqui of the Muslim Parliament of Great Britain. 'But when they go and knock on somebody's door, they don't have to treat people, the whole family, as if they are all terrorists, all criminals.

Because of this, our young people have lost trust in the system, which will take a long time to recover.'[5] The government squandered a lot of its credibility by its attitude to civil liberties. It looked less fair, and its mistakes were magnified to an extent that some Muslims complained that they were living in a police state. For many others, the government seemed to be accruing greater powers, sapping liberties and acting like a totalitarian state. Whether this was fair or not, the government was left with little in the way of ideological defence.

Many of the government's attempts to pre-empt terrorism with control orders suffered defeat in the courts and criticism from human rights bodies. Yet the government seemed set on its course; capitulation would look like defeat. Ministers appeared not to trust the justice system, preferring putting some suspects under control orders (which limited their right of movement, communication and association) to risking a trial in court. Such things were unprecedented in peacetime. And what differed from similar wartime controls was the lack of trust that ministers had any strong hold on the principles of liberty. They had sacrificed that trust by their language and policies across a broad range of issues. It was left to others to articulate the value of 'airy-fairy' civil liberties. 'We wouldn't get far in promoting a civilising culture of respect for rights amongst and between citizens if we set about undermining fair trials in the simple pursuit of greater numbers of inevitably less safe convictions,' said Sir Ken Macdonald, the Director of Public Prosecutions, arguing for 'legislative restraint' in the fight against terrorism. 'On the contrary, it is obvious that the process of winning convictions ought to be in keeping with a consensual rule of law and not detached from it. Otherwise we sacrifice fundamental values critical to the maintenance of the rule of law – upon which everything else depends.'[6]

The government had proved in many areas of policy, especially criminal justice, that it found civil liberties old-fashioned and burdensome on its actions. It was no wonder that Blair and his ministers did not like the word liberty. It was too broad a concept, too heavily laden with historical connotations, too restrictive of state power. When liberty was used in the context of the mission in Iraq and Afghanistan it meant all the good things which came with democracy. When it was used at home its meaning was severely restricted: it was the liberty to walk the streets or use public transport without fear; it meant, in the first instance, the rights of the majority, not the protection offered by the law. It was little wonder, therefore, that idealism was drained from the government's case and it became a straightforward, ideologically neutral issue of protection in which all the murky areas of injustice, miscarriages of justice or faulty intelligence were mere technical issues or 'common sense'.

When Blair said that the primary job of government was to protect the lives of citizens, he was forgetting that government had a duty to defend, even enlarge, liberty as well. In conceiving liberty in this restricted way, the state was not freeing itself to the fight the war on terror but binding its hands. For it had undermined something which stands out as a moral example even to die-hard fanatics. Eamon Collins was a member of the IRA who was freed, despite being guilty, because he had been tortured. 'The judge's words sent a real shock through my body,' Collins recalled. The judge, he said,

. . . had brought to life for me, even though he loathed the IRA, principles which were important boundaries between civilisation and barbarism . . . even though he suspected I was guilty as hell, he was willing to let me walk free on grounds that many people would have regarded as a technicality, a foolish abstraction.[7]

As with crime, the New Labour government was prepared to take a tough line on terrorism, and it came to see civil liberties as a barrier to action. As ministers, taking their cue from the Prime Minister, were keen to emphasise, it was better that the innocent were detained or punished than that a bomb exploded. It is certainly the case that we have to rethink all our strategies and exert new effort in the fight against terrorism. Yet the government offered little to put in place of the protections they were taking away. The problem was that they were not radical enough. It may very well be said that it is easy to close your senses against the evident truth of suicide terrorism and resist all change. But it is much harder to design workable policies which are compatible with liberty; to trust to old principles; to resist the chorus which demands tougher action. Laws, however stern they are, will not defend us against fanatics. And there is something alarming in the panaceas which have been offered: detentions, curfews, indiscriminate surveillance and bans on sentiments and words.

Fanatics may be resistant to the notion of civil liberty, but the people who offer them protection and low-level help may be won over by principles of justice and fairness. There is plenty of evidence that Muslims trust the state less and see it as hostile to their interests, particularly after they have seen botched trials and overreactions to faulty intelligence. There is an oft-trumpeted cliché that liberty has to be balanced with security. I would argue differently. The argument should have been about the two sides of the same coin: fighting terrorism with the weapons of a liberal democracy. Liberty and security are not opposites to be balanced or confronted one with the other, but, as history shows, in a strong and self-confident society they are intertwined. Any worthwhile theory of liberty is bound up with the necessary protection of society or it is fatuous waffle, and a democracy which seeks new powers must start from commonly agreed principles of liberty or it has cast itself adrift in a wide ocean with no landmark for guidance.

And being all at sea has been the impression that the government has, over time, created. Our ideas of liberty have not faced an all-out attack. Rather they have been chipped away bit by bit. Reforms are made to speed up justice and secure convictions; databases and ID schemes proliferate as necessity dictates; anti-terror laws are augmented every year, often for symbolic rather than practical reasons. It is indicative of a political system which has lost its moorings and is drifting for lack of principle. It is what happens when we cut those ties to history which are so important in maintaining the health of society. As it is, we have looked weak in the face of threat, giving terrorists genuine hope that they can effect change. By repudiating our principles, we have stopped providing any pretence at moral leadership. Ministers from countries as diverse as Belarus, Malaysia and Sri Lanka, when they justified repressive policies, pointed to the British example.[8]

When we cannot provide a satisfying *moral* alternative to seductive ideologies, then it can be no surprise when misguided people seek solace with evil alternatives. Throughout history outside groups have had faith that if they played by the rules they would be brought into the system and could in fact change the system if their ideas attracted support. The downgrading of liberty in our society means that this route is being closed off. We should remind ourselves that it is not a luxury, but it is at the root of our way of life. The promise of freedom is even more powerful than the promise of democracy in this age. But we are in danger of losing that great attraction because we have forgotten how to articulate it. When we have less liberty, we are less safe.

Liberty is a product of the courage to retain principles of justice in the face of danger and the confidence that it is an ideology which will always prevail over seductive alternatives. We will regain those characteristics when we realise that security won at the expense of freedom is futile and self-defeating and, indeed, the terrorists' aim. When we realise that the promise of absolute safety (in all aspects of life) is delusive. When we stop seeing liberty and security as clean separate things. This can only happen when we wake up to the fact that pathological ideologies can only be defeated by the integrity of our own beliefs. Then we will rediscover that we are equipped to meet the challenge. We don't have a single, uncompromising belief we can chant or worship – that is left to totalitarian systems and psychopathic fanatics. We have the opposite and something, in the end, far more valuable for its rich varieties and compromises: not a composite ideology but a long, long experience of liberty.

Notes

Abbreviations and Bibliographic Information

John Stuart Mill *The Collected Works of John Stuart Mill* (33 vols, Toronto, 1963)

John Milton *Prose Writings* (Everyman paperback edition, 1974)

Parl. Debs – *Parliamentary Debates*, preceded in notes by series number. Unless otherwise stated this abbreviation refers to debates in the House of Commons.

PH – Cobbett's *Parliamentary History of England, 1066–1803* (12 vols, 1806–12)

State Trials – Cobbett's *Complete Collection of State Trials and Proceedings for High Treason* (33 vols, 1809–26)

Place of publication is London unless otherwise stated.

PROLOGUE

1 Simon Hoggart, 'A Pyrrhic Victory Doomed to Pitiful Defeat', *Guardian*, 12 June 2008.
2 6 Parl. Debs, vol. CDLXXVII, c. 381–2.
3 'In Full: Davis Statement', www.news.bbc.co.uk/go/pr/fr/-/1/hi/uk_politics/7450899.stm, 12 June 2008.
4 For example see Nick Robinson, 'A Divisive Davis?', www.bbc.co.uk/blogs/nickrobinson/2008/06/a_divisive_davis. The comments on the blog pages of the major newspapers and the tabloids were similarly enthusiastic for Davis's stand and changed the editorial line of many papers and broadcasters; see Frank Fisher, 'David Davis and the Great Media U-turn', www.guardian.co.uk/commentisfree/2008/jun/16/internet.politics.
5 Stephen Drive and Luke Martell, *New Labour: Politics after Thatcherism* (Cambridge, 1998), p. 41.
6 Harold J. Laski, *Liberty in the Modern State* (1937 edn), p. 80.

7 Robert Marshall-Andrews, 'This Folly Has Provoked a Unique Alliance', *Independent*, 11 June 2008.

8 Rachel North, www.rachelnorthlondon.blogspot.com/2007_11_01_archive.html, 12 November 2007.

I. Strenuous Liberty

1. YOUR HOME IS YOUR CASTLE

1 Algernon Sidney, *Court Maxims* (ed. Hans W. Blom, Eco Haitsma Mulier and Ronald Janse, Cambridge, 1996), p. 103.

2 Harrington, *Political Works* (ed. J. G. A. Pocock, Cambridge, 1977), p. 310.

3 Sir Edward Coke, *The Second Part of the Reports of Sir Edward Coke* (1602), preface.

4 Dudley Digges, *Answer to the Printed Book* (1642).

5 Thomas Hobbes, *Behemoth, or the Long Parliament*, ed. Ferdinand Torniers (2nd edn, 1969), pp. 3, 23–25, 40, 124.

6 Digges, *Answer*.

7 Henry Parker, *Observations upon Some of His Majesties Late Answers and Expresses* (1642), pp. 13–15.

8 John Goodwin, *Anti-Cavalierisme* (1642), pp. 37–8.

9 Sir Edward Coke, 'Langdale's Case', *The Selected Writings and Speeches of Sir Edward Coke* (ed. Steve Shepherd, 3 vols, Indianapolis, 2003), vol. I, p. 473.

10 [House of Commons], *Form of Apology and Satisfaction*, in J. R. Turner (ed.), *Constitutional Documents of the Reign of James I* (Cambridge, 1931), p. 218.

11 *PH*, vol. III, cols 83ff.

12 See e.g. John Pym, *PH*, vol. III, col. 391.

13 J. P. Sommerville, *Politics and Ideology in England, 1603–40* (1986), p. 98.

14 Coke, *Second Institutes* (1642), p. 179.

15 Sir John Fortescue, *On the Laws and Governance of England* (ed. Shelley Lockwood, Cambridge, 1997); Sir Walter Raleigh, *The Works of Sir Walter Raleigh, Knight, Now First Collected* (ed. William Oldys and Thomas Birch, 8 vols, Oxford, 1829), vol. III, p. 159.

16 Stephen D. White, *Sir Edward Coke and the Grievances of the Commonwealth, 1621–1628* (Chapel Hill, North Carolina, 1979).

17 [House of Commons], *Form of Apology*, pp. 220–1; cf. Argument of Sir Robert Berkeley, Justice of the King's Bench, 1638, in *State Trials*, vol. III, cols 1,090ff.

18 Milton, *The Tenure of Kings and Magistrates*, in *Prose Writings*, pp. 201–2.

19 Berkeley, in *State Trials*, vol. III, cols 1,090ff.

20 Samuel Rutherford, *Lex Rex. The Law and the Prince. A Dispute for the Just Prerogative of King and People* (1644; 1843 edn), p. 86.

21 *PH*, vol. III, col. 366.

22 Edmund Burke, *Conciliation with the Colonies* (1775), in Burke, *Selected Works of Edmund Burke*, vol. II, *Thoughts on the Present Discontents; The Two Speeches on America* (ed. Francis Canavan, Indianapolis, 1999), pp. 241, 249, 254; Burke, *Account of the European Settlements in America* (2 vols, 1757), vol. II, p. 304.

23 *State Trials*, vol. III, cols 83ff.

24 Coke, *Twelve Reports, Selected Works*, p. 489.

25 *State Trials*, vol. III, cols 159–60.

26 S. R. Gardiner, *The Constitutional Documents of the Puritan Revolution 1625–1660* (Oxford, third edn, 1979), pp. 46–7.

27 *PH*, vol. III, col. 231.

28 Ibid., cols 355ff.

29 Ibid., col. 357.

30 Ibid, cols 372–3.

31 Gardiner, *Constitutional Documents*, pp. 86, 94.

32 Henry Parker, *The Case of Ship Money Briefly Discoursed, According to the Grounds of Law, Policy and Conscience* (1640), pp. 7, 20–1.

33 E.g. Marchamont Nedham, *The Case of the Commonwealth Stated* (1650), p. 30; Harrington, *Political Works*, p. 198.

34 Quoted in David Hume, *The History of England, from the Invasion of Julius Caesar to the Revolution of 1688* (8 vols, 1792–3), vol. VI, p. 242.

35 Voltaire, *Letters on England* (trans. Leonard Tancock, 1980), p. 49; cf. Harrington, *Political Works*, p. 196, where he calls the history of Magna Charta 'no other than a wrestling match' between King John and the barons.

36 Hume, *History*, vol. VI, pp. 74–5.

37 Lord Brooke, in *Two Speeches made in the House of Peers, on Munday the 19 of December, For, and Against Accommodation* (1642), p. 6.

38 *PH*, vol. III, col. 959.

39 Lord Saye and Seele, speech made in 1644, in *Vindiciae Veritatis*, (1654), pp. 6–7.

40 Hobbes, *Behemoth*, p. 109.

41 *PH*, vol. III, cols 1,416–18.

2. TEEMING LIBERTY

1 Lord Brooke, *A Discourse Opening the Nature of that Episcopacie, Which is Exercised in England* (1642), p. 95.

2 Harrington, *Political Works*, p. 170.

3 John Milton, *Areopagitica*, in *Prose Writings*, p. 182

4 John Milton, Sonnet 12, 'I Did But Prompt the Age', (*c.*1645).

5 Brooke, *Discourse*, p. 95.

6 Christopher Hill, *Milton and the English Revolution* (1977), p. 65.

7 William Bridge, *Babylons Downfall. A Sermon Lately Preached at Westminster* (1641), p. 21; Brooke, in *Two Speeches*, p. 4.

8 Brendan Simms, *Three Victories and a Defeat: The Rise and Fall of the First British Empire, 1714–1783* (2007), pp. 19ff.

9 Milton, *Eikonoklastes* (1649), pp. 150–1.

10 Brooke, *Discourse*, pp. 93–4, 114; cf. Brooke in *Two Speeches*, p. 4.

11 Goodwin, *Anti-Cavalierisme, passim*.

12 Ibid., pp. 37–8, 45–6.

13 John Milton, *The Tenure of Kings and Magistrates*, in *Prose Writings*, p. 191.

14 Rutherford, *Lex Rex*, p. 60 and *passim*; cf. Parker, *Observations*; Henry Parker, *Animadversions Animadverted* (1642); Henry Parker, *The Contra Replicant* (1643); Henry Parker, *The True Portraiture of the Kings of England Drawn from Their Titles, Successors, Reigns and Ends* (1648); Milton, *Tenure*; and Goodwin, *Anti-Cavalierisme*, pp. 5ff.

15 John Maxwell, *Sacro-Sancta Regum Majestas; or the Sacred and Royall Prerogative of Christian Kings* (Oxford, 1644), Epistle Directory, and pp. 3, 4, 23, 87.

16 *State Trials*, vol. IV, cols 1075, 993.

17 Milton, *Tenure*, p. 186.

18 Harrington, *Political Works*, pp. 169–70; cf. Sidney, *Court Maxims*, pp. 24, 27, 65.

19 Isaac Penington junior, *The Fundamental Right, Safety and Liberty of the People* (1651), preface.

20 John Goodwin, *Right and Might Well Mett* (1648), pp. 43–4; cf. Nedham, *Case of the Commonwealth*, pp. 21–5, 30, 80.

21 Nedham, *The Excellencie of a Free State: or, the Right Constitution of a Commonwealth . . . With Some Errors of Government, and Rules of Policy* (1656), pp. 83ff.

22 Harrington, *Political Works*, pp. 424, 609.

23 [Nedham], *Mercurius Politicus*, no. 100 (29 April–6 May 1652), pp. 1,570–1; Nedham, *Excellencie*, p. 13.

24 Nedham, *Excellencie*, p. 5.

25 Harrington, *Political Works*, pp. 172–4.

26 Nedham, *Excellencie*, p. 99; cf. Harrington, *Political Works*, pp. 230, 342.

27 Hobbes, *Leviathan*, part 2, ch. 21.

28 Quentin Skinner, 'The Idea of Negative Liberty: Philosophical and Historical Perspectives', in Quentin Skinner et al. (eds), *Philosophy and History* (Cambridge, 1984).

29 Blair Worden, 'Marchamont Nedham and the Beginnings of English Republicanism, 1649–1659', in David Wotton (ed.), *Republicanism, Liberty, and Commercial Society, 1649–1776* (Stanford, 1994), pp. 56–7.

30 Sidney, *Court Maxims*, p. 24.

31 John Milton, *The Second Defence of the English People*, in *Prose Writings*, p. 345.

32 Quentin Skinner, 'What Does It Mean to Be a Free Person?', *London Review of Books*, 22 May 2008.

33 Milton, *Areopagitica*, p. 177.

34 John Warr, *The Corruption and Deficiency of the Laws of England* (1649), quoted in Hill, *Milton*, p. 67.

35 *A Remonstrance and Declaration of Several Counties, Cities and Burroughs Against the Unfaithfulness, and Late Unwarrantable Proceedings of Some of Their Knights, Citizens and Burgesses in Parliament* (23 December 1648), pp. 4–6.

36 Anon., *Vox Plebis: Or, the Voice of the Oppressed Commons of England Against Their Oppressors* (April 1653), p. 2.

37 E.g. Richard Goodgroom, *Copy of a Letter Written to an Officer in the Army* (19 March 1656).

II. De Facto Freedom

3. THE GOOD OLD CAUSE

1 Henry St John, Viscount Bolingbroke, *The Works of Lord Bolingbroke. With a Life* (4 vols, Philadelphia, 1841), vol. I, p. 263.

2 Adam Ferguson, *An Essay on the History of Civil Society* (1793), p. 444.

3 John Millar, *An Historical View of the English Government, From the Settlement of the Saxons in Britain to the Revolution in 1688. To Which are Subjoined Some Dissertations Connected with the History of the Government, from the Revolution to the Present Time* (4 vols, 1803), vol. I, pp. 6–7.

4 David Hume, 'Of the Liberty of the Press', in *The Philosophical Works of David Hume* (4 vols, Edinburgh, 1826), vol. III, p. 11; cf. Millar, *Historical View*, vol. IV, pp. 133ff: 'The clamour and tumultuary proceedings of the populace in the great towns are capable of penetrating the inmost recesses of administration, of intimidating the boldest minister, and of displacing the most presumptuous favourite of the back stairs' (pp. 136–7).

5   John Toland (ed.), *The Oceana of James Harrington, And His Other Works* (1700), pp. vii–viii;
    cf. Toland, *Anglia Libera: Or, the Limitation and Succession of the Crown Explain'd and Asserted*
    (1701), p. 83.

6   Andrew Marvell, *An Account of the Growth of Popery and Arbitrary Government in England*
    (1677), p. 3.

7   William Blackstone, *Commentaries on the Laws of England* (4 vols, Oxford, 1765–9), vol. I,
    p. 134; Hume, *History*, vol. VIII, pp. 106–7; 'ABCDEFG' [John Trenchard and Walter
    Moyle], *An Argument Shewing, That a Standing Army Is Inconsistent With a Free Government, and
    Absolutely Destructive to the Constitution of the English Monarchy* (1698), p. 6.

8   *PH*, vol. IV, col. 1,126.

9   Barillon to Louis, 25 June 1685, in John Dalrymple, *Memoirs of Great Britain and Ireland*
    (2 vols, 1773), Appendices to vol. II, part 1, p. 196.

10 *State Trials*, vol. XI, col. 1,195.

11 John Evelyn, *Diary*, ed. E. S. De Beer (6 vols, Oxford, 1955), 3 November 1685.

12 Major John Wildman, *A Defence of the Proceedings of the Late Parliament of England, Anno 1689*
    (London, 1689); in *A Collection of State Tracts Publish'd on Occasion of the Late Revolution in
    1688. And during the Reign of King William III* (2 vols, 1705), vol. 1, p. 209.

13 W. A. Speck, *Reluctant Revolutionaries: Englishmen and the Revolution of 1688* (Oxford, 1988),
    pp. 517–9; Gilbert, Bishop Burnet, *History of His Own Time* (6 vols, 1725–35), vol. II,
    pp. 617–8.

14 [Major John Wildman], *A Memorial from the English Protestants, To their Highnesses the Prince
    and Princess of Orange* (November 1688), in *State Tracts*, vol. I, pp. 33–4.

15 Burnet, *History*, vol. III, p. 1,025.

16 See, *inter alia*: Anon., *Some Considerations Touching Succession and Allegiance*, in *State Tracts*, vol. I
    p. 337; J. Edmund Bohn, *The History of the Desertion; or an Account of all the Publick Affairs in
    England, From the Beginning of September 1688 to the 12th of February Following* (April 1689), in
    State Tracts, vol. I, p. 110; Anon., *The Desertion Discus'd In a Letter to a Country Gentleman*
    (n.d.), in *State Tracts*, vol. I, pp. 11–23; Anon., *Providence and Precept: or the Case of Doing
    Evil that Good May Come of it* (n.d.), p. 16; Revd J. S. Clarke, *The Life of James the Second*
    (2 vols, 1816), vol. II, p. 270.

17 *PH*, vol. V, cols 143–6.

18 Henri and Barbara van der Zee, *William and Mary* (1973), p. 351.

19 Charles Chenevix Trench, *George II* (1973), p. 37.

20 Toland, *Anglia Libera*, p. 92: a commonwealth is 'an independent community, where the
    common weal or good of all indifferently is designed and pursued, let the form be what
    it will'.

21 Millar, vol. IV, pp. 98–100.

22 *PH*, vol. V, col. 566.

23 Van der Zee and van der Zee, pp. 284–5.

24 Molesworth, preface to Francis Hotoman, *Franco-Gallia: Or an Account of the Ancient Free
    State of France, and Most Other Parts of Europe; Before the Loss of Their Liberties* (trans.
    Molesworth, 1721); Anon., *A Discourse Concerning Militias and Standing Armies, With Relation
    to the Past and Present Governments of Europe, and of England In Particular* (1697); [John
    Trenchard and Walter Moyle], *Argument*, pp. 7ff; [John, Lord Somers], *A Letter, Balancing
    the Necessity of Keeping a Land-Force in Times of Peace with the Danger That May Follow On
    It* (1697).

25 Simms, *Three Victories*, pp. 37ff, 181, 186, 223, 234ff, 251.

4. LICENTIOUS LIBERTY

1 David Hume, 'Of National Character', *The Philosophical Works of David Hume*, (4 vols, Edinburgh, 1826), vol. III, p. 235.

2 Hume, *History*, vol. VIII, p. 320.

3 'Cato's Letters', no. 62, 20 January 1722.

4 Ibid.

5 Hume, *History*, vol. VIII, pp. 320ff.

6 Ibid., p. 249.

7 Ferguson, *Essay*, pp. 213–15.

8 Voltaire, *Letters*, p. 51.

9 Ferguson, *Essay*, pp. 92–4.

10 'Cato's Letters', no. 76, 12 May 1722.

11 Anon., *The Freeholder's Alarm to His Brethren; or, the Fate of Britain Determin'd by the Ensuing Election* (1734), pp. 28–30; cf. 'Cato's Letters', no. 76, 12 May 1722.

12 'Cato's Letters', no. 15, 4 February 1721.

13 Ibid.

14 Voltaire, *Letters*, p. 51.

15 'Cato's Letters', no. 32, 10 June 1721; cf. nos 100–1, 27 October and 3 November 1723.

16 Ferguson, pp. 159, 185, 189, 199.

17 Ibid., pp. 319–20; cf. pp. 356–7, 370–1 and part 5, *passim*.

18 'Cato's Letters', no. 16, 11 February 1721.

19 Ibid., no. 25, 15 April 1721; no. 33, 17 June 1721; no. 60, 6 January 1722; no. 62, 20 January 1722.

20 Ibid., no. 70, 17 March 1722.

21 Bolingbroke, *Works*, vol. I, pp. 294–300.

22 Quoted in Isaac Kramnick, *Bolingbroke and His Circle: The Politics of Nostalgia in the Age of Walpole* (Harvard, 1968), p. 51.

23 'Cato's Letters', no. 70, March 17 1722.

24 Hume, 'Independency of Parliament', *Philosophical Works*, vol. III, p. 47.

25 Hume, 'Of the Original Contract', *Philosophical Works*, vol. III.

26 M. d'Archenholz, *A Picture of England: Containing a Description of the Laws, Customs, and Manners of England, Interspersed with Curious and Interesting Anecdotes* (Dublin, 1791), p. 8.

27 M. de Secondat, Baron de Montesquieu, *The Spirit of the Laws* (2 vols, Edinburgh, 1778), vol. I, pp. 20–1.

28 D'Archenholz, pp. 2–3.

29 J. L. De Lolme, *The Constitution of England, or an Account of the English Government* (Dublin, 1776), pp. 154–5.

30 D'Archenholz, pp. 38–9.

31 Jeremy Bentham, *A Fragment on Government* (1776), pp. xvii–ix.

32 Blackstone, *Commentaries*, vol. III, p. 268.

33 Cited in Douglas G. Long, *Bentham on Liberty: Jeremy Bentham's Idea of Liberty in Relation to his Utilitarianism* (Toronto, 1977), p. 142.

34 Oliver Goldsmith, *The Citizen of the World, or Letters from a Chinese Philosopher Residing in London to his Friends in the East* (Folio Society edition, 1969), Letter L, p. 160.

35 Douglas Hay et al., *Albion's Fatal Tree: Crime and Society in Eighteenth-century England* (1976), *passim*; E. Genovese, *Roll, Jordan, Roll: The World the Slaves Made* (1974), pp. 25–49; E. P. Thompson, *Whigs and Hunters: The Origins of the Black Act* (1975), *passim*; Morton

J. Horwitz, 'The Rule of Law: An Unqualified Human Good?', *Yale Law Journal*, vol. 86, no. 3 (January 1977), pp. 561ff; Bob Fine, *Democracy and the Rule of Law: Liberal Ideas and Marxist Critiques* (1984).

36 Hume, 'Of the Original Contract', vol. III.

37 A. V. Dicey, *Lectures on the Relation Between Law and Public Opinion in England During the Nineteenth Century* (1905), pp. 80–3.

38 Fox in a private letter; cited in Lord John Russell, *An Essay on the History of the English Government and Constitution, from the reign of Henry VI to the present time* (1821), p. 114.

39 Goldsmith, *Citizen*, Letter IV, pp. 32ff.

40 John Stuart Mill, 'Coleridge', *Collected Works*, vol. X, p. 143.

41 Edmund Burke, 'Letter to the Sheriffs of Bristol', in *The Writings and Speeches of Edmund Burke* (ed. Paul Langford et al., 9 vols, Oxford, 1981 onwards), vol. II, p. 317.

42 Mill, 'Coleridge', p. 145.

43 E. P. Thompson, *Writing By Candlelight* (1980), p. 178.

III. Enlightened Liberty

5. EVERY TAINTED BREEZE

1 Richard Price, *A Discourse on the Love of Our Country, Delivered on November 4th, 1789, at the Meeting House in the Old Jewry* (1789), pp. 49–51.

2 Burke, *Conciliation*, p. 237; cf. Burke in *Annual Register for 1775*, p. 14.

3 Sir Thomas Browne, *Religio Medici* (1643), vol. I, p. 15.

4 Gordon S. Wood, *Revolutionary Characters: What Made the Founding Fathers Different* (New York, 2007), pp. 130, 238; Hamilton added to this '. . . my vanity whispers I ought to be one of those fools . . .'

5 Edmund Burke, *A Letter from Edmund Burke, esq, one of the Representatives for the City of Bristol, to John Farr and John Harris, esqrs, Sheriffs of that City, on the Affairs of America* (Bristol, 1777), pp. 7–8, 15–21; Burke, *Conciliation*, pp. 244–6, 287–8.

6 Joseph Ellis, *His Excellency George Washington* (2005), ch. 2.

7 Cited in Bernard Bailyn, *The Ideological Origins of the American Revolution* (Cambridge, Mass., 1967), p. 83.

8 John Locke, *Second Treatise on Civil Government* (1690), ch. 2, paragraph 6.

9 Ibid., ch. 4, para. 95.

10 Burke, *Conciliation*, p. 238.

11 Ibid., pp. 239–40.

12 Ibid., p. 242.

13 Thomas Jefferson, *The Works of Thomas Jefferson* (ed. Paul Leicester Ford, 12 vols, New York, 1904), p. 78.

14 Ibid., p. 89.

15 Carl Becker, *The Declaration of Independence: A Study in the History of Political Ideas* (1922), pp. 133–4.

16 Joseph Priestley, *An Essay on the First Principles of Government; and on the Nature of Political, Civil and Religious Liberty* (1768), *passim*.

17 Edmund Burke, *Thoughts on the Present Discontents* (1770), *passim*. 'The virtue, spirit, and essence of the House of Commons consists in its being the express image of the feelings of the nation' (p. 118).

18 Anon., *Observations on Doctor Price's Revolution Sermon* (1790), pp. 10–11.

19 John Gray, *Doctor Price's Notions of the Nature of Civil Liberty, Shewn to be Contrary to Reason and Scripture* (1777), pp. 38–9.

20 Fox, *The Speeches of the Rt Hon. C. J. F., in the House of Commons* (ed. J. Wright, 1815), p. 14.

21 Thomas Jefferson, *Notes on the State of Virginia* (ed. William Peden, Chapel Hill, 1955), p. 120.

22 Goldsmith, *Citizen*, Letter L, pp. 159–61.

23 Burke, *Thoughts, passim.*

24 *PH*, vol. XIX, cols 3ff.

25 Ibid., col. 32.

26 Fox, *Speeches*, p. 438.

27 Bailyn, p. 160.

6. LIBERTIES OLD AND NEW

1 Publicus [Alexander Hamilton, John Jay and James Madison], *The Federalist* (Gideon edition, 1818), no. 14.

2 Benjamin Constant, *Political Writings* (trans. and ed. Biancamaria Fontana, Cambridge, 1988), p. 323.

3 *Federalist*, no. 63 (Madison).

4 Edmund Burke, *Reflections on the Revolution in France* (ed. L. G. Mitchell, Oxford, 1999), p. 8.

5 *Federalist*, no. 9.

6 Joseph Priestley, *The Importance and Extent of Free Enquiry in Matters of Religion* (1785), in *The Theological and Miscellaneous Works of Joseph Priestley* (ed. John Towill Rutt, 1817–32), vol. XV, p. 78.

7 Jefferson, *Works*, vol. II, pp. 438ff.

8 Wood, *Revolutionary Characters.*

9 *Federalist*, no. 51.

10 Ibid., nos 10, 14, 37, 39, 41–3, 45–7, 62 (Madison); 28 (Hamilton).

11 Ibid., nos. 41, 58 (Madison), 71 (Hamilton).

12 Jefferson, *Virginia*, p. 120. Jefferson wrote to Madison on 15 March 1789, 'The tyranny of the legislature is really the danger most to be feared, and will continue to be so for many years to come. The tyranny of the executive power will come in its turn, but at a more distant period.'

13 *Federalist*, nos 48–51 (Madison).

14 Ibid., no. 57.

15 Ibid., nos 62–4 (Madison), 65–75 (Hamilton).

16 Ibid., nos 50–1 (Madison).

17 Cf. Alexis de Tocqueville, *Democracy in America* (4 vols, 1835–1840), vol. I, pp. 44–6, 73, 130–1.

18 Constant, *Political Writings*, pp. 316–20.

19 Priestley, *Essay*, pp. 55–6, 61–2.

20 Constant, *Political Writings*, p. 323.

21 Alexander Hamilton, *The Revolutionary Writings of Alexander Hamilton* (ed. Richard B. Vernier, Indianapolis, 2008), p. 89.

22 Thomas Jefferson, *The Writings of Thomas Jefferson, The Memorial Edition* (ed. Andrew A. Libscome and Albert Ellery Bergh, 2 vols, Washington, 1904), vol. I, p. 279; cf. Jefferson, letter to Benjamin Rush, Jan 1811, in *Works*, vol. IX, p. 295.

23 Wood, *Revolutionary Characters*, ch. 4, 'Alexander Hamilton and the Making of a Fiscal-military State'.

24 *State Trials*, vol. XIX, *Dryden Leach* v *Money, Watson and Blackmore; Entick* v *Carrington*; the case of John Wilkes. [Anon], *English Liberty, or the British Lion Roused: Containing the Sufferings of John Wilkes, Esq; From the First of his Persecution, Down to the Present Time* (2 vols, 1769).

25 Arthur H. Cash, *John Wilkes: The Scandalous Father of Civil Liberties* (2006).

26 *State Trials.* vol. XIX, col. 983.

27 The following discussion is taken from *State Trials*, vol. XIX, John Entick against Nathan Carrington and three other messengers on an action of trespass, Common Pleas, Michaelmas Term 1765, cols 1,029ff. See also *A Letter Concerning Libels, Warrants, the Seizure of Papers, and Sureties for the Peace and Behaviour* (1767).

28 A. V. Dicey, *Introduction to the Study of the Law and the Constitution* (8th edn, 1915), pp. vii–viii, xxxvii–viii, 189, 191ff, 263–4,332ff, 381ff.

29 Brass Crosby, *Memoir of Brass Crosby* (1829), p. 22.

30 See Kevin Gilmartin, *Print Politics: The Press and Radical Opposition in Early Nineteenth-century England* (Cambridge, 1996); J. Ann Hone, *For the Cause of Truth: Radicalism in London, 1796–1821* (Oxford, 1982); Richard Ingrams, *The Life and Adventures of William Cobbett* (2005); Iain McCalman, *Radical Underworld: Prophets, Revolutionaries and Pornographers in London, 1795–1840* (Cambridge, 1993); E. P. Thompson, *The Making of the English Working Class* (1963); Ben Wilson, *The Laughter of Triumph: William Hone and the Fight for the Free Press* (2005).

31 Dicey, *Introduction*, pp. 192ff, 235ff.

32 See J. Barrell, *Imagining the King's Death: Figurative Treason, Fantasies of Regicide, 1793–1796* (Oxford, 2000); *The Trials at Large of Thomas Hardy and Others; for High Treason* (Nottingham, 1794), *passim.*

33 Barrell, *Imagining*, p. 174.

34 *The Trial at Large*, pp. 192–3.

35 Ibid., p. 193.

36 *Edinburgh Review*, vol. XXIV (February 1915), p. 533.

37 Thomas Paine, *Common Sense* (ed. Isaac Kramnick, 1982), p. 71.

38 Russell, *Essay*, p. 177.

IV. Mind Your Own Business

7. CHARACTER

1 Matthew Arnold, *Friendship's Garland: Being the Conversations, Letters, and Opinions of the Late Arminius, Baron von Thunder-ten-Tronckh* (1871), p. 147.

2 Alexis de Tocqueville, *Journeys to England and Ireland* (trans. George Lawrence and K. P. Mayer; ed. J. P. Mayer, New York, 1968), pp. 11, 67; cf. Dicey, *Lectures*, pp. 58–9.

3 Dicey, *Lectures*, pp. 2, 54; *Westminster Review*, vol. I, no. 1 (1 January 1824), pp. 227ff, vol. I, no. 2, pp. 506–11; Russell, *Essay*, pp. 84–114, 286–9; L. T. Hobhouse, *Liberalism* (1911), pp. 18–20; Abraham D. Kriegel, 'Liberty and Whiggery in Early Nineteenth-Century England', *The Journal of Modern History*, vol. LII, no. 1 (March 1980).

4 Tocqueville, *Journeys*, pp. 78, 83–6, 105–7; Russell, *Essay*, pp. 112–13.

5 Walter Bagehot, *The English Constitution* (ed. Paul Smith, Cambridge, 2001), p. 180.

6 Dicey, *Lecture*, p. 244.

7 Samuel Smiles, *Self-Help* (1908 edn), pp. 1–3.

8 Quoted in W. L. Burn, *The Age of Equipoise: A Study of the Mid-Victorian Generation* (1964), p. 316.

9 Bernard Porter, ' "Bureau and Barrack": Early Victorian Attitudes towards the Continent', *Victorian Studies*, vol. XXVII, no. 4 (Summer 1984).

10 Wordsworth Donisthorpe, *Liberty or Law?* (1885), pp. 16, 23.

11 *Darlington Telegraph*, 13 November 1867; cited in Burn, *Age*, p. 100.

12 Herbert Spencer, *Social Statistics* (1851), pp. 322–5, 380–1; Spencer, *Man Versus the State* (1884), p. 67–9.

13 Spencer, *Man Versus the State*, pp. 65–6.

14 Ibid., pp. 104–6.

15 Dicey, *Lecture*, pp. 239ff.

16 J. Toulmin Smith, *Local Self-Government and Centralization* (1851), pp.28–9.

17 John Stuart Mill, *Collected Works* (33 vols, Toronto, 1965–91), vol. XVIII: his two reviews of Tocqueville's *Democracy in America* (1835 and 1840); 'State of Society in America (January 1836); 'Civilization' (1836).

18 Mill, 'Civilization', *Collected Works*, vol. XVIII, pp. 132–3.

19 Mill, 'Democracy in America' (II) (1840), *Collected Works*, vol. XVIII, p. 194.

20 Isaiah Berlin, 'John Stuart Mill and the Ends of Life', *Four Essays on Liberty* (Oxford, 1969), p. 193.

21 John Stuart Mill, *Autobiography*, in *Collected Works*, vol. I; Alexander Bain, *John Stuart Mill, a Biography* (1882); Richard Reeves, *John Stuart Mill: Victorian Firebrand* (2007), ch. 1.

22 Reeves, *Mill*, pp. 66, 70.

23 John Stuart Mill, *The Subjection of Women*, in *Collected Works*, vol. XXI, p. 340.

24 Mill, 'Democracy in America' (II), *Collected Works*, vol. XVIII, p. 169.

25 Mill, 'Civilization', *Collected Works*, vol. XVIII, pp. 139ff.

26 John Frederick Denison Maurice, *Eustace Conway: Or the Brother and Sister* (3 vols, 1834), vol. II, pp. 79–81.

27 Mill, 'Bentham', *Collected Works*, vol. X, pp. 108–9.

28 Mill, *The Principles of Political Economy*, in *Collected Works*, vol. III, p. 209.

29 Mill, 'On Reform', (1848), *Collected Works*, vol. XXV, pp. 1,005–6.

30 Mill, *Principles*, in *Collected Works*, vol. III, p. 754.

31 Balzac, *Histoire de la littérature française au dix-huitième siècle* (Paris, 1853); quoted in Koenraed W. Swart, ' "Individualism" in the Mid-Nineteenth Century', *Journal of the History of Ideas*, 23 (1962), pp. 84–5.

32 Paul Landis, *Social Control* (rev. edn, Chicago, 1956), p. 7 and *passim*; Talcott Parsons, *The Social System* (1951), p. 321; Burn, *Age*, pp. 153ff, 191–4, ch. 5 *passim*; A. P. Donajgrodzki (ed.), *Social Control in Nineteenth-Century Britain* (1977); Peter Mandler (ed.), *Liberty and Authority in Victorian Britain* (Oxford, 2006), essays by Mandler, Philip Harling, Peter Baldwin, J. P. Parry and Helen Rogers.

33 Alexander Herzen, *My Past and Thoughts* (trans. Constance Garnet, revised by Humphrey Higgins, 1968), vol. I, p. 226.

34 Samuel Blackstone, 'Paternal Government. Whither Are We Drifting?', *Saint Paul's Magazine*, vol. XII (January–June 1873), pp. 723–4; cf. Josephine E. Butler, *Government by Police* (1879).

35 Mill, *Principles, Collected Works*, vol. III, p. 961.

36 Mill, 'Coleridge', *Collected Works*, vol. X, p. 156.

37 Mill, *Principles, Collected Works*, vol. III, p. 938.

38 Older ideas that the nineteenth century saw a revolution in government have been superseded by modern historians, e.g. Oliver MacDonagh, 'The Nineteenth-Century Revolution in Government: A Reappraisal', *The Historical Journal*, vol. I, no. 1 (1958); Henry

Parris, 'The Nineteenth-Century Revolution in Government: A Reappraisal Reappraised', *The Historical Journal*, vol. III, no. 1 (1960); Jenifer Hart, 'Nineteenth Century Social Reform: A Tory Interpretation of History', *Past and Present*, 31, 1965; Burn, *Age*, ch. 4, *passim*; Harold Perkin, 'Individualism Versus Collectivism in Nineteenth-Century Britain: A False Antithesis', *Journal of British Studies*, 17, 1977; Mandler (ed.), *Liberty and Authority*.

39 Eric J. Evans (ed.), *Social Policy 1830–1914: Individualism, Collectivism and the Origins of the Welfare State* (1978), p. 2.

40 'Alfred' [Samuel Kydd], *The History of the Factory Movement From the Year 1802* (1857), vol. I, p. 65.

41 John Stuart Mill, 'The Regulation of the London Water Supply', *Collected Works*, vol. V, pp. 433ff.

42 J. P. Parry, *The Rise and Fall of Liberal Government in Victorian Britain* (Yale, 1993), pp. 10–11, 16–17; Parry, 'Liberalism and Liberty', in Mandler (ed.), *Liberty and Authority*, pp. 71–2.

43 For details of enabling acts and what follows see John Prest, *Liberty and Locality: Parliament, Permissive Legislation, and Ratepayers' Democracies in the Nineteenth Century* (Oxford, 1990).

44 3 Parl. Debs, vol. CCXXV, col. 525.

45 Edward Jenkins, 'The Legal Aspect of Sanitary Reform', *Transactions of the National Association for the Promotion of Social Science, Manchester Meeting 1866* (1867), pp. 479–80.

46 J. Toulmin Smith, *The Parish: Its Powers and Obligations at Law, as Regards the Welfare of Every Neighbourhood, and in Relation to the State . . .* (1857 edn), pp. iii–iv, 5; Toulmin Smith, *Local Self-Government*, pp. 4–5; Hon. George C. Brodrick, 'Local Government in England', in J. W. Probyn (ed.), *Cobden Club Essays: Local Government and Taxation* (1875), pp. 3–30.

47 Toulmin Smith, *Local Self Government*, pp. 7–8, 31, 47–8, 54, 63–4; cf. Josephine E. Butler, *Government by Police* (1879), *passim*.

48 *The Times*, 21 June 1852.

49 Jenkins, 'Legal Aspect', p. 481.

50 Ibid., pp. 487ff.

51 Lord Edward Fitzmaurice in J. W. Probyn (ed.), *Local Government and Taxation in the United Kingdom* (1882), pp. 122–3.

52 Brodrick, 'Local Government', pp. 69–72.

53 Burn, *Age*, pp. 150–1; Brodrick, 'Local Government', pp. 63–5; Jenkins, 'Legal Aspect', pp. 487–9; Parry, *Rise and Fall*, pp. 205–6; cf. Philip Harling, 'The Power of the Victorian State', in Mandler (ed.), *Liberty and Authority*, pp. 45–6.

8. ADMINISTRATIVE DESPOTISM

1 John Emerich Edward Dalberg-Acton, first Baron Acton, *The History of Freedom, and Other Essays* (ed. John Neville Figgis and Reginald Vere Laurence, 1907), p. 93.

2 Dicey, *Introduction*, Introduction to the eighth edition; Dicey, *Lectures*, pp. 18–19, 44, 56–9, 62ff.

3 Acton, pp. 11, 12–13, 93–4.

4 Ibid., pp. 1–2.

5 Ibid., p. 95.

6 Tocqueville, *Democracy*, vol. IV, pp. 320–1.

7 Matthew Arnold, *Culture and Anarchy* (Cambridge, 1993), p. 86.

8 'Northumbrian', 'Freedom and Tyranny of Contract', *Reynold's News*, 20 June 1875; quoted in Eugenio F. Biagini, *Liberty, Retrenchment and Reform: Popular Liberalism in the Age of Gladstone, 1860–1880* (Cambridge, 1992), p. 169.

9 See Biagini, *Liberty*, pp. 8ff, 31ff, 41ff, 56–7, 88–9, 92–3, 251–3, 266–7, 269ff;
   Biagini, 'Radicalism and Liberty', in Mandler (ed.), *Liberty and Authority*, pp. 101ff.

10 Revd F. D. Maurice, 'The Suffrage', *Macmillan's Magazine*, no. 8 (June 1860), p. 93.

11 Lord Bramwell, *Laissez Faire* (1884), pp. 15–17.

12 John Stuart Mill, *Chapters on Socialism, Collected Works*, vol. V, pp. 751–3.

13 Andrew Reid (ed.), *Why I Am a Liberal: Being Definitions and Personal Confessions of Faith by the Best Minds of the Liberal Party* (1885), p. 44.

14 Parry, *Rise and Fall*, pp. 10–11, 193ff, 245ff.

15 G. J. Goshen, *Address by the Right Hon. G. J. Goshen to the Members of the Philosophical Institution at Edinburgh on Laissez-faire and Government Intervention* (1885), *passim*. For Goshen and liberalism see Parry, *Rise and Fall*, pp. 228–31, 245ff.

16 Spencer, *Man Versus the State*, pp. 7ff.

17 Ibid., p. 14 and *passim*.

18 Edward Bristow, 'The Liberty and Property Defence League and Individualism', *Historical Journal*, vol. XVIII, no. 4 (1975), p. 773 and *passim*.

19 M. D. O'Brien, 'Free Libraries', in Thomas Mackay (ed.), *A Plea for Liberty: An Argument Against Socialism and Socialistic Legislation* (1891).

20 Bristow, p. 778.

21 Reid (ed), *Why I am a Liberal*, pp. 93–5.

22 J. S. Mill, *Principles of Political Economy, Collected Works*, vol. II, p. 207.

23 John Stuart Mill, *On Liberty*, in *Collected Works*, vol. XVIII, p. 302.

24 L. S. [Leslie Stephen], 'Social Macademisation', *Fraser's Magazine*, n/s (August 1872), vol. VI, no. 32.

25 James Fitzjames Stephen, *Liberty, Equality, Fraternity* (1873), pp. 194–5.

26 Ibid., pp. 20–1, 46, 51, 94, 153ff.

27 Ibid., pp. 166, 170, 183–204.

28 Ibid., pp. 203–4.

29 T. H. Green, 'Lecture on Liberal Legislation and Freedom of Contract', in *Works* (3 vols, 1880), vol. III, p. 372.

30 Ibid., pp. 372ff.

31 Ibid., pp. 383ff; cf. W. L. Weinstein, 'The Concept of Liberty in Nineteenth Century English Political Thought', *Political Studies*, vol. XIII, no. 2 (June 1965).

32 Green, 'Lecture', p. 367.

33 Mill, *Representative Government, Collected Works*, vol. XIX, p. 401.

34 Green, 'Lecture', pp. 370–1; Hobhouse, *Liberalism*, pp. 41ff.

35 Hobhouse, *Liberalism*, p. 124.

36 Ibid., pp. 158–9.

37 Mill, 'Regulation', pp. 433ff.

38 Karl Popper, *The Open Society* (2 vols, 1945), vol. I, pp. 96–8.

39 Winston Churchill at St Andrew's Hall, Glasgow, 11/10/1906; cited in Winston S. Churchill, *Liberalism and the Social Problem* (1909), pp. 78–80.

V. *The New Jerusalem and the New Despotism*

9. A HALF REVOLUTION

1 Lord Allen of Huntwood, *Britain's Political Future: A Plea for Liberty and Leadership* (1934) pp. 2–3.

2 Ernest Benn, *Happier Days: Recollections and Reflections* (1949), pp. 69, 205, 212, 216–17.

3 Ibid.; 'North Briton', *British Freedom, 1914–1917* (1917), pp. 3ff.

4 5 Parl. Debs, vol. XCI, cols 1,499ff; cf. H. G. Wells, *Mr Britling Sees It Through* (1916); H. G. Wells, *The War That Will End War* (1914), pp. 58, 62; E. M. H. Lloyd, *Experiments in State Control at the War Office and the Ministry of Food* (Oxford, 1924), pp. 2–7; [Labour Party], *Labour and the New Social Order* (1918); Sir Leo Chiozza Money, *Fifty Points About Capitalism* (1919), pp. 41–2, 45; Alfred Zimmern, 'The Labour Movement', *The Round Table*, June 1916 and 'Reconstruction', ibid., September 1916.

5 Winston S. Churchill, *Complete Speeches, 1897–1963* (8 vols, ed. Robert Rhodes James, 1974), vol. III, p. 2,664.

6 Alfred Zimmern, *Nationality and Government* (1918), pp. 243ff.

7 Thomas Mackay (ed.), *A Plea for Liberty: An Argument Against Socialism and Socialistic Legislation* (1891), p. 8.

8 Ramiro de Maeztu, *Authority, Liberty and Function in the Light of War* (1916), esp. ch. 2 and pp. 107–29, 192, 197, 204–18; Lloyd, *Experiments*, pp. xii, 1–14; [Labour Party], *Labour and the New Social Order*; Zimmern, 'The Labour Movement'; Paul Lensch, *Three Years of World Revolution* (1918), esp. pp. 83ff; Werner Sombart, *Händler und Helden* (1915); Johann Plenge, *1789 and 1914: The Symbolic Years in the History of the Public Mind* (1915); Money, *Fifty Points*; Laski, 'Introduction to the Pelican Edition', *Liberty*, pp. 17ff.

9 5 Parl. Debs (Lords), vol. XVIII, cols 219–20.

10 5 Parl. Debs, vol. LXV, cols 2191–3; ibid., cols 87–9.

11 'North Briton', *British Freedom*, pp. 82, 85.

12 5 Parl. Debs, vol. LXX, cols 295–6.

13 E.g. 5 Parl. Debs, vol. LXXI, cols 865.

14 W. K. Hancock and M. M. Gowing, *British War Economy* (1949), pp. 3–29.

15 Lloyd, *Experiments*, pp. 26, 38–47.

16 5 Parl. Debs, vol. LXXVII, col. 931.

17 On the limitation of profits see 5 Parl. Debs, vol. LXXI, cols 1,766ff.

18 5 Parl. Debs, vol. XCI, cols 1,499–1,501.

19 David Kirkwood, *My Life of Revolt* (1935), pp. 11, 17–18.

20 Ibid., pp. 81ff, 97.

21 Ibid., pp. 99–101.

22 5 Parl. Debs, vol. LXXVII, col. 930; 5 Parl. Debs, vol. XC, cols 1,559–60.

23 Kirkwood, *My Life*, pp. 115–16.

24 Ibid., pp. 104–10.

25 Ibid., pp. 111–14; 5 Parl. Debs, vol. LXXVII, cols 838–46.

26 Iain McLean, *The Legend of Red Clydeside* (Edinburgh, 1983), pp. 80–4; 5 Parl. Debs (Lords), vol. XXI, cols 656ff, 662.

27 Kirkwood, *My Life*, pp. 116–68.

28 5 Parl. Debs, vol. XCV, cols 611–12.

29 5 Parl. Debs, vol. LXXV, col. 1,408.

30 5 Parl. Debs, vol. XC, cols 1,510ff.

31 Lloyd, *Experiments*, p. 24.

32 5 Parl. Debs, vol. XC, cols 1,532, 1,559–60, 1,901–2.

33 *The Times*, 16 February 1929; cf. 1 and 2 November 1929.

34 F. W. Maitland, *The Constitutional History of England* (Cambridge, 1974), p. 410.

35 Gold Standard (Amendment) Act 1931 (September); National Emergency Act 1931 (September) [concerning official salaries]; Foodstuffs (Preventing of Exportation) Act 1931 (October); Abnormal Importations (Customs Duties) Act 1931 (November); Horticultural Products (Emergency Customs Duties) Act 1931 (December).

36 5 Parl. Debs, vol. CCLVI, col. 419.

37 5 Parl. Debs, vol. CCCXIX, cols 1,029–30.

38 Sir Cecil Thomas Carr, *Concerning English Administrative Law* (Oxford, 1941), p. 92.

39 Report of the Committee on Ministers' Powers [Donoughmore Report] (command paper 4,060, 1932).

40 Report of the Committee on Finance and Industry (command paper 3,897, 1931), para. 8, pp. 4–5.

41 5 Parl. Debs, vol. CCCIV, cols 3,087ff.

42 5 Parl. Debs, vol. CCCXIX, cols 1,026ff.

43 Herbert Agar, *A Time for Greatness* (1943), p. 14.

44 Laski, *Liberty*, p. 51.

10. A VERY BRITISH REVOLUTION

1 William Beveridge, *Social Insurance and Allied Services: A Report by Sir William Beveridge* (1942), paras 7 and 31.

2 Dwight Waldo, *The Administrative State* (New York, 1948), p. 73.

3 Erich Fromm, *The Fear of Freedom* (2001 edn), pp. 28–30.

4 Karl Popper, *The Open Society*, vol. I, p. 176.

5 Evan Durbin, *The Politics of Democratic Socialism* (1940), pp. 330–1.

6 Michael Foot, *Aneurin Bevan* (2 vols, 1975), vol. I, p. 349.

7 [Labour Party], *The Old World and the New Society. A Report on the Problem of War and Peace and Reconstruction* (1942), pp. 13, 15–17, 28.

8 Beveridge, *Report*, p. 172.

9 Herman Finer, *Road to Reaction* (1946), p. 21.

10 Foot, *Bevan*, p. 508; 5 Parl. Debs, vol. CCCLXXXVI, cols 1,985ff.

11 Lloyd, *Experiments*, p. xi; cf. Herbert Morrison, 5 Parl. Debs, vol. CCCLVI, cols 1,309–10.

12 5 Parl. Debs. vol. CCCLI, cols. 63ff; Hancock and Gowing, *British War Economy*, pp. 83ff.

13 5 Parl. Debs, vol. CDI, cols 2,016–21.

14 Lloyd George, 5 Parl. Debs, vol. CCCLX, col. 1,282; Clement Attlee, ibid., col. 1,093.

15 5 Parl. Debs, vol. CCCLXI, cols 151ff.

16 5 Parl. Debs, vol. CCCLXX, cols 729ff.

17 5 Parl. Debs, vol. CCCLXXIII, cols 1,276–7.

18 5 Parl. Debs, vol. CDI, col. 447.

19 See 5 Parl. Debs, vol. CDI. Reference to Hayek is made by Captain Bernays, col. 2,028 ('It is the road to serfdom') and by Archibald Southby, col. 2,060 ('the people of this country are, in effect, to become a nation of serfs').

20 F. A. Hayek, *The Road to Serfdom* (1944), p. 159.

21 F. A. Hayek, *The Sensory Order* (1952; 1982 edn), p. 325.

22 Foot, *Bevan*, p. 248.

23 William Beveridge, *Full Employment in a Free Society* (1953), pp. 21ff.

24 Laski, *Will Planning Restrict Freedom?* (Cheam, 1944), p. xxx; Laski, *Liberty*, pp. 84–8.

25 Laski, *Liberty, passim*, and esp. p. 85.

26 Ibid., p. 158; cf. pp. 83–4.

27 Ibid., p. 94.

28 Finer, pp. 128–9.

29 5 Parl. Debs, vol. CCCXCIX, cols 1,061ff.

30 David Kynaston, *Austerity Britain, 1946–51* (2007), ch. 2.

31 Ibid., pp. 161ff.

32 John Lehmann, *The Ample Proposition* (1966), p. 30.

33 Ibid.

34 John Eaves, *Emergency Powers and the Parliamentary Watchdog: Parliament and the Executive in Great Britain,* 1939–1951 (1957), pp. 191–2.

35 R. H. S. Crossman, *Socialism and the New Despotism* (Fabian Tract, no. 298, 1955), pp. 19–20.

36 Ibid., p. 24.

VI. The Twilight World

11. PLAYING BY THE RULES

The key study for civil liberties from 1914 to 1945 is K. D. Ewing and C. A. Gearty, *The Struggle for Civil Liberties: Political Freedom and the Rule of Law in Britain, 1914–1945* (Oxford, 2000).

1 John Dos Passos, *Mr Wilson's War* (1963), p. 175.

2 Harold J. Laski, *Freedom of the Press in Wartime* (n.d.), *passim*; Laski, *Liberty*, pp. 113ff, 185ff; cf. Sir William Byles in the House of Commons, 5 Parl. Debs, vol. LXIX, col. 936.

3 Foot, *Bevan*, vol. I, pp. 330–1; cf. Laski, *Liberty*, pp. 29–30.

4 5 Parl. Debs (Lords), vol. XVIII, cols 204ff; T. Baty and J. H. Morgan, *War: Its Conduct and Legal Results* (1915), pp. 3–20, 38, 44ff.

5 5 Parl Debs (Lords), vol. XVIII, cols 452ff, 464–5.

6 Lloyd, *Experiments*, p. 5; cf. Baty and Morgan, pp. 73–4, 81–2.

7 5 Parl. Debs, vol. LXXII, col. 28.

8 5 Parl. Debs (Lords), vol. XVIII, cols 206ff, 443–65, 677–703, 989ff; (Commons), vol. LXIX, cols 295ff, 670ff, 1,500ff.

9 5 Parl. Debs, vol. LXXXVI, cols 538–40, 825ff, vol. LXXXVIII, cols 288ff.

10 5 Parl. Debs, vol. LXXXI, cols 430–4.

11 5 Parl. Debs, vol. LXIX, col. 1,304.

12 5 Parl. Debs, vol. LXXII, cols 1,184–6; 'North Briton', *British Freedom*, pp. 25–6.

13 5 Parl. Debs, vol. LXXX, cols 223–5, 410–11, 690–1, 1,236–65; vol. LXXXI, cols 445ff; cf. 5 Parl. Debs (Lords), vol. XVIII, cols 452ff.

14 5 Parl. Debs, vol. LXXV, cols 809–10, 1,399.

15 For this and similar examples see 'North Briton', pp. 34ff and 5 Parl. Debs, vol. LXXXI, cols 423ff.

16 5 Parl. Debs, vol. LXXXI, cols 414ff.

17 5 Parl. Debs, vol. LXXXII, col. 2,984; vol. LXXXIII, cols 1086–9.

18 5 Parl. Debs, vol. LXXV, cols 1,994–5; vol. LXXXI, cols 424–5.

19 5 Parl. Debs, vol. LXXV, cols 809–10, 1,994–5; vol. LXXXI, cols 414ff; vol. LXXXII, cols 2,977–3,004.

20 5 Parl. Debs, Vol. LXXXII, col. 2,993.

21 5 Parl. Debs (Lords), vol. XXI, col. 660.

22 5 Parl. Debs (Lords), vol. XVIII, col. 451.

23 5 Parl. Debs (Lords), vol. XXIV, cols 402–3.

24 5 Parl. Debs, vol. LXXXIII, col. 1,101.

25 5 Parl. Debs, vol. LXXV, cols 1,388ff; vol. LXXVI, cols 547ff.

26 5 Parl. Debs, vol. XCII, cols 1,598ff.

27 Ibid., col. 1,617.

28 Laski, *Liberty*, pp. 116ff; 5 Parl. Debs, cols 371ff.

29 'North Briton', *British Freedom*, pp. 25–8.

30 5 Parl Debs, vol. LXXXIII, cols 1,115–17; cf. cols 1,151–2, 1,160–2.

31 Kirkwood, *My Life*, pp. 171–4.

32 For this and the following discussion see 5 Parl. Debs, vol. CXXXIII, cols 1,345–7, 1,399ff.

33 Ibid., cols 1,797–8.

34 Ibid., col. 1,420; cf. cols 1,631ff.

35 Anne Perkins, *A Very British Strike, 3 May–12 May 1926* (2006), p. 66.

36 Ibid., 4–5, 53–4, 65ff; Ewing and Gearty, *Struggle*, pp. 185ff.

37 5 Parl. Debs, vol. CXCV, cols 308–9.

38 Kirkwood, *My Life*, pp. 234–5.

39 5 Parl. Debs, vol. CXCV, cols 363ff.

40 Ibid., cols 477–512.

41 5 Parl. Debs, vol. CXCVI, cols 743ff.

42 Ibid., col. 827.

43 *The Times*, 25 August 1926.

44 *The Times*, 7 June 1926.

45 5 Parl. Debs, vol. CXCVI, col. 847.

46 Ibid., cols 797ff, 839–40; vol. CXCIX, col. 431; *The Times*, 26 August 1926.

47 *The Times*, 25 October, 15, 16 and 23 November 1926; 5 Parl. Debs, vol. CXCIX, cols 444–5.

48 *The Times*, 1 October 1926; cf. Joynson-Hicks, 5 Parl. Debs, vol. CXCVI, cols 822–8.

49 Perkins, *A Very British Strike*, p. 152; *The Times*, 15 September 1926.

50 5 Parl. Debs, vol. CXCVIII, cols 2,527–9, 2,533–4.

51 5 Parl. Debs, vol. CXCVII, cols 1,765–846; vol. CXCVIII, cols 2,509, 2,527–9; vol. CXCIX, cols 36, 38; vol. CC, cols 723ff, 853–5.

52 5 Parl. Debs, vol. CXCIX, cols 752–4.

53 5 Parl. Debs, vol. CXCVI, cols 797ff.

54 5 Parl. Debs, vol. CC, cols 713ff, 723ff.

55 5 Parl. Debs, vol. LXXI, cols 429–30.

56 W. Ivor Jennings, *The Law and the Constitution* (1933), pp. 236, 243–47; cf. Laski, *Liberty*, pp. 106–7.

57 Ewing and Gearty, *Struggle*, pp. 218–19, 224–8; Jennings, *The Law and the Constitution*, p. 242.

58 Ronald Kidd, *British Liberty in Danger: An Introduction to the Study of Civil Rights* (1940), pp. 1ff, 74; Jennings, pp. 241–2; Laski, *Liberty*, pp. 110–11; *New Statesman*, 22 September 1934; quote from *Police Journal* in Ewing and Gearty, *Struggle*, pp. 252–3; *Redmond-Bate* v. *Director of Public Prosecutions* (Queen's Bench Divisional Court), 1999; *DPP* v. *Jones and Another* (House of Lords), 1999; *Regina (Laporte)* v. *Chief Constable of Gloucestershire Constabulary* (Lords), 2006. On the 'Breathing Act' see Burn, *Age*, pp. 153–4.

59 Kidd, *British Liberty*, pp. 68–71; Ewing and Gearty, *Struggle*, ch. 6 *passim*.
60 Kidd, *British Liberty*, p. 74.
61 5 Parl. Debs, vol. CCCL, cols 1,050–1.
62 Ibid., cols 1,047ff (2R), 1,505ff (Comm. and 3R), 1,852ff (Lords' amendments considered).
63 *The Times*, 20 July 1939.
64 5 Parl. Debs, vol. CCCL, cols 1,607; cf. 5 Parl. Debs (Lords), vol. CXIV, col. 650.
65 Carr, *Administrative Law*, pp. 65–72.
66 Agar, *Time*, p. 12.

12. THE BLACKOUT

1 5 Parl. Debs, vol. CCCLXXXVI, col. 1, 767.
2 Clinton Rossiter, *Constitutional Dictatorship: Crisis Government in the Modern Democracies* (Princeton, 1948), pp. 301ff.
3 Quoted in 5 Parl. Debs, vol. CDI, col. 2,028.
4 E.g. 5 Parl. Debs, vol. CCCLXXIII, cols 941ff and vol. CCCDXXXVI, cols 996ff, 1,359ff, 1,593ff.
5 Laski, *Freedom of the Press*, p. 9.
6 Foot, *Bevan*, vol. I, p. 307.
7 Francis Williams, *Press, Parliament and People* (1946), pp. 6–7.
8 5 Parl. Debs, vol. CCCLXVII, col. 868.
9 Eaves, *Emergency Powers*, pp. 19ff; 5 Parl. Debs, vol. CCCLXI, cols 20–2, 25–32.
10 5 Parl. Debs, vol. CCCLXIII, cols 65ff.
11 Ibid., cols 727–34.
12 Ibid., col. 1,437.
13 Ibid., cols 867–8.
14 5 Parl. Debs, vol. CCCLXIV, cols 1,326–7, 1,329.
15 5 Parl. Debs, vol. CCCLXIII, cols. 867–8.
16 Ibid., cols 727–34.
17 Neil Stammers, *Civil Liberties in Britain during the Second World War. A Political Study* (1983), pp. 34ff, 64ff.
18 5 Parl. Debs. vol. CCCLXVII, col. 846.
19 Winston S. Churchill, *The Second World War*, vol. V: *Closing the Ring* (1986), p. 635.
20 Sir Cecil Carr, 'A Regulated Liberty: War-time regulations and judicial review in Great Britain', *Columbia Law Review*, XLII, no. 3 (March 1942), p. 339.
21 5 Parl. Debs, vol. CCCLXXVI, cols 787ff.
22 Carr, *Administrative Law*, pp. 19–20.
23 Laski, *Freedom of the Press*, p. 7.
24 Williams, *Press, Parliament and People*, pp. 34ff; Eaves, *Emergency Powers*, pp. 75ff; Stammers, *Civil Liberties*, pp. 146ff; 5 Parl. Debs, vol. CCCLXXVIII, cols 1,665ff.
25 Eaves, *Emergency Powers*, pp. 75ff.
26 Foot, *Bevan*, p. 355; 5 Parl. Debs, vol. CCCLXXVIII, col. 2,290.
27 5 Parl. Debs, vol. CCCLXXVIII, cols 2,233–5.
28 Ibid., cols 2,156–60.
29 Ibid., col. 2,252.
30 *Tribune*, 30 August 1940.
31 Foot, *Bevan*, pp. 301ff, 324–5, 378–9, 381–4, 395–7; John Campbell, *Nye Bevan and the Mirage of British Socialism* (1987), p. 98.

32 Foot, *Bevan*, p. 381; Campbell, *Bevan*, p.142n.

33 5 Parl. Debs, vol. CCCLXV, col. 1,229.

34 Foot, *Bevan*, p. 345.

35 5 Parl. Debs, vol. CCCXCIII, cols 1,096–9; Cunningham-Reid was referring here to the plight of the miners and Regulation 1AA in 1944 (see previous chapter).

36 William J. Brennan Jr, 'The Quest to Develop a Jurisprudence of Civil Liberties in Times of Security Crisis', *Israel Yearbook of Human Rights* (1998), p. 11.

37 Stammers, *Civil Liberties*, pp. 1, 125, 230–6.

38 *Willcock* v. *Muckle* (1951), 2 *Times Law Review* 373.

39 Jennings, *The Law and the Constitution*, pp. 112–13.

40 Carr, *Administrative Law*, p. 92.

41 George Orwell, *The Lion and the Unicorn*, in *The Penguin Essays of George Orwell* (1984), p. 145.

VII. The Triumph of the Individual

13. RISK

1 Kenneth Arrow, 'Invaluable Goods', *Journal of Economic Literature*, 35 (2000), p. 761.

2 Will Durant, 'In Praise of Freedom', *Harpers Magazine* (European edn), vol. XCIV (June 1927), p. 46.

3 Margaret Thatcher, *The Downing Street Years* (1993), p. 306.

4 Walter B. Wriston, *The Twilight of Sovereignty: How the Information Revolution is Transforming the World* (New York, 1992), pp. 173–6.

5 Mark Johnson and Conor Gearty, 'Civil Liberties and the Challenge of Terrorism', in National Centre for Social Research, *British Social Attitudes, the Twenty-third Report* (2007).

6 Isaiah Berlin, 'Two Concepts of Liberty', *Four Essays on Liberty* (Oxford, 1969), pp. 124–5.

7 J. L. Talmon, *The Origins of Totalitarian Democracy* (1952), p. 2.

8 F. A. Hayek, *The Constitution of Liberty* (1960), p. 116.

9 *Guardian*, 11 February 1985.

10 Martin J Wiener, *English Culture and the Decline of the Industrial Spirit, 1850–1980* (1981).

11 Daniel Yergin and Joseph Stanislaw, *The Commanding Heights: The Battle Between Government and the Marketplace That is Remaking the Modern World* (New York, 1998), pp. 107–8.

12 Ibid., pp. 92–105.

13 Baroness Thatcher, 'Speech to the Conservative Party Conference', 10 October 1975, www.margaretthatcher.org/speeches/displaydocument.asp?docid=102777.

14 Ian Gilmour, *Inside Right: A Study of Conservatism* (1977), p. 118.

15 Hugo Young, *One of Us: A Biography of Margaret Thatcher* (1990), p. 282.

16 Ibid., p. 538.

17 Berlin, 'Two Concepts', p. 165.

18 Mill, *Representative Government, Collected Works*, vol. XIX, p. 412.

19 Eric Hobsbawm, *Politics for a Rational Left: Political Writing, 1977–1988* (1989), p. 46.

20 Tony Blair, speech, 19 July 2004, www.number10.gov.uk/output/Page6129.asp.

21 Marshall McLuhan, *Understanding the Media: The Extensions of Man* (1964); Ithiel de Sola Pool, *Technologies of Freedom* (1983); Richard Barbrook, *Imaginary Futures: From Thinking Machines to the Global Village* (2007), pp. 155ff, 265ff.

22 Milton Friedman, *Capitalism and Freedom* (2002 edn), pp. 20–3; Kenneth Arrow, *The Limits of Organization* (1974), pp 39, 64, 69–70.

23 Philip Mirowski, *Machine Dreams: Economics Becomes a Cyborg Science* (Cambridge, 2002), p. 285.

24 Susanne Lace (ed.), *The Glass Consumer: Life in the Surveillance Society* (Bristol, 2005).

25 S. Davies, 'Personal Virtue', in *Guardian* supplement 'Big Brother: Someone Somewhere Is Watching You', part 1, 7 November 2002.

26 I. Lawrence, 'Checkout at the Data Supermarket', in *Guardian* supplement 'Big Brother', part I.

27 'Bust Up with the Boss?', 8 May 2008,
www.news.bbc.co.uk/1/hi/magazine/7389547.stm.

28 G. Böhme, 'The Techno-structures of Society', in N. Stehr and R. Ericson (eds), *The Culture and Power of Knowledge: Inquiries into Contemporary Societies* (New York, 1992); Richard V. Ericson and Kevin D. Haggerty, *Policing the Risk Society* (Oxford, 1997), pp. 41–2, 78–9, 97–8, 108–9; Perri 6, 'The Personal Information Economy: Trends and Prospects for Consumers', in Lace (ed), *Glass Consumer*.

29 Ericson and Haggerty, *Policing*, pp. 6, 41–2, 117, 122; Lace (ed.), 'Introduction', *Glass Consumer*, pp. 1–2.

30 I. Hacking, *The Taming of Chance* (Cambridge, 1990); G. Priest, 'The New Legal Structure of Risk Control', *Daedalus*, 119 (1990), pp. 207–27; O. Gandy, *The Panoptic Sort: A Political Economy of Personal Information* (Boulder, 1993); R. V. Ericson, 'The Decline of Innocence', *University of British Columbia Law Review*, 28 (1994), pp. 367–83; Ericson and Haggerty, *Policing*, pp. 108–9.

31 A.-G. Slama, *L'Angélisme Exterminateur; Essai sur l'Ordre Moral Contemporain* (1993), p. 256.

32 Frank Furedi, *Culture of Fear: Risk-taking and the Morality of Low Expectation* (1997); Cass R. Sunstein, *Laws of Fear: Beyond the Precautionary Principle* (Cambridge, 2005).

33 Hans Boutellier, *The Safety Utopia: Contemporary Discontent and Desire as to Crime and Punishment* (Dordrecht, 2004), p. 35; cf. Zygmunt Bauman, *Postmodernity and its Discontents* (1997), p. 193.

34 Zygmunt Bauman, *Society Under Siege* (2002).

35 Graeme Newman, Ronald V. Clarke and S. Giora Shoham (eds), *Rational Choice and Situational Crime Prevention: Theoretical Foundations* (Aldershot, 1997); Derek B. Cornish and Richard V. Clarke, *The Reasoning Criminal: Rational Choice Perspectives on Offending* (New York, 1986); R. V. G. Clarke, *Hot Products: Understanding, Anticipating and Reducing Demand for Stolen Goods* (1999); Kevin Heal and Gloria Laycock, *Situational Crime Prevention: From Theory into Practice* (1986).

36 Newman, Clarke and Shohan (eds), *Rational Choice*, preface and introduction.

37 Richard Wortley, 'Reconsidering the Role of Opportunity in Situational Crime Prevention', in Newman, Clarke and Shohan (eds), *Rational Choice*, pp. 65–7.

38 www.foresight.gov.uk/first_phase/1999–2002/dl/Crime_Prevention/Reports/Future%20Crime%20Preventions/Future_Crime_Prevention_Mindset_Kit_March_2000.pdf.

39 Tony Blair, foreword to HM Government, Policy Review, *Building on Progress: Security, Crime and Justice* (March 2007), p. 4.

14. THE TRANSPARENT CITIZEN

1 Tocqueville, *Democracy*, vol. IV, pp. 324–5.

2 Tony Blair, speech to the Labour Party conference, 1999, news.bbc.co.uk/1/hi/uk_politics/460009.stm

3 McLuhan, *Understanding the Media*; Sola Pool, *Technologies of Freedom*; Shoshana Zuboff, *In the Age of the Smart Machine* (1988); Charles Leadbeater, *Living on Thin Air: The New Economy*

(1999), pp. vi–viii, 1–3, 39ff, 81, 91, 213ff; Richard Sennett, *The Culture of the New Capitalism* (New Haven, 2006), ch. 1; Barbrook, *Imaginary Futures*, pp. 155ff, 265ff. On a supposed connection between the left and the information revolution see Ellen Ullman, *Close to the Machine* (1997): 'When I think of it, it's not such a great distance from communist cadre to software engineer. I may have joined the party to further social justice, but a deeper attraction could have been to a process, a system, a program. I'm inclined to think I've always believed in the machine.'

4 Performance and Innovation Unit, *Privacy and Data-Sharing: The Way Forward for Public Services* (2002), pp. 7–8, 35–6; Leadbeater, pp. 188ff.

5 Hayek, *Individualism and the Economic Order* (1948), pp. 77–8, 154–5.

6 HM Government, Policy Review, *Building on Progress: The Role of the State* (May 2007).

7 Geoff Mulgan, *Connexity: How to Live in a Connected World* (1997), pp. 1–2, 5–7, 12–13, 53, 56, 60–1. Mulgan led Tony Blair's Strategy Unit.

8 Office of the Commissioner of Human Rights, *Report by Mr Alvaro Gil-Robles, Commissioner for Human Rights, on His Visit to the United Kingdom, 4–12 November 2004* (Strasbourg, June 2005), para. 3.

9 David Blunkett, 'Civic Rights', *Guardian*, 14 September 2002; David Blunkett, 'What Does Citizenship Mean Today?', *Observer*, 15 September 2002; David Blunkett, 'Integration With Diversity: Globalisation and the Renewal of Democracy and Civil Society', in The Foreign Policy Centre, *Rethinking Britishness* (2002).

10 Hazel Blears; quoted in her pamphlet *The Politics of Decency* (2004), p. 21.

11 James L. Nolan, *The Therapeutic State: Justifying Government at Century's End* (New York, 1998); Leadbeater, pp. 149ff, 162ff, 183ff, 205, 213ff.

12 Leadbeater, pp. 212, 230. Leadbeater was asked by Peter Mandelson to develop the white paper *Building the Knowledge Driven Economy*.

13 Department of Work and Pensions, Social Exclusion Unit, *Report of Policy Action Unit 18 on Better Information* (2000) and *United Kingdom National Action Plan on Social Exclusion 2001–2003* (2001); Prime Minister's Strategy Unit, *Predicting Adult Life Outcomes from Earlier Signals: Identifying Those At Risk* (31 August 2006).

14 'Blair Seeks Radical Changes to Boost Justice System', *Guardian*, 24 June 2006.

15 HM Government, *Information Sharing Vision Statement* (September 2006).

16 Prime Minister's Strategy Unity, *Risk: Improving Government's Capacity to Handle Risk and Uncertainty* (November 2002).

17 Prime Minister's Strategy Unit, *Predicting Adult Life Outcomes*.

18 Clive Norris and Gary Armstrong, *The Maximum Surveillance Society: The Rise of CCTV* (1999), pp. 24–7; Christine Bellamy, Perri 6 and Charles Raab, 'Personal Data in the Public Sector: Reconciling Necessary Sharing with Confidentiality?', in Lace (ed.), *The Glass Consumer*, pp. 139–40.

19 Sean Coughlan, 'Under the Thumb?, news.bbc.co.uk/1/hi/magazine/6129084.stm, 13 November 2006; 'Thumb Print Request Angers Shopper', news.bbc.co.uk/go/pr/fr/-/1/hi/england/kent/4684710.stm, 2 June 2006.

20 *Guardian*, 13 March 2006.

21 Hansard, Westminster Hall Debates, Home Affairs, 16 December 2003, c. 212ff.

22 'Reid: Public Safety Takes Priority over Civil Liberties', *Guardian*, 17 May 2006.

23 Home Office, *Rebalancing the Criminal Justice System in Favour of the Law Abiding Majority, Cutting Crime, Reducing Reoffending and Protecting the Public* (July 2006).

24 Blunkett, 'What Does Citizenship Mean Today?'; 6 Parl. Debs, vol. CDIII, col. 159.

25 'Blair Vows to "Rebalance" Justice Towards Victim', *Daily Telegraph*, June 19 2002.

26 Home Office, *Criminal Justice: The Way Ahead* (2001), pp. 20–3.

27 Commissioner of Human Rights, *Report by Mr Alvaro Gil-Robles*, para. 109.

28 Tony Blair, 'I've Been Tough on Crime: Now We Have to Nip it in the Bud', *Daily Telegraph*, 28 April 2007.

29 Prime Minister's Strategy Unit, *Personal Responsibility and Changing Behaviour: The State of Knowledge and its Implications for Public Policy* (2004), p. 67.

30 'Prime Minister's Speech on the Five-Year Crime Strategy', 19 July 2004, www.number10.gov.uk/Page6130.

31 Francis Fukuyama, *The Great Disruption: Human Nature and the Reconstitution of Social Order* (2000 edn), p. 90; John Durham Peters, *Courting the Abyss: Free Speech and the Liberal Tradition* (2005), *passim*.

32 Durant, pp. 46–7.

33 David Murakami Wood (ed.), *A Report on the Surveillance Society for the Information Commissioner by the Surveillance Studies Network* (Sept 2006), p. 36.

34 Tony Blair, 'I Don't Destroy Liberties, I Protect Them', *Observer*, 26 February 2006.

35 'Family's Shock at Council Spying', 11 April 2008, news.bbc.co.uk/1/hi/england/dorset/7343445.stm.

36 The phrase is that of the politician James Parnell. *Observer*, 27 January 2008.

37 Wood (ed.), *Report on the Surveillance Society*, p. 3.

38 Virginia Eubanks, 'Technologies of Citizenship', in Torin Monahan (ed.), *Surveillance Society: Technological Politics and Power in Everyday Life* (New York, 2006).

39 For details of cases of identity theft and fraud in the early 2000s see The Information Commissioner's Office, *What Price Privacy? The Unlawful Trade in Confidential Personal Information* (May 2006).

40 Sennett, *Culture*, pp. 173ff.

41 www.wired.com/politics/law/news/1999/01/17538.

42 Norris and Armstrong, *Maximum Surveillance*, chs 6 and 7; Clive Norris, 'From Personal to Digital: CCTV, the Panopticon, and the Technological Mediation of Suspicion and Social Control', in David Lyon (ed.), *Surveillance and Social Sorting: Privacy, Risk, and Digital Discrimination* (2003).

43 M. Gill and A. Spriggs (Home Office Research Department), *Assessing the Impact of CCTV* (2005), pp. 60–1.

44 news.bbc.co.uk/1/hi/world/americas/3347313.stm, 25 December 2003; news.bbc.co.uk/1/hi/world/americas/3362043.stm, 2 January 2004; news.bbc.co.uk/1/hi/world/europe/3363723.stm, 2 January 2004.

45 news.bbc.co.uk/1/hi/world/americas/7052155.stm, 19 October 2007.

46 HM Government, *Building on Progress: Security, Crime and Justice*, p. 45.

15. THE SUNSET WORLD

1 Laski, *Liberty*, p. 37.

2 Commissioner of Human Rights, *Report by Mr Alvaro Gil-Robles*, para. 4.

3 'Government to Offer Terror Bill Compromise', *Guardian*, 7 November 2005.

4 Johnson and Gearty, 'Civil Liberties'.

5 6 Parl. Debs, vol. CCCLXXV, cols 87–8.

6 Ibid., col. 330.

7 *The Times*, 23 November 1974.

8 5 Parl. Debs, vol. DCCCLXXXII, col. 634.

9 Ibid., cols 655, 880.

10 *The Times*, 26 November 1974.

11 Clive Walker, *The Prevention of Terrorism in British Law* (Manchester, 1986), pp. 22–4; cf. Roy Jenkins, *A Life at the Centre* (1991), p. 393.

12 Jenkins, *Life*, p. 397.

13 5 Parl. Debs, vol. DCCCXCII, cols 1126–7.

14 6 Parl. Debs, vol. XXXVIII, cols 569–72.

15 E. P. Thompson, *Writing by Candlelight* (1980), pp. 163–5.

16 *Council of Civil Service Unions* v. *Minister for the Civil Service* (1985), AC 374, at 402.

17 Young, *One of Us*, pp. 287–8.

18 K. D. Ewing and C. A. Gearty, *Freedom Under Thatcher: Civil Liberties in Modern Britain* (Oxford, 1990), pp. 147ff.

19 Ibid., pp. 117ff.

20 *Sunday Telegraph*, 27 November 1988.

21 Downing Street Press Briefing, 22 June 2006, www.number10.gov.uk/Page9729.

22 Tony Blair, 15 May 2006, http://www.guardian.co.uk/politics/2006/may/15/immigrationpolicy.labour.

23 Jack Straw, 'I'm Simply Protecting Democracy', *Guardian*, 14 December 1999.

24 *A* v. *Secretary of State for the Home Department* (2204) UKHL 56, paras 97 (Hoffman), 155 (Scott).

25 6 Parl. Debs, vol. CDXXXI, cols 401, 416, 780, 784,

26 Ibid., cols 648–9.

27 Ibid., cols 640ff.

28 Ibid., cols 951–2, 1,510–11.

29 *Guardian*, 14 March 2005.

30 Andrew Rawnsley, 'Bad Laws Won't Stop the Bombers', *Observer*, 6 March 2005.

31 6 Parl. Debs, vol. CDXXXI, col. 726.

32 *Guardian*, 1 November 2003.

33 6 Parl. Debs (Lords), vol. DCLXX, col. 133.

34 6 Parl. Debs, vol. CDXXXI, col. 304.

35 'Blair and Clarke Split on 90-day Detention', *Daily Telegraph*, 4 November 2005.

36 *Sun*, 27 July 2005.

37 'Britons Would Trade Civil Liberties for Security', *Guardian*, 22 August 2005.

38 Cherie Booth, Nineteenth Sultan Azlan Shah Law Lecture, Kuala Lumpur, 26 July 2005; 'Blairs at odds over anti-terror measures', *Guardian*, 27 July 2005.

VIII. *The New Orthodoxy*

16. FREE DIVERSITY

1 Mill, *On Liberty, Collected Works*, vol. XVIII, p. 229.

2 Amartya Sen, *Identity and Violence: The Illusion of Destiny* (2006), p. 149.

3 Mill, *On Liberty*, pp. 207, 226.

4 Hume, 'Of National Character', p. 235.

5 Quoted in Brian Moynahan, 'Putting the Fear of God into Holland', *Sunday Times*, 27 February 2005.

6　Mathias Döpfner, 'Europa – dein Name ist Feigheit', *Die Welt*, 20 November 2004.

7　Ian Buruma, *Murder in Amsterdam: The Death of Theo van Gogh and the Limits of Tolerance* (2006), pp. 96ff; Buruma, 'Final Cut', in Lisa Appignanesi (ed.), *Free Expression Is No Offence* (2005).

8　*R* v. *Headteacher and Governors of Denbigh High School* (2006), UKHL, 15, para. 97.

9　Sen, *Identity*, pp. 157–8.

10　Buruma, *Murder*, pp. 167–9.

11　John Gray, *Liberalism* (1986), p. 226; Berlin, 'Two Concepts', p. 155.

12　Yasmin Alibhai-Brown, *Who Do We Think We Are?* (2000), p 246; Bhikhu Parekh, 'A Varied Moral World: A Response to Susan Okin's "Is Multiculturalism Bad for Women?" ', *Boston Review*, October/November 1997; Gita Sahgal and Nira Yuval-Davis, *Refusing Holy Orders: Women and Fundamentalism in Britain* (2000), p. 15.

13　See the landmark case *Hoffman* v. *Austria* (1994), 17 EHRR 293: 'The criteria of social marginalisation could be applied to members of any minorities as a means to strip them of their parental rights. This is incompatible with the spirit of a pluralistic democratic society in which minority rights must be respected' (307–8). And in more recent English rights law see *R* v. *Secretary of State for Education and Employment, ex parte Williamson* (2006), UKHL, 15 and *R* v. *Headteacher and Governors of Denbigh High School* (2006), UKHL, 15.

14　The Runnymede Trust, *The Future of Multi-Ethnic Britain: The Parekh Report* (2000).

15　Ibid., p. ix.

16　Sen, *Identity*, pp. 118–19, 158.

17　Submission by Women Against Fundamentalism and Southall Black Sisters to the Commission on Integration and Cohesion, January 2007; downloaded from www.womenagainstfundamentalism.org.uk/

18　Will Kymlicka, *Multicultural Odysseys: Navigating the New International Politics of Diversity* (Oxford, 2007), pp. 161–2, 164–7.

19　Melanie Phillips, 'This Country Is So Pro-Muslim It Is Giving Succour to the Extremists Who Would Destroy Us', *Daily Mail*, 8 July 2008.

20　Kymlicka, *Multicultural Odysseys*, pp. 159ff.

21　*Parekh Report*, p. 165.

22　Ibid., p. 239.

23　Sen, *Identity*, pp. 13, 117ff, 159–60.

24　Ibid., p. 165.

25　Quoted in Andrew Anthony, 'The End of Freedom?', *Observer*, 12 February 2006; cf. Kenan Malik, 'The Real Value of Diversity', www.kenanmalik.com/essays/diversity.html.

26　6 Parl. Debs, vol. CDXXXVIII, col. 334.

27　'Lyrical Terrorist Found Guilty', 8 November 2007, news.bbc.co.uk/1/hi/uk/7084801.stm; 'Terror Manuals Woman Avoids Jail', 6 December 2007, news.bbc.co.uk/1/hi/uk/7130495.stm; *Guardian*, 18 June 2008.

28　*Independent*, 29 May 2006.

29　Buruma, *Murder, passim*; Moynahan, see n. 5 above.

30　*Norwood* v. *DPP* (2003), EWHC, 1564.

31　Rex Ahdar and Ian Leigh, *Religious Freedom in the Liberal State* (Oxford, 2005), p. 381.

32　Cited in 6 Parl. Debs, vol. CDXLII, col. 212.

33　*Guardian*, 12 October 2005.

34　*The Moral Maze*, BBC Radio 4, 14 July 2004.

35　*Daily Telegraph*, 22 December 2004.

36 Ahdar and Leigh, pp. 384, 386; House of Lords Select Committee on Religious
Offences, First Report for 2002–3, para. 52.

37 Ed Husain, *The Islamist: Why I Joined Radical Islam in Britain, What I saw Inside and Why I Left*
(2007), pp. 65–6.

38 Letters, *Guardian*, 27 December 2004.

39 Inayat Bunglawala, 'I Used to Be a Book Burner', *Guardian*, 19 June 2007,
www.guardian.co.uk/commentisfree/2007/jun/19/notsurprisinglytheawarding.

40 Hobbes, *Leviathan*, part 1, ch. 14.

41 6 Parl. Debs, vol. CDXLII, col. 227.

17. TAKING SIDES

1 Flemming Rose, 'Why I Published Those Cartoons', *Washington Post*, 19 February 2006.

2 'Freedom v Faith: The Firestorm', *Sunday Times*, 5 February 2006.

3 'More European Papers Print Cartoons of Muhammad, Fueling Dispute With Muslims',
New York Times, 2 February 2006.

4 Flemming Rose, 'Why I Published the Muhammad Cartoons', *New York Times*,
31 May 2006.

5 Thomas Paine, *The Rights of Man*, part 1, in *Political Writings* (ed. Bruce Kuklick,
Cambridge, 2000), p. 126.

6 Hans Magnus Enzensberger, 'Der radikale Verlierer', *Der Spiegel*, 7 November 2005;
English translation at www.signandsight.com/features/493.

7 Thomas Hegghammer, 'Jihadi Studies: The Obstacles to Understanding Radical Islam
and the Opportunities to Know It Better', *Times Literary Supplement*, 4 April 2008.

8 'Imams Plan "Civil" March to Show Distress at Cartoons', *Guardian*, 9 February 2006.

9 'Furor Over Cartoons Pits Muslim Against Muslim', *New York Times*, 22 February 2006;
cf. Brian Whitaker, 'Drawn Conclusions', *Guardian*, 7 February 2006.

10 'What Price Must Be Paid for Freedom', *The Times*, 4 February 2006; cf. the reactions of
Tony Benn, the Bishop of Oxford and Sir Jonathan Sacks in the same article.

11 Quoted in 'Freedom v Faith', *Sunday Times*.

12 Nick Cohen, 'Yet Again We Cave In to the Religious Bigots', *Observer*, 28 May 2006.

13 *Guardian*, 17 July 2006.

14 Monica Ali, 'The Outrage Economy', *Guardian*, 13 October 2007.

15 *Guardian*, 27 October 2007; cf. Germaine Greer, 'Reality Bites', *Guardian*, 24 July 2006.

16 Hari Kunzru, 'Terror Stricken', *Guardian*, 15 November 2007.

17 Timothy Garton Ash, 'We Must Stand Up to the Creeping Tyranny of the Group Veto',
Guardian, 2 March 2006.

18 'Artists Too Frightened to Tackle Radical Islam', *The Times*, 19 November 2007.

19 'Artist Hits at Tate "Cowards" over Ban', *Observer*, 25 September 2005; for the Tate's
view see Stephen Deuchar, 'This Is Not Censorship, It's Safety', *Guardian*,
11 October 2005.

20 6 Parl. Debs, vol. CDXLII, col. 207.

21 Andrew Anthony, 'When Did the Police Start Collaring Television?', *Observer*, 12 August
2007.

22 James Silver, 'It's the Last Chance for Panorama', *Guardian*, 21 August 2006.

23 Andrew Blick, Tufyal Choudhury and Stuart Weir, *The Rules of the Game: Terrorism,
Community and Human Rights*, a report by Democratic Audit, Human Rights Centre,
University of Essex, for the Joseph Rowntree Reform Trust (York, 2006), p. 54.

24 *The Times*, 14 January 2006.

25 *Guardian*, 27 November 2006.

26 Quoted in Anthony, 'The End of Freedom?'.

27 Mill, *On Liberty, Collected Works*, vol. XVIII, p. 229.

28 'Ayaan Hirsi Ali v. Ed Husain: The West and the Future of Islam', Centre for Social Cohesion, 20 November 2007, www.socialcohesion.co.uk/audio/Event201107.mp3.

29 Bunglawala, 'I Used to Be a Book Burner'.

30 A. Sivanandan, 'Why Muslims Reject British Values', *Observer*, 16 October 2005.

31 'Cartoons Row Hits Danish Exports', 9 September 2006, news.bbc.co.uk/1/hi/world/europe/5329642.stm; cf. 'How One of the Biggest Rows of Modern Times Helped Danish Exports to Prosper', *Guardian*, 30 September 2006.

32 Martin Jacques, 'Europe's Contempt for Other Cultures Cannot Be Sustained', *Guardian*, 17 February 2006.

33 www.youtube.com/watch?v=PY8fjFKAC5k.

EPILOGUE

1 Cited by Karma Nabulsi, 'Don't Sign Up to This Upside Down Hobbesian Contract', *Guardian*, 22 March 2006.

2 Tony Blair, in 'Blair: Shackled in War on Terror', *Sunday Times*, 27 May 2007.

3 Ibid.

4 'Government to Offer Terror Bill Compromise', *Guardian*, 7 November 2005.

5 Rachel Shabi, 'Guantánamo in Our Back Yard', *Guardian*, 11 September 2004.

6 'There Is No War on Terror', *Guardian*, 24 January 2007.

7 Eamon Collins with Mick McGovern, *Killing Rage* (1999), pp. 340–1.

8 Boris Johnson, 'Blair's Crackdown on Freedom Is an Inspiration to Tyrants', *Daily Telegraph*, 25 May 2006.

Acknowledgements

—⌇—

I would like to thank the following for their help, advice and patience: Claire Ashworth, Clare Conville, Walter Donohue, Becky Fincham, Alex Kirby, David Maxwell, Silvia Novak, Anne Owen, Stephen Page, Eleanor Rees, James Rivett, Rebecca Smith, David Starkey, Stephanie Waddell, Chris and Marney Wilson, Matthew Wilson.

Index